# Data Communications and Networking Fundamentals Using Novell NetWare® (4.11)

**Ann Beheler**

*Richland College*

Prentice Hall

*Upper Saddle River, New Jersey*    *Columbus, Ohio*

**Library of Congress Cataloging-in-Publication Data**
Beheler, Ann.
    Data communications and networking fundamentals using Novell
NetWare® (4.11) / Ann Beheler.
       p.     cm.
    Includes index.
    ISBN 0-13-592007-8 (alk. paper)
    1. NetWare (Computer file)   2. Local area networks (Computer
networks)  I. Title.
TK5105.8.N65B44   1999
004.6—dc21                      98-28513
                              CIP

Editor: Charles E. Stewart, Jr.
Production Editor: Alexandrina Benedicto Wolf
Cover photo: Photo Researchers, Inc.
Design Coordinator: Karrie M. Converse
Cover Designer: Rod Harris
Production Manager: Deidra M. Schwartz
Marketing Manager: Ben Leonard

This book was set in Arial by Carlisle Communications, Ltd. and was printed and bound by The Banta Company.
The cover was printed by Phoenix Color Corp.

©1999 by Prentice-Hall, Inc.
Simon & Schuster/A Viacom Company
Upper Saddle River, New Jersey 07458

Printed in the United States of America

10 9 8 7 6 5 4 3 2

ISBN: 0-13-592007-8

Prentice-Hall International (UK) Limited, *London*
Prentice-Hall of Australia Pty. Limited, *Sydney*
Prentice-Hall of Canada, Inc., *Toronto*
Prentice-Hall Hispanoamericana, S. A., *Mexico*
Prentice-Hall of India Private Limited, *New Delhi*
Prentice-Hall of Japan, Inc., *Tokyo*
Simon & Schuster Asia Pte. Ltd., *Singapore*
Editora Prentice-Hall do Brasil, Ltda., *Rio de Janeiro*

# Preface

Since the introduction of the personal computer in the early 1980s, data communication and computer networking usage have grown exponentially. Today's computer information sciences students must have a solid understanding of data communications and networking to form a framework for any specialized study that they may pursue. Communications is no longer just voice; computers and their users no longer operate singly. Truly, the world is connected, and data communications and networking form the glue.

Communications courses have been taught at the college level for many years, and courses focusing solely on networking are rapidly being added. However, a course that addresses both data communications and networking is an ideal introduction to both subjects for all computer information sciences students. Given that the average curriculum for the computer information sciences student is already so full, many colleges and universities are finding it attractive to teach a combination introductory course.

This book was written to serve the combined need to teach both data communications and networking. The first half of the book serves as an orientation to communications and networking. The second half focuses on the use of networks. It features Novell's NetWare version 4.11 to illustrate local area network operating systems, and it provides hands-on tutorial activities for the students to implement in a lab environment with NetWare 4.11.

NetWare 4.11 was chosen as the software to use because it currently has a large market share and because it is an enterprise type of network operating system. Therefore, it is likely that a student not only would want to study it, but would see it again in business use.

## Objectives of the Text

1. To teach the basic terminology of communications and networking.

2. To present the components needed to establish communications and the options available in applying each of the components.

3. To describe major data communications devices and systems.

4. To show the use of both wide area and local area networks.

5. To illustrate the components required to configure a local area network and the options available in applying each of them.

6. To present the need for disaster recovery planning.

7. To explain network design fundamentals.

8. To explain the characteristics of NetWare 4.11.

9. To explain the administrative utilities of NetWare 4.11.

10. To describe file system and NDS trustee assignments and their ramifications in NetWare 4.11.

11. To explore various types of clients used with NetWare 4.11, including DOS and Windows 95.

12. To show how to install and operate both the client and server portions of NetWare 4.11.

13. To present a troubleshooting methodology and give students practice scenarios to diagnose.

## Organization of the Text

The book consists of 16 chapters which provide the essential terminology and concepts for an introductory course in data communications and networking. The first seven chapters focus on data communications and networking in general, and the last nine chapters focus on specifics related to Novell NetWare 4.11. The book begins with a history of data communications and then proceeds to explain a wide variety of basic data communication and networking terminology for both systems and hardware. It then focuses on the specific protocols, standards, and topologies specifically related to networking and internetworking, and it examines various topics related to network design, security, and disaster recovery. It then proceeds to discuss Novell NetWare 4.11 topics ranging from overview through user creation, login script creation, printing, file system rights, Novell Directory Services rights, and troubleshooting.

The book assumes a basic level of computer literacy usually attained in a college-level introduction to computer science course or an equivalent continuing education course. The book provides the foundation for both concepts and terminology of communications and networking needed to pursue advanced data communications courses or advanced networking courses.

Exercises at the end of each chapter focus on helping students grasp the concepts presented in the chapter. Optional projects are also provided to help students further solidify and apply their knowledge. It is highly recommended that students make every attempt to complete all or most of the projects to have a stronger learning experience.

An appendix containing information on how to obtain products and technical support information from a variety of computer-related vendors and a glossary of commonly used terms are included.

## Supplements

For the instructor, there is a comprehensive instructor's guide that includes;

1. Suggestions on how to organize the course, depending on the desired emphasis and focus.

2. Answers to all end of chapter questions.

3. Solutions to projects.

4. Transparency masters of the figures in the book.

5. Test bank for use in quizzes and examinations.

## Acknowledgments

I am indebted to my students and fellow colleagues for their input during the creation of this book. I also appreciate the contributions of each of the following reviewers: Alan Rowland, Ivy State Technical College, Indianapolis, Indiana; Mike Awaad and William Lin, DeVry Institute, North Brunswick, New Jersey; Renee Curtis, Computer Learning Center, Philadelphia, Pennsylvania; and Carl Beheler, Satellite Communications Engineer, Rockwell International, Richardson, Texas.

I am also indebted to my family for their support and encouragement. Without their willingness to be without Mom during this project, this book would never have been completed.

Finally, I would like to thank all the people at Prentice Hall who made this book happen. I would personally like to thank Charles Stewart, my editor and Kim Yehle, his assistant, for their patience and support throughout the development of this book.

*To my husband, Carl, for his support and willingness to let me be me and pursue my goals even when they sometimes do not match his.*

*To my four children, Joey, Sarah, Jeremy, and Katie. Each is unique and very bright. They are living proof that fine adults and young people can come from a two-career home.*

*To my parents who always supported me beyond my dreams.*

*To my Aunt Grace who continues to model the best in love and teaching skills after over fifty years in the profession.*

*To my Uncle Jennings and Aunt LaRue whose impact on me was and is immeasurable.*

# Contents

# 1
# Introduction to Communication Concepts

## Objectives

After completing this chapter you will

1. Understand the concept of data communication.

2. Obtain an overview of the history of data communication.

3. Understand the basic requirements of a communication system.

4. Understand the basic concepts of networking.

5. Have a general overview of some of the services offered through data communication networks.

## Key Terms

Data communication

Network

Video conferencing

The Internet

Satellite

Host

Terminal

Modem

Transmission Medium

Bulletin Board

Public network

Telecommuting

Electronic Mail

# Introduction

This chapter provides an overview of data communication and networking concepts and terminology from a historical perspective. It describes the various components of data communication systems and documents some of the historical efforts toward data communication from the earliest discoveries to the present Information Age. Mastering this chapter will give the student a basic understanding of the technological concepts pertaining to the configuration of data communications and networking systems upon which information in other chapters will build.

The chapter begins with an introduction to the concept of data communication and its importance in the business world. It then provides a brief history of the most important developments that have shaped the data communication industry, followed by the most important functions that a data communications system must provide. Then the major requirements of a data communications system are discussed. Finally, the chapter concludes with a discussion of some basic services that can be accessed through existing data communications networks.

# Data Communications Systems

## Definition

**Data communications** is the transmission of electronic data over some medium. The medium ranges from coaxial cable to optical fiber to microwaves to air. The hardware and software systems that enable the transmission of data are often called data communication **networks**. These networks are an important component of today's information-based society, a society dominated by computers and the need to have virtually instantaneous access to accurate information.

The demand for information is so great in our society that many companies have been formed to service this need. These companies vary from those that develop and manufacture hardware and software for communications to service companies dealing in the distribution of data itself. These service companies form the basis for the rapidly growing information services industry.

Information is a commodity that can be bought and sold. Often, the information sold is a byproduct of a company's normal course of business. An example of this is the mail-order company that sells all or portions of its database to other corporations interested in the same types of customers. Additionally, companies obtain customer information with extensive demographic characteristics when a consumer fills out and mails in a normal warranty card. This allows a company to purchase a mailing list with persons most likely to be interested in the company's products.

Additionally, companies exist for the sole purpose of selling targeted mailing lists customized to the specifications desired by the company purchasing the mailing list. These companies go beyond the single company's mailing list, combining customer lists and demographic data from various sources to produce astonishingly complete information about individuals and households that cannot be obtained from a single source. The privacy issues of this buying and selling of highly specific information about individuals have not yet been resolved, but such mailing lists have already been developed and have been widely distributed.

It can be generalized that the value of the communication system depends on the knowledge transmitted by the system and the speed of movement of the knowledge. High-speed data communication networks transmit information that brings the sender and the receiver close together. Therefore, a good communication system is a major component of a successful business organization. The ability to provide information in a timely and accurate fashion is the key to survival into the twenty-first century. Because of this, data communications is one of the fastest growing segments of the communication market.

# Functions

An effective data communications system has a series of characteristics or functions that are easily recognized. These characteristics are the result of the behavior and functionality of the system as it provides information to its users, as it captures the information, and as it allows its users to communicate with one another. These characteristics can be further categorized by the features associated with them.

First, an effective data communications system must provide information to the right people in a timely manner. Having information at the proper place in a timely fashion can mean the difference between making a profit and sustaining a loss. Today's companies have networked data communication systems that can deliver text, voice, and graphical information at speeds that were impossible just a few years ago. By integrating communication and computer technology, a letter or report can be delivered anywhere in the world in seconds or minutes. In the case of **videoconferencing**, for example, the information is delivered near-instantaneously. Instantaneous delivery of information is becoming more and more prevalent with the growing use of the **Internet** and mobile telephones to access databases at a central location anywhere, anytime.

Second, a data communications system needs to capture business data as it is being produced. Data communications systems are being used more and more as input mechanisms to capture data about the daily business operations of a company as the data is generated. On-line computer applications allow a business to enter customer information, produce an invoice to the customer, and provide inventory, sales-effectiveness, and shipping information at the point of the customer transaction. Additionally, the information, once captured by the system, can be instantaneously made available to other users, often worldwide.

The survival of many businesses depends on having data available on a real-time basis. Imagine, for example, an airline reservation system that cannot provide accurate and up-to-date flight information to passengers or a warehouse club that sells products that are not in stock because the inventory has not been updated on a real-time basis. Transportation, finance, insurance, and many retail industries require complex, fast, and accurate data communications systems for their business survival. As a result, companies have developed redundant systems and reliable backup systems to ensure that their communication networks have a minimal amount of "downtime" (time when the network is not functioning). The survival of most companies requires that the data communications network supporting the company be accessible at all times of the business day.

Third, data communications systems allow people and businesses in different geographical locations to communicate with one another. Data communications systems allow employees of companies separated by large distances to work as if they were in close proximity. Corporations can communicate with manufacturing operations in a remote geographical location almost as easily as if the operation were in the same building. Inventory, personnel, and other company data can be transmitted from one location to another through high-speed data communications networks. In this manner, the corporation can operate as a single entity with little regard for geography. Managers can instantly review inventory levels in the manufacturing location. Engineers can deliver new designs in realtime, and managers can share up-to-date and accurate information to make the best strategic decisions.

Data communications systems combined with computer technology are an integral part of today's companies. As a result, a business can become more effective and efficient in the world market than was possible a few years ago.

## A Brief History

The first data communications systems were created in 1837 as a result of the invention of the telegraph by Samuel F. B. Morse. Even though the United States government declined to use the telegraph, in 1838 Morse created a private company to exploit his invention. By 1851, more than fifty telegraph companies were in operation. Today's Western Union Telegraph was formed in 1856 and became the largest communications company in the United States ten years later.

In 1876, the U.S. patent office issued a patent to Alexander Graham Bell for his invention of the telephone, with the Bell Telephone Company being formed in 1877. The first telephone system didn't have switching offices or exchanges. If a subscriber wanted to establish a communication with another subscriber, he had to have a pair of telephone wires attached directly to the phone at the location of the receiving call. Therefore, if a business needed communication with fifty other businesses, then it had to install fifty pairs of wires. When a call was made, the right wires had to be connected to the telephone. In addition, telephones didn't have bells or ringers. Therefore, both parties had to be on-line at the same time since there was no way for one party to know when the other was making a call.

Bell installed the first telephone exchange with an operator. By using wire jumpers, a telephone operator could connect a user to different locations. Therefore, subscribers didn't require a pair of wires for each location they wanted to reach.

In 1885, American Telephone and Telegraph Company (AT&T) was formed to build and operate long distance lines in order to interconnect the regional phone companies. This allowed the connection of the individual Bell company subsidiaries operating throughout the country to connect all their subscribers together.

Technology continued to progress, and by 1892 automatic switching began with the introduction of the first dial exchange in La Porte, Indiana. This system worked by using a series of electromechanical selector switches called relays to automatically place the incoming call on the right outgoing line. This process took time to complete and that is the reason the first telephone used round dials. The round dials provided a deliberate waiting period after each digit was dialed, giving the switch time to set up the connections. The electromechanical switch was replaced later by the electronic switch. With this type of device the delay used for the relays was no longer required, and pushbutton telephones could be used to make the connection.

The vacuum tube was invented in 1913, and in 1941 came the integration of computer and communications technology. This was an important step in the evolution of communications systems. The computer enabled the creation and management of faster and more sophisticated systems. With this integration, the usage and development of new systems accelerated, lowering the cost of communication and increasing quality and efficiency.

In 1943, submersible amplifiers and repeaters were developed, facilitating communication across large distances and among international customers. But it was the invention of the transistor in 1947 that revolutionized the telecommunication industry. The transistor allowed for the development of smaller and faster computers that, through mass production, became relatively inexpensive and within the reach of many companies and users. The integration of communications systems and computers would not be what it is today without the invention of the transistor and subsequent developments in integrated circuitry. This technology led to the development of **satellites** with the first satellite being launched in 1957, expanding the opportunity for worldwide data communications.

In 1968, an important decision known as the Carterfone Decision was made by the Federal Communications Commission (FCC). The FCC decided that a small Dallas, Texas-based company (Carter Electronics Corporation) could attach its Carterfone product to the public telephone network. The Carterfone allowed the connection of private radio systems to the phone network. When AT&T refused to allow Carter Electronics to attach its product to the phone system, Carter Electronics sued and won. This decision opened the door for the attachment of non-AT&T equipment to the public phone system and spawned a new era in the communications industry. It also helped in breaking the monopoly that AT&T and the Bell companies had over the phone system.

Other antitrust suits against AT&T during 1974 to 1982 ended in 1984 in the divestiture of AT&T from its 22 Bell companies. This allowed many other companies to provide phone services to individuals and corporations, ultimately increasing the quality, sophistication, and types of offerings that a communications company could provide. It also helped in reducing the cost of using data communications system.

Also, as a result of a Department of Defense initiative to connect major governmental, commercial, and educational entities during the early 1970s, the Internet was born. This development paved the way for the information superhighway in which many people and companies are interconnected via the Internet.

Table 1-1 shows a summary of the history of data communications.

| Year | Event |
| --- | --- |
| 1837 | Invention of the Telegraph |
| 1856 | Western Union was Created |
| 1877 | The Bell Company was Formed |
| 1885 | AT&T was created |
| 1913 | Invention of the Vacuum Tube |
| 1941 | Integration of Computing and Communication technology |
| 1947 | Invention of the Transistor |
| 1957 | First Satellite was Launched |
| 1968 | Carterfone Decision |
| 1984 | Divestiture of Bell into Separate Companies |

**Table 1-1.** A summary of data communication history

Today, the network of available telephone lines, microwave stations, and satellite stations continues to expand. Computer technology continues to become faster and more economical. Data communications has become a worldwide enterprise. These systems, although complex, have four common characteristics. These characteristics are called the data communication system basic components.

# Basic Components

All data communications systems must have the following four major components:

1. The source of communication and the destination of that communication. These are the originator or sender of the message to be sent and the receiver (sometimes called the sink or **host**) of the message to be sent.

2. The medium of communication or transmission medium. This is the physical path through which the message has to travel.

3. One or more protocols for communication. These are the rules for communication between sender and receiver.

4. Something to send and receive, in other words, a message.

## The Sender or Originator

Although the communication established between two people through the use of the telephone is important, in this book we are more concerned with the communication requirements when two or more computers want to establish a communication link. This is because in many situations a computer is both the sender and receiver. If two computers have a communication link established and data is flowing from one machine to the other, one or the other of the machines is transmitting data at times and at other times may be receiving data.

## The Communications Medium

The medium can be a leased line from the telephone company (also called a common carrier), a proprietary coaxial, optical fiber, microwave, satellite or other line. Figure 1-1 depicts a basic data communication system. This system includes computers or terminals that act as senders, modems, connector cables, telephone equipment, interexchange channel facilities, a receiver, and a host computer. The items in Figure 1-1 will be explained in more detail in further chapters, but a general description follows.

The computer and terminal are used to enter information. This device can be a **terminal** attached to a minicomputer or mainframe, or a microcomputer with a keyboard and a printer, or it can be a facsimile machine, or any other input device.

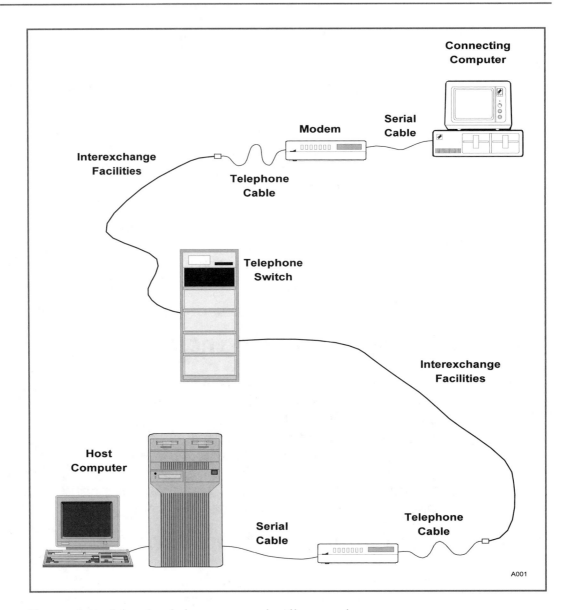

**Figure 1-1.** A basic data communications system.

The connector cables in Figure 1-1 connect the sender to a modem. The **modem** is an electronic device that converts digital signals originating from the computer or facsimile machine into analog signals that the analog telephone equipment can transmit.  The signals go from the modem to a local telephone switch that connects the home or office to the telephone company central office or some other carrier  Then, at the central office, switching equipment connects the sender's equipment to a line that terminates at the receiver's location and equipment.

# The Protocol or Rules

Just as communication between two individuals relies on the two individuals speaking the same language, data communications relies on the sender and receiver sending and receiving messages according to a predetermined set of rules called protocols. In the case of data communications through the public telephone system, the rules are defined by the telephone company. In the case of data communications utilizing other media besides that of the public telephone system, the rules may be defined by the type of communications desired, the actual media used, etc. This topic will be explored further in later chapters.

# The Message

There must be information that the sender wishes to send to the receiver if there is to be data communications in the first place. This message may be encoded in various manners depending on the type of information being sent. Voice data, for example, is usually handled differently from the transmission of data files themselves.

# The Central Office

The central office or exchange office contains switching and control facilities operated by the phone company All calls and data exchanges have to flow through these facilities unless there is a leased line. If there is a leased line, the phone company bypasses the switching equipment in order to provide an unbroken path of communication between sender and receiver. An example of a commonly used lease line is the T1 line, which will be discussed in Chapter 3.

# The Interexchange Facilities

Interexchange channels or IXCs are circuit lines that connect one central exchange office with another. These circuit lines can be microwave, satellite, coaxial cable, optical fiber, or other physical media. They simply relay communication data from one geographical location to another for the purpose of routing the call.

# The Host or Receiver

Finally, the receiving end has another modem to convert the analog signals from the telephone company back to digital format. These signals are then transferred to a host computer that processes the received message and takes appropriate actions.

Many other components can be incorporated into the data communication system depicted in Figure 1-1. Later chapters provide further details of these components, as well as an in-depth discussion of communications networks that incorporate computer technology. However, one component of the data communication system, the communication network, is worth discussing at this point.

# The Data Communications Network

A network is a series of points that are connected by some type of communication channel.

Each point or node is typically a computer although it can consist of switching equipment, printers, facsimile machines, or other devices. A data communications network is a collection of data communications circuits managed as a single entity. Then what is the difference between a data communications system and a data communications network? The collection of data communications networks and the people who enter data, receive the data, and manage and control the networks make up the communications system. Figure 1-2 shows examples of multiple networks that are part of a data communications system.

Even though almost anyone can establish a data communications network, successful network implementations have a common set of characteristics. These characteristics or requirements of a data communications network must be observed if a network is to be efficient and effective in its role. To create a successful implementation, a network designer must be aware of all the different configurations and possibilities that are at his or her disposal in designing the network. The network designer must be well schooled in design techniques as well as have an excellent understanding of the data communications field. This last point may seem trivial, but many companies leave network designing, especially local area network designing, to individuals without the proper background and training. The result is a poorly configured system that is blamed for the difficulties and problems in communicating data within the company and a lack of user confidence in technology.

## Requirements of a Data Communications Network

As discussed above, there is a set of major criteria that a successful data communications network must meet. These are performance, consistency, reliability, recoverability, and security.

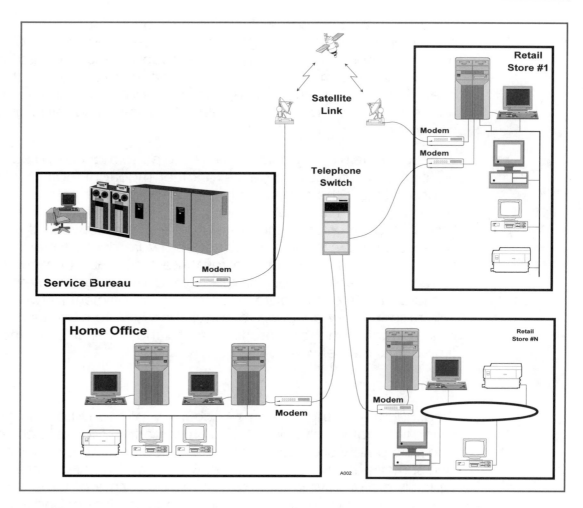

**Figure 1-2.** Multiple networked data communications systems.

## Performance

A data communications network must deliver data in a timely manner. Performance is typically measured by the network response time. Response time is normally considered to be the elapsed time between the end of an inquiry to the network and the beginning of the response from the network or system. The response time of a communications network must meet the expectations of the users.

Many factors affect the response time of a network. Some of these factors are the number of users on the system, transmission speed, type of **transmission medium**, and type of hardware and software being employed. For example, assume that a network was designed to handle the data communications needs of 20 individuals and their associated equipment. If the company that employs them doubles in size, the number of users is also likely to double. Most likely, the response time of the communications system will increase, in some cases by several orders of magnitude.

In addition, 20 users communicating through a medium at 10 million bits per second (megabits) will get a different response time than the same number of users using a 4 megabits per second medium. Also, the type of data transmitted makes a difference in the response time of the network. If text files are transmitted through the 4 megabit path, the response time will be faster than for the same network transmitting large graphics files and text files.

Although there is a tendency to relate the performance of a data communications network to its hardware, another important factor that will affect response time is the type of software controlling the system. The network operating system and the different protocols supported by the network will have a large impact on the performance of the network. It is true that, if a network is slow, introducing faster hardware and a faster communication medium will decrease the response time. But, in many cases, the increase in speed of transmission gained by using this method is small compared to the gain obtained by using an efficient network operating system specifically designed to handle heavy data communications. Just as important as the response time itself is the consistency of the response time across the network.

## Consistency

Predictability of response time, accuracy of the data transmitted and mean time between failures (MTBF) are important factors to consider when choosing a network. Inconsistency of response time is annoying to users, and sometimes it is worse than a slow but consistent response time. Users typically prefer having a consistent response time of three seconds that they can depend on to having, for example, a one-second response time that, on occasion, varies to 15 seconds. Unpredictable performance may motivate some users to rely on other means of acquiring and transmitting their data, making the data communications network inadequate as a data communications solution for the company.

## Reliability

Accuracy of data is important if the network is to be deemed reliable. If a system loses data, then the users will not have confidence in the information generated by the system. An unreliable system is often not used, and if it is used, users tend to duplicate the data entered into the network by using manual or other off-line systems. The result is that users spend additional time manually duplicating everything they send through the network, thus increasing the amount of time they spend on a function. This decreases their productivity, increases the cost to the company, and tends to demoralize the users of the system.

In addition to the accuracy of the data transmitted, another factor that contributes to network reliability is how often the network is unusable. This is often called network failure and is measured by the mean time between failures.

Network failure is any event that prohibits the users from processing transactions. Network failure can include a breakdown in hardware, the data carrying medium, and/or the network controlling software (network operating system). With today's complex data communications networks, the number of components that can fail during the operation of the network is continually increasing. Current-day equipment has a failure rate that is less than that of similar but older equipment. In addition, new monitoring software and hardware as well as redundancy in the network contribute to increasing the time that the system is operational.

As mentioned above, the failure rate of the network and its equipment is measured by the mean time between failures. The MTBF is a measure of the average time a component is expected to operate between failures. This time is normally established by the manufacturer of the equipment, and users normally trust the numbers provided by the makers of the equipment. However, many user groups and trade publications have their own statistics, and users are advised to compare these numbers with those provided by equipment manufacturers. In addition, these statistics provide some indication of the time of recovery after failure. This refers to the length of time for the equipment or the network to become operational after a failure. Also, the fact that a network is composed of several separate but connected components further modifies the effective MTBF and MTTR (Mean time to repair).

## Recovery

All networks are subject to failure. After a failure, the network must be able to recover to a prescribed level of operation. This prescribed level is a point in the network operation where the amount of lost data is nonexistent or at a minimum. Recovery procedures and the extent of recovery will depend on the types of hardware and software that control the network.

Some networks use log files that are saved continually to a hard disk. These log files contain all transactions performed since the system was turned on or since a predetermined date. If the network fails, many operating systems are capable of using the log file to rebuild transactions that were lost when the system went down. Less sophisticated systems rely on a network operator to rebuild the system log file. In addition, many networks employ what are commonly known as mirror techniques with their hard drives. With this technique data can be saved to two different hard disks at the same time. In this manner, if a hard disk failure occurs, the other hard disk is brought on line and the system can stay operational. Mirror techniques enhance the reliability of the network, but they also enhance another critical aspect of the network, its security.

## Security

Network security is another important component in communications networks, especially when computer data is involved. A business's data must be protected from unauthorized access and from being destroyed in a catastrophic event such as a fire. Therefore, companies are placing more stringent security measures on networks in order to safeguard their data. When a communications network is being designed, security must be carefully considered and incorporated into the final design.

A network's security is enhanced by the use of identification numbers and passwords for all its users. In addition, call-back utilities can be used to reduce the number of unauthorized callers connecting through dial-up ports. These units assure that the caller or user of the network is using an authorized location and/or terminal. However, even these measures are not enough in safeguarding the data transmitted through and stored in the network.

Another technique employed when security is a high priority is encryption. With this method, data that needs to be transmitted is encoded with a special security key. The result is that the data is unusable to unauthorized users. At the receiving end, the same key is used to decode the data and convert it to its original format. Security keys and encrypting are commonly used in the defense industry.

Data on a network is also threatened by computer viruses. A computer virus is a program that invades programs inside computers in the network and then performs unwanted functions on the programs themselves and the data stored on disks. These functions can be as simple as displaying annoying characters on the screens of network users, or as unpleasant as destroying the data stored on the users' hard disks and network servers. Several programs and monitoring software can be used to alert network administrators to the presence of such viruses.

## Applications of Communications Networks

During the 1990s and on into the twenty-first century, networks will be one of the fastest growing segments in the computer industry. Even though both industries are now integrated, we are moving from the computer era to the data communications era.

A recent survey indicates that during this decade, the majority of new career opportunities will be related to the communications field, especially in local and widearea networks and their connection to other systems, including the Internet. Data communications networks are appearing in all places where one computer needs to exchange data with another computer. Teaching institutions are connecting their students and administrative workstations to enhance communication and data sharing. Companies connect each department with a local area network and then connect individual local area networks into a single enterprise network; companies that cover the world connect their regional networks into wider area networks through the use of satellites and other wide area communications.

Also, many business systems currently use data communications networks as the backbone for carrying out their daily business activities. Data communications networks can be found in every segment of industry. On-line passenger systems, such as American Airlines' SABRE system, have changed the way people travel. In addition, an airline's computer is normally connected to all other airlines via telecommunications. In this manner, reservation agents from United Airlines can make reservations for flights on American Airlines. Car rental companies, such as Avis, and hotel chains, such as Holiday Inn, could not function effectively without their reservation systems. The type and scope of communications networks are wide and extensive. Several applications of data communications networks are commonly found in modern-day companies. These types of applications are discussed in the following paragraphs and include video-text, satellite, public networks, teleconferencing, and telecommuting.

## Videotext

Videotext is the capability of having a two-way transmission between a television or computer in the home and organizations outside the home. It allows people to take college courses at home, conduct teleconferences from the home, play video games with players in other locations, utilize electronic mail, connect with the bank and grocery stores, do on-line mail shopping, utilize voice store and messaging systems, and carry out many other functions. The conferencing system can be accessed from a home or office by using a microcomputer and special hardware and software to call a host computer and "talk" to other people on the system. This is a common process used on many public and commercial **bulletin boards** and even the IRC (Internet Relay Chat) channels over the Internet. With it, an electronic public forum or a question and answer session that involves dozens of people simultaneously can be conducted. In addition, it is a quick way to have impromptu on-line training between a customer and a service company.

## Satellite

By using a home satellite TV receiver and transmitter, people will be able to communicate with other people via a satellite dish located on their property. This antenna can receive and transmit voice or data to any other part of the world by relaying it to other satellites orbiting the earth. Many steps have been taken to reduce the cost of transmitting data using this method. Today the cost of receiving data using a home satellite dish is relatively low.

One use of satellite technology has been tested by politicians when they conduct electronic town meetings. When one of the "meetings" takes place, the satellite and frequency of transmission are normally available to the public. A person with the right equipment and information can tune into the satellite channel and receive the transmission without the inter-ruption of commentators normally found in commercial television. Transmission back to other sites, though, usually involves equipment outside the range of purchase by most individuals and is therefore left to commercial concerns.

Satellite communication is also used for commercial worldwide announcement of a new product or for simultaneous worldwide training. Novell, Inc., for example, customarily uses satellite transmission to announce new products and to provide marketing and technical training of their products.

## Public Communications Networks

**Public networks** have standard interfaces that allow almost any type of computer or terminal to connect to other computers or terminals. Many companies already have their own private telephone branch exchange (PBX). These systems can connect terminals and computers in the company to other systems anywhere in the world by using satellite, radio, and microwave transmission.

Using public networks, an individual can use a terminal or computer and a modem from his or her home and connect to other computers and networks in a different geographical location. This capability is used by many progressive companies to allow their employees to work from their homes. This has increased the efficiency of many employees since they can now spend the time required to travel back and forth from the office performing their jobs. Additionally, companies are now able to keep valuable employees that they could otherwise lose such as new parents who want to stay home with their children. By using a personal computer, a modem, and a public network, these employees can now minimize the amount of time spent at the office.

In addition to traditional transmission media offered by public networks, cellular radio loops can be used to replace copper wire as the communication medium for computers. This increases the ability of an employee to be at a required location and still be in touch with the main office's network and host systems.

## Teleconferencing

Video teleconferencing allows people located in different geographical regions to "attend" meetings in both voice and picture format. A video teleconference is accomplished by using a television camera and associated equipment to transmit voice and video signals through satellite networks. Many teleconferences have the same type of equipment at both sites, allowing all attendees to talk to and see each other, including selected computer displays. Other teleconferences have the projection equipment at a single location, and participants at remote locations can communicate back to the central transmitting site by using telephone communications.

Documents can also be made available to all people attending the teleconference almost instantaneously. This can be performed with the use of facsimile machines or by using a scanner and then transmitting the scanned image. However, if the required document exists in digital form, the data can simply be transmitted with the use of a modem and a receiving modem and computer system.

## Telecommuting

This application, as explained before, allows employees to perform office work at home. Through the use of a terminal or a personal computer and a modem, an employee can be in constant communication with the company and perform his or her work more efficiently and without wasting the time required to travel to and from the office. This allows employees to have greater time flexibility, less stress, optimized scheduling, and many other benefits. The employee is then free to schedule his or her work to allow for maximizing use of the available time. In most of these cases, the employee visits the office once or twice per week for meetings or other duties, but this time is minimal when compared to the weekly schedule.

## Electronic Mail

**Electronic mail** (e-mail) provides the ability to transmit written messages over short or long distances instantaneously through the use of a microcomputer or terminal attached to a communication network. The people communicating through electronic mail do not have to be on-line at the same time. They can leave messages and retrieve the replies later. Figure 1-3 shows a screen that is typical of many electronic mail systems.

Electronic mail has the ability to forward messages to different locations, send word processed or spreadsheet documents to any user of the network, and transmit the same message to more than one user by using a mail list. A mail list contains the names and electronic mailbox addresses of people to whom the message must be sent. The electronic mail system reads the names and addresses from the list and sends the message to all users on the mail list. Electronic mail significantly improves corporate and individual communications.

## Home Banking

Computers can handle the traditional methods of making payments through home banking. A user with a terminal or microcomputer can connect to his or her bank's computer network through electronic mail and pay bills electronically, instead of writing paper checks. The user can indicate the amount of a payment and the receiver of the payment electronically, and the bank processes the transfer of funds. Additionally, new home banking systems offer many other services such as providing checking account balances, ticket purchasing, and stock information services. Figure 1-4 shows a screen of a home banking service software program. The banking service displayed in the figure has options for bill paying, credit card acquisition, money markets, IRAs, loans, and mortgages.

Also, many electronic home banking services are being connected to other consumer services such as grocery stores. By using this service, an individual can use a personal computer and modem to dial a database of products belonging to a grocery company or store. The user selects the type and quantity of the products needed and then instructs the system to produce a balance. The balance is then forwarded to the electronic home banking system which transfers the balance to the grocer's account, and the bag of groceries can be picked up by the customer. Or, for a small fee, it can be delivered to the customer's address.

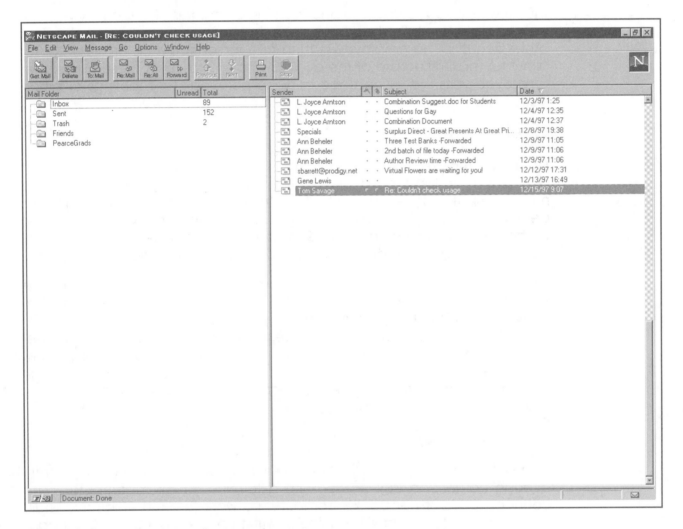

**Figure 1-3.** Electronic mail example.

## Electronic Funds Transfer

The ability to transfer funds electronically from one financial institution to another has become a necessity in today's banking world. Commercial banks transfer millions of dollars daily through their **electronic funds transfer** (EFT) systems. The large number of transactions that are made every day by banks requires the use of computers and communications networks to increase speed and cost efficiency.

Imagine the amount of time that it would take to manually handle all fund transfer transactions that take place in a single day at the New York Stock Exchange. Although some people think that the use of technology in such settings is more harmful than good, today's financial transactions couldn't be accomplished without the use of effective data communication networks. The modern Western world couldn't exist as we know it without such communication systems.

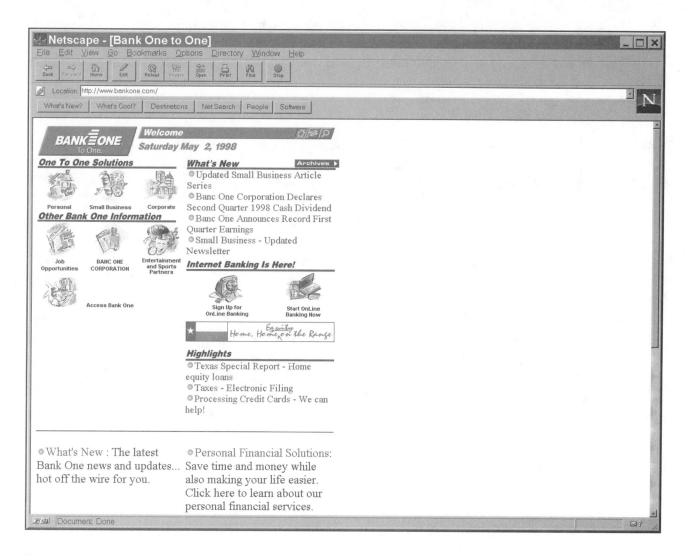

**Figure 1-4.** A Web page permitting home banking via the Internet.

## Information Utility Services

Information utility services offer general and specialized information that is organized and cross-referenced, much as subjects are in libraries. Items are organized into databases and each database contains several categories of services, such as access to news, legal libraries, stock prices, electronic mail services, conferencing, and games.

The desired information is located by signing onto the **information service** and then selecting the topic of interest from a menu. Once the topic is selected, search criteria can be entered and the system will display the information on the screen. This information can then be captured (downloaded) onto the hard disk of the user's microcomputer for further examination.

## Electronic Bulletin Boards

The electronic bulletin board system (BBS or EBBS) consists of a computer or microcomputer that is used to store, retrieve, and catalog messages sent in by the general public through their modems. The telephone company provides the link between the person using the BBS and the host computer of the BBS. The primary purpose of the BBS is for people to leave notes to others.

Additionally, some BBS are now being used for group conferencing. They offer a variety of messages and services to their users. Some of these services are electronic "chats" with other users, making airline reservations, playing games, and sending and receiving messages.

## Value Added Networks

Value added networks (VANs) are alternative data carriers to the traditional public data carriers such as AT&T. VANs are now considered common carriers and are subject to all government regulations. They can be divided into public and private VANs.

Private VANs own and operate their networks and are not accessible to the public. One example of a private carrier is the SABRE system used by travel agents to make reservations and check prices. Public VANs offer a wide variety of communication services to the general public. These services include access to databases and electronic mail routing. An example of a public VAN is Telenet.

## The Internet

Perhaps the most far-reaching of the information services is the Internet. Using a software package called a browser and a connection to the worldwide Internet through an Internet Service Provider, a user can obtain information on almost any service or products available in the world. Locating this information can often be challenging. Figure 1-5. shows a sample screen depicting the home page for a search engine service called Yahoo. By connecting to the Yahoo search page and then typing in the name of the item to be searched, a user is given a listing of links to pages with information about the desired search item. The user can then connect directly to the desired site or can note the site for further reference.

Additionally, the Internet is rapidly changing the face of business worldwide through its support of electronic commerce. Companies of all sizes can have equal footing to advertise and sell their products through the Internet. Further, because the Internet is available 24 hours per day, normal selling hours are no longer imposed, and consumers have greater latitude in purchasing goods and services when they need them from the privacy of their own homes or offices.

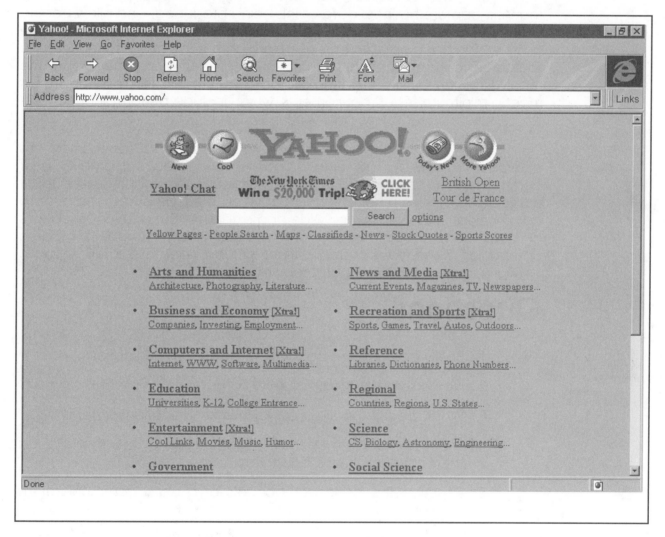

**Figure 1-5**. The Next Generation bulletin board - An Internet search engine (Screen text and artwork copyright© 1997 by YAHOO! INC. All rights reserved. YAHOO! and YAHOO! logo are trademarks of YAHOO! INC.)

# Summary

Data communications is the transmission of electronic data over some medium. The medium can be coaxial cable, optical fiber, microwave, or some of the other data-carrying media. The hardware and software systems that enable the transmission of data make up what are called data communications networks. For a data communications system to be effective, it must provide information to the right people in a timely manner, capture business data as it is being produced, and allow people in businesses in different geographical locations to communicate with one another. The basic components of a data communications system are the source of communication, the medium of communication, and the receiver of the communication. All data communications systems must meet a minimum set of requirements, which include performance, consistency, reliability, recovery, and security.

Data communications systems are composed of data communications networks. A network is a series of points connected by some type of communication channel. Each point is typically a computer, although it can consist of many other electronic devices. The type and scope of data communications networks are wide and extensive. But a few applications of data communications networks are commonly found in modern companies. These types of applications include videotext, satellite, public networks, teleconferencing, and telecommuting.

# Questions

1. Briefly describe the concept of data communications.

2. Name some of the possible data transmission media.

3. What are the functions of data communications systems?

4. Briefly name the most important historical events that shaped the communications industry up to the 1990s.

5. Describe the basic components of a data communications network.

6. What is a communications network?

7. What is the difference between a communications network and a communications system?

8. What are the major requirements that a data communications network must possess?

9. What is meant by mean time between failures (MTBF)?

10. Discuss three applications of a data communications network.

11. What is e-mail?

12. What is a bulletin board system?

13. What is an information service?

14. What services are provided by commercial bulletin board systems?

15. Name and describe the importance of four commercial information services.

# Projects

## Project 1. Understanding an Existing Computer Communications System

This project will make the student familiar with a currently implemented data communications system. It provides a way to visualize the concepts and hardware discussed in the chapter. In addition, it allows the student to acquire a "feel" for how people use the components of data communications systems and to observe some of the equipment and processes that will be explained in more detail in subsequent chapters.

Visit the data center at your institution or at a local business and find out what types of network and data communications facilities are available for the private use of the institution and which facilities are available for general public access. Try to answer all of the following questions by asking data center personnel or by observing the daily operations and hardware present at the center.

1. What types of mainframes or minicomputers (hosts) are available?

2. What types of personal computers are available?

3. Laptops - list models and types

4. Macintosh - list models and types

5. PC or PC-compatible 80286 machines

6. PC or PC-compatible 80386 machines

7. PC or PC-compatible 80486 machines

8. Pentium PC or PC-compatible machines

9. Other

10. Are the hosts networked?

11.  Are the personal computers networked?

12.  How are the personal computers connected to the host?

13.  Is electronic mail available?

14.  How is the electronic mail accessed?

15.  What databases are available in the institution library?

16.  How often do they experience downtime?

17.  Find out how the staff conducts business when their computer or terminal is down.

18.  How is the data protected from unauthorized access and accidents?

# Project 2. Understanding an Elementary Computer Network

Contact your local bank and write a report that describes how the bank personnel perform their daily routines. Use the following outline as a guide for your report.

1.  What computer systems are in use at headquarters and at the branches?

2.  Mainframes

3.  Minicomputers

4.  Personal computers

5.  Terminals

6.  What networks are used at each branch and between the branches and headquarters?

7.  How is electronic funds transfer handled?

8.  What types of value added networks and public networks are used to perform e-mail and electronic fund transfer?

9.  Are there any facilities available for home banking?

10.  What types of disaster recovery plans do they have?

11.  How do the managers at different branches communicate with one another.

# 2
# Basic Communication Concepts and Hardware

## Objectives

After completing this chapter you will

1. Differentiate among the various modes of data transmission.

2. Understand the ASCII code system and its importance.

3. Understand the concept and use of modems in the communication process.

4. Be able to design and use interfaces for serial (RS-232) ports.

5. Understand the role of microcomputers in data communications systems.

## Key Terms

Half-Duplex

Full-Duplex

Parallel Port

Asynchronous Communication

Synchronous Communication

ASCII

Control Characters

Modem

Serial Port

RS-232 Interface

# Introduction

Data communications hardware and software come in many different forms and levels of sophistication. However, at the basic level of transmissions, a few concepts and devices are standard across all computing and data communications platforms. The mode of transmission is one of these concepts. Regardless of the devices transmitting, the modes in which the data is transmitted remain basically constant. In this case data can be transmitted in simplex, half-duplex or full-duplex, and it can be a serial or parallel transmission. Data can be sent asynchronously or synchronously. These are the concepts that this chapter explores along with a description of the standard digital codes that constitute the data being transmitted.

In addition to the mode of data transmission, this chapter explores the concepts and uses of modems. Since modems are a basic and common way of communication in the microcomputer world, they deserve special treatment. Also, the port used to connect the modem to the computer, the RS-232 or EIA-232, as it is sometimes called, is explored and analyzed in detail.

# Modes of Transmission

There are many different ways in which the transmission of data can be classified. However, data transmission is normally grouped into three major areas according to

1. How the data flows among devices

2. The type of physical connection.

3. The type of timing used for transmitting data.

Data can flow in simplex, half-duplex, or full-duplex mode (see Figure. 2-1). The physical connection can be parallel or serial (see Figure. 2-2), and the timing can be synchronous or asynchronous.

## Data Flow

In simplex transmission, data flows in only one direction on a data communications line. Examples of this type of communication are commercial television and radio transmission. A television station normally broadcasts a signal from an antenna connected to a production studio and it is received by a television receiver in the home. Once the signal is received by the television set, it is displayed but no data is sent back to the production studio.

In **half-duplex** mode, transmission is allowed in either direction on a circuit, but in only one direction at a time. This type of transmission is widely used in data processing applications. If a computer is communicating with a terminal in this mode, then only one of them can be transmitting at any given time. Once the terminal sends data to the computer and the message is received, then the computer can send data back to the terminal. During this last phase, the terminal becomes the listener and the computer the sender. If two devices are communicating in half-duplex and both transmit at the same time, then the data sent is not received or simply becomes "garbage" in the lines.

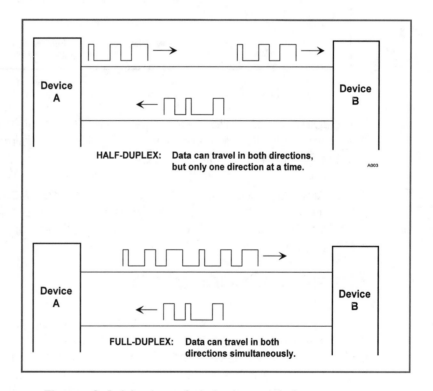

**Figure 2-1.** Modes of data transmission.

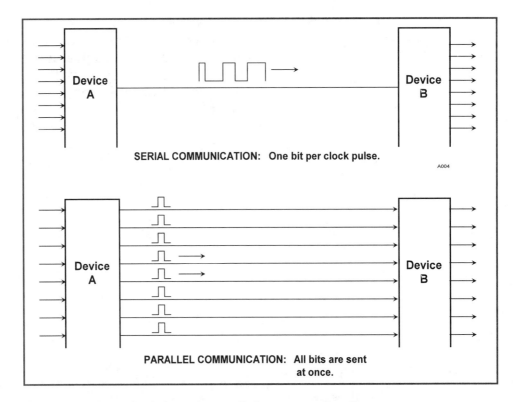

**Figure 2-2**. Serial and parallel communications.

**Full-duplex** mode allows for the transmission of data in both directions simultaneously. Most terminals and microcomputers are configured to work in full-duplex mode. This type of transmission allows the computer and the terminal to send at the same time, so it requires more software and hardware control on both ends. Specialized software and hardware make sure that the messages are delivered to their destinations in a legible format. Although this is the most complex of the three modes, it is also the most efficient.

## Physical Connection

Although data transmission can be classified according to the format of the data flow through the communication wires, it can also be classified as to how many bits of information are transmitted with every clock pulse. If data transmission is classified in this manner, then two possibilities arise. One is parallel communication and the other is serial communication.

The input/output ports of a data processing device can transmit data bit by bit or send an entire byte in a single parallel operation employing eight lines, one for each bit. The benefit of parallel transmission is its simplicity. A byte is placed on the output port of a device and a single pulse of the computer clock transfers the data to a receiving device. However, because of the number of wires involved and the loss of signal over relatively short distances, it is impractical to use **parallel port**s for communications over long distances. Parallel communication is achieved through the use of a parallel port normally located at the back of the computer or a Centronics interface on a printer or other peripheral.

In serial transmission the data is sent one bit at a time using a single conductor to provide communication between devices. Standard telephone lines can be used to transmit data serially. Although transmitting data in this mode is slower than parallel transmission, it is currently a widely used data transmission mode. This is especially true in the case of communications between a microcomputer and a minicomputer or mainframe. In many situations, the microcomputer is simply working in a terminal emulation mode. That is, it is working as if it were the native terminal of the minicomputer or mainframe. In such cases, most managers want to use the least expensive communication schema. If the microcomputers are in close proximity to the host, serial communication is normally employed.

# Timing

The type of timing used for the transmission of data is the last of the major categories for classifying data communications. Here, timing refers to how the receiving system knows that it received the group of bits that form a valid character. Two major timing schemas are used. One is **asynchronous communication** and the other is synchronous data communication.

Asynchronous communication is characterized by the use of a start bit preceding each character transmitted. In addition, one or more stop bits follow each character. In asynchronous transmission, sometimes called async, data comes in irregular bursts, not in steady streams.

The start and stop bits form what is called a character frame. Every character must be enclosed in a frame. The receiver counts the start bit and the appropriate number of data bits. If it does not sense the end of a frame, then a framing error has occurred and an invalid character was received. When this happens, smart systems ask that the sender retransmit the last group of bits.

Asynchronous transmission is relatively simple and inexpensive to implement. It is widely used by microcomputers and commercial communication devices. However, it has a low transmission efficiency since at least two extra bits must be added to each character transmitted. Typically, asynchronous communication takes place at low speeds, ranging from 300 to 19,200 baud, but the transmission speed can be higher.

The start and stop bits in asynchronous transmission add overhead to the bit stream. There is an alternate method of serial communication that doesn't use start and stop bits. It is called synchronous serial communication. With synchronous transmission, data characters are sent in large groups called blocks. These blocks contain synchronization characters that have a unique bit pattern. They are placed at the beginning and middle of each block with the synchronization characters ranging in number from one to four. When the receiver detects one of these special characters, it knows that the following bit is the beginning of a character maintaining, in this manner, synchronization.

This type of transmission is more efficient than asynchronous communication. As an example, assume that 10,000 characters are going to be sent serially. If the characters are sent via asynchronous transmission, then 10,000 char x ( 8 data bits + 2 bits per char) yields 100,000 bits that are sent in asynchronous communications. Using **synchronous communication**, the calculation (10,000 char + 4 synchronous char) x 8 bits per char yields 80,032 bits that are sent.

In this example, the synchronous transmission has a 22 percent increase in transmission efficiency over asynchronous transmission. The efficiency of synchronous over asynchronous transmission increases as the block of data gets larger. Many terminals use synchronous communication, including the IBM 3270 series. However, the actual efficiency of the transmission will also depend on many other factors such as how many times bits must be retransmitted.

## Standard Digital Codes

As mentioned before, computers process information in digital form. That is, information is in the form of individual bits or digits with a bit being the smallest unit of data that the computer can represent. Normally, personal computers use 7 or 8 bits to represent the individual characters that are stored inside the computer. Individual characters for the English language that are stored in a computer include:

Lower- and uppercase letters of the alphabet (a...Z)

Digits (0...9)

Punctuation marks (., ?, :, ...)

Arithmetic operators (*,-,+,/,...)

Unit symbols (%, $, #, ...)

In addition to these characters, there is a set of special characters that some computer makers include with their machines. These are mostly graphical and language-specific characters.

For many years, the computer industry has tried to standardize the representation of digital codes. As a result, two major code representations exist in the market today. The most popular and widely recognized is the code system employed by computer manufacturers in the United States and many other countries called the American Standard Code for Information Interchange (ASCII). The other major code is the Extended Binary Coded Decimal Interchange Code (EBCDIC), which is used by IBM mainframes and compatibles. Most other types of mainframes, minicomputers, and microcomputers employ the **ASCII** code.

ASCII is a seven-bit code in which 128 characters are represented. EBCDIC uses eight bits to represent each character. Table 2-1 shows the standard ASCII code representation. In addition to the standard 128 ASCII characters, there is a set of 128 special characters used by IBM personal computers and compatibles called the Extended ASCII code. The characters represented in Extended ASCII vary among computer manufacturers and are used to represent foreign characters or graphic characters.

In this chapter we will concentrate on explaining the ASCII representation since it is the most popular. The ASCII code in Table 2.1 contains 128 unique items. The table shows 32 **control characters** and 96 printable characters. Table 2-1 uses the hexadecimal system to represent the ASCII value of each character. To find the ASCII value of a character the process is as follows. Assume that the ASCII value of "A" is required. The column number of "A" is four, therefore four is multiplied by 16 giving 64. The row number of "A" is one, so one is added to the previous result. The total is 65 and that is the ASCII value of the character "A". Notice that the rows jump from 9 to A, B, C, D, E, and F. In this case A represents 10, B is 11, C is 12, D is 13, E is 14, and F is 15. Using this example it is easily verified that the ASCII value of the character "O" is 79 because 4 x 16 = 64, and 64 + 15 = 79.

The printable characters can be generated by pressing the corresponding key on the keyboard or by pressing the shift key and the appropriate key. The control characters are generated by pressing a key labeled Control or CTRL on the keyboard and a corresponding key. For the rest of this chapter, the character ^ will be used to denote the CTRL key. These control codes are used for communicating with external devices such as modems and printers.

The control codes can be further subdivided into format effectors, communication controls, information separators, and others as described in the following sections.

## Format Effectors

The format effectors provide functions analogous to the control keys used in document preparation. Each code name is followed by its hexadecimal representation, then a colon, and finally the key combination that can generate the code. A description of each follows.

BS (backspace) 08H:^H. It moves the cursor on a video display or the print head of a printer back one space.

HT (horizontal tab) 09H:^I. This is the same as the Tab key on a keyboard or typewriter.

LF (line feed) 0AH:^J. It advances the cursor one line on a display or moves the printer down one line.

CR (carriage return) 0DH:^M. It returns the cursor on a display or moves the printer head to the beginning of the line. This code is sometimes combined

|   | 0 | 1 | 2 | 3 | 4 | 5 | 6 | 7 |
|---|---|---|---|---|---|---|---|---|
| 0 | NUL | DLE | SP | 0 | @ | P | ` | p |
| 1 | SOH | DC1 | ! | 1 | A | Q | a | q |
| 2 | STX | DC2 | " | 2 | B | R | b | r |
| 3 | ETX | DC3 | # | 3 | C | S | c | s |
| 4 | EOT | DC4 | $ | 4 | D | T | d | t |
| 5 | ENQ | NAK | % | 5 | E | U | e | u |
| 6 | ACK | SYN | & | 6 | F | V | f | v |
| 7 | BEL | ETB | ' | 7 | G | W |   | w |
| 8 | BS | CAN | ( | 8 | H | X | h | x |
| 9 | HT | EM | ) | 9 | I | Y | l | y |
| A | LF | SUB | * | : | J | Z | j | z |
| B | VT | ESC | + | ; | K | ( | k | { |
| C | FF | FS | ' | < | L | \ | l | l |
| D | CR | GS | - | = | M | ) | m | } |
| E | SO | RS | . | > | N | A | n | ~ |
| F | SI | US | / | ? | O | - | o | DEL |

**Table 2-1.** ASCII codes.

with the line feed to produce a new line character that is defined as a CR/LF sequence.

FF (form feed) 0CH:^L. It ejects a page on a printer. It also causes the cursor to move one space to the right on a video screen.

VT (vertical tab) OBH: AK. It line feeds to the next programmed vertical tab on a printer. It causes the cursor to move up one line on a video screen.

## Communication Controls

Another series of control codes is used for communication. These controls facilitate data transmission over a communication network. They are used in both async and sync serial protocols for data transfer handshaking. These codes are:

SOH. It indicates the start of a message heading data block. Workstations in a network check the data following this header to determine if they are the recipients of the data that will follow the heading. Sometimes this character is used in asynchronous communications to transfer a group of files without handling each file as a separate communication session.

STX. It indicates the start of text.

ETX. It indicates the end of text.

EOT. It indicates the end of transmission.

ENQ. It indicates the end of an inquiry.

ACK. It indicates acknowledgment by a device.

NAK. It is negative acknowledgment.

SYN. It is synchronous idle.

ETB. It indicates the end of a block.

These control codes are used in building data-transfer protocols and during synchronous transmission.

## Information Separators

There are four information-separator codes.

FS. It is used as a file separator.

GS. It is used as a group separator.

RS. It is used as a record separator.

US. It is used as a unit separator.

Most of the communication control and information separator codes are not relevant to the material presented in the rest of this chapter. However, they are shown here for general information purposes.

## Additional Control Codes

Of the remaining codes used by computers, the following are the most important.

NUL (null) OOH: ^ @. It is used to pad the start of a transmission of characters.

BEL (bell) 07H:^G. It generates a tone from the speaker on the video monitor or the computer.

DC1, DC2, DC3, and DC4 (device control): ^Q, ^R, ^S, ^T. These codes are used to control video monitors and printers. Of these four, the first (DC1) and the third (DC3) are of special interest. DC1 is generated by ^Q and is called X-On. DC3 is generated by ^S and is called X-Off. If a computer sends information to a printer too quickly, then the printer's buffer gets full before it can print the characters stored in it. The result is that characters are lost before they can be printed. In this situation, the printer sends a ^S (X-Off) to the computer before the buffer is completely full. This causes the computer to stop sending characters. When there is room in the printer buffer for more characters, a ^Q (X-On) is sent to the computer. This indicates to the machine that it can resume sending characters. This use of X-On and X-Off is called software handshaking.

ESC (escape) 1BH: ^(. Video terminals, computers, and printers interpret the next character after the escape code as a printable character.

DEL (delete) 7FH. It is used to delete characters under the cursor on video displays.

When two computers communicate with each other, the information will be exchanged by passing the individual bits that make up the characters. The flow of information is controlled by the use of control codes between communicating devices. The conventions that must be observed in order for electronic devices to communicate with one another are called the protocol. The bits that make up these control characters flow through some type of communication medium

If the communicating devices are in close proximity then the medium of communication can be coaxial cable, twisted-pair cable, or optical fiber. If the computers are far apart, then microwave, satellite, or telephone line connections are used to connect the machines. The phone company provides one of the most common and inexpensive methods of connecting machines. However, if analog phone lines are used, a modem must be employed.

# Modems

Normally data communication between terminals or microcomputers and other host systems is done over some type of direct cabling. Direct means that the cable goes directly from one device to the other. However, sometimes the distance between the devices is too large to have a direct connection. In such cases a device called a **modem** can be used to facilitate the transmission process using telephone lines.

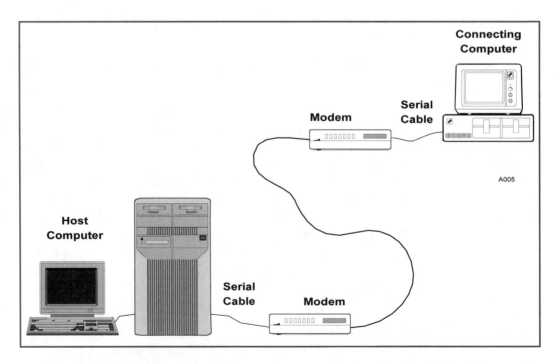

**Figure 2-3.** Connection between a remote terminal and host through a telephone line.

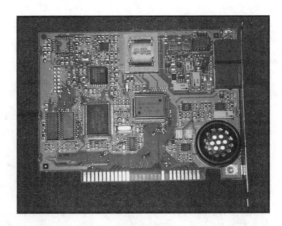

**Figure 2-4**. Internal card style modem.

Figure 2-3 depicts the connection of a remote terminal or microcomputer to a host system via standard telephone lines. The terminal and host systems are connected through telephone lines with a modem at each end of the connection. A modem is an electronic device that converts (modulates) the digital communications between computers into audible tones that can be transmitted over telephone lines. The received data are then converted (demodulated) from the audible tones into digital information. This is the origin of the name modem (MOdulator-DEModulator).

Modems not only facilitate the transmission process, but many of them have smart features built in. For example, many modems can dial phone numbers automatically. Additionally, they can redial busy numbers and automatically set the proper communicating speed. These features and others are discussed later in this section.

Although modems can be classified in many different ways, one way to classify them is according to the location of the modem with respect to the computer that it serves. Modems can be external or internal. An internal modem (Figure 2-4) is placed inside the computer by using available bus expansion slots or bays. Then it is connected to a phone line with the use of a standard phone cord.

An external modem (Figure 2-5) is separate from the computer and connected to one of its **serial port**s with the use of a serial cable and to the telephone line with a phone cord. Once the modem is connected to the computer and the telephone, its function is normally controlled by software residing in the computer.

Modems transmit data at various speeds. The speed of data transfer through a modem can range from 300 bits per second to 56000 and higher bits per second on microcomputers. On mainframe networks, some types of modems operate at speeds of up to 1.5 million bits per second, and higher.

**Figure 2-5**. Typical, serial cable-connected, external 28.8 Kb modem (Courtesy of U. S. Robotics).

The speed of the modem determines the time required to transfer files. A higher speed of transmission means lower transfer time. The file transfer time can be estimated by using the following formula.

Time = (characters to be transmitted x bits per character) / (modem speed in bits per second)

As an example, assume that a 100-page document is to be transmitted over telephone lines. Further assume that each page contains approximately 3300 characters and each character requires 7 bits for storage. This means that there are 2,310,000 bits. The following table shows the approximate amount of time required to transmit the file.

| Bits per second | 300 | 1200 | 4800 | 9600 | 14400 | 28800 |
|---|---|---|---|---|---|---|
| Time (seconds) | 7700 | 1925 | 480 | 240 | 160 | 80 |

These are approximate times. The actual time required to transfer a file depends on many factors such as noise in the communicating lines, how the data is packed, and how many times a character must be retransmitted when an error occurs. However, the times shown in the table can be used to obtain an idea of how the transmission time is reduced by increasing the speed of the modem.

## Types of Modems

There are several types of modems, each with a unique set of functions that make it suitable for a specific job. Some of the most common types are optical, short haul, acoustic, smart, digital, and V.32 modems. Of these, smart modems are the most commonly found in the microcomputer market.

## Optical Modem

An optical modem transmits data over optical fiber lines. This type of modem, at the sender's end, converts electrical signals from a computer into pulses of light to be transmitted over optical fiber lines. At the receiver's end, the modem receives the light pulses and converts them back into a signal that the computer can understand. It operates using asynchronous or synchronous transmission modes.

## Short Haul Modem

This type of modem uses paired wire cable to transmit electrical signals when the distances involved are approximately 20 miles or less. A short haul modem transmits at speeds of 9600 bits per second up to 5 miles, 4800 bits per second up to 10 miles, and finally at 2400 bits per second for distances of 10 to 20 miles. Normally, this type of modem is used to connect computers between different offices in the same building.

## Acoustic Modem

This is an older type of modem, also called an acoustic coupler. It interfaces with any phone set and it is used for dialing another computer.

## Smart Modem

A smart modem can perform functions by using a command language. The language can be accessed through communication programs and adds functionality to the modem. Among microcomputer users, the Hayes modem has become a standard. This device can automatically answer or dial other modems, switch communication parameters, set the modem's speaker volume. and perform many other functions under software control.

## Digital Modem

If, instead of using analog conversion, the communication circuits use digital transmission, then a digital modem is used. This type of modem modifies the digital bits as needed. Its function is to convert EIA-232 digital signals into signals more suitable for transmission.

## V.32 Modem

A V.32 modem works at full duplex at 9600 bits per second over normal telephone lines. It is typically used to back up leased phone lines on networks. That is, if data transmission through a leased line is interrupted, a V.32 and normal phone lines could be used as a temporary replacement for the leased line.

# Features of Modems

Most newer modems have features that facilitate their use by inexperienced computer users. These features include the ability to change the speed of transmission, automatic dialing and redialing of numbers, and automatic answering of incoming calls.

## Speed

Modems are designed to operate at a set speed or a range of speeds. The speed can be set via switches on some modems or fall under program control. Typical speeds for modems under microcomputer control are 1200, 2400, 4800, 9600, 14400, 28800, and 56000 bits per second.

It is important to note that modems are sometimes classified in terms of baud rating rather than bits per second. Baud refers to the number of state changes per second, and if only one bit of data is encoded into a given state change, then baud is equal to bits per second. Using a variety of encoding schemes, multiple bits can be encoded into one state change. For example, if a modem is transmitting at 2400 baud and the encoding method being used encodes 4 bits per state change, the modem is transmitting 9600 bits per second. When considering actual throughput, it is usually more useful to describe throughput in terms of bits per second rather than baud.

## Automatic Dialing/Redialing

Some modems can dial phone numbers under program control. If the modem encounters a busy line, it automatically redials the number until a connection is made

## Automatic Answering

Modems can automatically answer incoming calls and connect the dialing device to a host system. This is especially useful when setting up a private or home electronic bulletin board. In this case, you want the modem to answer calls automatically when a potential user calls in.

## Self-Testing

Most new modems have a self-testing mode. Each modem has electronic circuitry and software in ROM that allows the modem to check its electronic components and the connection to other modems, and to report any problems to the user. This includes memory checking and modem-to-modem transmission tests.

### Voice-over-Data

Modems also allow the simultaneous transmission of voice and data. This allows a conversation to take place while data is being transmitted over the same phone line.

Other newer modems contain many other features in addition to the ones outlined above. Some of these features are: auto-disconnect, manual connect/disconnect, speaker, full- or half-duplex, reverse channel, synchronous or asynchronous transmission, and multiport.

# The RS-232 Port

Modems normally connect to the computer through an **RS-232** or serial port. On most microcomputers, the connections between external modems, computers, and other devices conform to this RS-232 standard. The RS-232 is a connector that is found on the back panel of most computers. Figure 2-6 shows a diagram of a 25-pin RS-232 connector.

The important pins to consider are pin numbers 1, 2, 3, 4, 5, 6, 8, and 20. Following is a description of these connectors with the capitalized abbreviations corresponding to the modem front panel.

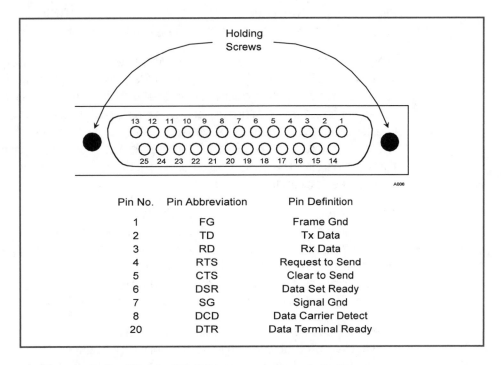

| Pin No. | Pin Abbreviation | Pin Definition |
|---------|------------------|----------------|
| 1 | FG | Frame Gnd |
| 2 | TD | Tx Data |
| 3 | RD | Rx Data |
| 4 | RTS | Request to Send |
| 5 | CTS | Clear to Send |
| 6 | DSR | Data Set Ready |
| 7 | SG | Signal Gnd |
| 8 | DCD | Data Carrier Detect |
| 20 | DTR | Data Terminal Ready |

**Figure 2-6.** 25-pin RS-232 connector definition.

Pin 1. Frame ground: FG. This pin is used to connect the frame of the terminal or modem to earth ground. It protects the device from dangerous voltages. Normally, this pin is left unconnected.

Pin 2. Transmit data: TD. Outgoing data travels from the terminal or computer to the modem via pin 2.

Pin 3. Receive data: RD. Incoming data travels from the modem to the terminal or computer via pin 3.

Pin 4. Request to send: RTS. This is used to indicate to the terminal or computer that the modem has activated its carrier and that data transmission can start.

Pin 5. Clear to send: CTS. This pin is taken to an active level when the terminal or computer is ready to accept data.

Pin 6. Data set ready: DSR. An active DSR indicates to a device that it is connected to an active modem.

Pin 7. Signal ground: SG. This pin completes the electrical circuit for all data signals on the other pins.

Pin 8. Data carrier detect: DCD. This pin is used by the modem to inform the computer or terminal that a remote connection has been made.

Pin 20. Data terminal ready: DTR. An active DTR indicates to the modem that it is connected to an active device.

Handshaking is the manner in which the communicating computer knows when the other machine is sending or receiving data, or when it is doing some other task that might interfere with the transmission signals. This is also referred to as the communications protocol. Handshaking can be accomplished through the use of software by using control characters (X-On and X-Off). Pins 4, 5, 6, 8, and 20 are used for hardware handshaking. That is, these pins are used to make sure that there is cooperation between the devices exchanging data.

Another type of RS-232 connector is the nine-pin RS-232 connector found on some microcomputers. By using nine pins instead of twenty-five pins, space is saved on the back panels of computers and peripherals. The layout of the pin connections on this type of RS-232 differs from manufacturer to manufacturer. Figure 2-7 shows the layout of the nine-pin RS-232 connector found on the IBM PC-AT and later machines.

The nine-pin connector in Figure 2-7 has an extra pin (pin 9, RI) beyond the eight defined above. This is the ring indicator. This pin becomes active when the modem has received the ring of an incoming call.

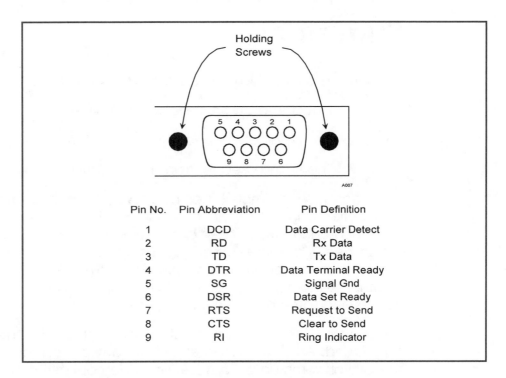

**Figure 2-7.** 9-pin RS-232 connector definition.

The process of using a modem to connect a microcomputer or terminal to a host system is as follows:

1. When the communicating devices are powered up, the terminal's DTR signal and the modem's DSR signal are activated.

2. When the terminal is ready to send data, it activates its RTS signal.

3. The modem activates the CTS signal of the analog carrier.

4. The user's modem dials the phone of the remote modem and waits for its response.

5. When the user's modem senses communication over the phone line, it activates its DCD signal.

6. A high-level DCD signal tells the microcomputer or terminal that it is connected to a remote device and the data exchange can begin.

# Summary

Data transmission is typically described according to

1.  How the data flows between devices

2.  The physical connection

3.  The timing used for transmitting data

Data can flow in simplex, half-duplex, or full-duplex mode. The physical connection can be parallel or serial, and the timing can be synchronous or asynchronous. Regardless of the mode of transmission, the data being transmitted is described by coding standards. One is the ASCII standard used by all microcomputers, non-IBM mainframes, and minicomputers. Another standard is the EBCDIC standard, which is used by IBM mainframes and some of their minicomputers.

In the case of serial communications over telephone lines, modems have to be used. A modem is an electronic device that converts (modulates) the digital communications between computers into audible tones that can be transmitted over telephone lines. The received data is then converted (demodulated) from the audible tones into digital information. There are several types of modems, each with a unique set of functions that makes it suitable for a specific job. Some of the most common types are optical, short-haul, acoustic, smart, digital, and V.32 modems. Smart modems are the most commonly found in the microcomputer market.

Modems normally connect to the computer through an RS-232 or serial port. On most microcomputers that use the ASCII code, the connections between external modems, computers, and other devices conform to this RS-232 standard. The RS-232 is a connector that is found on the back panel of most computers.

# Questions

1.  What is data transmission in full-duplex mode?

2.  Why is the synchronous mode more efficient than the asynchronous mode?

3.  Since parallel transmission is faster than serial transmission, why don't we perform all data communications using parallel transmission?

4.  What is the purpose of the ASCII standard?

5.  Describe the function of a modem.

6. In the case of microcomputers, which modem are we most likely to use when sending data over phone lines? Why?

7. Describe three different types of modems.

8. What is the purpose of the RS-232 port?

9. Briefly describe the process of handshaking.

# Projects

The projects in this chapter are intended to familiarize the student with the basic hardware required to connect computers and printers using standard RS-232 ports. The basic equipment required to perform the projects is outlined in Project 1. As an additional challenge, the instructor may provide unknown or lesser known serial printers and instruct the student to design the interface between the printer and a microcomputer.

## Project 1. Interface Between an External Modem and a Microcomputer

There are two methods of connecting an external modem to your computer. The first method is to purchase a serial cable from a local computer store and connect the RS-232 or serial connector at the back of the computer with the serial connector at the back of the modem. This is the easier method. The second method is to construct your own serial cable. The tools required to make this cable are as follows:

1. Soldering iron and solder material.

2. Nine-wire (or more) cable.

3. Two serial connectors of the right gender. The gender can be "male" or "female." The male has pins coming out of the connector. In most cases the connector required for the PC will be female and that for the modem will be male. However, the gender of the connectors is not standard among all equipment manufacturers.

4. Wire strippers.

5. Clamps to hold the wires and connectors.

6. Breakout box (optional).

After all the tools and materials are gathered, use the connections outlined in Figure 2-8 to connect a modem and a terminal.

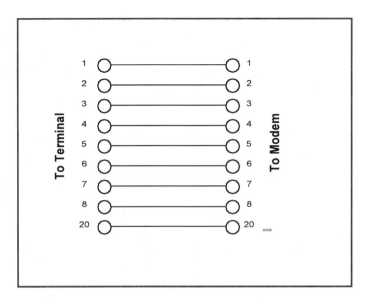

**Figure 2-8.** Pin diagram for a connection between a modem and a terminal.

# Project 2. Serial Interface Between Two IBM PC or IBM PC-Compatible Microcomputers

To connect one computer directly to another without a modem, a modem eliminator or null modem is required. A null modem is a cable that has at a minimum the wires that connect pins 2 and 3 on both computers crossed over. Pin 2 on both computers is responsible for sending data, and pin 3 receives data. As you can imagine, if both of these pins were not crossed, then both the computers could talk but neither would be listening.

Making the connecting cable is only one aspect of connecting two microcomputers. Communication software will be required to perform the communication functions. A general null modem can be created by crossing pins 2 and 3, 20 and 6, and connecting 8 to 6 on the RS-232 cable as in Figure 2-9.

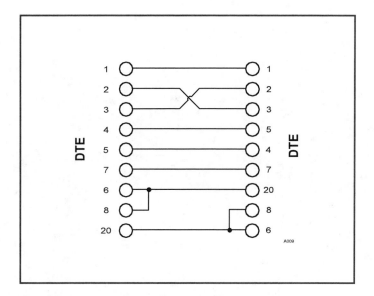

**Figure 2-9.** Pin diagram for a connection between two IBM or IBM-compatible microcomputers.

# 3
# Advanced Communication Hardware

## Objectives

After completing this chapter you will

1. Understand the use of concentrators, protocol converters, PBXs, cluster controllers, and matrix switches in a data communication system.

2. Understand the different line adapters that can be placed on a network and their application to data communication lines.

3. Understand the need for security in a data communication line and the equipment that can be used to enforce it.

4. Know the purpose of a breakout box.

5. Know the role of microcomputers, front end processors, and mainframes in a data communication system.

6. Know about multiplexers and their use.

## Key Terms

Microcomputer

Mainframe

Multiplexer

Concentrator

Cluster Controller

Protocol Converter

PBX

Line Monitor

Channel Extender

Line Splitter

Digital Line Expander

Encryption

# Introduction

Today's data communication systems have increased in sophistication and take advantage of equipment that was formerly reserved for voice communication systems only. Microcomputers, front end processors, mainframes, multiplexers, protocol converters, PBXs, matrix switches, and concentrators are among these devices. Additionally, the educated data communication system user and manager must understand the different devices that can be used to monitor these systems and the transmission media available to them.

It is important to point out that, although current tendencies in the data communication market are toward networks, a networking solution is in many situations not the best or the only solution to a data communication problem. The uneducated manager may try to solve any communication problem by using local or wide area networks, since these are solutions that usually seem to work. However, a network is not easy to install nor is it always the most cost-effective solution for creating a media-sharing environment. Today's data communication managers must be aware of many devices that solve common data transmission problems quickly and effectively.

This type of thinking, along with the knowledge of the diversity of devices that can be used in different situations, indicates an informed manager who can make smart decisions. This type of individual is a rare commodity in a field that is crowded with so-called experts who do not have the proper training in the field of data communication. Any data communication manager can make decisions, but only knowledgeable and open-minded managers can make decisions that are efficient and cost effective. With this in mind, let's take a closer look at some of the data communication equipment that is commonly found in the marketplace.

# Terminals and Microcomputers

A terminal is an input and/or output device that can be connected to a host computer. The terminal may depend on the host system for computational power and/or data. Obviously, many devices can meet this definition of a terminal. Among them is the microcomputer. Both the terminal and the computer to which it is connected are known as data terminal equipment (DTE). This type of equipment operates internally in digital format and produces digital output. The modem used to connect the terminal or computer to the communication line is known as data circuit-terminating equipment. Because the definition of data terminal is broad, there are several categories of terminals, each of which is defined in the following section.

# Classifications

## Microcomputer Workstation

A **microcomputer** workstation is a general-purpose microcomputer or specialized input/output workstation with "smart" circuitry and a central processing unit. Technically, there is a difference between a microcomputer workstation and a microcomputer. The workstation includes the tools necessary for a professional to perform his or her daily work. These tools are specialized software applications such as CAD systems and mathematical modeling systems. In addition, today's workstations have the ability to use multitask software programs. This means they can run multiple programs simultaneously and can switch among them as the user requires. The microcomputer may not have all of these capabilities built in. It may be used only for word processing or database access. Regardless of which system we are discussing, the microcomputer is an integral part of communication networks. It can be used as part of a local area network or as a terminal device connected to a host system. Figure 3-1 shows a typical desktop microcomputer system. Portable notebook microcomputers are also available that provide virtually the same performance and functions as desktop microcomputers (see Figure 3-2).

**Figure 3-1.** A typical desktop microcomputer.

Microcomputer workstations are being increasingly used in networks since they can perform many processing functions internally before the data is passed on to a host system. Some of the ways in which they are used are:

1. Data stored in central systems is transmitted (downloaded) to the microcomputer. The data can be processed by the microcomputer using a word processor, database, spreadsheet, or some other software application. After processing, the data is transmitted back to the central system for further processing or storage.

2. Data stored on the microcomputer can be submitted as a batch job to the host system as required.

3. Applications on the microcomputer can be assisted by the processing power of the host system. For example, a scientific database can reside in part on the microcomputer system, but when large calculations or repetitious calculations are required, the microcomputer can rely on the host system for assistance.

4. Large projects can be divided among several microcomputers. The completed pieces can then be assembled on the host system.

5 Microcomputers can work as terminals to the host computer. In this role they emulate the native terminals of the central sysem.

6. Microcomputers that are part of a local area network can share storage and printer devices on the network or devices on the central system.

**Figure 3-2.** A typical notebook-style portable microcomputer.

### Remote Job Entry Station

A remote job entry station is a processor on a network or terminal workstation where several types of devices are connected. Data is often transmitted from the host system to a remote job entry station such as a video display terminal (VDT) or printer. Input can also be received by the host in a batch mode from entry stations.

### Data Entry Terminal

This is a low-cost terminal used in homes or offices. This device can establish an interactive dialog with the host system, obtain data from a business application and at the same time provide data to the application. An example of a specialized data entry terminal is the transaction terminal employed by ATM machines in the banking industry for cash dispensing.

### Facsimile Terminal (Fax)

A facsimile terminal (see Figure 3-3) is able to transmit an exact picture of a hard copy document over telephone lines and satellite circuits anywhere in the world.

Fax machines are divided into four major groups according to technology and speed. Groups 1 and 2 are older analog machines, whereas groups 3 and 4 are digital technology machines. Most newer Fax machines are group 3 or 4. Group 3 machines can transmit a page in approximately one minute or less. Group 4 machines can transmit an 8 1/2- by 11-inch page in approximately 20 seconds.

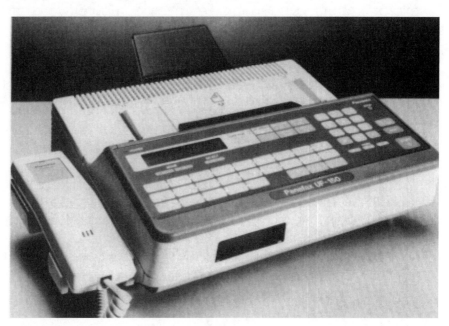

**Figure 3-3.** A typical multipurpose fax machine, copier, printer and telephone.

Additionally, group 4 fax machines have a higher image transmission quality. Some newer models of fax machines use "plain paper" to produce a hard copy of a digital transmission. This type of machine, also known as a laser fax, can double as a scanner for the computer or as a plain paper copier. Its circuitry is based on laser printer engines, and it can serve as a multipurpose machine on a network.

Signals from a digital facsimile device can be read into a computer and stored because they are made up of bits. This has led to the development of fax boards that can be added to microcomputers. With these boards, any document created on a personal computer can be transmitted to any fax machine through phone lines. Messages sent by fax machines can also be received by the fax boards inside microcomputers and a picture of the document can be stored on a disk or sent to an attached printer.

### Dumb/Intelligent Terminals

Dumb terminals are video terminals that do not participate in control or processing tasks. They do not contain storage systems, internal memory, or microprocessor chips. When a character is typed on one of these terminals, it is transmitted immediately to the host system. This forces the host or central system to create buffers for this type of terminal so the message can be assembled before acting on it.

Intelligent terminals are able to participate in the processing of data. These terminals contain internal memory and are capable of being programmed. Many intelligent terminals also contain auxiliary storage units and fast central processing units. Most of today's intelligent terminals are microcomputers and specialized microcomputer workstations.

## Attributes of Terminals

Many terminal attributes should be considered when purchasing a terminal. Some of the most important are described next.

### Keyboard

All terminals have a keyboard with certain basic capabilities. Advanced or extended keyboards contain additional function keys that indicate functions to be performed on entered data. Also, some function keys act as interrupt keys. Additionally, most keyboards contain numerical keypads and control keys used to transmit sequences that can be acted on by a program. Specialized keyboards contain foreign language characters and job-specific characters.

### Light Pen

This device is used to select options from menus appearing on the screen. When the pen is aimed at the video display screen, the light image can be read by the computer and the coordinates of the point are determined by the system. The coordinate system is translated into a selection displayed on the screen.

### Touch Screen

Such a screen works in a similar manner to the light pen. The user touches a  portion of the screen with a finger to make the selection.

### Mouse, Joystick, and Trackball

The mouse allows the user to control the screen cursor by moving the mouse on a table surface. When the screen cursor is on a selection, the user presses a mouse button. The coordinates of the cursor are read by the computer, and this location is associated with some software option. The joystick moves the cursor by moving the stick in a specific direction. A trackball is similar to the mouse except that the cursor is moved by rotating a ball mounted in a fixed holder. The cursor moves in the direction of rotation of the ball.

### Voice Entry

Data can be entered into the system by using a microphone. Special voice recognition software is required in the system.

### Page Scanner

A page scanner can scan an image and translate it into a digital format. The image can be stored and later processed by the computer.

# Front End Processors

Front end processors are often employed at the host end of a communication circuit to perform control and processing functions required for the proper operation of a data communication network. Figure 3-4 illustrates the location of a front end processor in a communication network. The front end processor provides an interface to the communication circuits. It relieves the host computer of its communication duties, which allows the host to perform the data processing function more effectively.

The typical duties of the front end processor are message processing and message switching. In message processing, it interprets incoming messages to determine the type of information requested. Then it retrieves the information from an on-line storage unit and sends it back to the inquiring terminal without involving the host system. In message switching, the front end processor switches incoming messages to other terminals or systems on a network. It can also store messages and forward them at a later time.

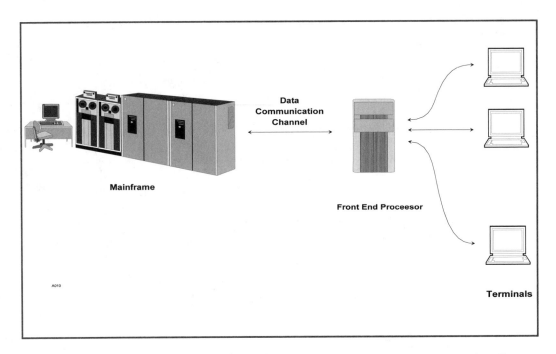

**Figure 3-4.** Location of a front end processor in a data communication network.

## Functions of the Front End Processor

The functions of the front end processor include the following:

1. Circuit polling and addressing terminals. Polling involves asking each terminal if it has a message to send. Addressing involves asking a terminal if it is ready to receive the message.

2. Answering dial-in calls and automatic dialing of outgoing calls.

3. Converting code from ASCII to EBCDIC or EBCDIC to ASCII.

4. Circuit switching. This allows an incoming circuit to be switched to another circuit.

5. Accommodating circuit speed differences.

6. Protocol conversion, such as asynchronous to synchronous.

7. Multiplexing.

8. Assembling incoming bits into characters.

9. Assembling characters into blocks of data or complete messages.

10. Compressing messages for more efficient communications.

11. Activating remote alarms if errors are detected.

12. Requesting retransmission of blocks of text containing errors.

13. Keeping statistics on network usage.

14. Performing diagnostics on attached terminals.

15. Controlling of editing that includes rerouting messages, modifying data for transmission, etc.

16. Buffering messages before they are passed to the host computer or user terminal.

17. Queuing messages into T/O queues between the front end processor and the host computer.

18. Logging messages to tape or disk.

19. Identifying trouble or security problems.

There are many vendors of front end processors. Some of the best known models are the IBM 37XX family of communication controllers and the NCR COMTEN 3600 series of front end processors.

# Mainframe Computers

**Mainframe** computers are considered central computer systems that perform data processing functions for a business or industry. In some networks, several mainframe computers can be found sharing the responsibility of processing information as a distributed system. In such systems the hardware, software, processing, and data are normally dispersed over a geographical area. The individual technologies are connected through some type of communication network. As part of this network, mainframe computers can perform networking functions as well as the more traditional processing functions.

A mainframe computer that is built to perform "number crunching" routines may not be suitable to perform communication routines. The type of processing required for communications differs greatly from that required to perform mathematical calculations. For a computer that is built to perform traditional data processing functions, additional or auxiliary hardware is required. The type of auxiliary hardware will depend upon the configuration of the network.

There are three types of configurations, the first of which consists of a computer that is not part of any local or wide area computer network. The circuitry required to handle all communications is built into the machine. Figure 3-5 shows a typical configuration for this type of centralized system.

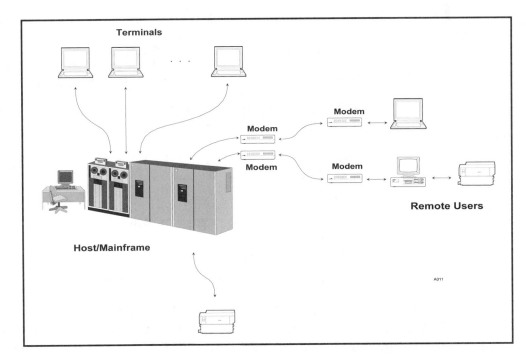

**Figure 3-5.** A centralized data communication system.

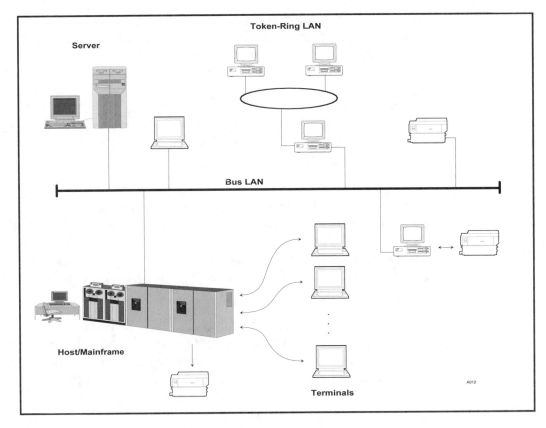

**Figure 3-6.** A data communication system using a LAN.

This configuration uses dedicated hardware to handle the interaction between the host system and the data entry terminals.

The mainframe computer can store users' programs as well as the software to handle communication with the users. The type of configuration shown in Figure 3-5 can be found in manufacturing environments and in dedicated database systems. Even though we refer to the computer as the mainframe computer, this central system is often a minicomputer system.

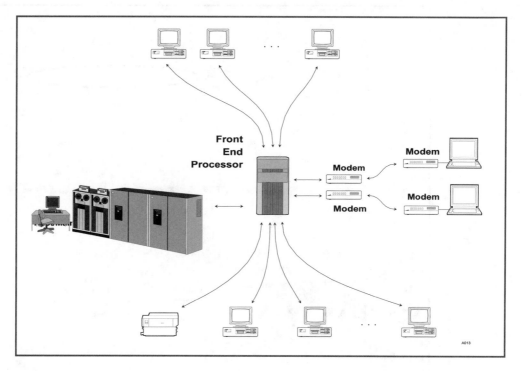

**Figure 3-7.** A data communication system using an FEP.

The second type of configuration is a network that employs microcomputers, minicomputers, and mainframe computers connected through some type of local area network (LAN). Figure 3-6 depicts this type of system. The network is usually confined to the business office or business complex where the processing is taking place. Users can communicate to the outside world by sending their message to an outside system through the local telephone exchange or some other medium. The local exchange then routes the message through long distance networks until it reaches the local exchange of the receiving system. Finally, the message is routed to the receiving computer or local network. These systems are important, and there are several chapters in this book that further explore the concepts.

The final type of configuration is one that employs a large general-purpose computer along with a front end processor (FEP). Figure 3-7 shows a diagram of this configuration. The front end processor is known by names such as line controller, communications controller, or transaction processor. The function of the FEP is to interface the main computer to the network where the users' communication equipment resides. It can be a nonprogrammable device that is built to handle a specific situation. Or the front end processor can be programmable and it can handle some processing functions in addition to input/output activities.

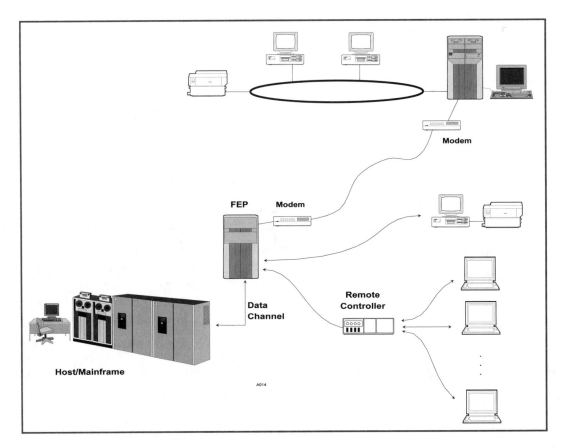

**Figure 3-8.** A distributed data communication system.

During the past few years, network designers have opted to remove as much processing as possible from the host computer. The idea is to distribute the processing hardware along a network, making the entire system more efficient.

Figure 3-8 shows an example of this type of network distribution. The front end processor handles the control of all communication functions. The data channel between the front end processor and the host system handles the movement of data into and out of the main processing computer. Remote terminal controllers handle users' terminals. Microcomputers process data locally and later transmit the results to the host system. Telephone exchanges, multiplexers, and other devices are used throughout the network to handle communications efficiently between users and the host computer. Further in this book, chapters on networks and local area networks explain the terminology and concepts in more detail.

# Multiplexers

Although modems are used to connect computers over large distances and direct cable is normally employed over short distances, the number of cables required to satisfy all users can at times be overwhelming. In addition, leasing lines from the phone company to communicate between two offices located far away from each other can be expensive. Multiplexers help in solving some of this economic cost by allowing the transmission of multiple data communication sessions over a common wire or medium.

## Function

Multiplexing technology allows the transmission of multiple signals over a single medium. **Multiplexers** (see Figure 3-9) allow the replacement of multiple low-speed transmission lines with a single high-speed transmission line. The typical configuration includes a multiplexer attached to multiple low-speed lines, a communication line (typically four-wire carrier circuit), and a multiplexer at another site that is also connected to low-speed lines.

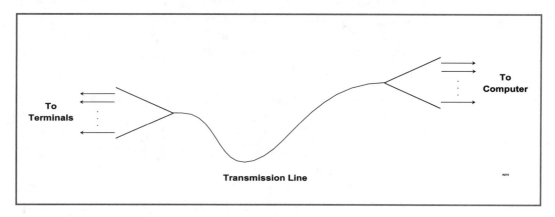

**Figure 3-9.** Multiplexers help reduce the number of transmission lines needed.

The trend in computer technology is toward faster, smaller, and distributed network systems. However, the central or host system plays an important part in network strategies. The processing and data throughput power of minicomputers and mainframes is superior to that of microcomputer systems. This makes the mainframe or the minicomputer a key component of a successful network configuration. In addition, many network managers rely on a central or host system for security, backup, and maintenance purposes.

Figure 3-10 depicts this configuration. In addition, the figure shows a remote site that is connected to a multiplexer through the use of modems. The remote site contains terminals, microcomputers, modems, and printers attached to a multiplexer. The host site has a multiplexer, FEP, and a host CPU.

The operation of the multiplexers, frequently called MUXs, in Figure 3-10 is transparent to the sending and receiving computers or terminals. The multiplexer does not interrupt the normal flow of data. Multiplexers allow for a significant reduction of the overall cost of connecting remote sites, since the quantity of lines required to connect the sites is decreased.

# Techniques

Multiplexing techniques can be divided into frequency division multiplexing (FDM), time division multiplexing (TDM), and statistical time division multiplexing (STDM).

## Frequency Division Multiplexing (FDM)

Users of existing voice-grade lines (phone lines) can multiplex low-speed circuits into the standard voice-grade channels by using FDM. In FDM, a modem and a frequency division are used to break down the frequency of available bandwidths of a voice-grade circuit, dividing it into multiple smaller bandwidths. The bandwidth is a measure of the amount of data that can be transmitted per unit of time. The bandwidth is determined by the difference between the highest and lowest allowed frequencies in the transmission medium.

As an example, assume that a telephone circuit has a bandwidth of 3100 Hz, and a line capable of carrying 1200 bits per second (bps). Suppose that instead of running a terminal at 1200 bps, we want to run three terminals at 300 bps. If three terminals are going to use the same communication line, then some type of separator is required in order to avoid crosstalk (interference of signals from one to another). This separator is called a guardband. For transmission at 300 bps the standard separation is 480 Hz. Therefore, in the above situation, two guardbands of 480 Hz each are required (see Figure 3-11). Since the guardbands now occupy 960 Hz, and the original line had a bandwidth of 3100 Hz, then the frequency left for the 300 bps transmission is 2140 Hz. If three terminals are required, then 2140 Hz divided by three gives a frequency of 713 Hz to be used per channel.

With FDM it is not necessary for all lines to terminate at a single location. Using multidrop techniques, the terminals can be stationed in different locations within a building or a city.

## Time Division Multiplexing (TDM)

Time division multiplexers are digital devices and therefore select incoming bits digitally and place each bit into a high-speed bit stream at equal time intervals. (See Figure 3-12.) The sending multiplexer will place a bit or byte from each of the incoming lines into a frame. The frames are placed on high-speed transmission lines, and a receiving multiplexer, knowing where each bit or byte is located, outputs the bits or bytes at appropriate speeds.

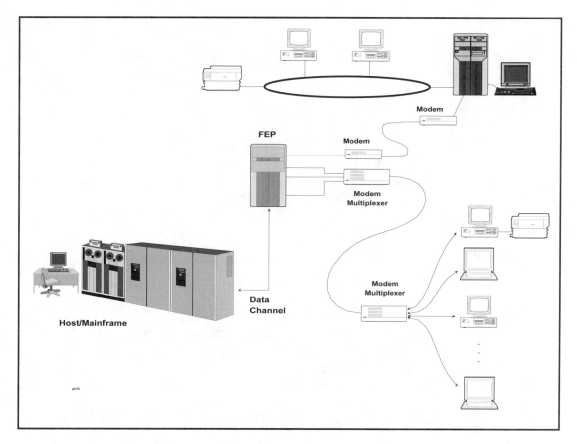

**Figure 3-10.** Multiplexer operation is transparent to the operation of the data communication system.

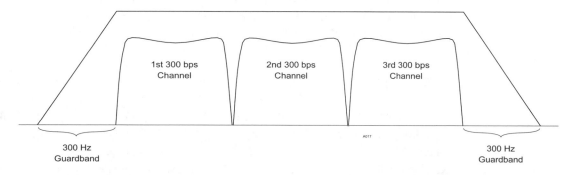

**Figure 3-11.** Guardbands and spectrum occupancy in the transmission process.

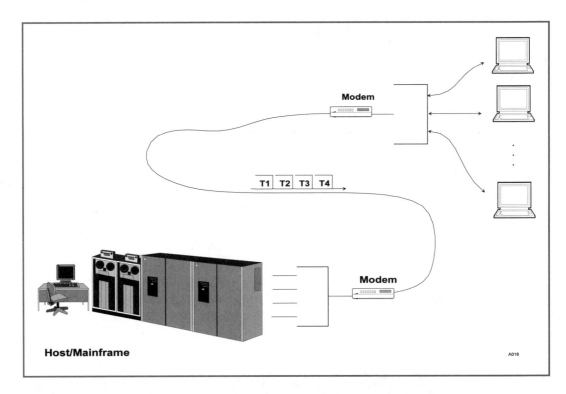

**Figure 3-12.** Time division multiplexers in the communication process.

Time division multiplexing is more efficient than frequency division multiplexing, but it requires a separate modem. To the sending and receiving stations it always appears as if a single line is connecting them. All lines for time division multiplexers originate in one location and end in one location. TDMs are easier to operate, less complex, and less expensive than FDMs.

## Statistical Time Division Multiplexers (STDM)

In any terminal-host configuration the terminals attached to the host CPU are not always transmitting data. The time during which they are idle is called down time. Statistical time division multiplexers are intelligent devices capable of identifying which terminals are idle and which terminals require transmission, and they allocate line time only when it is required. This means line time is provided only when a terminal is transmitting. This allows the connection of many more devices to the host than is possible with FDMs or TDMs (see Figure 3-13).

The STDM consists of a microprocessor-based unit that contains all hardware and software required to control both the reception of low-speed data coming in and high-speed data going out. Newer STDM units provide additional capabilities such as data compression, line priorities, mixed-speed lines, host port sharing, network port control, automatic speed detection, internal diagnostics, memory expansion, and integrated modems.

The number of devices that can be multiplexed using STDMs depends on the address field used in an STDM frame. If the field is 4 bits long, there are

16 terminals (2 to the power of 4) that can be connected. If 5 bits are used, 32 terminals can be connected (2 to the power of 5).

# Configurations

Multiplexers can be used in a variety of configurations and combinations. Cascading is a typical configuration used to extend circuits to remote entry points when there are two or more data entry areas. Figure 3-14 shows an example of cascading multiplexers. In the figure, data entry terminals in a geographical location are multiplexed, and a single carrier sends the data to a temporary receiving location. The data is then demultiplexed and multiplexed by a third multiplexer before being sent to the final destination. Then a multiplexer receives the data and distributes it among the ports of the host system.

The number of ports that a multiplexer can accommodate varies. Commonly there are 4, 8, 16, 32, 48, or 64 ports. The price of a multiplexer will vary with the number of ports in it and the sophistication of the device.

Newer multiplexers are difficult to define. Some devices have a large array of options and functions that make them work in a specific format under some working conditions. They can be switched to a different type when the conditions change. Some standard types that can be found in the marketplace are outlined below. However, keep in mind that some multiplexers can perform the functions of several of these types.

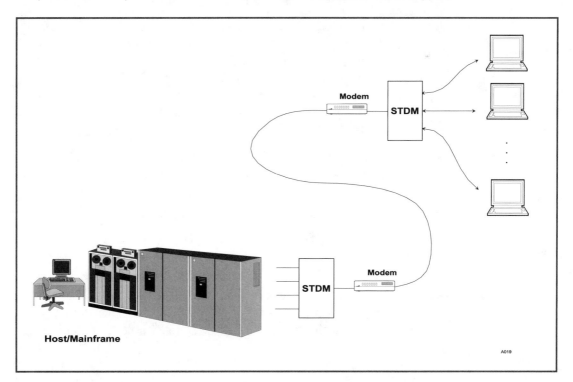

**Figure 3-13.** Statistical time division multiplexers in communication systems.

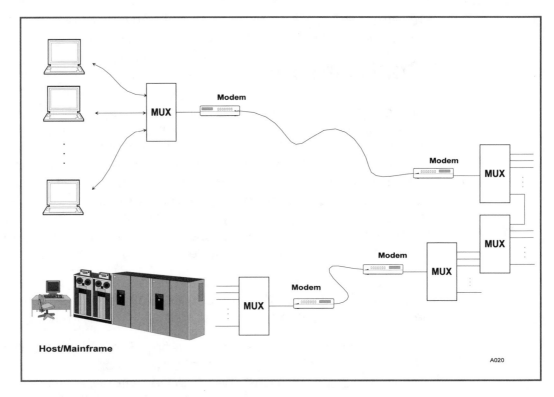

**Figure 3-14.** Cascaded multiplexers technique.

## Inverse Multiplexer

An inverse multiplexer provides a high-speed data path between computers. It takes a high-speed line coming out of a computer and separates it into multiple low-speed lines. The multiple low-speed lines are then recombined by another inverse multiplexer before making connection with the receiving computer.

## T-1 Multiplexer

A T-1 multiplexer is a special type of multiplexer combined with a high-capacity data service unit that manages the ends of a T-1 link. A T-1 link is a communication link that transmits at 1.544 million bits per second. Therefore, T-1 circuits can carry 24 channels of 64,000 bits per second.

## Multiport Multiplexer

A multiport multiplexer combines modem and time division multiplexing equipment into a single device. The line entering the modem can be of varying transmission speeds. The multiport multiplexer then combines the data and transmits it over a high-speed link to another receiving multiplexer.

### Fiber-Optic Multiplexer

A fiber-optic multiplexer takes multiple channels of data, with each channel transmitting at 64,000 bits per channel, and multiplexes the channels onto a 14 million bits per second fiber-optic line. It is similar in operation to a time division multiplexer, but operates at much higher speeds.

# Concentrator

Standard multiplexers are bit- or byte-oriented devices with limited storage capabilities and little computing logic. There are occasions when it is desirable to perform some type of processing on the information traveling through the communication medium for purposes of error detection and editing. In this case, handling the information on a bit-per-bit or byte basis is inadequate. For the processing functions that we are discussing, the information must be handled on a message basis, or on a store-and-forward basis. Store-and-forward means that the message is received at a location, it is validated, and an acknowledgment is sent back to the sender. A device that can perform this type of operation is the concentrator.

A **concentrator** is a line-sharing device with a primary function that is the same as a multiplexer. It allows multiple devices to share communication circuits. In addition, a concentrator is an intelligent device that sometimes performs data processing functions and has auxiliary storage. Some of the earlier concentrators were statistical multiplexers. That is the reason some vendors refer to a concentrator as a statistical multiplexer or stat mux. In addition to having a CPU, concentrators are used one at a time, whereas multiplexers are used in pairs. Also, a concentrator may vary the number of incoming and outgoing lines, while a multiplexer must use the same number of lines on both ends.

A typical concentrator configuration is depicted in Figure 3-15. The example shows multiple terminals using a concentrator to access several host systems. Concentrators perform data compression functions, forward error correction, and network-related functions in addition to acting as a line-sharing device. They are considered data processing devices, and newer types of concentrators are built around microcomputers and minicomputers. However, "pure" concentrators don't perform any type of routing of data on a network. They just take data from a central location and distribute it to some remote site and take data from the remote site and send it to the central location. Any routing of data from one terminal to another terminal or from one workstation to another workstation is performed by message switching equipment or front end processors. Above, we use the word "pure" to emphasize that the job of a concentrator does not typically include performing data switching functions. But there are some modern concentrators that do perform switching functions. This is the result of equipment manufacturers trying to cover as much of this market as possible. As the hardware becomes cheaper, equipment manufacturers try to pack as much power in their devices as possible in order to appeal to a larger audience. The result is equipment that performs the duties of multiple devices.

# Cluster Controller

A **cluster controller** is designed to support several terminals and the functions required to manage the terminals. A modern cluster controller performs many of the functions of a front end processor and is in most cases a smaller version of a front end processor. In addition, it buffers data being transmitted to or from the terminals, performs error detection and correction, and polls terminals (see Figure 3-16). Polling is a technique by which the controller checks to see which terminals are ready to send data. If a terminal needs to send a packet of data to a host, the cluster controller ensures that the packet gets to its destination. In addition, some cluster controllers can be attached to more than one communication line, allowing one user to have multiple sessions that access multiple computers. Normally, a special key combination switches the user from one host computer to another. Also, not only can a user be attached to multiple computers, but some cluster controllers allow the user to have multiple sessions with the same computer. In this manner, a user can be executing a database query and performing file transfer or some other function in different but simultaneous sessions.

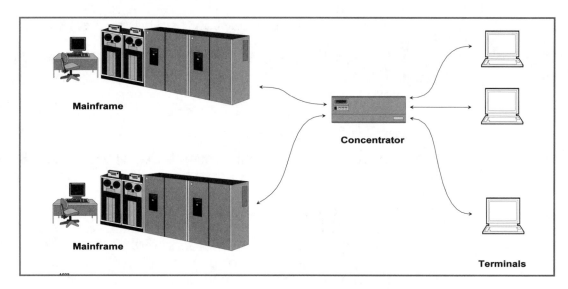

**Figure 3-15.** A data communication system using a concentrator.

Examples of popular cluster controllers are the IBM 3174 and 3274 cluster controllers. These controllers can handle up to 32 terminals and normally interact with 3278ng terminals or terminal emulators. In the case of the 3174 or 3274, the most common configuration for large-scale systems is to attach groups of cluster controllers through a telecommunication line to a front end processor. Common IBM front end processors are the 3705 and 3725. Also, these devices can be nodes in a network, enhancing the capability of the equipment and making their life cycle longer in an era when data communications equipment must coexist with other equipment in network configurations. This concept is explored in later chapters. It is an important point to explore, because of the number of microcomputers being used to communicate with cluster controllers.

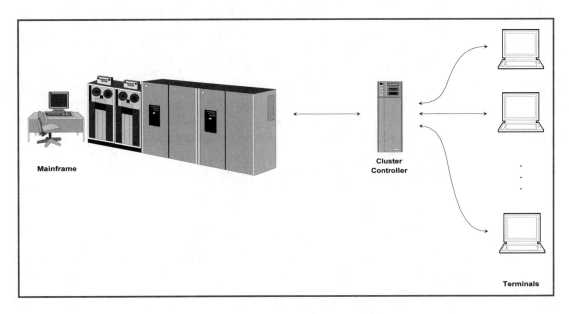

**Figure 3-16.** A cluster controller managing several terminals.

Until recently, 3270 or other types of terminals were the main source of communication between users and IBM mainframes. But as the price of microcomputers dropped during the last decade, people used microcomputers with some type of emulation system as a replacement for the communication terminal. Microcomputers gave users the ability to send large amounts of data to the cluster controller that was originally designed to handle short transactions. The end result is an overloading of the cluster controller with the response time increasing in some situations to as much as 20 minutes. This problem is alleviated by using networks and distributing the load of the data communications equipment. The use of the microcomputer as a communicating device between the user and the mainframe also made the protocol converter a popular device.

# Protocol Converter

In order for electronic devices to communicate with one another, a set of conventions is required. This set of conventions is called the protocol. A protocol determines the sequence of codes required for data exchange and the bit or character sequences required to control the exchange.

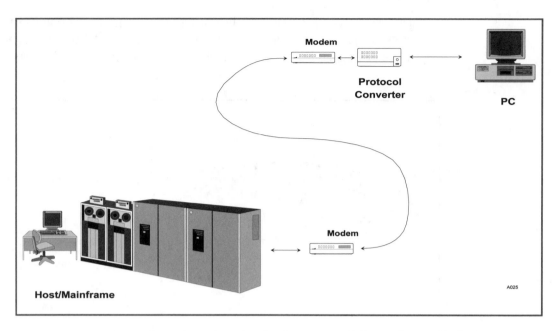

**Figure 3-17.** A protocol converter between a PC and a mainframe.

Since computers and other electronic devices sometimes have their own proprietary protocols, **protocol converters** are used to interconnect two dissimilar computers or terminals so they can talk to each other. As an analogy, imagine a person who speaks only English and another person who speaks only Russian trying to communicate with each other. For the communication to be effective, a translator who understands both languages serves as the bridge between both persons. The protocol converter assumes the role of the translator in the electronic data exchange. Although we discuss only some of the most commonly used protocols in data communications, many more exist. The protocol converter provides an effective means of translating information or packets of data (a message that is subdivided into smaller data units for a more efficient transmission) between dissimilar devices that need to exchange data.

Protocol converters also convert character codes. As mentioned in Chapter 2, two character codes used in the computer environment in the United States are the ASCII and EBCDIC standards. The EBCDIC code is used by IBM in midrange and mainframe systems. The ASCII code is used by virtually every other computer manufacturer. Therefore, to connect an IBM personal computer that uses the ASCII system to an IBM mainframe, an ASCII-to-EBCDIC converter is required (see Figure 3-17).

Protocol converters can be hardware or software designed. A hardware protocol converter is treated as a "black box" on the communication line. It performs its function in a manner that is transparent to the system. For example, third party vendors offer asynchronous to synchronous protocol conversion boxes. This allows an inexpensive async terminal to access an IBM mainframe. There are also add-on circuit boards that fit inside microcomputers that perform communications and protocol conversion at the same time. These boards allow a personal computer to emulate a 3278 or 3279 terminal and connect to a 3174 or 3274 controller via a coaxial cable. Some of the cards have the controller built in and can access the mainframe directly.

The other method of protocol conversion is achieved through software. Typically, this software resides in the host system and converts incoming data to the language that the host system can understand. This is an inexpensive manner of achieving protocol conversion. However, it requires attention from the host computer, reducing the amount of time it can apply to other tasks. Whenever possible, hardware protocol converters are used, but be aware that many protocol converters also perform other functions, such as multiplexing and concentrating. Because of these multiple options in a single device, purchasing decisions must be made carefully to avoid duplication or needless acquisition of features. This is especially true as the sophistication of the equipment increases, such as in the PBX.

# Private Branch Exchanges (PBX)

A private branch exchange is an electronic switchboard within an organization, with all the telephone lines of the organization connected to it (see Fig 3-18). Normally, several of the telecommunication circuits of the **PBX** go from this switchboard to the telephone company's main office. These are called trunk lines when they are devoted to voice transmission. If they are used for data communication, they are known as leased lines, dedicated lines, or private lines.

Private branch exchanges, like the centralized switching equipment found at the phone company, are computers that are specially designed to handle voice telephone calls. However, since they are computers, they can also handle data communications in a digital format. Their flexibility in this area, especially when it comes to connecting a terminal or microcomputer to a host system, makes them popular devices used in data communications. But, as we will see shortly, the PBX as a hub for connecting data communication equipment is effective only when the required rate of transmission is low. Before we discuss the capabilities of the private branch exchange, it is important to know some of the history behind the development of the PBX so you may understand the capabilities of any existing PBXs at your site.

## PBX History

PBX systems have been in offices for a number of years. As organizations developed and grew, PBX equipment was upgraded and enhanced to meet users' demands. The evolution of PBX equipment can be categorized into several generations.

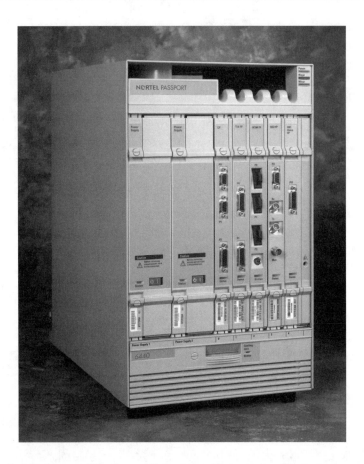

**Figure 3-18.** These Northern Telecom Enterprise Switches are the modern equivalents of the older telephone PBX. (Courtesy of Northern Telecom, Inc.)

The first generation of PBXs was placed in service prior to the mid-1970s. They carried only voice and were capable of handling only analog signals. Their design was electromechanical, and they used analog circuitry for switching signals.

The second generation of PBXs was designed between the mid-1970s and the mid-1980s. These were also voice-only PBXs, but they digitized voice signals before transferring them through the switch. This PBX equipment could be modified to carry digital data signals as well as voice. However, the transfer rate for data signals was slow.

The third generation of PBXs has been in existence since the early 1980s. They have the capability to move voice and data at relatively high speeds. Incoming analog signals are converted to digital signals, and therefore offer greater flexibility and capabilities. Most of today's PBXs are from this generation.

The fourth generation of PBXs is characterized by having all voice and data switching capabilities combined in a LAN distribution system. They can serve as voice phone switches, electronic mail, voice mail, and data switches for LANs. However, their implementation has been slow due to the high cost of each line in the system.

# Capabilities

Newer digital PBXs, such as the IBM 9751, Northern Telecom's Meridian, and the AT&T System 75 and 85, are designed around 32-bit microprocessor chips that control the entire system. They contain many features, including the following:

1.   They can transmit voice and data simultaneously. Obviously, all PBXs can handle voice communications, but most of them have the capability to handle data communications. With this features a user with a terminal or a microcomputer can access devices or host computers that are connected to the PBX. In the case of a microcomputer, some type of terminal emulation is normally used to communicate with the host. To access the host, the user dials the number of the site where the host is located. In some systems, system names can be given instead of the number. The PBX's software interprets the name provided and finds the destination requested. If the host has an available line, the user's microcomputer is connected to the host. When the user is finished with the transmission, the line is made available to another user. In this fashion, other intelligent devices, such as smart facsimile machines and printers, can be made available to users, along with the microcomputer. These facilities can also be made available to users who must dial in from other offices or their homes. Once a line is available to one of these users, he or she has the same capabilities as any user in the office.

2.   They can perform protocol conversion, allowing equipment from different vendors to communicate. Modern PBX systems have built-in protocol conversion capabilities that allow microcomputers to connect to host computers with dissimilar protocols without the need for additional equipment. Using an async or sync line provided through the PBX, a microcomputer can be attached to an IBM host, placing the burden of protocol conversion on the PBX instead of the host. Although this type of scenario is not effective when high transmission speeds are required, it is a solution for many users who only need terminal emulation and connection to a host.

3.   They can control local area networks from within the switchboard. Private branch exchanges can be used as the connecting hub for several local area networks. In this case, networks that are isolated and need to exchange data with other networks using existing phone wires can use the PBX as a central hub that switches data from one network to another using an available line.

4.   They have voice and electronic mail. One of the necessities of the modern office is the need for employees to communicate

continuously. Private branch exchanges can provide voice mail for a customer or another user to access the PBX using a telephone, access a private voice mail box by typing a set number of digits from the telephone pad, and then leave a voice message to the owner of the voice mail box. The owner can then retrieve messages in any order, delete messages, forward messages, or save messages.

Additionally, PBXs offer electronic mail. The concept of electronic mail is similar to that of voice mail, but instead of leaving a voice message using a telephone, a terminal or computer is used to leave a written message. The owner of the electronic mail box has the same capabilities as the owner of voice mail boxes in terms of managing the mail stored by the system.

5. Asynchronous and synchronous transmissions can be performed simultaneously. With this capability, a corporation can have multiple hosts, some of which may require async data transmission and some that require sync data transmission. The private branch exchange can handle both types of transmission simultaneously, allowing inexpensive async terminals access to their native host in addition to performing the translation required (in some cases) to use an async type terminal on a host requiring sync transmission. Although many PBX systems place the burden of async-to-sync conversion on other devices, they still allow both types of transmission over the same switching lines.

6. Automatic routing is available, ensuring that calls are routed through the least costly communication system. This is an important feature when a long distance call is made and large amounts of data are being transmitted. The ability to find the least costly route can save thousands of dollars annually for corporations that must maintain data lines with remote offices or sites.

7. They can switch digital transmission without the use of modems. Recall that in order for a computer to send data over ordinary telephone lines, a modem is required. When a private branch exchange system is used, any switching of data from one line of the PBX to another of its lines can be done without the need for a modem. The PBX performs all the tasks necessary to ensure that the data gets to its destination. However, you will still need a modem if a call is placed outside the domain of the PBX and a digital trunk line is not available. In this case, even though the call goes through the PBX, it eventually has to use public phone lines, and the data must be modulated at one end and demodulated at the other end of the communication line. For this task, the modem must be used.

8.   They can provide security by requesting and maintaining security access codes. Private branch exchanges can be programmed to request an access code from any person trying to use its services. This provides an added layer of security on what is considered one of the most vulnerable areas of a data communication system.

9.   They can connect digital signals to high-speed circuits such as T-1 circuits. Recall that a T-1 line is a high-speed line provided by the public telephone system in order to have high-efficiency communication between two remote sites. A private branch exchange can be used to provide users with access to this type of communication circuit and, therefore, maximize its use. If a T-1 line is dedicated to a single device, when the device is not using the line, the cost/usage ratio becomes large. A PBX can switch devices over to the T-1 circuit as the line becomes available, ensuring that the circuit is used as much as possible, thus maximizing the investment in the T-1 line.

10.  They allow computer users to select different host computers or destinations without having to rearrange cables. This is an important benefit of a private branch exchange. Normally, a user would need a cable for each host that he or she needs to access. If only one port is available at the user's terminal, then manual or some other type of switching is necessary when the user logs out of one computer and logs in at another system. This problem is eliminated with the use of a network or a PBX. Since the PBX is an automatic switching device, the user can log out of one computer, and at the same terminal type the code or name of the next host system that needs to be accessed. The PBX will then connect the user, provided that a line is available for the requested host computer. All of these operations are performed from the user's keyboard without the user having to physically switch cables or any other type of equipment.

11.  They also offer many other features such as call forwarding, call holding, conference calling, and paging.

Besides digital and analog PBX systems, there are several other varieties including voice only, voice and data, and data only. Even though PBXs offer many advantages for digital data communications, they have limitations in the speed of data transmission. As the distance of transmission increases, the rate of transmission decreases. For this reason, a private branch exchange is not normally used as the communication system when large files need to be transmitted frequently or when there is a heavy data transmission requirement with an expectation of small response times. In such cases networks or direct connections are employed.

The private branch exchange or any individual device, including networks, shouldn't be considered as the only solution for the data communication needs of a corporation or institution. Rather, they can be one component of a larger and more complex group of equipment and software that work together to solve the communication needs of the user. No single device will be able to solve all needs, and, in some cases, the solution is too expensive. Each element of a data communication system should be evaluated as an integral part of a much larger solution. Many other devices exist in the market that, although not glamorous or expensive, provide an adequate solution to problems. One such product that has a close relationship with the private branch exchange is the matrix switch.

# Matrix Switch

A matrix or data switch is a data and peripheral-sharing facilitator. At its basic level of operations, a matrix switch allows terminals and other electronic devices to access multiple available host processors without the need to physically move any communication line. In this respect, matrix switches operate in a manner similar to early PBXs.

Matrix switches evenly distribute users over multiple processors or devices. If one processor or device becomes overloaded, users can be quickly and efficiently moved to another processor or device. If a line fails, the terminal connected to that line can easily be switched to another available line. Additionally, more terminals can be distributed using matrix switches than using physical wire.

They are effective and relatively inexpensive when compared to local area networks designed to perform the same functions that the matrix switch performs. Data switches work best when there is a small number of connections that they are responsible for. On the average, eight to twenty-four connections is a normal load for a matrix or data switch. Additionally, they normally use standard serial and parallel connectors to handle the communication with computers and other devices. Using these ports, several computers can be attached to different output devices using the switch as the hub of the operation. When a user needs to send data to a specific device, the switch automatically directs the output of the computer, either through serial or parallel lines, to the right output device.

From the user point of view, the matrix switch is a box that contains several input ports and several output ports. A user connects one of the input ports to the switch through a serial or parallel port depending on the application and the need of the user. Devices or other hosts connect to the output ports using an available serial or parallel port. Software residing in the switch or the attached computer instructs the device what to do. In addition, many programs are designed to read the settings of the switch, relieving the user from having to set up any parameters manually. Once the software is set up, the user can send print jobs directly to one of the printers attached to the matrix switch. The print job, on many occasions, has embedded commands that provide the switch with the instructions required to perform its duties. In other situations, the software running in the user's computer can send data to the required device without knowing that the switch is present. In this case, the matrix switch handles all communication operations automatically.

The disadvantage of matrix switches is in their lack of power and speed of data transmission. Most matrix switches work in the 19,200 bits per second range, with a few of them transmitting at higher speeds. But their speed is far below the speed of transmission of most local area networks. However, they are simple to install and use without the need for a system administrator. Although matrix switches will never replace true media-sharing local area networks, they are very useful in many data communication situations. If all that is needed is the sharing of devices among several users who are in close proximity, a matrix or data switch should be considered.

Many other devices can be used to extend the capabilities of a data communication system and provide users with an affordable solution to their data communication needs. Some of these additional devices fall under the category of line adapters because they are incorporated directly into the line of communication. These are discussed in the next section.

# Line Adapter

A line adapter is a device that is placed in the line of data transmission to perform monitoring functions, extend the range of data transmission, perform security functions, or allow the sharing of a data line. Some of the most commonly used types of line adapters are line monitors, port-sharing devices, line splitters, digital expanders, and security devices such as encryption systems and call-back units. Additional line adapters such as bridges and gateways are discussed in later chapters as a subset of networks. The main purpose of the line adapter is to increase the range and the number of connections possible between users and host systems, especially as distributed systems become more the norm rather than the exception. The first of the line adapters that we will discuss is the line monitor, and it is used mainly by system administrators as a debugging and management tool.

## Line Monitor

A **line monitor** is used to diagnose problems on a communication line or link. It attaches to a communication circuit, and a digital format of the data flowing through the circuit is displayed on a screen, printed to paper, or stored on an auxiliary device for further analysis.

There are two categories of line monitors, active and passive. Active line monitors can generate data, are interactive, and can emulate various types of monitors. Passive line monitors gather data and store it for analysis at a later time. Modern line monitors provide information about traffic volume, idle status, and errors that take place in the communicating medium. These statistics are normally stored in some secondary storage medium for further analysis and are displayed in a graphical format at the same time that they are being stored.

The hardware monitor is a special type of line monitor. It measures voltage changes in the line and reports changes. Using a hardware monitor, any type of system such as a front end processor, concentrator, and data communication line can be closely monitored. Additional monitors, such as network monitors, are discussed in later chapters, but any monitor of system performance that installs or interfaces between the user's equipment and the data communication line is considered a line monitor.

A typical line monitor can work with data speeds of up to 64,000 bits per second, and has video displays and memory, supports synchronous and asynchronous transmission, has breakout box capabilities (see later section in this chapter), and is capable of being programmed. Using this capability, a system administrator can instruct the line monitor to look for specific signals or to look at the function of individual devices. The purpose is to diagnose problems that a user may report or to find "bottlenecks" in the transmission process in order to improve response time.

Microcomputers can be enhanced to function as line monitors. A PC adapter board, internal RS-232, and software can convert a standard microcomputer into an active and intelligent line monitor and response time analyzer. This is a common procedure in the monitoring of local area networks. Using sophisticated software and an interface card, a personal computer can now perform monitoring functions that expensive line monitors have been performing until recently. In addition, the personal computer can process data as it collects it or store it and process it later.

# Channel Extender

A **channel extender** links remote stations to host facilities. It connects directly to the host system and operates at high speeds. It functions like a small front end processor to connect remote work stations and computers to a host. It can support auxiliary devices, including printers, disk drives, and microcomputers. Figure 3-19 shows the placement of a channel extender in a communication circuit.

Although channel extenders are essentially scaled down front end processors, they are slower and less powerful than FEPs. However, as the cost of hardware decreases and the software in these devices becomes more sophisticated, channel extenders will be competing more directly with front end processors.

Channel extenders provide a method for improving response time and off-loading data communication processes from networks, and they provide a less expensive alternative to front end processors. Through the use of channel extenders, the distance limitation of 400 feet between the terminal and mainframe is overcome. This allows for the implementation of distributed processing beyond the basic physical location of the mainframe. This allows several mainframes, minicomputers, and microcomputers to be located many miles apart, yet function as if they were in close proximity. This type of connection can be accomplished by using channel extenders and a T-1 line to connect the computers over long distances. The T-1 line provides the high-speed connection, and the channel extender provides the capability of taking the data signals beyond their 400-feet limit.

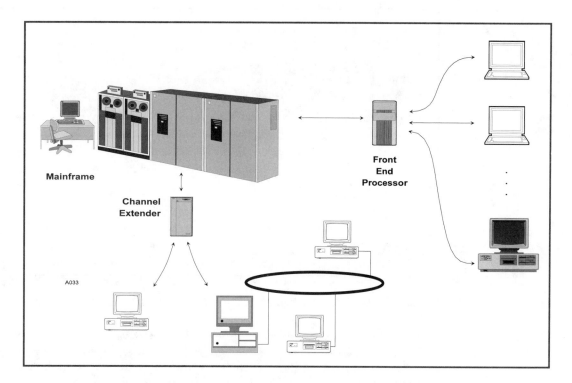

**Figure 3-19.** A channel extender in a communication circuit.

Figure 3-19 shows how distributed processing can be achieved beyond the typical 400-feet limitation for a mainframe data channel interconnection. The mainframe channel can be extended to another mainframe channel by using a channel extender. This device can also connect microcomputers and terminals at remote locations. Moreover, local area networks can be connected to the mainframe channel through a channel extender.

# Port-Sharing Device

A port-sharing device allows multiple terminals or stations to use a single port on a front end processor or mainframe system. This type of equipment is used when the capacity of the front end processor or host system needs to be exceeded. For example, it is possible that at a given installation the number of ports available on the host are already used. Therefore, if the host system has 32 ports, then 32 incoming lines may already be attached to devices or allocated to users. What happens if an additional device is required or if new users need to be added to the system? The obvious solution is to expand the system or acquire a bigger system to accommodate all the required devices and users. But what if the processing capabilities of the system are adequate and just the number of ports needs to be increased? Or what if several devices need to share a common port? In this case the solution may be to install a port-sharing device.

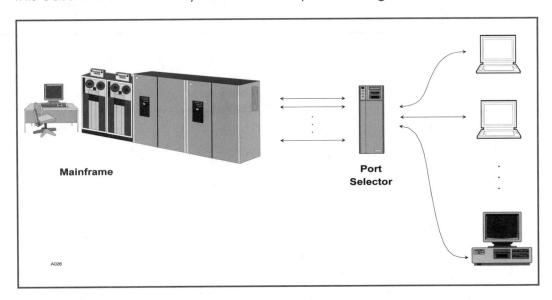

**Figure 3-20.** Port selector in a communication system.

For example, if the number of users in the system increases to 48 or if more printers need to be attached, a port-sharing device constitutes a temporary fix until a more appropriate solution is designed. Using a port-sharing device, printers or terminals that are not going to be used simultaneously can be made to share a port and therefore decrease the cost of adding new ports that may be idle during much of the time.

Another example of the use of channel extenders applies to an office or corporation that uses personnel who share a single job. In this case, one or more individuals may perform the same job at different times during the business day or week. However, these individuals may have their own terminals and offices. It seems redundant to equip each employee with a terminal and a line attached to an individual port on the host system. It is a better use of resources to use a port-sharing device or a matrix switch to provide these users with shared access to the resources in the host using a single line or multiple line attached to a port-sharing device. Since only one user will be accessing the host at any given time, this schema will work effectively. In many cases, channel extenders can serve as sophisticated port-sharing devices.

## Port Selector

Working alongside the port-sharing device, port selectors allow a user to be automatically attached to the first available port on a host system. Where the port-sharing device allows the connection of many terminals to a single port (only one at a time), the port selector may take a single line and can attach this line to any number of ports that are assigned to the port selector (see Figure 3-20).

It is normally used in conjunction with dial-up lines where there may be a large number of lines available for connection from the outside, but only a few ports are available for these dial-up users. When a user calls into the system, the port selector searches for an available port on the host. If one is found, the user is connected to that port. If a port is not found, the user is notified of the situation or a busy signal is transmitted back to the user, and he or she is asked to try later.

Modern port selectors can handle incoming calls that use different transmission speeds and different communication protocols such as ASCII and EBCDIC. In addition, they can switch users to dial-up circuits or dedicated lines, perform statistics on the use of the host ports, and provide feedback when a port is not available for the user.

# Line Splitter

A **line splitter** works in similar fashion to a port-sharing device with the difference being the location of the line splitter. A line splitter is normally found at the remote end of a communication line, where the terminal or workstation is located (see Figure 3-21). Port-sharing devices are normally located at the host end of the communication line.

Line splitters act as switches that allow several terminals to connect to a modem to access the host system. Even though multiple terminals are attached to a line splitter, only one communication line exists. Therefore, only one terminal can be communicating with the host at any one time.

As an example of using this technique, assume that four users need access to the host system from a remote location at different times during the working day. One solution is to provide each user with an individual line and a modem in order to access the host system. Therefore, four communication lines and at least five modems are required. Four of the modems are the users' and at least one is needed for the host. This solution, although efficient, could be costly depending on the needs of the users.

Another solution is to use a single line and modem and use a line splitter at the site where the users are located. In this scenario, the line splitter acts as a switch providing one of the users access to the line and modem at any given time. This is a less costly solution than the one mentioned above. However, keep in mind that only one user can access the modem and the data communication line at any given time. The other users must wait for the line and the modem to be given up by the user who is performing the communications before they can transmit data. If a single data communication line must carry the signals of more than one transmission, then another device, the digital line expander, may be used to increase the efficiency of the data line.

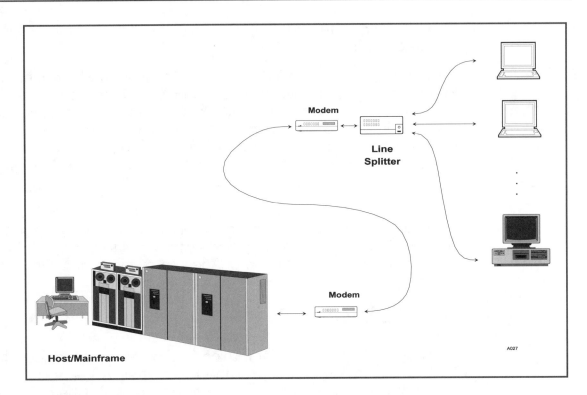

**Figure 3-21.** A line splitter in a communication system.

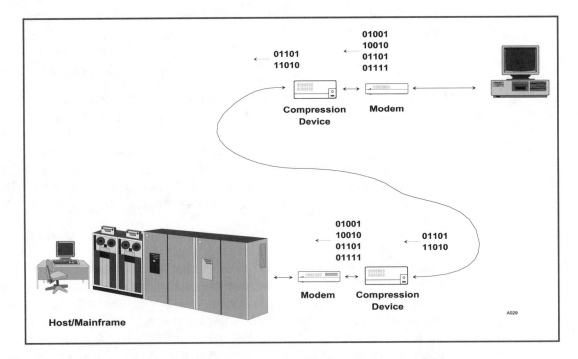

**Figure 3-22.** Increasing throughput using data compression.

# Digital Line Expander

A **digital line expander** allows users to concentrate a larger number of voice and data channels into the bandwidth of a standard communication channel. This is done through the use of hardware and software techniques that make use of the entire bandwidth capability of a standard voice circuit.

For example, if a communication site has only two leased lines between two remotely located terminating points, it can save money by using a line expander to increase the carrying capacity of those lines. One digital line expander can provide up to eight intermixed voice and digital data transmission circuits over a single digital communication circuit. This will obviously reduce the overhead cost for the company and increase the effectiveness of the leased lines. However, as in many other situations, this increase in capacity doesn't come free. If the number of transmissions is increased, the speed of the transmission must be decreased in order to make room for the additional data flowing through the circuit. If a line has a transmission speed of 57,600 bits per second, we couldn't send two transmissions at 57,600 bits per second. But we could send three data signals traveling at a speed of 19,200 bits per second simultaneously by using a digital line expander. Another device that enhances the efficiency of a data communication line is a data compression device.

# Data Compression Device

A data compression device can increase the throughput of data over a communication line by compressing the data (see Figure 3-22). By reducing the amount of memory that a file or message uses, the net throughput of a line can be increased, since more data is being sent per second. This technique is somewhat similar to compression techniques used in expanding the storage capabilities of a hard disk. Compression software, following a specific compression algorithm, intercepts the data that needs to be transmitted and reduces its space requirements. The result is that the same information is packed into a smaller number of bytes and then stored, or in this case sent through the data transmission lines. At some point, the same algorithm must be used again to decompress the data and restore it to its original state. A data compression device is a microprocessor-controlled device that uses several techniques for data compression. One type of compression technique is to count the number of repeating characters that are in sequence and send this count instead of sending each character. This is called run length encoding.

Another, more sophisticated technique is called Huffman encoding. The Huffman encoding algorithm uses tables of the most commonly transmitted characters within a language and adjusts the number of bits needed to transmit each character, based on the relative frequency of the character in the language.

Although a thorough discussion of compression algorithms is beyond the scope of this book, suffice it to say that data compression devices use software techniques to reduce the space requirement of data. Then by sending fewer characters, yet maintaining the integrity of the information, the efficiency of transmission is increased. You may have already seen this type of transmission in a less sophisticated format. Many bulletin boards have their files in compressed format, using one of several popular compressing programs such as PKZIP. The compressed file is then transferred from the host machine, where the bulletin board resides, to the user's computer. Here, using a decompression program such as PKUNZIP, the user decompresses the file, restoring it to its original form. After decompression, the user can use the file the way it was designed to be used. This is a technique commonly employed in the microcomputer communication arena. Figure 3-23 shows a file before it was compressed by PKZIP and the resulting compressed file and size. As you can see, there is a large decrease in the size of the file after compression. This new compressed file will take less time to transmit than the original file.

| Name | Description | Date | Time | Original Size | Compressed Size | Ratio |
|------|-------------|------|------|---------------|-----------------|-------|
| TextFile.ps | PostScript Print File | 7/12/97 | 10:30 | 130,538 | 23,630 | 82% |
| TextFile.txt | ASCII Text File | 6/11/97 | 7:24 | 50,170 | 13,346 | 73% |
| fig3-1.bmp | Grayscale Photograph | 7/12/97 | 10:23 | 280,694 | 196,369 | 30% |
| fig3-1.eps | Grayscale Photograph | 7/12/97 | 10:22 | 590,311 | 236,467 | 60% |
| fig3-1.pcx | Grayscale Photograph | 7/12/97 | 10:23 | 376,182 | 210,885 | 44% |

**Figure 3-23.** Typical file sizes before and after software compression

# Security Devices

The concept of sharing resources and files is one of the great appeals of communication networks and centralized computer systems. However, there are times where user access to records and files must be limited to prevent unauthorized access of such items or to prevent inadvertent damage of any critical data. Additionally, data traveling through communication circuits is prone to interception, and the devices attached to these lines are also in danger of intrusion by unauthorized users. Securing these data transmission lines is an important aspect of data communications today. For the purpose of preventing unauthorized access to computing equipment, several pieces of hardware can assist in protecting data flowing through communication circuits. These devices are call-back units and encryption equipment. Additional equipment used in the management and protection of data communication, such as metering software and monitoring equipment, is discussed under the topic of networks.

# Call-Back Unit

A call-back unit is a security device that calls back the user after he or she makes a login attempt. After the call is answered, the call-back unit hangs up the phone and the phone number of the originating call is looked up in a table.

If the phone that the user is on is an authorized number in the table, then the call-back unit calls the user back and expects the terminal or user's computer to answer the call. If the call is completed properly, the system permits the user to log in.

The actual procedure that the call-back unit goes through to secure lines is as follows:

1. A person attempting to access the system makes a connection from a remote terminal or microcomputer using communication software.

2. The person is required to provide an identification number (ID) and a password.

3. The connection is severed after the ID and the password are entered.

4. The ID and password are checked in a table to verify that the user is authorized.

5. If the user is authorized, the call-back unit calls the user's registered phone number. The phone number is stored inside the host and authorized by the company's security personnel.

6. The user's modem is accessed and the session between the terminal and the host begins.

Call-back units provide access only to authorized users, inhibiting access by hackers, unless they are using an authorized phone. However, these units have some problems. First, the host system becomes responsible for the cost of the connection. Second, if a person is on a business trip and tries to access the host system with a portable computer, the computer won't be able to make the connection, since the phone number being used is not registered.

This last problem can be resolved by providing users with a cellular telephone and modem. Using a portable or cellular system, a user can be anywhere the cellular system can receive a signal. Then as long as the portable phone is registered with the system, a call-back unit will be able to locate the user and establish a connection. Several companies, including IBM, make laptop computers that have built in cellular phones and modems for use by sales and executive personnel. These systems are, of course, susceptible to the noise and interference that normally affects cellular equipment.

Another problem with the last solution outlined is that transmission over cellular phones is susceptible to interception by unauthorized users with the proper equipment. If company secrets are transmitted in this manner, there is a good possibility that they could be intercepted and used without the company knowing it. When high security is a necessity, then additional devices such as encryption equipment must be employed.

# Encryption Equipment

Some data communication networks, such as those employed by the government and military, require very secure communication. For this purpose, encryption equipment is used to scramble the data at the sending location and reconstruct it at the receiving end. Figure 3-24 depicts this configuration. **Encryption** is the transformation of data from meaningful code into a meaningless stream of bits. To make this transformation, the data is sent through an encrypting algorithm with the result being the set of meaningless bits. To see the data in its original format, the scrambled data is sent back through the algorithm which in essence now works in "reverse," restoring the original message. This is somewhat similar to the scrambling that we experience with cable television premium channels. The signal is scrambled as it leaves the broadcasting studio. A descrambler or decoder is necessary to restore the original signal.

Modern encryption devices expect digital information as input, and produce digital information as output. The function of these devices is governed by standards set by the U.S. National Bureau of Standards (NBS). This set of standards is called the Data Encryption Standard (DES), which uses 64 bits to encrypt blocks of 64 bits. Eight of the 64 bits are used for error detection, and a 56-bit pattern is used for the encryption key. This provides 256 possible different key combinations or more than 72 quadrillion possibilities for the key used in encrypting and decrypting the message.

During the transmission of an encrypted message, the same key must be used in the sending and receiving end of the transmission. This means that there must be a mechanism for sending the key to the receiving user. Sometimes the overhead involved during this operation can be costly since expensive and secure lines or some special courier must be used.

Encryption can be achieved through software or hardware implementation. Hardware encryption is faster but less flexible than software encryption. However, there are many chips that implement the DES algorithm that can simply be plugged into a computer and are ready for use. Software encryption is normally used only when there are small amounts of data to be encrypted; otherwise, hardware encryption is employed.

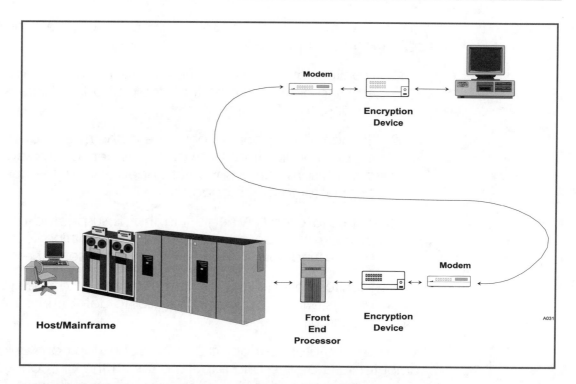

**Figure 3-24.** Encryption devices in a communication system.

# Miscellaneous Equipment

In addition to the data communication devices already mentioned, there are other hardware devices that help in the installation and maintenance of data lines. One of the most common is the breakout box, and it is used to set up the proper cable configurations required in data communications. Although used in several forms of communications, the breakout box is most commonly used to configure pin out configurations in RS-232 ports and serial data communications. Although the RS-232 is considered a standard, each manufacturer of computing equipment implements one of several versions of the RS-232 standard. This creates incompatibilities between devices that use the serial port as the main communication device. Some of these cases are terminals and peripherals attached to computers running the UNIX system. In this system, most terminals connect through the RS-232 or serial port, with many of the printers in the system also connected through the serial port. Unfortunately, an RS-232 pin configuration that works for one type of terminal may not work with another terminal from a different configuration. For these reasons, many system technicians make use of the breakout box.

## Breakout Box

A breakout box is a passive device that can be attached to a circuit at any connecting point, but it is normally attached to a serial port on a device or computer. It can be programmable or nonprogrammable with the latter being the most commonly used. Once the breakout box is installed it can perform the following functions:

1. Monitor data activity on the circuits. Each line circuit has a light emitting diode (LED) on the breakout box. If there is a signal on the line, the LED lights up.

2. Exchange line connections. One of the major causes of improper communication between devices is crossed lines. Line connections can easily be changed without the need to build a connector for each change.

3. Isolate a circuit. A single line that is suspected of causing the problem can be prevented from transmitting to the receiving device and isolated to see if it is the cause of the errors.

4. Monitor voltage levels. Some breakout boxes have voltage meters built in. This allows the user to detect unusual voltages in the circuit.

With the use of a breakout box a user or technician can "quickly" attach a computer to a device and experiment with the pin configuration until the right combination that allows the proper transmission of data without any losses is achieved. Some newer types of breakout boxes claim to be completely automatic. That is, they will automatically detect the right pin configuration for the sending and transmitting devices and adjust themselves to make sure that both devices work properly. Such devices seem to work well in many situations. However, they can't always automatically detect the right configuration. These devices will save a lot of time if they are able to automatically figure out the right cable configuration, but there is a good possibility that you may still have to use a normal breakout box and some trial-and-error techniques before an optimal solution can be found.

# Summary

Several types of electronic devices are used in the design and installation of data communication networks. The most commonly used are microcomputers, front end processors, mainframes, concentrators, cluster controllers, PBXs, matrix switches, line adapters, and security devices.

Typical electronic devices used in data communication are microcomputers, terminals, front end processors, and mainframes. The terminals are used strictly to send and receive data to and from a host computer. There are many variations in terminal attributes. These include keyboards, light pens, touch screens, mice, joysticks, trackballs, voice entry devices, and page scanners.

Front end processors are employed at the host end of a communication circuit to perform different control and processing functions required for the proper operation of a data communications network.

Mainframe computers are considered central computer systems that perform data processing functions for a business or industry. Mainframe computers are used in networks as host systems or as controllers. There are three types of configurations in which a mainframe can be used. In the first configuration the mainframe is a stand-alone system. The second configuration employs minicomputers and microcomputers in a local area network. The third configuration includes a front end processor to help with the communication.

A concentrator is a line-sharing device whose primary function is the same as that of a multiplexer. It allows multiple devices to share communication circuits. Unlike multiplexers, concentrators are intelligent devices that sometimes perform data processing functions and provide auxiliary storage.

Cluster controllers are designed to support several terminals and the functions required to manage those terminals. Also, they buffer data being transmitted to or from the terminals, perform error detection and correction, and poll terminals.

Private branch exchanges are electronic switchboards that connect to all the telephone lines of the organization. They can handle data communications in a digital format. Their flexibility in this area, especially when it comes to connecting a terminal or microcomputer to a host system, makes them a popular device used in data communications.

A matrix switch is similar to a private branch exchange and allows terminals and other electronic devices to access multiple host processors without the need to physically move any communication line. They are less sophisticated than private branch exchanges but are also less costly than PBXs.

Several other devices can be used to expand the communication distance between users and the host system. These devices are called line adapters and they come in different varieties, such as line monitors, channel extenders, line splitters, port-sharing devices, port selectors, digital line expanders, and data compression devices.

Securing data transmission lines is an important aspect of data communication today. Several pieces of hardware can assist in protecting data flowing through communication circuits. These devices include call-back units and encryption equipment.

Another device used in monitoring and improving line channel performance is the breakout box. The breakout box is a passive device that can be attached to a circuit at any connecting point.

# Questions

1. Why do we need devices to communicate more than a few hundred feet from a mainframe?

2. What is the main purpose of a matrix switch?

3. Why do we use breakout boxes?

4. What are concentrators?

5. What is the function of a protocol converter?

6. What is the function of a PBX?

7. What is a cluster controller?

8. Describe four different types of line adapters.

9. How does a line monitor work?

10. Why is hardware encryption used?

11. What device(s) could we use to increase the efficiency of a data communication line?

12. What device(s) could be used to increase the use of a data communication line in terms of the amount of data to be transmitted?

# Projects

The projects in this chapter are intended to familiarize the student with the basic hardware required to connect computers and printers using standard RS-232 ports. The basic equipment required to perform the projects is outlined in Project 1. As an additional challenge, the instructor may provide unknown or lesser known serial printers and instruct the student to design the interface between the printer and a microcomputer.

## Project 1. Minimum Interface Between a Printer and a Microcomputer

To connect a printer to a computer using the serial port, a minimum null modem eliminator can be used in most cases. The minimum null modem eliminator can be used on devices that support the Xon/Xoff protocol. If your computer and printer support this communication protocol, then pins 4 and 5 can be loop shorted on both systems and also pins 6, 8, and 20 can be shorted. However, all the handshaking must be done through software and not through the hardware. In most cases additional software is not required when printing documents using the interface discussed in this section. The sending software program needs to be instructed that it is communicating with the printer serially and that Xon/Xoff should be used in addition to the typical serial parameters .

To construct the minimum null modem eliminator, follow the configuration in Figure 3-25.

# Project 2. General Interface Between a Printer and a Microcomputer

In some situations a minimum null modem eliminator is not sufficient for the printer and the computer to communicate. If the printer seems to "lose" characters or if it prints correctly for a while and then it stops, the configuration in Figure 3-26 may solve the problem. Some printers require pin 11 (printer ready) to become active by a signal from the union of pins 6 and 8 as in Figure 3-26.

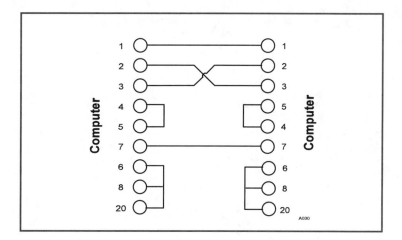

**Figure 3-25.** Minimum null modem eliminator.

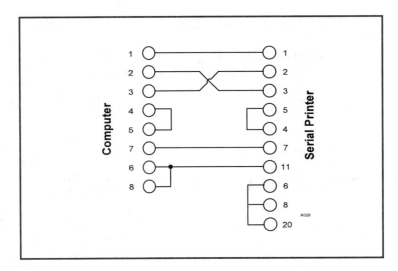

**Figure 3-26.** Connections between a printer and a computer.

# 4
# Communication Media

## Objectives

After completing this chapter you will

1.  Understand the different types of data communication media available in the marketplace.

2.  Be able to make educated decisions about the proper types of transmission media to solve a data communication problem.

3.  Understand the selection criteria for the different types of transmission media.

4.  Understand different criteria for selecting circuit media.

## Key Terms

Twisted Pair

Bandwidth

Coaxial Cable

Optical Fiber

Microwave

Satellite

Cellular Radio

## Introduction

All data communication equipment needs some type of transmission medium in order for the transmission to take place. Whether this communication medium is some type of conducting metal, water, air, or vacuum is not as important as recognizing the limitations that the medium imposes on current technology.

The educated data communication manager must understand the limitations and capabilities of all transmission media available to perform his or her duties as the person responsible for a successful data communication environment.

Each of the data communication media explored in this chapter has advantages and disadvantages that make it appropriate for some companies and inadequate for other data transmission needs. Although many managers make decisions about the transmission medium based on its data volume capacity and speed of transmission, many other factors affect the overall success of the implementation of a data communication system. The right medium is, of course, a key element in a successful operation. However, speed should not be the sole criterion for determining the appropriate medium.

Additionally, the services offered by common carriers should not be overlooked. These companies have been providing data communication services for many years, and their expertise in this area is often superior to that of company experts. Many companies may benefit from the offerings of such carriers, if for no other reason than the managing of the communication facilities, a task that many small and medium-sized companies tend to overlook.

Therefore, the following chapter should be read with an open mind if a broad understanding of all solutions is to be gained. The chapter presents different types of data transmission media, and then explores some selection criteria for choosing one of these media.

# Circuit Media

The data transmission medium is the physical path that the signal must use in order to travel from the sender to the receiver. There are many types of transmission media to choose from, but they can be classified in general terms into two types:

1.  Guided transmission media

2.  Unguided transmission media

Guided transmission media include several types of cabling systems that guide the data signals along the cable from one location to another. The other type, unguided transmission media, consists of a means for the signals to travel, but nothing to guide them along a specific path. Examples of these types of transmission media are air and water.

Guided transmission media work by attaching the transmitter directly to the medium. The transmitter can be a microcomputer, terminal, peripheral device, or even a cable television station. The signal travels through the cable and, at the other end, the receiver is also attached directly to the cable.

The cables used in guided transmission are basically wire conductors. Conductors can be classified into four major groups: open wire, twisted pair cable, coaxial cable, and optical fiber cable. Each of these has its own capabilities in terms of data-carrying capacity and speed of transmission. At the low end we can consider the open wire, and at the high end we have optical fiber. Of course, prices increase as the transmission performance of the cable increases.

Unguided media use antennas for the transmission and reception of the data signals. Among the different types of signals that can be transmitted using this format, we have microwave and satellite signals. Although unguided media such as air don't guide the signals along a specific path, the direction of the signal transmitted can be chosen by employing different configurations and arrangement of antennas. In this fashion, a beam of microwaves can be concentrated along a direction where a receiving antenna is expected to be located. The ability to focus a beam of signals in an unguided medium depends on the frequency of the signals being transmitted. The frequency of a signal is the number of cycles per second that signals go through, meaning the number of times the signal varies between two settings in one second. As the frequency gets higher, it is easier to focus the beam in a specific direction.

Although this chapter doesn't discuss all possible types of media configurations, it will discuss the most common types that are found in the marketplace. In most, if not all cases, the different data transmission media described below will satisfy the requirements of any data communication system.

# Guided Media

## Open Wire

Open wire lines have been around since the inception of the data communication industry. An open wire line consists of copper wire tied to glass insulators, with the insulators attached to wooden arms mounted on utility poles. While still in common use throughout the world, they are quickly being replaced by twisted pair cables and other transmission media. Communication on this medium is susceptible to a large degree of interference, since the cable is open in the atmosphere.

## Twisted Pair Cables

Because of the susceptibility of open wire to interference, it is typically wrapped with an insulating plastic coating and twisted together, hence the name **twisted pair** (see Figure 4-1). The cables are twisted in pairs because the electrical effect of one current is canceled by the electrical effect of the other, thereby reducing the amount of interference that the signal is subjected to. In this manner, the signals from one pair of cables are prevented from interfering with the signals of another pair, a type of interference that is sometimes called crosstalk. Twisted pair wiring is a common type of data transmission medium found in homes and buildings. Therefore we need to study it further, along with some of its data communication applications.

**Figure 4-1.** Unshielded twisted pair (category 5 UTP) cable, with and without an RJ-45 connector attached.

A twisted pair cable is composed of copper conductors insulated by paper or plastic and twisted into pairs. At the location where the pairs enter a building, a terminating block, also called a punchdown block, is normally found. These pairs are bundled into units and the units are bundled to form the finished cable. Figure 4-2 shows a terminal connector where twisted pair cables are being used. The terminating block serves several purposes. One of the functions of the terminating block is to act as a distribution panel. From the terminating block wires are distributed to offices or to other distribution panels or blocks located throughout the building. Another function of the terminating block is to act as a demarcation point where the responsibility of the common carrier (the public company that owns the cable) ends and the responsibility of the building owner begins. Any cable that is distributed from the terminating block belongs to private owners and they are responsible for its maintenance and upgrade. This same concept applies to homeowners. The phone company owns the twisted pair cable that is used to bring the phone signals up to the house. But the homeowner is responsible for the twisted pair phone cable installed throughout the house.

**Figure 4-2.** A terminal connector for connecting large numbers of UTP cables.

The size of twisted pair cable is measured in gauges, with typical twisted pair cables coming in 26, 24, or 22 gauge. The smaller the gauge number, the bigger the wire. This type of gauge corresponds to thicknesses from 0.0016 to 0.036 inch.

A variation of twisted pair is called the shielded twisted pair or data-grade twisted pair. Shielded twisted pair is twisted cable placed inside a thin metallic shielding of aluminum foil or woven-copper shield and then enclosed in an outer plastic casing. The shielding provides further isolation from the interference caused by the signal-carrying wires. Also, it is less susceptible to interference signals produced by electrical wires or nearby electronic equipment. Additionally, shielded twisted pair cables are less likely to cause interference themselves.

Because of this insulation, shielded twisted pair wire is capable of carrying data signals faster than normal twisted pair wire. However, this type of wire is more expensive and difficult to work with than unshielded twisted pair wire, and it requires custom installation to have a "clean" connection and avoid interference from poorly attached cable. Additionally, the shielding affects the transmission characteristics of the line and reduces the distance over which a signal can be effectively transmitted.

Twisted pair, whether shielded or unshielded, is used to transmit analog and digital signals. If an analog signal is being transmitted, amplifiers are normally required every three or four miles. If digital signals are being transmitted, some type of repeater is required every one or two miles. It has limited distance carrying capabilities, limited bandwidth, and limited data transmission speed. That is, it is very limited in the total amount of data it can transmit per unit of time and has low transmission speeds. Additionally, transmission frequencies can be high for long distances. In this case, electrical interference in the form of crosstalk between adjacent circuits is a problem for twisted pair cables. Even if shielded twisted pair wire is used, the problems above still apply, although to a lesser degree. However, it is inexpensive and commonly available in most offices and buildings. This makes it a popular data transmission medium in data communication systems. To solve some of the problems with twisted pair wire, coaxial cable is employed.

## Coaxial Cable

**Coaxial cable** consists of two conductors. The inner conductor, normally copper or aluminum, is shielded by placing it inside a plastic case or shield. The second conductor is wrapped around the plastic shield of the first conductor. This further shields the inner conductor. Additionally, the second conductor (shield) is covered with plastic or some other protective and insulating cover (see Figure 4-3).

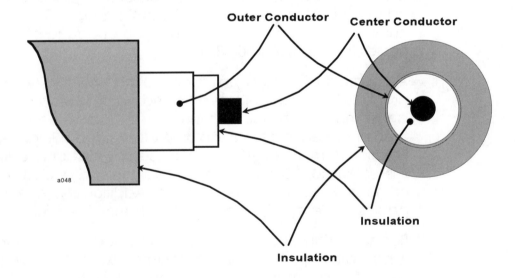

**Figure 4-3.** A typical coaxial cable.

The outer conductor shields the inner conductor from outside electrical signals and reduces the electromagnetic radiation of the inner conductor. The distance between the conductors varies, along with the type of shielding and insulation material used. This difference gives each type of coaxial cable a unique characteristic normally called impedance. The impedance is a measure of the resistance that the conductor has to the flow of electrical signals. Typical diameters of coaxial cables range from 0.4 to 1 inch.

Coaxial cables are sometimes grouped into bundles. Each bundle can carry several thousand voice and/or data transmissions simultaneously. This type of cable has little signal loss, signal distortion, or crosstalk. Therefore, it is a better transmission medium than open wire or twisted pair cables.

It is one of the more versatile transmission media and it has wide acceptance in the communication industry. It is used extensively in television distribution (cable television), local area networks, and long distance phone transmission. We have all seen the coaxial cable that cable companies use in distributing their signals from a distribution building to homes. Today, over half of the residential homes in the United States have cable television, and most of them are connected through coaxial cable.

Coaxial cable is heavier and more expensive than twisted pair wire. It can carry a greater capacity of data over longer distances and it is stronger than twisted pair. This makes it a common choice of data transmission media in factories and other areas where there is a harsh environment. The typical bandwidth of coaxial cable is between 400 MHz and 600 MHz. This large bandwidth is what gives coaxial cable its high data-carrying capacity.

It can carry analog and digital signals and, because of its shielded concentric construction, it is less susceptible to interference and crosstalk than twisted pair cable. For transmitting a signal over long distances, repeaters are required every few miles with the number of miles depending on the frequency of the data being transmitted. With higher frequency of data signals, the distance needed between repeaters becomes shorter.

Local area networks have been using coaxial cable as a medium for transmitting data to workstations. Coaxial cable can support large numbers of devices with different data and protocols transmitting over the same cabling system over short and long distances. However, it is important to note that there are many types of coaxial cable with different electrical characteristics. Not all coaxial cable can be used with a particular networking scheme.

Working with coaxial cable takes practice because it is bulkier than twisted pair wire. Therefore, connecting devices using coaxial cable should be done by a professional. One bad connection can render an entire system inoperative. It is wise to invest in good connectors regardless of their price. Additionally, a good crimping tool should be used. Also, invest in good quality coaxial cable. There are many vendors of poor quality coaxial cable that tends to break down after time and corrosion expose the conductors.

## Optical Fiber

**Optical fiber** consists of thin glass fibers that can carry information at frequencies in the visible light spectrum. The data transmission lines made up of optical fibers are joined by connectors that have very little loss of the signal throughout the length of the data line.

At the sending end of a data circuit, data is encoded from electrical signals into light pulses that travel through the lines at high speeds. At the receiving end, the light is converted back into electrical analog or digital signals that are then passed on to the receiving device.

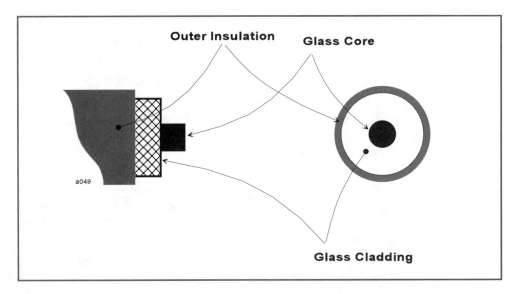

**Figure 4-4.** A typical optical fiber cable.

The typical optical fiber consists of a very narrow strand of glass called the core. Around the core is a concentric layer of glass called the cladding (see Figure 4-4). After the light is inserted into the core it follows a zig-zag path through the core. The advantage of optical fiber is that it can carry large amounts of information at high speeds in very reduced physical spaces with little loss of signal.

Single mode transmission uses fibers with a core radius of 2.5 to 4 microns. Since the radius of the fiber is so small, light travels through the core with little reflection from the cladding. However, it requires very concentrated light sources to get the signal to travel long distances. This type of mode is typically used for trunk line applications. A trunk line is the cable that carries the signal from a central office to a PBX or building where the signal will then be distributed.

There are three primary types of transmission modes using optical fiber. They are single mode, step index, and graded index (see Figure 4-5).

The promise of optical fiber as one of the best communication media comes from its high bandwidth. Optical fiber has a bandwidth range of about 1014 to 1015 Hz. With a bandwidth much larger than any other type of cable, a single optical fiber can carry the signals of thousands of simultaneous telephone conversations. In addition, optical fiber can carry signals much faster than other cabling schemes without distortion.

In terms of local area networks, the speed of optical fiber is not a good reason to choose it as the data transmission medium. In this situation, fibers carry data at about the same speeds as coaxial cable. However, optical fiber can carry the data longer, more reliably, and more securely than any other type of media. Additionally, fiber has the potential to carry data at higher speeds as the technology develops to take advantage of such a possibility.

Optical fiber can carry digital signals a longer distance than copper wires without the need for repeaters. Additionally, optical fibers don't pick up electrical noise from nearby conductors. On the other hand, copper-based conductors, regardless of the amount of shielding used, always become antennas. The amount of interference in the copper is directly proportional to its length. Since the signal traveling in an optical fiber is not electrical, none of these problems apply.

Optical fiber has additional benefits relating to security. Electrical signals traveling in a coaxial or twisted pair cable can be detected since electromagnetic radiation is emitted. This radiation, with the right equipment, can be used to obtain the original message. Light, on the other hand, doesn't emit electromagnetic radiation. Therefore, it is much more difficult for unauthorized users to pick up the signal in the fiber. Additionally, tapping into an optical fiber, although not impossible, is more difficult than tapping into twisted pair or coaxial cable.

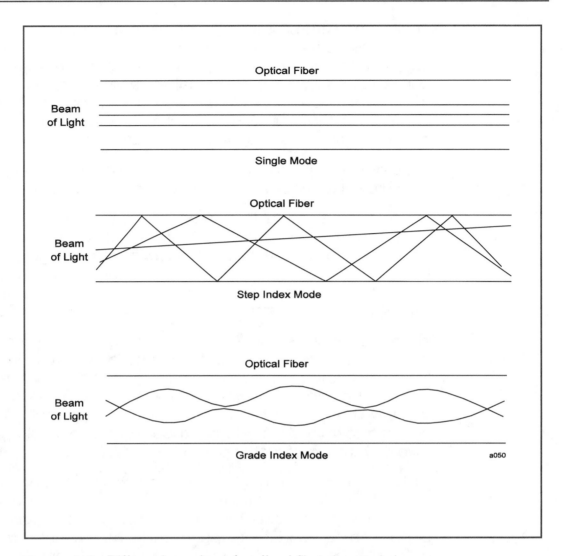

**Figure 4-5.** Different modes of optical fiber transmission.

Although more expensive than coaxial cable and twisted pair, optical fiber has the following advantages over them:

1. It has a greater capacity for carrying data due to its large bandwidth.

2. It has the potential for greater speeds of transmission than coaxial or twisted pair cables.

3. It is smaller in size and weight than other conventional cabling systems.

4. It can carry a signal over longer distances than other cabling systems with a smaller attenuation. That is, the signal loss over long distances is less with optical fiber.

5. It is not susceptible to electromagnetic radiation from nearby cables, light fixtures, and motors.

All these features of optical fiber make it a compelling transmission medium. As we move closer to the 21st century, users are demanding more than mere access to text-based data. Newer technologies such as multimedia are becoming standards in the workplace and in education. Multimedia technology incorporates sound, graphics, animation, and full motion video. Documents that incorporate multimedia techniques are being sent through traditional communication media that can not, in general, handle the massive amount of data that such documents contain. Just a few seconds of full motion video require millions of bytes of information. If companies and institutions expect to move their data communication needs into the future, they will have to design data communication systems that can handle the large amount of information that a multimedia document may require. Electronic mail with voice and video is now available. However, only optical fiber has the bandwidth and speeds of transmission required to manipulate such massive amounts of data effectively and efficiently. By the beginning of the next century, optical fiber will be the dominant data transmission medium for fixed-location applications.

Before leaving this topic, though, we must compare and contrast optical fiber with category 5 UTP cable. Several communication protocols now operate in the 100 million bits per second (Mbps) range on either category 5 UTP copper wire or optical fiber. In the 100 Mbps speed range both category 5 UTP and optical fiber are similar. Transmission speeds in the future, though, are expected to be 10 to 100 times or more faster. Eventually the rates will increase to the point that optical fiber will have a significant distance advantage .

# Unguided Media

## Microwave

**Microwave**, or radio transmission as it is sometimes called, is a high frequency radio signal that is transmitted over a direct line-of-sight path between two points. The concept of line-of-sight is important since the earth has a curvature. This necessitates that microwave stations be no more than 30 miles apart with the actual distance varying according to the terrain being crossed. Figure 4-6 shows a picture of a microwave tower and transmission station.

From the picture you can see one of the most common types of microwave antennas, the parabolic antenna or "dish." A normal size for this type of antenna is 10 to 12 feet in diameter and it is fixed to some stationary structure. The function of this antenna is to focus the microwave signals into a narrow beam that is transmitted to a receiving antenna that is directly in the line-of-sight of the sending dish. Microwave antennas are located in high places such as the rooftop of a building and on rigid towers.

The primary purpose of microwave towers is to connect computers or communication equipment that are located in different geographical areas. For example, a company with several offices distributed throughout a city could use microwave communications to connect all of its data processing equipment. In this case, the company, if it is a private enterprise, is not allowed to lay its own cabling system across the public right-of-ways (streets and highways). Only common carriers such as AT&T have permission from the local and federal government to perform such actions. However, it is possible for the company in the example to lease lines from a common carrier to connect its distributed offices. Depending on the amount of equipment to be connected and the data communication and processing needs of the company, it may be more cost effective to set up a microwave communication system to solve its communication needs. As long as the microwave antennas are within a line-of-sight of each other, the company in question will be able to connect all of its equipment without having to lease lines from a common carrier.

**Figure 4-6.** This microwave tower is located in New Jersey. Both parabolic and horn reflector antennas can be seen. (Courtesy of AT&T Bell Laboratories)

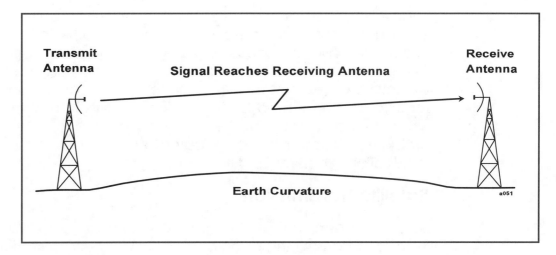

**Figure 4-7.** Point-to-point microwave relays are used to connect sites separated by 10 to 50 miles, depending upon terrain characteristics. Sites further apart require additional repeater links.

But what happens if the antennas are not in a line-of-sight? Then, in this case, repeating microwave stations must be employed. The typical line-of-sight is about 10 to 50 miles depending on the type of terrain that the microwave tower is located on. Beyond this distance, relay or repeating stations must be employed, otherwise the signal is lost into space (see Figure 4-7).

A typical microwave system transmits signals with a frequency in the range of 2 to 40 GHz. As the frequency increases, so does the bandwidth and therefore the potential for higher carrying loads. Also, as the frequency increases, the data transmission rate increases, but at high frequencies the attenuation of the signals also increases. Therefore, high frequencies are used only for short transmitting distances. These frequencies are subdivided into several types of transmission areas.

Three main groups of radio systems are used for communications lines. They are broadcast, beam, and satellite. Broadcast radio is limited to a unique frequency within the range of the transmitter. Radio beam transmission needs to be repeated if the signal is to travel farther than 30 miles. Normally, radio beam repeaters are found on top of buildings, mountaintops, and radio antennas. Satellite microwave radio is employed to avoid the limitations imposed by the earth's curvature, and it is described in the next section.

Microwave transmission offers speed, cost effectiveness (since there are no cables), and ease of operation. However, it has the potential for interference with other radio waves. This has become more apparent since the popularity of microwave transmission has increased over the last few years. With many microwave systems in place, especially in large cities, the chance of different transmissions overlapping each other and causing interference has increased. Additionally, commercial transmissions can be intercepted by any person with a receiver in the line of transmission, thus creating security risks. Another problem with microwaves is attenuation due to weather conditions. Microwaves tend to be attenuated by the water droplets from rainfall, especially when the transmission frequency is above 10 GHz. But even with these problems, microwave technology is a popular solution to data communication problems and needs.

## Satellite Transmission

Satellite transmission is similar to microwave radio transmission. But instead of transmitting to an earth-bound receiving station, it will transmit to a satellite several thousand miles out in space (normally approximately 22,300 miles). Figure 4-8 shows a picture of a transmitting satellite dish antenna.

**Figure 4-8.** These satellite dish antennas are about 5 meters in diameter. Other dish antennas ranging from 1 meter to 30 meters are used in satellite communications.

The basic components of satellite transmission are an earth station, used for sending and receiving data, and the **satellite**, sometimes called a transponder. The satellite receives the signals from an earth station (uplink), amplifies or repeats the signal, changes the frequency, and retransmits the data to another receiving earth station (downlink). The frequency is changed so the uplink does not interfere with the downlink (see Figure 4-9).

In satellite transmission, a delay occurs because the signal needs to travel out into space and back to the earth. Typical delay time is 0.5 second. There is an additional delay due to the time required for the signal to travel through ground stations.

But just as with the earthbound microwave antennas, a satellite must be within a line-of-sight of its earth stations. We use the words line-of-sight to indicate that the earth-based station and the satellite must be in locations that allow for the transmission and reception of a direct beam of microwave signals. Because of this, communication satellites remain stationary with respect to their position over the earth.

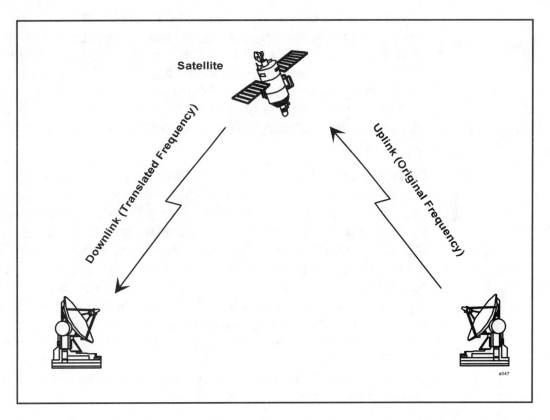

**Figure 4-9.** A typical satellite communication system (reverse link not shown).

Two satellites that use the same frequencies cannot be too close to each other. Otherwise, they will interfere with each other. To avoid this situation, nations that place satellites in orbit around the earth follow a standard that requires them to place satellites with a minimum of 4 degrees of angular spacing as measured from the earth if the satellite transmits in the 4 to 6 gigahertz band. Also, the standard requires 3 degrees of spacing if the satellites transmit in the 12 to 14 gigahertz band. This standard limits the number of satellites that can be placed in orbit.

As stated before, satellites use different frequencies for receiving and transmitting. The frequency ranges are from 4 to 6 gigahertz (GHz), also called the C-band; 12 to 14 GHz, also called the Ku-band; and 20 to 30 GHz. As the value of the frequency decreases, the size of the dish antenna required to receive and transmit the signals needs to increase. The Ku-band is used to transmit television programs between networks and individual television stations. Since signals in the Ku-band have a higher frequency, their wavelength is shortened. This allows receiving and transmitting stations to concentrate the signals and use smaller dish antennas.

One of the most common uses of satellites is in the transmission of television signals. Satellites are being used extensively in the United States and throughout the world for this function. For example, to broadcast a show throughout the continental United States, a television network sends its signal to a satellite that in turn retransmits the signal to a series of receiving stations on the ground. From this station, through microwave or coaxial cable, the signals are relayed to the sets in people's homes.

Satellites are also used extensively for point-to-point trunks between telephone central offices in public telephone networks. Also, they are used by businesses to connect private networks. A user or business leases one or more channels in the satellite. It then connects data processing and communication equipment in a building with similar equipment in a branch or office located thousands of miles away. But, until recently, such use of a satellite has been expensive. However, recent developments in the very small aperture terminal (VSAT) system provide low-cost alternatives to expensive traditional satellite transmissions. Using this scheme, several stations are equipped with low-cost antennas. These stations share a satellite transmission capacity for transmission to a central station. The central station exchanges messages with each of the stations and also relays messages between the stations.

Security poses a problem with satellite communications, because it is easy to intercept the transmission as it travels through the air. In some cases, a scrambler is used to distort the signal before it is sent to the satellite, and a descrambler is used in the receiving station to reproduce the original signal. This is the procedure used by several premium cable television channels such as HBO and Cinemax. A business could employ similar techniques by using some type of software or hardware encryption of the data signal that it needs to transmit.

### Cellular Radio

Traditional mobile telephones always had a problem with the availability of channels assigned to communication. It is common to find 20 channels being shared by 2,000 users, making it difficult to obtain a channel to use for communicating with someone else. Cellular radio solves this problem. **Cellular radio** is a form of high-frequency radio transmission where the signals are relayed from antennas that are spaced in strategic locations throughout metropolitan areas.

Each area of service is divided into cells, and each cell has a fixed transmit and receive site. If a person is using a car telephone and moves to the edge of a current cell, the cellular radio system automatically moves the user's communication to another antenna that is closer. In this manner, transmission is not interrupted and the user doesn't have to worry about moving from one cell to another. Additionally, the quality of the transmission is comparable to that found in common hardwired telephone systems.

Cellular radio can be used for voice or computer data communications. A user dials into the cellular system, and the voice or data is transmitted directly from the user's location to the cell antenna. From here it is retransmitted throughout the service area, or in some cases it can be transmitted to a satellite for communications over long distances.

Several laptop and palmtop computers have cellular radio transmission capabilities. This allows a user to be at any location and dial into a central location for the downloading or uploading of data, freeing the sender from locating a telephone outlet and communicating in traditional ways. Many sales personnel, police, or individuals who need access to a central site on demand use cellular radio for their data communication needs.

# Circuit Media Selection

With all the different options available for use as a transmission medium, which one is the most efficient and cost effective for a company? The answer to this question may be a single product, but is most likely a combination of products. In any case, many factors influence the decision of choosing a medium for a data communication network. These factors include cost, speed, expandability, security, and distance requirements. Decisions regarding these factors cannot be made independently. Deciding on a cabling scheme depends on the hardware that you have or plan to purchase. Software requirements may indicate a specific cabling system, and the hardware may have to be reconfigured for it.

In addition, data communication system designers will have to contend with two types of designs, one for the communications within the building or campus, and one for the communications to remote locations. Normally, the decisions that apply to communication beyond the immediate premises of the business have broader issues and implications than the decisions required for implementing a data communication system within the immediate business physical environment. This is due to the user not caring about the type of communication medium used by the common carrier providing the transmission media. That is, the user doesn't care that a particular carrier uses one hundred percent optical fiber or coaxial cable. The user is concerned only with the cost and quality of the service that the common carrier provides.

When it comes to providing data communications solutions for in-house needs, many types of issues need to be addressed since the options are wide in terms of cost and the services that they provide. One such crucial decision will involve choosing the right data transmission medium. For pedagogical reasons, each factor will be considered individually.

## Cost

The cost of a given communication network will include not only the cost of the medium itself, but also the supporting hardware, software, and personnel required to manage the network. Installing the cable and supporting hardware and software is just the beginning of the maintenance process. Many managers say the cost of installing the transmission medium is the largest piece of the entire cost of having a data communication system. They are incorrect. The major part of the cost is the personnel required to maintain the system.

The expertise required to maintain a system will increase with the size of the system. At the end of its life cycle, the cost of installing the communication system may be insignificant compared with the cost of personnel required to maintain the system.

In addition, the cost of further expansion must be taken into consideration. For example, a business that is established in Dallas may consider Dallas, Houston, Chicago, and New Orleans as its target cities. To connect its regional offices to its headquarters, this emerging company can use leased lines from a common carrier. However, if it is projected that within five years the contact offices will be in many more cities, a satellite network may be a more cost-effective solution than leased lines.

The cost comparisons used in the design and selection of a data communication system must be projected over the expected life of the system and must include at least the following elements:

1. The cost of the transmission medium.

2. The cost of installing the transmission medium and all communication and data processing equipment that will support the system.

3. The cost of personnel to maintain the system.

4. The cost of personnel to train users how to use the system.

5. The cost of upgrades or additions as the needs of the company and users expand.

6. The cost of the software and software upgrades required to keep the system running.

7. The cost of any leased lines or satellite channels leased from common carriers.

Although many more factors also affect the overall cost of a data communication system, the above need to be considered during the feasibility and design phases of the life cycle of the system.

# Speed

The transmission speed of data communication systems ranges from a low of 300 bits per second to several million bits per second. Some media, such as twisted pair cable, are less expensive than optical fiber. However, optical fiber can transmit at much higher speeds than twisted pair cable. The cost of increased speed must be balanced against the needs of the data communication system and its users.

Two factors dictate the speed of the data transmission medium: the response time expected by users and the aggregate data rate. The response time is the time it takes from the moment a terminal sends a request to the time the response from the host gets back to the user. A good response time is two seconds or less. However, longer response times may be tolerated to sustain a lower cost of the medium. Also, it is typically better to have a slow response time that is consistent than a response time that is unpredictable. Most users would get frustrated with the data communication system if one day the response time is one second or less and the next day the response time increases to several minutes for no apparent reason.

The aggregate data rate is the amount of information that can be transmitted per unit of time. A company's users may be satisfied with transmission speeds of 9600 bits per second. But at peak processing times, with large files, the speed requirements may range as high as 19,200 bits per second or more. The same communication medium may not work for both speeds.

The planning phase during which the data communication system is designed must consider peak loads in order to have a predictable response time for users. A twisted pair cabling system may be adequate for most types of transmission, but if, during a peak time, speeds of 10 megabits per second or more are required, a different wiring system should be considered.

Additionally, future requirements of the system must be taken into account. For example, if a network is being implemented in an educational institution to satisfy the initial needs of teaching programming languages, designers may choose to implement twisted pair wires. However, as the sophistication of the users increases and technology advances, the rest of the college may decide to use the system and incorporate multimedia concepts into the network. Then the twisted pair scheme will not work. In this case, it would have been better and more cost effective to spend the additional money and implement the data communication system using optical fiber. Table 4-1 provides the speed of data transmission of the circuit media discussed.

| Media | Speed Range |
|---|---|
| Private and leased lines | 300 to 80,000 bits per second |
| T-1-type media | 1.5 megabits per second |
| Coaxial cable | 1 to over 500 megabits per second |
| Optical fiber | over 2 gigabits per second |
| Microwave | up to 50 megabits per second |
| Satellite | up to 50 megabits per second |

**Table 4-1.** Data transmission speeds of different media.

Don't forget that the complexity and cost of the transmission medium tends to increase as we move down the elements in this list. Also, cost and speed are just two of the factors that should be considered when choosing the transmission medium for a data communication system. Regardless of the speed of the transmission medium, it may not work for a company unless it has expansion capabilities.

# Expandability

Eventually, most data communication systems need to be expanded by adding more devices at a location or by adding new locations. Some transmission media offer more cost-effective expandability than others. For example, coaxial cable and satellite-based networks are easier to expand into new locations. If a corporation has headquarters in Dallas, Texas, and opens new offices in London, Great Britain, it may be easier and relatively inexpensive to lease a satellite channel to extend the data communication system from headquarters to the new office. Of course, we say that it may be inexpensive, but the actual costs and savings will depend on the needs and volume of the data transmission requirements imposed on the system.

In many situations, leased telephone lines make expansion into new areas more difficult and costly. The installation of leased lines and the expense of their monthly lease, along with the low data transmission speed, may make using leased lines cost prohibitive. In a situation where high volumes of data must flow constantly between two remote locations, a leased line may not be the best solution. Microwave and other technology should be considered and their costs compared over the life of the systems. This will provide a more accurate picture of the actual costs than just comparing the initial costs of setting up the data communication system.

Future expansions must be considered whenever a data communication network is being designed. For example, a company can install twisted pair cable throughout an entire building. Two or three years after installation it may find that it needs coaxial or optical fiber media. In this case the cost of rewiring the building is larger than it would have been to install it initially. When planning communication systems, both short-range and long-range needs must be considered. This emphasizes the importance of planning when considering a data communication system. Planning must include solutions not only for the immediate needs (short-range goals), but also must include anticipated or future needs that extend beyond three years (long-range goals). Additionally, the planning process must be done according to some type of life cycle development (see Chapter 7). This will ensure that all aspects of the planning process are taken into consideration, as they should be if the project is to be successful.

## Security

The lack of security in a data communication network will allow hackers or unauthorized persons to have access to vital data. The data could be used to gain an advantage in the marketplace, or it could be altered or destroyed, with catastrophic consequences for a business.

Providing a completely sealed network that unauthorized persons can never access is impossible. However, some media, such as optical fiber, are more difficult to penetrate than other media, such as coaxial cable or satellite. The most vulnerable medium to the average hacker is switched lines. Once an individual gains access to the switching equipment, this person has good access to the rest of the network. Switching equipment should be protected by using account identification numbers, passwords, and perhaps a call-back unit, as the one described previously in Chapter 3.

Another type of security threat is the invasion of the system by a computer virus. A computer virus could be introduced into the data communication system by an employee of the company. Once inside the system, a computer virus could become an irritation to users or it could destroy data in user computers or host systems. To protect communication systems from this type of security threat, antivirus or virus scan software can be used to check any disk before it is used in any workstation or to check any file that flows through the system. Monitoring software can also be used to alert system operators to any unusual activities that may be the action of a computer virus.

Not only must a system protect itself against unauthorized users and computer viruses, but it must guard against any physical disaster such as a fire. Many systems have redundant lines and backup systems. Then in case of fire or some other catastrophic event, the critical aspects of the data communication system will continue operation by using alternative equipment and transmission media. Many corporations that use microwaves or satellite communications also have leased lines as backups, in case their primary transmission medium fails.

However, no matter how much backup a system has, it needs a good disaster recovery plan. Security on any data communication system is greatly enhanced by having a proven and well-designed disaster recovery plan as is described in Chapter 7. An effective disaster recovery plan is the result of good management of a data communication system.

## Distance Requirements

The distance between a sender and a receiver can determine the type of medium used for data transmission. For example, if two sites that need to be connected are hundreds of miles apart, it is not possible to lay coaxial cable between them. In this case leased lines, satellite, and microwave transmission need to be explored. Don't forget that only common carriers are allowed by law to lay cable across public right-of-ways such as highways. Therefore, if there is a public right-of-way between two locations, even for a short distance, leased lines or microwave communications must be considered since private cable couldn't be used.

Additionally, distance requirements will have to be measured against the volume of data that needs to be transmitted. If two locations are just a few feet apart, but the volume of data to be transmitted is heavy, such as in the use of multimedia technology, optical fiber may be a better solution than twisted pair wire.

Also, distance affects the number of devices that may be served. For short distances twisted pair, coaxial cable, and optical fiber may be used, but even these cabling schemes have limitations in how far they can transmit data without the need of repeaters. The cost of all these devices must be taken into account when designing the data communication system. And, for long distances, the average business may have to rely on local carrier lines, microwave, or satellite media.

## Environment

The environment in which a medium must exist will eliminate some options from consideration. For example, local building codes may prohibit a company or educational institution from laying cables under-right-of-ways. In this case, microwave radio transmission may need to be used. Another example is a case where phone lines are sharing conduits with electrical wires. This may cause too much interference with digital data transmission.

During the planning stages of a data communication network, the location of the medium and local constraints must be taken into account to avoid costly modifications during installation. For example, if twisted pair wire is used, care must be taken to locate the cable away from electrical motors, fluorescent lights, and other equipment that may cause interference with the data flowing through the medium. Also, some types of communication strategies may not work on all types of cables. A specific strategy may require coaxial cable and may not work with twisted pair wire. Therefore care must be taken to ensure that the communication strategy adopted is compatible with the transmission medium available.

## Maintenance

The type of maintenance required for a communication network must also be considered during the planning stage. If a coaxial line or twisted pair wire is broken or becomes defective, it can be repaired easily by finding the troubled section and replacing it. However, if a satellite malfunctions and needs repair, the time required to place it back into normal operation may be lengthy. This is why many communication companies have multiple media backup networks.

Additionally, the personnel requirements to maintain a microwave data communication system are different from the personnel requirements for a local network using twisted pair wires. Even though a data communication strategy may seem the best solution in terms of its capabilities, the maintenance and cost of personnel required to perform such maintenance may render the system too costly to be effective. These economic comparisons must be performed during the planning stages of the system and must be used to find a solution that not only solves the data communication needs of the company but is affordable.

# Summary

The data transmission medium is the physical path that the signal must use in order to travel from the sender to the receiver. There are many types of transmission media to choose from, but they can be generally classified into two types.

1. Guided transmission media.

2. Unguided transmission media.

Guided transmission media include several types of cabling systems that guide the data signals along the cable from one location to another. Examples of this type of transmission media are open wire, twisted pair wires, coaxial cable, and optical fiber cable.

The other type, unguided transmission media, consists of a means for the signals to travel but nothing to guide them along a specific path. Examples of this type of media are microwave, satellite transmission, and cellular radio.

Open wire line consists of copper wire tied to glass insulators with the insulators attached to wooden arms mounted on utility poles. Open wire was replaced by twisted pair cables and other transmission media because of the large potential for interference from electrical noise and weather as it lies open in the atmosphere.

Twisted pair cable is composed of copper conductors insulated by paper or plastic and twisted into pairs. At the location where the pairs enter a building, a terminating block, also called a punchdown block, is normally found. These pairs are bundled into units and the units are bundled to form the finished cable.

Coaxial cable consists of two conductors. The inner conductor, normally copper or aluminum, is shielded by placing it inside a plastic case or shield. The second conductor is wrapped around the plastic shield of the first conductor. This further shields the inner conductor. Additionally, the second conductor (shield) is covered with plastic or some other protective and insulating cover.

The last type of guided media covered in the chapter is optical fiber. Optical fiber consists of thin glass fibers that can carry information at frequencies in the visible light spectrum. The data transmission lines made up of optical fibers are joined by connectors that have very little loss of the signal throughout the length of the data line.

In unguided transmission, one common type of transmission is microwave transmission. Microwave, or radio transmission as it is sometimes called, is a high-frequency radio signal that is transmitted over a direct line-of-sight path between two points. The concept of a line-of-sight is important since the earth has a curvature. This necessitates that microwave stations be no more than 50 miles apart.

Another type of unguided transmission media is satellite communications. Satellite transmission is similar to microwave radio transmission, except that it transmits to a satellite several thousand miles out in space (normally approximately 22,300 miles) rather than to an earth station.

The last type of unguided transmission media discussed in the chapter is cellular radio. Cellular radio is a form of high-frequency radio transmission where the signals are relayed from antennas that are spaced in strategic locations throughout metropolitan areas.

Several criteria can be used to select the appropriate type of transmission media. These criteria are cost, speed, expandability, security, and distance requirements. Decisions regarding these factors cannot be made independently. Deciding on a cabling scheme depends on the hardware that you have or plan to purchase. But software requirements may indicate a specific cabling system, and the hardware may have to be reconfigured for it.

# Questions

1. Describe the advantages of twisted pair over coaxial cable.

2. Describe the advantages of coaxial cable over twisted pair.

3. If computer data and video data were to be distributed over the same medium for multimedia purposes, which cabling scheme would you use? Why?

4. How can cellular radio benefit a company?

5. What is a transponder? How does it work?

6. Describe three selection criteria used in deciding the type of transmission media used in data communication.

7. What is a T-1 circuit?

# Projects

The following are research projects rather than hands-on projects. However, they play an important role in the acquisition and retention of the topics discussed in this chapter. The result of these projects should be a short term paper that follows the criteria established in most technical writing classes. Many students graduate without knowing how to prepare technical documents, and that becomes a handicap in their professional work. These projects will not introduce the student to technical writing topics, but the instructor should emphasize such topics and demand that all work have a professional look and content. For this purpose, the instructor may make available some type of sophisticated word processor with desktop layout capabilities and/or presentation equipment, so the students can begin to appreciate the need for and use of such technology. For this reason, the projects below serve a dual purpose and they should be performed.

## Project 1. Comparison of Data Communication Media

Using the local library, find out the cost per foot for the installation and/or leasing of the different transmission media discussed in this chapter. Additionally, research the speed and other technical aspects of the media, and produce a report that outlines their strengths and weaknesses. Compare the cost per megabyte of transmission of each of the media and propose situations or scenarios where one type of media may be more suitable than others. Justify your answers with technical facts or cases.

## Project 2. Exploring Solutions to Data Transmission Needs

Find out the data processing capabilities of your institution or choose a specific existing company and perform the same functions. Describe how they implemented the transmission media and how they are using it. Additionally, find future expansion plans and recommend transmission media solutions to such plans. Also, find out how many telephones they are using including outside lines. Find out whether they have their own PBX or if they lease a Centrex system. Find the limitations of their current system and suggest solutions. If they have a PBX, what features does it have? How is it maintained? What is the cost of the system, and does it compare with the cost of having a Centrex system performing the same functions? Always justify your answers with technical facts or cases.

# Project 3. Exploring a Communication System

Pick a system to report on: a. A cellular system, b. A voice messaging system, c. A teleconferencing system, or d. A marine communication system.

Produce a two- or three-page report on the capabilities and potential of the system in the data communication field. Always justify any conclusion with technical facts.

# 5
# Network Basics

## Objectives

After completing this chapter you will

1.  Understand the benefits of networking.

2.  Understand the difference between local area networks and wide area networks.

3.  Know the standards that are used in designing networking technology.

4.  Know the different types of network topologies.

5.  Understand the different devices used for interconnecting networks.

6.  Obtain a general overview of design considerations for hybrid networks.

## Key Terms

Network

Software

WAN

MAN

LAN

OSI Model

SNA

TCP/IP

Ring

Bus

Star

PDN

Bridge

Router

Brouter

Gateway

# Introduction

The concepts explored in previous chapters become the foundation for understanding the importance and functionality of networks. These networks are the basic building blocks of the information age of the 1990s and beyond. The information system industry is being shaped by the use of networks for interconnecting workstations, peripherals, mainframes, and minicomputers. Students in all areas of business need to understand network connectivity issues and the advantages and disadvantages of the different configurations.

This chapter discusses the benefits of having a networked environment and the basics of understanding networks. The difference between wide area networks and local area networks is explained, along with the different types of network topologies that are found in the workplace. Finally, the technologies required to connect dissimilar networks are discussed, along with related design concepts.

The student should read the material in this chapter thoroughly before reading any of the following chapters. Those chapters assume knowledge and understanding of the general networking concepts explored in this chapter. These concepts are crucial in obtaining an educated view of the benefits and problems of designing and interconnecting data communication networks.

# Benefits of Networking

The microcomputer, with all of its benefits and usefulness, has serious shortcomings. Initially, microcomputers were designed with a single user in mind. Multi-user systems were delegated to mainframes and minicomputers This is generally true today, even though many microcomputers have more processing capacity and memory than a large number of the minicomputers in the business market.

Another problem with the microcomputer is that it was not designed to share its resources among other computers. If a printout is required, the personal computer must have its own printer. If a file must be stored on a hard disk, the personal computer must have its own hard disk. To a lesser extent, mainframes and minicomputers have the same problems. Even though a mainframe has many terminals that share disk space and printers, users of other computers within the same corporation may need to share resources in an efficient manner.

For example, assume that a corporation has an IBM AS-400 minicomputer, a Digital Equipment Corporation VAX minicomputer, and many personal computers and terminals. On many occasions the data stored on the AS-400 may be required by users of the VAX minicomputer and vice versa. In addition, some data processed in microcomputers and the resulting information must be shared by users of both minicomputer systems. This scenario creates many different types of information needs that must be resolved in an efficient and cost-effective manner. Users should not be expected to duplicate data entry procedures or to master diverse and difficult-to-use systems.

How does a system manager resolve the diverse information needs of users? One solution is to provide two terminals for each user, one for the AS-400, one for the VAX, and a microcomputer for those individuals who need access to software that runs on personal computers. Although this will address the different needs of each user, this solution does not solve the problem of sharing data among the minicomputers.

Another solution is to provide every user a personal computer. Through the microcomputer and with the aid of communication software, each user can access one minicomputer, download the data to a personal computer using the communications program, modify the data locally, and, using a different emulation-communication program, upload the data to the second minicomputer. This solution may eventually work, but it assumes that every user is proficient with both minicomputer systems and the personal computer. In addition, to perform the entire transaction properly, the user must have a good knowledge of microcomputers and communication software. These assumptions typically cannot be made. Statistics show that the majority of users in corporations cannot perform all of the above functions without technical help. Finally, even though a user may accomplish the entire transaction without errors, the method employed is not very efficient.

The isolation of computers described in the example results in duplication of hardware, software, and human resources. Each user must perform duplicate functions in order to transfer the data from one processor to another. These additional functions use time and personnel that could be applied to improve the balance sheet of the corporation.

Another example of the inefficiencies of this approach in a large company would be the implementation of a large number of microcomputers as standalone units. If a company has 100 microcomputers and all users need to run a specific package, the company must purchase 100 individual programs if it wishes to remain within the limits of the law. Similarly, each user must be provided with a printer and any other peripherals required to use the software. This duplication of resources is expensive to install and maintain, and space is needed for all the equipment, its containers, and manuals that need to be kept by the company.

Even small companies will find that using computers in an isolated form is inefficient. As an example, imagine a small company that purchases a microcomputer to keep track of inventory. In this scenario, one person keeps the inventory updated, and others occasionally use the microcomputer to check the inventory level and monitor availability of a product. As users find the application beneficial, the demand to use the inventory database increases. The company also grows and expands its product line, adding more inventory items to the database. As the database is used on a continuous basis and the inventory grows, it becomes increasingly difficult to keep the inventory updated, since users monopolize the time during which the computer is accessible. One obvious solution is to purchase more computers and place the database on each of the machines. However, if more computers are purchased to handle the demand, then the complication arises of keeping the database updated on all machines.

The current solution to these problems is to connect all the computers in a **network**. A computer network can change a group of isolated computers into a coordinated multi-user computer system. A network user can legally share copies of the software with other users, if network versions of the software are purchased. Data can be stored in centralized locations or in different locations that are accessible to all users. Also, printers, scanners, and other peripherals connected to the network are available to all users.

If the inventory system described above was placed on a network with several other computers, the system could be kept updated and could be accessed by many users simultaneously. This is because one of the computers can act as a centralized repository of all software. This computer, normally called a server, will be the only machine that keeps a copy of the database and provides the software to workstations that request it. Since only one copy of the software and data is kept, any user who accesses the database will always have the latest or most current version of the programs and data. Also, having this type of centralized system eliminates the need for additional hardware and software, thus lowering the overall cost to the company.

The method of operating just described has been at the core of companies or departments that have long used minicomputers and mainframes. It is a centralized system that minimizes the expense of purchasing hardware and software, yet it provides shared resources to all users. The network provides all of that, but goes a step beyond in that it provides all the functionality of the centralized system to users who have a computer on their desk. In addition, the network provides all the advantages mentioned above, regardless of the maker of the computer. In this fashion, minicomputers, mainframes, and microcomputers can all be connected to share resources, even though some may be IBM computers, some Apple computers, and others may be made by Digital Corporation.

# Hardware Sharing

A network allows users to share different types of hardware devices. The most commonly shared items are hard disks, printers, CD drives, and communication devices.

## Sharing Hard Disks

Today's sophisticated software applications require large amounts of disk space. Software environments such as Microsoft Windows with a word processing package consume in excess of 15 Mbytes of space before any data is saved onto the hard disk. Additionally, as companies require more information about their operation, larger disks are required. A microcomputer database management system such as Microsoft Access managing a corporate database may utilize an additional 50 to 100 Mbytes or more of storage. If the above software needs to share disk space with some other operating environment such as SCO UNIX, then the storage requirements for a single computer can be in the hundreds of megabytes. Also, if the base machine is not a microcomputer but a minicomputer or mainframe, the disk storage needs are even greater.

Although the price of disk technology has dropped dramatically in recent years, disks with a capacity to store billions of bytes are still relatively expensive. In addition, it is not uncommon for microcomputer users to require hard disk capacities of hundreds of megabytes. It would be too expensive to purchase large disk space for all users or all possible situations that may arise within a corporation.

The cost of storage media is just one factor to consider. In addition, the security and backup of storage devices become more difficult to manage when the devices are isolated. If there are many computers in an isolated format, it is difficult to ensure that all important data is properly backed up and safeguarded against possible loss. In addition, the time to perform all the procedures required to safeguard the data is extensive. This requires full-time personnel to perform just those functions. Another problem that arises is making sure that everyone has the most current version of a program on their hard disks. Since there can be many computers, each with the same copy of the program, it becomes difficult to ensure that everyone has the most up-to-date version of a data file or a program.

All of these problems are greatly reduced, and in most cases solved, by using a network that connects all the individual computers. The network backs up the files and software is stored on the hard disks of one or a few central computers. Additionally, since all the software is maintained in one location, everyone is assured of the latest version of data files and software programs.

Today's networks are based on the concept of sharing access to disk storage devices. These disks are typically installed on special devices called file servers, which will be discussed in the next chapter. A file server is a computer on a network that provides files and programs to those workstations that request them. As outlined above, sharing disk space has several benefits. The most obvious originally was cost, but integrity of the data, sharing of a database, and security have become more important as the cost of storage has decreased.

In the earlier days of networking, costs were reduced by purchasing hard disks to be shared among all users, rather than purchasing one for each user or location. Instead of purchasing a 500 Mbyte hard disk for 100 users, many companies provided smaller hard disks for the users and stored the programs and large data files required by users on a large centralized hard disk with a server. In addition, when the server's hard disk was large enough, it could also be used to save files that a user may have wanted to store in a location other than his or her workstation. This method of storing data provided users with a "larger" hard disk that has common access. The word "larger" is used in quotations because the user's computer didn't have the extra hard disk space, but the user did have access to additional storage.

In current times, the cost of hard disk storage has become so low that it is common for the user's PC workstation to have well over 1 GB of local storage. Therefore, providing the user with more storage at a smaller cost is not as important as it once was. However, the data-sharing needs of companies have continued to grow, and the network continues to provide a viable means for storing large database systems for access by many users from various workstations within a company.

Additionally, the safety of the data is improved over having it on isolated disks, since a network administrator can make constant backups of all files on the device. This is important when the data manipulated and transmitted through the network is critical to the operation of the company. Remember that it is easier to replace damaged equipment, but some data can't be replaced if lost or damaged. Frequent and consistent backup is one the best ways to ensure that all important data will be available if the main hard disk is damaged and the data is lost. Additionally, having the data in a centralized location on the network safeguards this data from being lost by a user's misplacing or damaging floppy disks or from failure of the user's local hard disk.

Security of the data is enforced by using the network's built-in security systems. Data on isolated disks is an easy target for anyone who wants to damage it. Network management software can prevent unauthorized users from gaining access to and deleting or destroying important data. Also, many of the network management programs available have computer virus detection/correction capabilities that can prevent these viruses from infecting users' workstations and network servers. Hard disk sharing is only one of the many advantages of networking. Another important device that can be shared through networks is the printer.

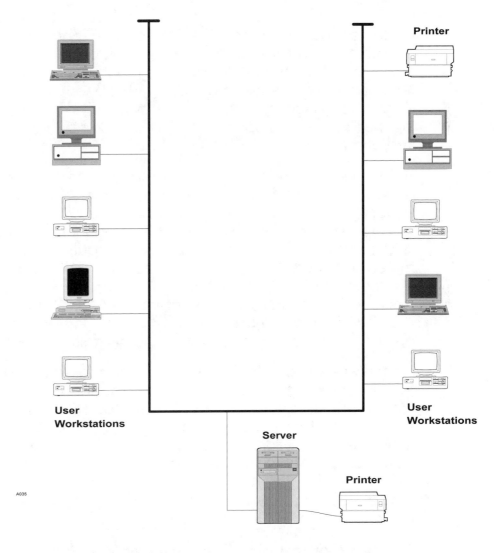

**Figure 5-1.** Network showing user stations and file server.

## Sharing Printers

Printer sharing is common on networks. Printers can be attached to a file server or connected to the network independently of the file server (see Figure 5-1). Users in the network depicted in Figure 5-1 can use any of the printers on the system. Instead of each user having a low-cost printer attached to a terminal or microcomputer, a few high-speed, high-quality printers can be purchased and connected to the network. Any user who needs a fast printout can send the output to the printer nearest to his or her station. This ability to share output devices reduces the cost of the overall system to the company and at the same time allows users to have access to better quality output devices than would otherwise be possible.

Printers are not the only devices that can be shared on a network. Input equipment can be shared along with output devices. Some of these additional devices include facsimile machines, scanners, and plotters. Scanners and facsimile machines have been around the computer industry for a long time. However, they have become popular only during the last few years as their prices have dropped and their quality has improved.

A facsimile machine can be shared as both an input and output device. If the facsimile is an independent machine, it can be attached directly to the network. Then output can be directed to it through the use of specialized software. In the same manner, if the facsimile device and its software are smart enough, any input received can be transmitted and routed to the intended receiver. A facsimile machine can also be shared by attaching it to a workstation and making the workstation act as a gateway or printer server. Also, new facsimile boards that fit inside the computer provide a closer integration of this technology into modern networks and connectivity strategies.

Plotters and other output devices can be shared the same way a typical printer is shared. To the network, a plotter or a printer is simply a logical output device, and they are treated relatively the same. Also, scanners can be shared by attaching the scanner to a workstation and using the workstation to distribute scanned images through the network. Some modern scanners have expansion slots that can be fitted with a network card that provides the scanner with its own identity to the network. This allows the scanner to function on the network without being attached to a specific computer.

## Sharing Communication Devices

Personal computer users on a network often need to access remote systems or networks. One possible solution is to provide them with modems and terminal emulation software to access other systems from their individual workstations. This solution is expensive and places a burden on the users who must know all the parameters and communication settings for their particular hardware.

A better solution is to provide users on a network with access to shared modems, gateways, bridges (these devices are more fully discussed in this chapter), and other network and data communication devices without the need to purchase one for each user (see Figure 5-2). Many companies set up what is called a "modem pool." This is a group of modems that are located in a single place and connected to several communication lines. The modems in the pool are available to users on a "first come, first served" basis. The modems are controlled, in most cases, by a gateway server computer. When a user needs to access another computer at a remote location, the user instructs his or her workstation to connect it to an available modem in the "pool." If a modem is available, the modem is logically given to the workstation for the duration of the communication session. From this point on, the user's workstation utilizes the modem as if it were attached directly to the workstation. After the communication session is over, the modem is returned to the pool, and it is made available to another user who may request it.

In summary, the benefits of sharing hardware on a network are clear. Costs can be reduced by avoiding duplicate hardware, and at the same time users can have access to a variety of devices. Also, data security and safety are improved by having up-to-date backups and enforcing the security measures that are available with each network.

## Software Sharing

Networks can also provide benefits in **software** sharing. Instead of purchasing an individual application program for every user in a company, a network version of the program can often be obtained at a lower cost per user. The software program can be stored on one of the network servers, making the program available to any network-authorized user. Also, software designed for networks allows multiple use of the software simultaneously, making a network of personal computers a multi-user system. In this case, users can share the data produced and used by the package at any given time, even though parts of the data files may be in use by another computer.

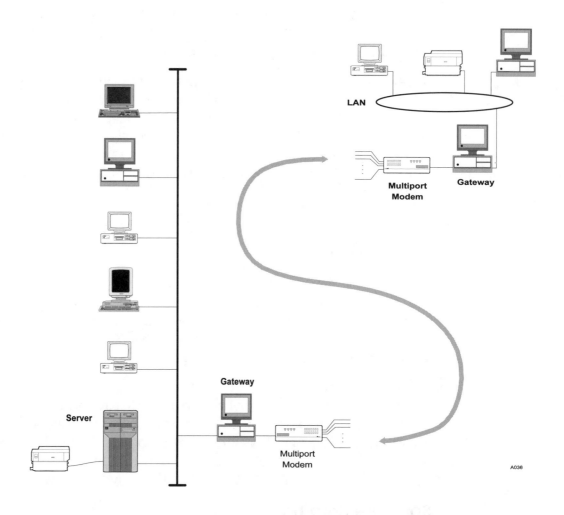

**Figure 5-2.** Connecting networks located in different geographical areas.

There are many advantages of sharing software. The most important are cost reduction, legality of the product, sharing data, and having current upgrades. Cost reduction has been explained before. As a further example, imagine purchasing 100 copies of a spreadsheet. Even with group discounts, the price of acquiring all of those packages can be $50,000 or higher. Purchasing a network version of the same package at a volume discount price for a number of users will usually result in a much lower cost. In addition, when an upgrade is available, there is a single cost that is a fraction of the cost of the upgrades for 100 separate copies, and having a single central copy means upgrading only one computer. Also, software designed for networking places data files in centralized locations that all authorized users can access.

Through various network management utilities, administrators can enforce security and the legality of all copies used, leaving the user to concentrate on generating and analyzing the data. If a company purchases a license to use 10 copies of a spreadsheet, the number of users that can concurrently access the program can be controlled by the network management system. If all 10 copies of the spreadsheet are being used and another user tries to load a copy of the program, the network management system informs the user that all legal copies are being used and that a current running copy must be closed before a new copy can be loaded into the user's workstation.

As stated previously backups are also easier to enforce and maintain if all the software resides on one or a few servers. Additionally, some types of networks allow a technician to back up not only the server's hard disks, but also the hard disks of user workstations. Although a network administrator wouldn't want to get into the practice of backing up all users' workstations, the ability to perform centralized and automatic backups enhances the security of the data in case of a disaster.

Networking multiple computers also has an added advantage. The productivity of users can be enhanced by taking advantage of "groupware." Groupware is software that includes electronic mail (e-mail), calendars, appointment managers, word processors, alarm clocks, and other time management software. It allows a user to manage his or her time electronically and communicate this information to other users on the network. It is intended to eliminate much of the inter-office paperwork, making information available to all users faster.

Using groupware, a user can create a memo, mail a copy of it to many other users, check their calendars for an opportune time for a meeting, and schedule the meeting automatically for the people in a given office or department. In addition, electronic alarms can be attached to the calendar to alert users of important events. These and other time management groupware products allow the system to perform the daily operations of the company and keep its employees in contact with each other.

However, even with all the advantages mentioned above, networks are often costly and are not problem-free from an administrative and technical point of view. Many companies don't look closely at these problems until it is too late to reverse costly and time-consuming events that are put in motion when a network is implemented. These problems or challenges are explained in the next section.

# Challenges of Networking

Although the implementation of a network carries many benefits, as outlined in the beginning of this chapter, its introduction into the work environment presents new challenges and costs that are sometimes not anticipated. These challenges can be summarized as the cost of networking.

The cost of networking includes, but it is not limited to, these factors:

1. The cost of acquiring and installing cables and associated equipment for the transmission of data. Different types of transmission media come with advantages and disadvantages that vary greatly. The cost of the media varies according to the data transmission capacity and speeds of movement through the cable. In addition, it is easier, and therefore cheaper, to install twisted pair wire than it is to install optical fiber. The purchase of transmitting media is just one aspect of this cost.

2. Specialized personnel may be required to lay the cable. The cost of contracting a company to perform the "pulling" or layout of the cable will also depend on the number of difficulties that the installers have to overcome as they perform their job. It is cheaper to install cable when a building is being constructed than to have to drill through several feet of concrete after it is built. Also, if the distances are large, additional equipment such as line adapters may be required. The cost of these adapters tends to increase as the sophistication of the media increases.

3. The cost of purchasing the network operating system and network versions of individual software packages. Depending on the type of network being implemented and the number of users, the cost of the software to run the network, the network operating system or NOS, can be several thousand dollars. Even companies with small networks can expect to pay a few thousand dollars for the NOS. Additional modules to the NOS such as network monitoring software and virus protection are not normally included in the basic network operating system package. Depending on the type of network being installed and the number of users, the complete set of software to operate the network can be more expensive than most of the hardware pieces. And, of course, the network operating system alone is not sufficient. Application software must also be acquired.

4. Software applications that were running on an individual basis may need to be upgraded in order to obtain network licenses. Additionally, many software programs designed for an individual computer will not execute on a network without modification of that software.

5. The source code. If a company has a heavy investment in software that is not able to run on the network, then the cost of acquiring new software to replace the old can run the cost of the network beyond the fiscal possibilities of the company. Further, if the network contains many users and sophisticated applications, someone must maintain the servers and the physical layout of the network itself as people and workstations are relocated.

6.  The cost of personnel to manage software installation, expand and reconfigure the network, provide backup, maintenance of hardware and software, and maintenance of the network/user interface. As users become comfortable with the network, their use of it will increase and thus increase the demand for additional network services. Also, people may need to be relocated within an office or building. Someone has to ensure that the network services for these users are not interrupted.

7.  In some cases, the number of users or software used through the system may exceed system resources. Technical personnel will be needed to "tune" and enhance the network to make sure that it works efficiently and effectively. Periodically, passwords may need to be reassigned, backups need to be performed, hard disks need to be defragmented, and old accounts need to be erased to make room for new accounts. All of these functions require personnel trained and educated in the operation of networks. This is an important point that was mentioned before. Many companies delegate the operation of networks to individuals who don't have any formal training in system design and network operations. These individuals learn as much as possible as they perform their duties, but by the time they learn enough about the network, it may have deteriorated to the point of needing a major and costly overhaul. Technical and network operating personnel must have the formal training that today's sophisticated systems require in order to perform efficiently and effectively.

8.  Finally, as users are added to the network, the security and safekeeping of data becomes critical. Personnel will be required to maintain the network on a full-time basis and to ensure that proper backups are made in a consistent and timely fashion. The network interface will need modification as types and quantities of users change. In most cases, companies should expect that to install a network that serves many users, additional trained personnel need to be hired in conjunction with the purchase of the network itself. A lack of proper personnel is one of the most common factors contributing to a poorly designed system and to the failure of networks.

9.  The cost of bridges and gateways to other networks and the software and other equipment required to implement the connection. After the network is implemented, there may be a need to connect it to other communication systems. The equipment used in the networking field to provide connectivity among different network platforms comes in the shape of gateways, routers, brouters, and bridges.

    The technical staff in charge of the network needs to be aware of the differences, capabilities, and cost of these devices. Each was designed for a specific purpose, and using them in the wrong situation or place could disrupt the operation of the network. The cost and challenge of performing this connection are an additional burden to network managers, and additional personnel and training may be required.

10. The cost of training users of the network and the personnel required to manage the network. This is an ongoing and hidden cost due to the turnover of personnel. Many companies don't consider this cost in their design stage. Although the cost of training a network administrator and technical operation staff is in many cases accounted for, the cost of training users is many times ignored. If a user is being trained on how to use the network, the hours spent in training are lost production to the company. Also, if the training is performed off-site, then a replacement may have to be hired during the training period.

    Many administrators claim that these costs are offset by the savings introduced by the employee after the training is completed. Even though an employee may perform his or her duties more efficiently after learning how to use the network, there is a cost associated with training users, and outside consultants or training personnel need to be included in the cost. If the company has a high turnover ratio, this cost will be large.

11. The cost of maintenance, including installation of future software upgrades, correcting incompatibilities between the network operating system and new software upgrades, and correcting hardware problems. As new versions of the network operating system become available, old software programs may not be able to coexist with the new operating system. In such cases, new versions of application software must be secured. (Of course, if the number of users is large, having a network license can provide substantial savings over purchasing many individual copies of the same program.) The number and frequency of upgrades is a cost that must be scheduled into the system life cycle (see Chapter 7).

12. The cost of hiring a network administrator or specialist to manage the system or to solve problems as they occur. Although many companies use existing personnel to manage new networks, these people will have to give up a minimum of approximately 10 to 20 hours per week to manage and back up the network. Their absence from a task for which they were originally hired will eventually have to be compensated for by hiring assistants or by increasing the salary of such personnel.

13. In small companies the task of implementing and managing the network can be performed by one or two persons. However, in large companies, several full-time employees may

be needed to perform network management duties. These costs will become a sizable portion of the operational budget of the company. It is important that any implementation of a network follows the rules for system design. Only in such a case will the company be assured that all possible problems and obstacles in the success of the network implementation have been properly addressed and anticipated (see Chapter 7).

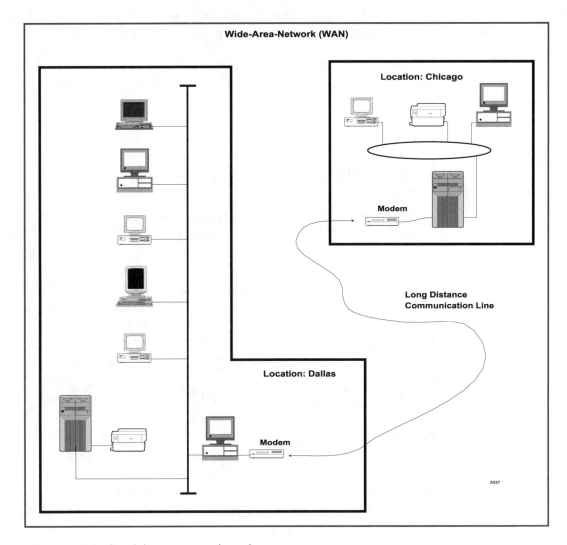

**Figure 5-3.** A wide area network.

# Types of Networks

Although the distinction between terms is becoming less and less clear as communications becomes faster and more affordable, the geographical area covered by a network has traditionally determined whether the network is called a wide area network (WAN—see Figure 5-3), metropolitan area network (MAN), or local area network (LAN). Wide area networks link systems that are too far apart to be included in a small in-house network. Metropolitan area networks connect across distances greater than a few kilometers but no more than 50 kilometers (approximately 30 miles). Local area networks usually connect users in the same office or building. In some cases, adjacent buildings of a corporation or educational institution are connected with the use of LANs. However, the boundaries of a type of network are not as clearly defined in real life as they are in this book.

Many companies have networks that encompass hundreds of miles, yet they are still called local area networks. This book will try to differentiate among the three types according to the distance they cover, but keep in mind that their definitions are sometimes altered by the people who implement and manage them.

# Wide Area Network (WAN)

**Wide area networks** cross public right-of-ways such as highways and streets, and most use common carrier circuits for their transmitting medium. They use a combination of the hardware discussed in previous chapters. Wide area networks use a broad range of communication media for interconnection that includes switched and leased lines, private microwave circuits, optical fiber, coaxial cable, and satellite circuits. Basically, a wide area network is any communication network that permits message, voice, image signals, or computer data to be transmitted over a widely dispersed geographical area.

# Metropolitan Area Network (MAN)

**Metropolitan area networks** connect locations that are geographically located from 5 to 50 kilometers apart. They include the transmission of data, voice, and television signals through the use of coaxial cable or optical fiber cable as their primary medium of transmission, although many metropolitan area networks are implemented through the use of microwave technology.

Customers of metropolitan area networks are primarily large companies that need to communicate within a metropolitan area at high speeds. MAN providers normally offer lower prices than the phone companies and faster installation over a diverse routing, and include backup lines in emergency situations.

## Local Area Network (LAN)

**LANs** connect devices within a small area, usually within a building or adjacent buildings. LAN transmission media usually do not cross roads or other public thoroughfares. They are privately controlled and owned with respect to data processing equipment, such as processors and terminals, and with respect to data communication equipment such as media and extenders. Local area networks are covered in detail in the next chapter.

Many local area networks are used to interconnect the computers and peripherals within an office or department. Through specialized hardware and software, each department's LAN is connected to a larger local area network within the company's building. Then, this larger LAN is connected to a metropolitan area network that may interconnect different offices or branches throughout a large city. And finally, the company's MANs may be connected to a wider area network that interconnects the company's regional or international offices.

Each of the types of networks mentioned above has a set of standards that most manufacturers adhere to in order for their equipment to work with equipment manufactured by other companies. This set of standards is a necessity in a computing field that sees equipment manufacturers trying to impose their own standards on customers for the sole purpose of monetary gain. These standards assure customers that, as long as they purchase equipment that follows the established set of criteria for the functioning of communication equipment, they will be able to connect the equipment to their networks and should expect it to work properly. The set of criteria or standards is formulated by country representatives that have grouped together and formed the International Standards Organization for Standardization.

# Current Standards

The computer industry is dominated by standards that are the result of several companies forming committees to ensure that the equipment and system type software they produce will be compatible. These sets of standards minimize the risk of creating networks that use equipment from different vendors who may follow different protocols. Also, by designing a network with equipment that complies with a set of standards, the users of these networks are assured that they will be able to share information from different sources and over different network schemes.

Additionally, the use of standards in network design and installation helps in managing the system by creating common management processes. At the same time it insulates the network operators from changes at low levels of the standard. Although there are several types of standards in the communication industry, three of the most commonly implemented are those established by the Open Systems Interconnect subcommittee, or OSI; IBM's System Networking Architecture, or SNA; and TCP/IP, whose standards are controlled by Requests for Comment from the community of TCP/IP users themselves.

# Open Systems Interconnect (OSI)

Network evolution has been toward standardized networking and Internet working technology. One of the most important standards-making bodies is the International Standards Organization or ISO, which makes technical recommendations about data communication interfaces. Standardizing the interfaces and the format of the data flowing through them ensures that, regardless of the equipment manufacturer, the entire network will work as long as the equipment in it adheres to these standards.

## History

In 1978, the ISO created the Open Systems Interconnect (OSI) subcommittee, whose task was to develop a framework of standards for computer-to-computer communication. The result of the subcommittee's work is referred to as the OSI Reference Model. It serves as the model around which a series of standard protocols is defined. Using this model, hardware and software companies can develop their products to work within certain parameters that are the guidelines of the model. The resulting product is then able to communicate with other products that follow the same parameters.  Be sure to remember, though, that the OSI model is a model and not a specific set of standards.

The OSI Reference Model is known as a layered protocol, specifying seven layers of interface, wherein each layer has a specific set with functions to perform (see Figure 5-4). Each layer has standardized interfaces to the layers above it and below it, and it communicates directly with the equivalent layer of another device.

As a result of the OSI Reference Model, the communications industry has concentrated on making products that comply with the interface guidelines, making them OSI compatible. Among the best known customers of OSI products is the federal government, which is committed to purchasing large quantities of OSI-compatible products through the Government Open System Interconnect Profile or GOSIP. By basing their networks on OSI compatibility, users can discuss product relationships and compatibilities and capabilities in the same working framework.

The **OSI model** divides the communication process into seven layered processes. These processes are as follows:

1. The physical layer.

2. The data link layer.

3. The network layer.

4. The transport layer.

5. The session layer.

6. The presentation layer.

7. The application layer.

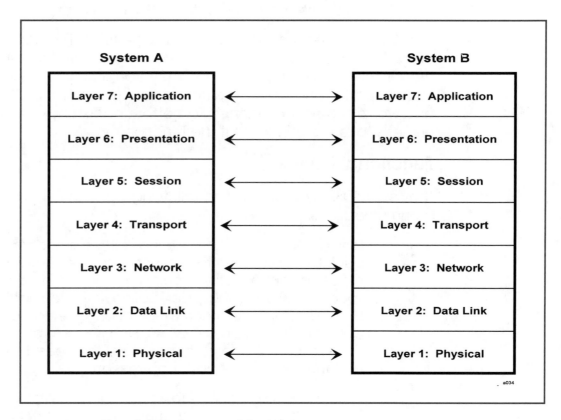

**Figure 5-4.** The OSI Reference Model.

When a company refers to one of its products as working at level 2, it means that the product works at the second level of the OSI model and it is "transparent" to any other products that work on layers 3 through 7. The word "transparent" means that the product under discussion will not negatively affect the operation of any other products that work in higher level layers. The lowest level layer is 1 and the highest level is 7.

## Benefits

Having a layered framework, the OSI model offers several benefits:

1. Network hardware and software designers can allocate tasks more effectively among network resources.

2. A network layer can easily be replaced by a layer from another network vendor.

3. Processes from mainframes can be off-loaded into FEPs or other network control devices.

4. Networks can be upgraded more easily by replacing individual layers instead of the entire software system.

The user and network designer are not restricted to using the product of a specific company. If they are not satisfied with the performance or the service of a product provider, they can simply replace the product in question by another of a different company that is OSI compatible and works in a similar manner. To better understand the individual layers, let's take a closer look at the function of each.

## Functional Layers

The seven OSI layers define the following standards in the field of data communications.

1. Physical layer. This layer defines all the standards that provide guidelines on how to physically move data bits between modems and perform circuit activation and deactivation. The specifications on this layer define the electrical connections between the transmission medium and the computer. The layer describes how many wires will be used to transmit the signals, the size and shape of connectors, the speed of transmission, and the direction of data transmission.

2. Data link layer. The standards in this layer establish and control the physical path of communication to the next node. This includes detection and correction of errors, handling flow control between modems, and the proper message sequence. This layer is basically responsible for the accuracy of the data transmitted between two locations on the network and the control mechanism for accessing the network.

3. Network layer. The standards defined for this layer provide the necessary control and routing functions to establish, maintain, and terminate communication links between transmitting and receiving nodes.

4. Transport layer. The standards established by this layer are responsible for generating the address of end users and ensuring

that all data packets are received. A packet is a block of data that is sent from an originating point to a receiving location.

5. Session layer. It provides the necessary standards to define the interface to manage and support a communication dialog between two separate locations. It establishes a session, manages the session, synchronizes the data flow, and terminates the session.

6. Presentation layer. The standards for this layer define how products may accept data from the application layer and format the data. If there are any data preparation functions, the functions are not embedded into the data; rather, they are performed by this layer. The types of functions that can be performed are data encryption, code conversion, compression, and terminal screen formatting.

7. Application layer. The standards defined by this layer provide guidelines for network services such as file transfer, terminal emulation, and logging into a file server. This layer is functionally defined by the user, and it supports the actual end-user application.

# Systems Network Architecture (SNA)

Another standard proprietary to IBM is the Systems Network Architecture or **SNA**. SNA was introduced in 1974, and today there are over 36,000 SNA-compatible network installations. This large installed base warrants the study of SNA and some of the standards established by it.

The SNA strategy is conceptually similar to the OSI model but it is not compatible with it. Like OSI, SNA is divided into seven layers, but these layers are defined differently from those found in the OSI model. In the SNA scheme, the seven layers are as follows:

1. The physical layer.

2. The data link control layer.

3. The path control layer.

4. The transmission control layer.

5. The data flow control layer.

6. The presentation layer.

7. The application layer.

Remember that, although these layers seem compatible to the OSI layers, they are not compatible with each other.

## Concepts

The SNA definition divides the network into physical units (PU) and logical units (LU). The physical units constitute the hardware on the network such as printers, terminals, computers, and other processor devices. There are four types of physical units defined as 1, 2, 4, and 5. Presently there isn't a physical unit 3. These four types correspond to the hardware in the following manner:

| PU | Hardware |
| --- | --- |
| 1 | Terminals |
| 2 | Cluster controllers |
| 4 | Front end processors |
| 5 | Host computers |

The logical units are the users logged onto the network and the application programs running in the system. The logical units or LUs are implemented through software in the network. The communication between users is a communication between logical units called a session. Notice that a physical unit can support many logical units.

The sessions mentioned above need to be established before two LUs can communicate with each other. Sessions occur between terminals and programs, terminals and terminals, and programs and programs. They can also be classified as interactive, batch, and printer sessions with each user having multiple simultaneous sessions, each with its own LU. This provides users of SNA systems the ability to communicate with two or more computers or with two or more programs simultaneously.

The SNA standard specifies that each device uses a 48-bit network address that identifies the LUs and PUs, also called network addressable units or NAU. Each NAU has its own unique address which, due to its 48-bit format, can be a large number, giving SNA-compatible networks access to a large number of nodes

Each of the NAU in an SNA-compatible network uses the Synchronous Data Link Control (SDLC) protocol as its primary data link protocol. In addition, SNA can operate with the BISYNC and X.25 protocols. This was implemented in response to a large number of IBM customers requesting access to other networking standards.

SNA networks are normally designed to maximize the network connecting the centralized mainframes that serve as hosts for all data processing activities. The network itself is not as intelligent as other standards in the market. In the SNA architecture, the mainframe is the main processor of data and the network is just an avenue for getting the data to the mainframe.

To manage the SNA network, IBM and other third party vendors provide software to aid in this task. One of these products that is commonly found in many installations is called Netview. Netview becomes an interface between the network administrator and the network itself. This product provides statistics about transmission errors, circuit problems, difficulties with modems, response time, and other network problems. In addition, the Netview product is an "open" product that allows third party manufacturers to create products that interface with it.

# Transmission Control Protocol/Internet Protocol (TCP/IP)

**TCP/IP** (Transmission Control Protocol/Internet Protocol) is a suite of common network protocols for information interchange between computers. Development began in the early to middle 1970s as a Department of Defense project whose goal was connecting computer systems with very different hardware and operating systems.

As contrasted with the OSI 7-layer model which was developed much later, the Department of Defense had a 4-layer model, with protocols at various layers. These protocols are the TCP/IP suite. TCP/IP is part of both 4.2 and 4.3 versions of Berkley Source Distribution UNIX and has been added to several other implementations of UNIX. Probably even more important to the long-term survival of TCP/IP is the fact that TCP/IP is the protocol on which the Internet is based.

## The Internet

The Internet is a worldwide network connecting users from education, business and industry, various U.S. government sites, and numerous other users. The Internet is the result of the interconnection of several large networks:

1. ARPANET. Defense Advanced Research Project Agency (mid 1960s, early 1970s - early developer of physical backbone, and dismantled in 1990. Originally 56KB, later replaced by T-1.)

2. CSNET. Computer Network, originally sponsored by National Science Foundation

3. NSFnet. Group of networks financed by National Science Foundation

4. MILNET. DOD Network, formerly part of ARPANET

5. Cypress Net. Internet access for small institutions, controlled by Purdue University

The DOD model for TCP/IP covers the same functions as the OSI model, but these functions are separated into four layers, not seven. A rough mapping of the OSI model layers to the corresponding TCP/IP layers is shown in Figure 5-5.

## The Layers of TCP/IP

### Process/Application Layer

The first layer is the Process/Application layer. This layer controls the user's interface and applications between two hosts. The protocols at this layer do such things as terminal emulation, file transfer, e-mail, etc. Common applications are:

| TCP/IP Layers | OSI Layers |
| --- | --- |
| Process/Application | Application<br>Presentation<br>Session |
| Host to Host | Transport |
| Internet | Network |
| Network Access | Data Link<br>Physical |

**Figure 5-5.** TCP/IP model compared to OSI model.

**File Transfer Protocol** - File Transfer Protocol (FTP) allows for transfer of files between the user's computer and the remote host. This protocol is not transparent to the end user because it requires the use of a command language with a particular syntax or grammar.

**Trivial File Transfer Protocol** - Trivial File Transfer Protocol (TFTP), like FTP, allows the user to transfer files between two systems. TFTP, however, does not require the user to specify an account or password, but limited types of files can be transferred.

**TELNET - TELNET** is a Virtual Terminal Protocol that provides terminal emulation connected to a remote host.

**Simple Mail Transfer Protocol** - Simple Mail Transfer Protocol (SMTP) is an e-mail protocol that provides for the sending and receiving of mail over a TCP/IP connection. This is the most common of all the TCP/IP applications, primarily because of the use of the protocol on the Internet.

## Host-to-Host Layer

The second layer, the Host-to-Host layer, establishes and maintains simultaneous connections, ensuring data integrity and setting up reliable communication between systems. The layer ensures delivery of data units, in sequence, without loss or duplication. The layer contains two major protocols: Transmission Control Protocol (TCP), a connection-based protocol, and User Datagram Protocol (UDP), which is a connectionless protocol.

**Transmission Control Protocol** - Transmission Control Protocol (TCP) utilizes a virtual circuit between different hosts in a connection-based environment where the circuit is maintained for the length of the message. Applications at this layer include TELNET terminal emulation; File Transfer Protocol, which is used to transfer files between hosts; and SMTP, which is the widely used Simple Mail Transfer Protocol.

**User Datagram Protocol** - User Datagram Protocol is an unreliable, connectionless protocol, which functions similarly to regular postal mail in that there is no requirement for acknowledgment when a message is transmitted. Applications at this layer include Trivial File Transfer Protocol and NFS, the Network File System used by such manufacturers as Sun Microsystems.

## Internet Layer

The third layer is the Internet layer. This layer routes packets between different hosts or networks. Protocols at this layer include the Internet Protocol (IP), the Internet Control Message Protocol (ICMP), the Address Resolution Protocol (ARP), and the Reverse Address Resolution Protocol (RARP).

**The Internet Protocol** - The Internet Protocol, which provides datagram service between hosts, is responsible for packet routing, fragmentation, and reassembly.

**The Internet Control Message Protocol** - The Internet Control Message Protocol is situated between IP and the Host-to-Host layer to take care of the overhead of sending error and control messages.

**Address Resolution Protocol** - The Address Resolution Protocol translates the host's software address to an actual hardware address.

**Reverse Address Resolution Protocol** - The Reverse Address Resolution Protocol, the reverse of ARP, determines the host's software address from its hardware address.

### Network Access Layer

The fourth layer is the Network Access layer. This layer is responsible for the physical connection between hosts, including protocols such as Ethernet and Token Ring. The layer ensures an error-free physical link. Each protocol has a formal blueprint, managed by the Inter NIC (or NIC) based in Herndon, Virginia. Requests for Change (RFCs) are submitted to the NIC and are distributed for comment prior to implementation.

### The Future of TCP/IP?

Since the United States government was behind the development of TCP/IP and is now supporting GOSIP, a version of the OSI model, one might wonder about the future of the TCP/IP standards. The answer is not simple. TCP/IP enjoys a wide usage base, largely but not totally due to the popularity of the Internet. GOSIP usage, to date, has not grown as fast as was predicted, in spite of federal mandate. State and local governments that earlier adopted the GOSIP standard are in some cases relaxing the requirement for GOSIP. For example, the state of Texas recently changed back from GOSIP to TCP/IP as a standard for communication, based primarily on the popularity of TCP/IP.

Another important fact is that the bank of IP addresses for the current TCP/IP standard is almost deplenished. Another TCP/IP standard, often referred to as TCP/IP version 6, will provide many more, larger IP addresses, which will support the growth of TCP/IP as a worldwide standard well into the future.

Two other common standards in the field of networking and data communications are the X.25 and X.400 standards. The X.25 standard is used for data transmission using a packet switching network and it covers the first three layers of the OSI model. The X.400 standard is used for creating definitions and compatibility in the electronic mail industry.

# Network Topology

The configurations used to describe networks are sometimes called network architecture or network topology. Networks can have many different logical and physical configurations. However, regardless of how they are implemented, networks can be placed into one of the following general categories. The most common network topologies are:

1. Ring

2. Bus

3. Star

4. Hybrid

Regardless of the configuration used, all networks are made up of the same four basic components:

1. The user workstations that perform a particular operation. In newer implementations, the user workstation comes in the form of a microcomputer.

2. The protocol control that converts the user data into a format that can be transmitted through the network until it reaches the desired location. These are the rules that govern how the data will be moved through the network from the originator of the message to its receiver.

3. The interface that is required to generate the electrical signals to be moved on the medium. This interface can be in the form of an RS-232 with its associated signals. In most cases it is handled by an interface board that connects the computer to the transmission media.

4. The physical medium that carries the electrical signals generated by the interface. The physical medium can be twisted pair wire, coaxial cable, optical fiber, microwaves, or some of the other media explored in previous chapters.

In addition to these four categories, networks can be further categorized into narrowband networks and wideband networks. A narrowband is a cable whose characteristics allow transmission of only a small amount of information per unit of time. Larger bandwidth capabilities of a cable mean larger data-carrying capacity. This carrying capacity is controlled and enhanced by the use of different transmission techniques such as multiplexing.

On narrowband networks only one device on the network can be transmitting at any point. This means that only one user can be communicating through the network at any given time. The typical transmission speed for this type of network is up to a maximum of 10 megabits per second. In wideband networks multiple users can be communicating at the same time. Most of the microcomputer networks such as Novell and IBM's PC LAN are considered narrowband. Many of the newer wide area networks are wideband networks.

# Ring Network

The ring architecture is depicted in Figure 5-6. This configuration is typical of IBM's Token Ring network. Each device in the network is connected sequentially in a ring configuration that is shown in Figure 5-6 as the solid line connecting all devices. In the actual physical configuration, the beginning and end of the network link are attached so it forms a circle.

In a **ring** network, each node (receiving/sending station) can be designated as the primary station and the others as secondary stations. Also in this type of network, the wire configuration is a series of loop-type connections from a centralized location called a multistation access unit (MAU). This is done so that if a station on the network malfunctions, the ring will not be broken. The MAU provides a short circuit to ensure the integrity of the network in case of a malfunction in any location on the ring.

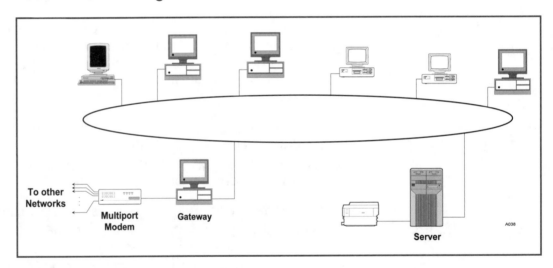

**Figure 5-6.** Ring network.

In this type of network, data travels around the ring in one direction. Each of the workstations or nodes on the network receives and examines the message transmitted to see if it is for that workstation. If it is, the workstation receives the message and takes appropriate action. If the message is not for the station that is examining it, then it regenerates the signal and sends it through the network again. The time required for the data to travel around the ring is called the walk time. The message knows the destination because each workstation in the ring network has a unique address.

Reliability is high in ring networks, assuming that the integrity of the ring is not broken. Also, expanding a ring network is easy to achieve by removing one node and replacing it with two new ones. Finally, the cost of the ring network is usually less than that of the star and hybrid networks.

# Bus Network

A network based on the **bus** topology (also called a tree topology) connects all networked devices to a single cable (called the bus) running the length of the network. Figure 5-7 depicts this configuration. Cables running between devices directly connect them to the bus. Therefore, data may pass directly from one device to another without the need of a central hub, as in the star configuration. With some applications, however, the data must first be moved in and out of a central controlling station, as in the case of a Novell network.

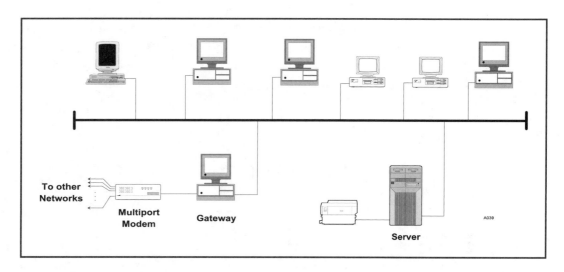

**Figure 5-7.** Bus network.

In the typical implementation of the bus configuration, all nodes on the bus have equal control. One end of the bus is called the head end. The two ends of the cable or bus are carefully terminated so the data can be absorbed, preventing it from traveling in the opposite direction and interfering with other signals traveling through the bus. Without these terminations the data moving through the bus could be lost when interference from incoming reflected waves cancels the electromagnetic waves that carry the signal.

Bus networks are, in essence, multipoint networks, in that a single cable extends through the length of the network with many nodes or stations attached to the bus at different locations. This type of network topology is very popular in PC-based networks. However, the distance that one of these networks can encompass is limited. This is because each time a node taps into the bus, some of the signal is lost on the cable. Because of this signal loss, typical cable distances are 2,500 meters and the practical number of nodes is 100 as in the case of Ethernet.

The reliability of bus networks is good unless the bus itself malfunctions. Losing one node does not have an effect on the rest of the network. But expandability is the strength of the bus topology. A new node can be added by simply connecting it to the bus. Because of the number of nodes and travel distance limitations, bus networks are normally limited to local area network installations.

## Star Network

In a **star** network (sometimes called a hub topology), all devices on the network are connected to a central device that controls the entire network (see Figure 5-8). The central location receives messages from a sending node and forwards them to the destination node. This central location becomes a hub that controls all the communication in the network.

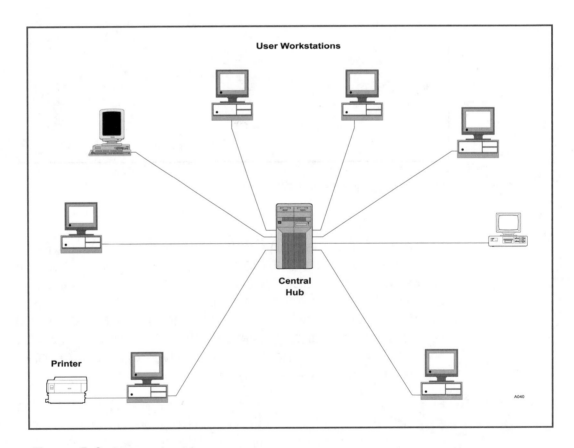

**Figure 5-8.** Star network.

The star topology is a traditional approach to interconnecting equipment in which each device is linked by a separate circuit through a central device such as a PBX. In this case the PBX receives a message from a workstation and switches it to a receiving station.

Star networks have several advantages. They provide the shortest path between nodes in the network. Messages traveling on the network must pass through one hub to reach their destination. Therefore, the time required to get a message from the source to its destination is short. A star network also provides the user with a high degree of network control. Since all messages must pass through a central location, this station can log traffic on the network, produce error messages, tabulate network statistics, and perform recovery procedures.

Expanding a star network is relatively easy. To add a new node, a communication link is attached between the new node and the central device, and the network table on other nodes is updated. However, the reliability of star networks is low. If the central station malfunctions, then the entire network fails. This type of topology is common among networks designed by AT&T.

# Hybrid Networks

A network with hybrid topology (Figure 5-9) contains elements of more than one of the network configurations outlined above. For example, a bus network may have a ring network as one of its links. Another type of hybrid topology is a star network that has a bus network as one of its links, where a workstation is normally found.

Rarely are hybrid networks actually planned and created as hybrids. Rather, they generally  evolve from the combination of existing networks or from switching to different LAN protocols during the life of a network.

Hybrids that are designed to be hybrids are usually designed as such because of the need to interface with a specific system running a given protocol when that protocol is for some reason undesirable for the entire network.  An example of this is a network that uses Token Ring LAN  cards to connect to a mainframe system and Ethernet to connect systems within the LAN.  The Token Ring system is dictated by the other computer's manufacturer, but since it is more costly than Ethernet 10Base T, for example, Ethernet cards were chosen to interface on the LAN itself.

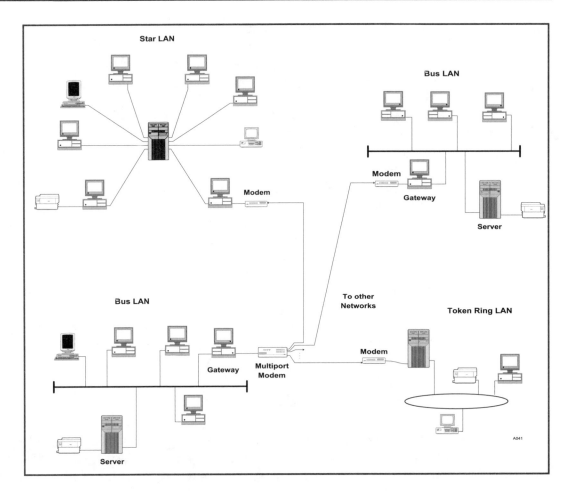

**Figure 5-9.** Hybrid Network.

This type of network is becoming more common in the workplace due to the ability of many protocols to interact with each other. In addition, the creation of standards promotes the design of multiple topology networks, since one topology may be more efficient or effective in a given situation than the other topologies. Yet, at some point in time, the different network topologies need to allow their users access to each other's resources.

## Packet Data Networks (PDNs)

Packet switching is a widely used technique for exchanging data between computers over local area networks that may be in diverse geographical locations. Networks using these techniques are called packet data networks, or **PDNs**. Packet switching is a store-and-forward data transmission technique in which messages are split into small segments called packets.

A packet is a logical container in which messages are transported from one originating location to their destination. Each packet is assembled at a workstation by a packet assemble/disassemble facility or PAD.

Then it is transmitted through the network independently of other packets, whether or not the other packets are part of the same transaction. The packets belonging to different messages travel through the same communication channel. When the packets that contain a message arrive at their destination, the PAD facility examines them and assembles the data contained in them into the original message.

Each packet in the network has a predetermined length that ranges from a few hundred bits to several thousand bits. This length is determined by the data transmission characteristics of the network through which the packets are moving. If a message is longer than the number of bits that the packet can store, several packets are sent, each identified with a sequence number. The communicating terminals or workstations that send the packets are connected via what is called a virtual circuit.

## Virtual Circuits

A virtual circuit is a communication path that lasts only long enough to transmit a specific message. Virtual circuits are controlled by software that connects two nodes as if they were on a physical circuit. The address of the destination node is contained in the packet of data. When a workstation begins to send packets of data, the network is responsible for ensuring that the packets arrive at their destination. By knowing the originating and destination addresses of the packet, the network establishes the virtual circuit. When all the packets are sent, the virtual connection is broken. This avoids hardware problems that arise due to data speed mismatches and helps in retransmitting the packet in case of errors.

## Example of a PDN

To better understand how these packets move through a network, let's follow a message as it is sent from a terminal to its destination address using a virtual switched connection (see Figure 5-10).

The first step is for the user to connect to a packet switching network. After the physical connection is made, the login procedure takes place. After the login procedure, the address of the receiving node is provided. The PDN then performs a call request packet from the sending node to the receiving node. The call request is delivered to the receiver as an incoming call packet. If the receiver accepts the call, it sends a call accepted packet that the sender node receives as a call connected message. Then the data exchange begins.

After the data is transmitted, either node can transmit a clear request to the other node. The receiver of the request acknowledges the disconnect with a clear confirmation control packet and the transmission is completed.

During data exchange, the process of splitting messages into individual packets is called packetizing. Packets are assembled and disassembled either at the sender's terminal or the receiver's terminal, or sometimes by the packet assembly/disassembly (PAD) facility mentioned above. In either case, packetizing is performed almost instantaneously, and data is transmitted in a virtually uninterrupted stream.

By using packet data networks, users are only charged for the amount of data transmitted and not for the amount of connection time. In addition, PDNs provide access to many different locations without the cost of traditional switched connections. However, since PDNs are usually shared networks, users must compete for access. Therefore, it is possible for traffic from other users to block the transmission of a message. Also, if the number of data packets to be transferred is large, the cost of using a PDN can exceed that of leased lines.

# Network Interconnectivity

As networks proliferate in the workplace, homogeneous networks are no longer the rule, but rather the exception. Heterogeneous or hybrid networks have become prominent in the workplace. They are composed of several network segments that may differ in topology, protocol, or operating system. For example, some networks contain a mixture of personal computers running on a bus network using Novell's NetWare, UNIX workstations using Ethernet on a token ring, and minicomputers running any of the several large platform protocols.

During the first years of networking and data communications, these systems were designed to communicate with devices using the same topology and protocol in a homogeneous networked environment. Modern design strategies may include many different topologies in a communications solution that encompasses large geographical areas. To network these types of topologies into a single seamless environment is not an easy task, yet there are many combinations of hardware and software that can provide solutions for connecting hybrid network designs.

## Connecting Hybrid Networks

Before any attempt is made to connect a mixture of network configurations, some basic network characteristics need to be understood. One of these characteristics is the network topology. The network topology is the way a network is configured. Different topologies were outlined previously in this chapter.

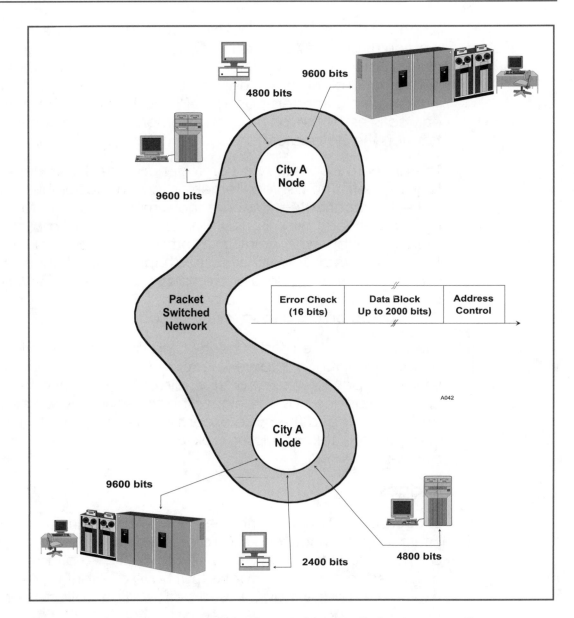

**Figure 5-10.** A message sent using a virtual switched connection.

Another network characteristic is the protocol. Recall that the protocol is a set of conventions or rules for communication that includes a format for the data being transferred and the procedures for its transfer. When connecting networks, the protocol, as well as the topology, must be considered. Two networks that use the same topology but different protocols cannot effectively communicate without help. We call these heterogeneous networks.

Heterogeneous networks can be thought of as being made of building blocks connected by "black boxes." The building blocks are self-contained local area networks with their own workstations, servers, and peripherals. Each consists of a single topology and a single protocol.

To connect two of these boxes, a boundary must be crossed. A connection must be established between both boxes either by a physical cabling scheme or by radio waves. The device that makes the connection, the black box, does not change either interconnecting network. It simply transfers packets of data between the networks. It not only satisfies all the physical requirements of both networks, but also transfers the data safely and securely from one network to the other.

The ability to connect two heterogeneous networks depends on two requirements. The first requirement is that the topologies must be able to be interconnected. Second, there must be a way to transfer information between dissimilar systems of communication (protocols). This means that at some point a common protocol must be employed. There are several ways to accomplish this. Most solutions use high-level protocols for moving data and employ tools for internetworking such as bridges, routers, brouters, and gateways. Each of these devices has distinct characteristics and specific applications.

The type of device used in connecting dissimilar networks will depend on the amount of transparency desired and the cost that a company is willing to pay for such devices. A rule of thumb is that the more sophistication a device has, the higher the transparency will be to the users and networks and the more expensive the equipment will be. With this in mind, let's take a closer look at some of these interconnectivity devices.

## Bridges

**Bridges** are normally employed to connect similar networks. Both interconnecting networks should have the same protocol. The result is a single logical network (see Figure 5-11). A bridge can also be employed to connect networks that have different physical media. For example, a bridge may be used between an optical fiber-based network and a coaxial cable-based network.

Bridges may also be used to connect networks that use different low-level communication protocols. Therefore, under the right circumstances, a bridge may be used to connect a token ring network and a star network running different communication protocol software.

Bridges feature high-level protocol transparency. They can move traffic between two networks over a third network that may exist in the middle of the others and that does not understand the data passing through it. To the bridge, the intermediate network exists only for the purpose of passing data.

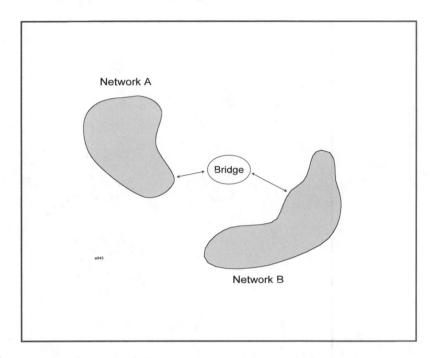

**Figure 5-11.** A bridge connecting two networks.

Bridges are intelligent devices. They learn the destination address of traffic passing on them and direct it to its destination. They are also employed in partitioning networks. For example, assume that a network is being slowed down by excessive traffic between two of its parts. The network can be divided into two or more smaller ones, using bridges to connect them. However, since bridges must learn addresses, examine data packets, and forward messages, processing is slowed down by these functions.

## Routers

**Routers** don't have the learning abilities of the bridge, but they can determine the most efficient data path between two networks. They operate at the third layer of the OSI model (see Figure 5-12).

Routers ignore the topologies and access levels used by networks. Since they operate at the network layer, they are unconstrained by the communication medium or communication protocols. Bridges know the final destination of data packets, but routers know only where the next router is located. They are typically used to connect networks that use the same high-level protocol.

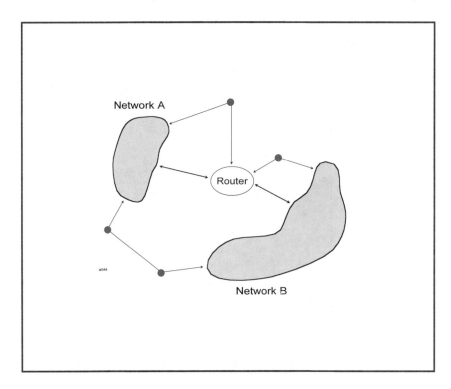

**Figure 5-12.** Networks with redundant connectivity linked by a router.

When a data packet arrives at the router, it determines the best route for the packet by checking a router table. The router sees only the packets sent to it by a previous router, where bridges must examine all packets passing through the network. The most common use of routers is to connect networks that have similar protocols but use different packet sizes. Depending on the source, routers are sometimes described as bridges and sometimes as gateways. Most large inter-networks can make good use of routers as long as the same high-level protocol is used.

## Brouters

**Brouters** are hybrid devices that incorporate bridge and router technology. Often they are improperly referred to as multiprotocol routers. In fact, they provide more sophistication than true multiprotocol routers. Brouters provide the advantages of routers and bridges for complex networks. Brouters make decisions on whether a data packet uses a protocol that is routable. Then they route those that can be routed and bridge the rest.

## Gateways

**Gateways** are devices that provide either six- or seven-layer support for the OSI protocol structure. They are the most sophisticated method of connecting networks to networks and networks to hosts (see Figure 5-

13). Gateways can connect networks of totally different architectures. With a gateway, it is possible to connect a Novell PC-based network with an SNA network and make the sharing of resources transparent to the user.

Gateways do not route data packets within networks. They simply deliver their packets so the network can read them. When a gateway receives a packet from a network, it translates it and routes the packet to a distant-end gateway. Here the packet is retranslated and delivered to the destination network. A gateway is the most sophisticated method for interconnecting wide area networks.

## Planning a Hybrid Network

Even though previous chapters in this book dealt with the different concepts of network design, this section provides a general overview of planning a heterogeneous network. For an in-depth view of network design fundamentals, read Chapter 7.

Typically a network administrator or designer does not plan a network from scratch, but inherits one. However, if one can be planned from the beginning, several issues should be considered. The first of these issues is to decide on the objectives for the new system.

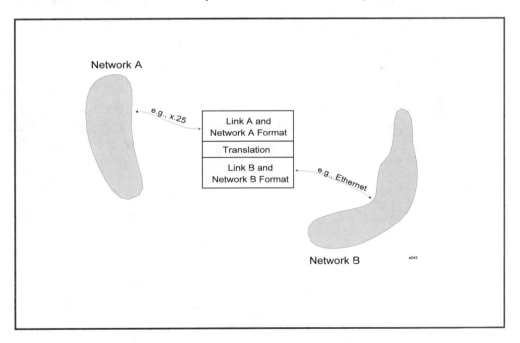

**Figure 5-13.** Networks connected by a gateway.

These objectives normally include connecting different work situations with different needs. Therefore, it is a good idea to start by defining the individual needs of the users of the network. Each department that is going to be affected by the network will have different requirements that may be solved by different types of technologies. Instead of deciding at this point on how to interconnect networks, it is better to understand the expectations of the department that will use them.

Once the needs of the individual users have been established, the commonalties can be identified. This can be done by considering how an individual topology, or set of topologies, and a single protocol may be used throughout the system. If possible, a single network topology and protocol will reduce the number of potential problems that may arise in the operation of the network. Additionally, the required technical knowledge of maintenance personnel is reduced, along with the amount of maintenance time required to keep the system operational.

After the individual workgroup and its related needs have been established, the designer must consider how best to incorporate the workgroups into individual local area networks or network segments. Once each of these segments is designed, the next step is to incorporate the individual network segments into a network at each location.

After individual segments are successfully connected into a single network, the interconnectivity needs of the different buildings in the office complex or campus should be considered. In this case the network designer must deal with traffic flow. Managing traffic flow includes two main issues. One issue is the speed of data transmission between locations. The other is the amount of congestion on the routes between locations.

Data speed problems can be addressed by employing a fast communication medium such as optical fiber, if the distance between buildings is short. Otherwise, high-speed dedicated links, such as T-1 lines, may need to be considered since private companies don't have the rights to extend their own cables across thoroughfares or public right-of-ways.

Congestion of traffic in the lines becomes a concern when public data communication circuits are used. Since these lines may be shared by many devices, it is easier to exceed the capacity of the transmission medium, causing a slowdown in the overall speed of transmission. Alternative methods of traffic routing need to be considered. For example, if the network spans an area from Chicago to Dallas, alternate routes such as through Kansas City or Memphis are possible paths if the main route becomes congested.

Traffic problems are addressed by some companies by using a technique called the spanning tree algorithm. Using this technique, bridges can be placed between long haul locations. Under the control of the spanning tree algorithm, the bridges making up the alternative routes, let's say, between Chicago and Dallas, conduct tests to determine the best communication path at any given time. The one with the best path becomes the forwarding bridge, and the others stay in a holding pattern. If the communication link begins to deteriorate, the other bridge starts forwarding messages and the original bridge stays on hold. This technique can also be used between buildings that are short distances from each other in order to have a consistent throughput efficiency in the communication circuit.

# Managing Hybrid Networks

Today's network managers have a large array of sophisticated tools to manage and correct problems in homogeneous and heterogeneous networks. The type of management tools utilized fall into three general levels of sophistication and flexibility of usage.

The first level consists of simple performance monitors. Performance monitors provide information on data throughput, node errors, and other occurrences. A product that falls into this category is Novell's LANtern. LANtern offers a cost-effective way of monitoring individual networks or network segments and reporting the existence of problems. This solution is good for small to medium-sized networks.

The second level consists of devices or software that perform network analysis. These add meaning to the data generated by the network monitor. An example of a network analyzer is Novell's LAN analyzer. Network analyzers provide a large amount of information about the network operation, but require skillful and knowledgeable network operators to interpret the data. Also, network analyzers are very expensive.

The third level of network management tool is designed for wide area hybrid networks. These tools come in two different types. One is a new array of global network management tools that allow a network administrator to obtain a global and sometimes graphical view of the operations on the entire network. The other type of management tool comes in the form of two emerging standards called the Simple Network Management Protocol (SNMP) and the Common Management Information Protocol (CMIP). Both techniques have the same goal, that is, to move information across a network so the network manager can find problems in the system. Even though these techniques have different designs and reporting options, they will play an important role in future management of wide area hybrid networks.

# Summary

A computer network can change a group of isolated computers into a coordinated multiuser computer system. A network user can legally share copies of the software with other users. Data can be deposited in centralized locations or in different locations that are accessible to all users. Printers, scanners, and other peripherals connected to the network are available to all users. Additionally, a network allows users to share many different types of hardware devices. The most commonly shared devices are hard disks, printers, and communication devices.

Software designed for networks allows multiple users to access programs simultaneously and share the data produced and used by the application. The advantages of software sharing are many. The most important are cost reduction, legality of sharing the product, sharing data, and up-to-date upgrades.

The geographical area covered by the network determines whether the network is called a wide area network (WAN) or a local area network (LAN). Wide area networks link systems that are too far apart to be included in a small in-house network. They can be in the same city or in different countries. Local area networks connect devices within a small local area, usually within a building or adjacent buildings.

Network evolution has been in the direction of standardized networking and internetworking technology. One of the most important standards-making bodies is the International Organization for Standardization (ISO), which makes technical recommendations about data communication interfaces. The OSI Reference Model, created by the ISO, is known as a layered protocol, specifying seven layers of interface, where each layer has a specific set of functions to perform.

The configurations used to describe networks are sometimes called network topology. Networks can take on many different logical and physical configurations. However, regardless of how they are implemented, networks can be placed into one of four general categories. The most common network topologies are ring, bus, star, and hybrid.

One commonly used technique that networks use to transmit data to users' workstations is called packet switching. Packet switching is a store-and-forward data transmission technique in which messages are split into small segments called packets. Each packet is switched and transmitted through the network, independently of other packets belonging to the same transaction or other transactions. The packets belonging to different messages travel through the same communication channel. The communicating terminals or workstations are connected via a virtual circuit.

As networks proliferate in the workplace, homogeneous networks are no longer the rule, but rather the exception. Heterogeneous or hybrid networks are prevalent. They include several network segments that may differ in topology, protocol, or operating system. The ability to connect two heterogeneous networks rests with two requirements. First, the topologies must be capable of being interconnected. Second, there must be a way to transfer information between dissimilar systems of communication (protocols). This means that at some point a common protocol must be employed. There are several ways to accomplish this. Most use high-level protocols for moving data and employ tools for internetworking such as bridges, routers, brouters and gateways.

# Questions

1. Why should individual microcomputers be connected into a network within an organization?

2. What is a local area network?

3. What is a wide area network?

4. What are the most common network topologies?

5. Describe the bus network topology.

6. What is a gateway?

7. What is a bridge?

8. What is a router?

9. What is packetizing?

10. Describe the operation of a PDN.

11. What is a hybrid network?

12. What tools are available to manage a hybrid network?

13. What is a communication protocol?

14. What is the first consideration in designing a hybrid network?

15. What is OSI?

16. What are the different layers of OSI?

17. Explain the importance of TCP/IP.

18. What are the layers of the TCP/IP model and how do they relate to the OSI model?

# Project

## Objective

This project will familiarize the student with the software techniques required to transfer files and establish a two-way serial communication between computers using different operating systems but the same communication protocol. It is important that the student understand the individual concepts of basic file transfer and communication between two microcomputers using a direct serial or a modem connection. If two different computers are not available, then the project can easily be modified to accommodate two computers of the same type. In this case the student should be instructed that the process for dissimilar systems is the same and the process of file transfer among different systems will be simulated.

### Project 1. Communication between a Macintosh and an MS-DOS Based PC Through the Serial Port

Several methods allow you to connect a Macintosh and an MS-DOS based PC or compatible through the serial port to provide file transfer capabilities. One of these methods is to purchase a commercial product specifically designed for this purpose, such as Maclink PC, and follow the instructions in the manual to perform file transfers. This package comes with all the cables and software required to perform the connection.

Another method is to use your existing communication software to perform the connection and the transfer. In addition, you will need to make a cable to physically connect the two machines. In this section we will take the second approach.

The cable can be constructed in two phases. The first step is to purchase a Mac-to-modem cable from your local computer store. This is done because of the small serial interface on the Macintosh side. The cable costs approximately $5.00, making this a simpler approach than working with the small Mac interface.

The serial cable will not work by itself. A null modem will be required to complete the circuit. To build a null modem refer to Chapter 3 projects. Connect the serial cable and the null modem and then connect one end of the serial cable to the Mac and the free end of the null modem to the PC (see Figure 5-14).

Now you are ready to establish the connection using whatever communication software is available. For this example, use the communication tool in Microsoft Works for the Macintosh and Microsoft

Works for the MS-DOS based PC. We have chosen Works on the Mac and the MS-DOS based PC due to their popularity and availability. If your system does not have these two software products, use any type of communication software for both systems. The screens will look different depending on your communication software, but the procedures are basically the same.

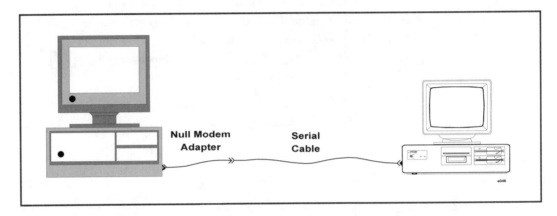

**Figure 5-14.** Connecting two PCs using their serial ports.

Before the communications link can be established, both systems must have the same communications settings. Figure 5-15 shows the communication settings that will be used for this project.

To set the right parameters on the Macintosh you will need to perform the following general steps:

1. Launch the Microsoft Works program (or your communication software).

2. Select New and choose the communications tool.

3. You will see a screen like the one shown in Figure 5-16.

4. Click on the Communications menu and select Settings.

5. You should have a screen similar to the one shown in Figure 5-15. At this point make sure that your screen has the same settings as those found in Figure 5-15, regardless of your communication program.

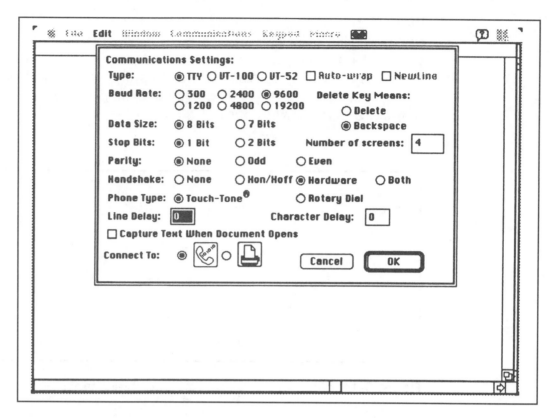

**Figure 5-15.** Communication settings.

On the IBM side you will need to perform the following steps:

1. Run the Works program or your communication application.

2. Select Create New File and then choose New Communications from the opening menu and press the ENTER key.

3. You should now have a screen like the one shown in Figure 5-17. Press the ENTER key.

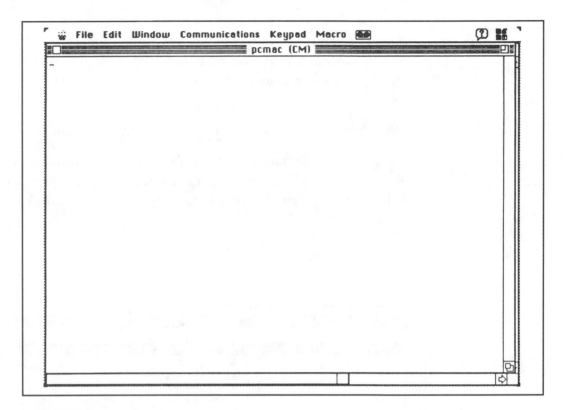

**Figure 5-16.** Main terminal screen.

4.  Type 9600 for the baud rate, and set the other parameters the same as those in Figure 5-15. Now you are ready to establish communications.

5.  Select the Options pull-down menu and choose Terminal. Move the cursor to Local echo and press the ENTER key to place a check mark.

6.  On the IBM PC side select the Connect pull-down menu and choose Connect.

7.  Type the following on the MS-DOS based PC side:

    **"Now is the time for all good men to come to the aid of their country."**

You should see the same text you typed on the MS-DOS based PC side displayed on the Macintosh side as you type. This is a successful connection.

Now we will transfer a file from the PC to the Macintosh. The file to be transferred can be of any type you desire. For this exercise we will transfer the file created by typing the following text using the word processing tool in Works for the PC and then save it as LETTER.WPS.

This is a sample data file to test the communication capabilities of the Works program. Files can be transferred with any type of communications program that supports uploading and downloading of text and binary files.

We are copying the same paragraph again below this one.

This is a sample data file to test the communication capabilities of the Works program. Files can be transferred with any type of communications program that supports uploading and downloading of text and binary files.

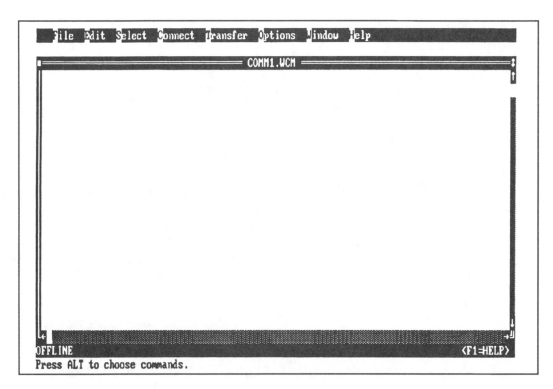

**Figure 5-17.** Communication screen for the PC.

To transfer this file from the PC to the Mac, follow these instructions:

1. Click on the Communications pull-down menu on the Mac and select Receive File. You should get a screen like the one in Figure 5-18. Make sure that you select Xmodem Data.

2. Type the name of the file that is going to receive the transferred data. Type LETTER for the name of the file and press the ENTER key.

3. On the MS-DOS based PC side select the Transfer pull-down menu and choose Send File.

4. Type the name of the file to be sent. In this case it is LETTER.WPS. Then press the ENTER key.

5. The Mac screen will look like the one in Figure 5-19 and will indicate the number of characters received. The MS-DOS based PC side will transmit and the Mac will receive the transmission, storing the "xxxxxxxx".

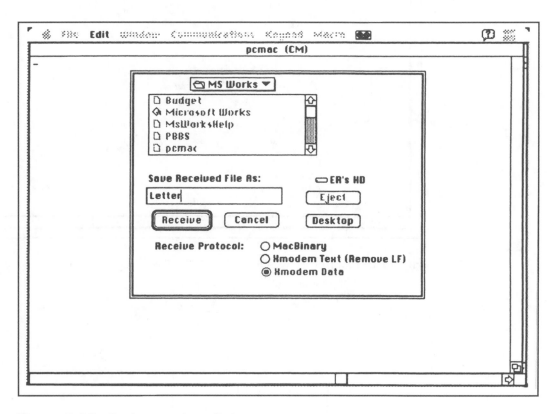

**Figure 5-18.** Data receive dialog.

After the transmission is completed, the Mac will sound a short beep to indicate the end of transmission and you will have a file called LETTER in the Works folder on the Mac. The same process can be repeated in reverse order to transfer files from the Mac to the PC.

To transfer files using a modem, the process is virtually the same, except that a modem connection must be made. The serial cable developed in Chapter 3 can be used to connect the modem to the computers. One of the computers will be the host, and its modem will be set to answer mode. This can be done by activating a switch on the modem.

The software on the host will be indicated to receive and the sender will transmit using the procedure outlined above. Even though we used a Mac and an MS-DOS based PC in the example above, the same procedure can be used to connect any types of microcomputers.

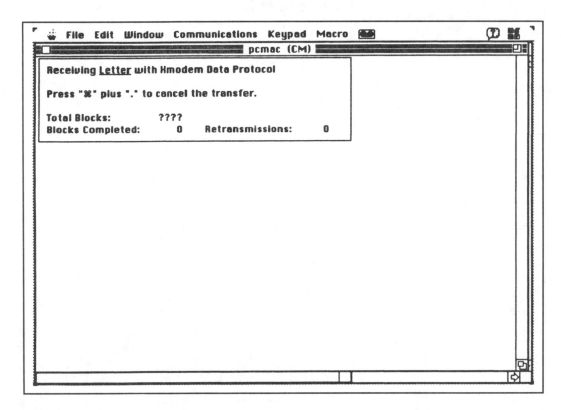

**Figure 5-19.** Transmission screen for the Macintosh.

# 6
# Local Area Networks

## Objectives

After completing this chapter you will

1. Understand the importance of a local area network.

2. Understand the function of a local area network.

3. Have a general view of the types of applications running on a local area network.

4. Understand the hardware and software components of a local area network.

5. Understand the different topologies of local area networks.

6. Understand the standards that guide the design of local area networks and their protocols.

## Key Terms

Local Area Network

CAD

File Server

Workstation

Network Operating System

Bus Topology

Ring Topology

Star Topology

Protocol

CSMA/CD

# Introduction

The rapid acceptance of local area networks has made networking a common event in the workplace, especially in education. The local area network allows individuals to share resources and offset some of the high costs of automating processes. An individual at any computer on a local area network can create a document and send it to another computer on the network for editing or printing purposes. The access provided by local area networks is controlled and, to some extent, secure.

These concepts, as well as some of the inner workings of the hardware that make up the local area network, are explored in this chapter. Additionally, the most commonly used protocols and the standards set up by the IEEE are defined, along with their impact on local area network design.

# Local Area Networks

## Definition

One of the largest growth segments of the communication industry since the early 1980s is **local area network** (LAN) technology. This growth has resulted in lower prices for the hardware and software required to implement a local area network. The lower prices of hardware components have translated into less expensive microcomputers, which have replaced terminals as the main hardware interface to the user. In addition, the increase in power of the processors that control the microcomputer has made the microcomputer a powerful workhorse that in many instances has replaced the minicomputer. That is the reason most LAN workstations today are microcomputers. Not all LANs are composed of microcomputers, for many LANs contain a mixture of microcomputers, minicomputers, and mainframes. However, the microcomputer is well suited to be an active participant in local area networks. If we compare only numbers, the majority of the computing devices in local area networks are microcomputers.

Local area networks connect devices that are confined to a small geographical area. The actual distance that a LAN spans depends on specific implementations. A LAN covers a clearly defined local area such as an office suite, a building, or a group of buildings. To better understand LANs, it is important to know their uses.

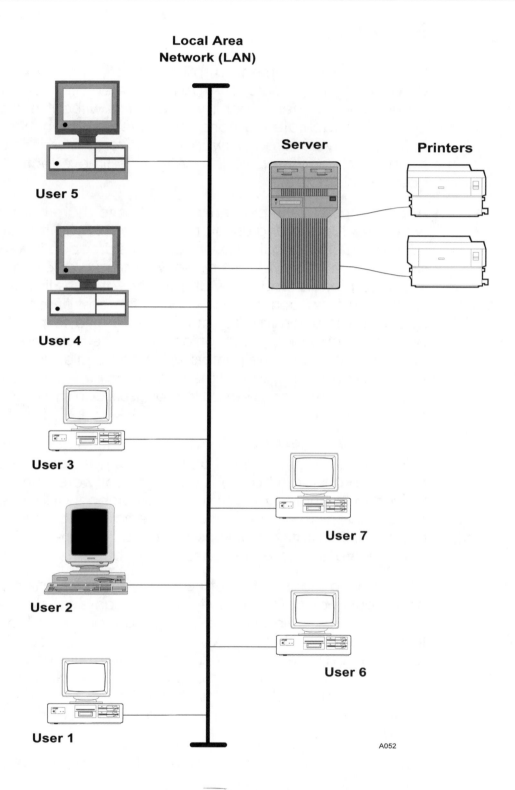

**Local Area
Network (LAN)**

**Server**

**Printers**

**User 5**

**User 4**

**User 3**

**User 7**

**User 2**

**User 6**

**User 1**

A052

**Figure 6-1.** Users sharing printers over a network.

# Benefits

Most LANs are implemented so that users in the network can transfer data and share resources. A LAN implementation can provide high-speed data transfer capability to all users without needing a system operator to facilitate the transmission process. Even when connecting a LAN to a wider area network that covers thousands of miles, data transfer between users of the network is time effective and in most cases problem free.

Another reason for implementing a LAN is to share hardware and software resources among users of the network. Even though the price of microcomputers and their peripherals has dropped in recent years, it is still expensive to provide every user with a hard disk, printers, CD drives, scanners, plotters, and many of the other devices that are common in today's personal computers. Although the cost of some of these items is relatively inexpensive, it is not cost effective to purchase ten laser printers for ten workers in an office where the distance between workers is small, because the printers will often be idle. Since not all workers will be printing at the same time and all the time, it is more practical to implement a local area network so all users can share one or two printers (see Figure 6-1).

LANs also allow users to share software and the data produced by the software. Software for which a site license has been obtained can be placed on a shared hard disk drive. The software can then be downloaded to the individual workstation, provided that license agreements are observed. This type of sharing is efficient and has the additional benefit of facilitating backups of network-installed software and the installation of software upgrades as they become available.

In addition to the benefits outlined above, local area networks encourage security of data and software from physical disasters as well as computer viruses. Since all the workstations on the LAN are connected to each other and in most cases the bulk of the data and software resides on a file server, it is easier to perform frequent and complete backups of all important data and programs. Additionally, modern network monitoring software has sophisticated virus detection mechanisms that help prevent the invasion of computer viruses into the workstations and servers.

Some of the more compelling reasons for installing a LAN are:

1. Sharing of software

2. Sharing of data

3. Sharing system resources

4. Security and backups

5. Easier maintenance and upgrades

## Sharing Software

Imagine an office that has 20 employees, all using personal computers with word processing, spreadsheet, and database software. If each user is to have individual copies of software, there must be a legally purchased copy of each package for each user.

Another solution is to purchase network versions of all software products and install a single copy of each on a local area network connecting all users. Purchasing a network version of a software product is, in many situations, less expensive than buying individual copies for each user.

Additionally, there isn't the need to keep track of 20 copies of the same software product. Only one copy needs to be administered.

## Sharing Data

With network copies of software programs, the data generated by one user can be used by others in a "transparent" mode. That is, all users can work with the same data file as if it were their own. With individual copies of software, data generated on one workstation must be physically moved from one machine to another. Data for sales, inventory, and other departments must be moved often to keep it current, requiring additional processing and duplication of files.

## Sharing System Resources

Network versions of software also save on hard disk space. Instead of using space on multiple users' hard disks, the software can be placed on the network server's hard disk. This allows the software and data to be shared by everyone on a local area network.

## Security and Backup

Individual copies of software on multiple workstations are difficult to safeguard from unauthorized individuals. It is relatively easy to go to a person's desk and damage or change data files.

Using the security resources of a network, software can be safeguarded by installing passwords, trustee rights, and file attributes. This enhances the safety of data files and programs in a manner that is almost impossible with individual software.

With multiple users working with stand-alone programs, backing up software becomes a difficult task. Users are not always prompt when it comes to backing up important software and data. Using the network resources, software and data can be backed up from a single location with minimal effort. This also enhances security since the latest copy of a file is assured when using the latter method.

### Easy Maintenance and Upgrades

In many situations, users of a particular package do not have the latest updates or modifications. Sometimes this is due to a lack of time to install software upgrades, and other times there is a lack of funding to purchase the latest release of a product.

If network software is used, only one upgrade copy of the software needs to be installed and/or modified to get the latest features. Also, in large corporations with many users, the cost of upgrading a network version of a software product can be substantially less than purchasing individual copies of the same program.

# Applications

Not only are local area networks a good mechanism for sharing hardware and enforcing security, but they promote the sharing of application programs that, in many cases, take advantage of the capabilities of the LAN to enhance the flexibility and usefulness of the programs. There are many of these LAN applications. Some of the more common types of applications are in office automation, education, computer-aided design, and computer-aided manufacturing.

### Office Automation

Microcomputers have provided office workers the ability to automate their processing needs. The local processing power of the microcomputer, coupled with software such as electronic mail, calendar automation, shared databases, and document exchange, have changed the way offices conduct business. Offices connected by a local area network can now exchange documents electronically, schedule meetings electronically by finding the best hours that workers can meet, and share high-quality output devices such as laser printers at a fraction of the cost of stand-alone systems.

A LAN can provide office workers with the following capabilities:

1.  Memo and document distribution to recipients using electronic mail.

2.  Automatic meeting scheduling with electronic calendars. The scheduler can automatically find commonly available times and schedule the participants.

3. Downloading of software from a file server at speeds comparable to that of local hard disks.

4. Multiple user access to printers, plotters, facsimile machines, CD drives, and scanners.

5. Multiple user access to documents for editing purposes and for sharing among other users.

6. Centralized backup of all documents by the network administrator. This assures workers that, in case of a disaster, their work and files are recoverable and safe.

7. Enhanced security of files and data by allowing the LAN to safeguard files residing on the file server.

8. Extracting data from a centralized database and manipulating the data locally on a microcomputer.

9. Composing parts of a document or project and submitting them to a centralized location for integration with other parts of the document produced by other workers on the network.

10. Entering transactions to be processed on other LANs.

11. Sending data from the LAN to other users on a WAN or other LANs.

## Education

Educational institutions have found LANs to be an invaluable tool in the education process. Colleges and universities use LANs to provide students access to a centralized server from which they can communicate with faculty or other students through electronic mail, access software required for class assignments, and place assignments on a centralized disk for faculty retrieval and review.

Research faculty and students have access through LANs to the local library and through gateways to electronic libraries throughout the world. In addition, the academic community has access to information located in large geographical areas through wide area networks such as the Internet.

## CAD

Computer-aided design (**CAD**) software allows users to have a workstation to create drawings, architectural blueprints, and electronic maps without the need of pencil and paper. A LAN used to connect CAD stations allows designers to place notes and instructions to drafters on a centralized server. Each drafter can retrieve the information, ask for further clarification, and complete a portion of the drawing. Then the drawing can be sent to other workers on the LAN for completion and then to a plotter. In most cases, many engineers work on portions of a single project collectively. A LAN enables them to quickly exchange and share information in order to complete the project. CAD systems are used extensively by car manufacturers, aerospace workers, and computer corporations.

## CAM

Computer-aided manufacturing (CAM) systems are used to control assembly lines, manufacturing plants, and machinery. A LAN in a computer-aided manufacturing environment allows the automatic control of scheduling, inventory, and ordering systems. Errors that are found by the individual system in the manufacturing process can be transmitted by the LAN to a centralized location for analysis and correction. Instructions can then be transmitted through the LAN to correct the problem and continue the manufacturing process.

All of the above application categories demonstrate the extensive and various uses of local area networks. However, it is important to understand that LAN applications fall into three categories. Most software that needs to be used in a LAN can be divided into the categories of network incompatible, network compatible, and network aware.

Network incompatible software cannot be used at all on a normal LAN while it is stored on a file server. Usually the problem involves the program's use of low-level operations to control the disk drive or access its own files. These low-level operations access the hardware of the computer directly, rather than using the operating system function calls that network operating systems normally employ to access the resources managed by the file server.

Other problems can arise when the program is simply incompatible with the resident network driver programs (programs that allow the computer hardware and operating system to take advantage of network functions), although this situation is rare. In this case the program cannot be run on a computer that is attached to the network. When the software can be run with the network drivers loaded in main memory, but not on the network, it is necessary to install it on the workstation's hard disk. This makes the program an individual software application on the user's workstation and not a networked application.

Network-compatible software includes all programs that can be run on the network, even though they might not be network-specific versions. Many programs have no install options that indicate which logical hard disk they are running on. These programs can simply be copied to a network directory. Others, such as older versions of WordStar, can be installed on any of the network server's hard drives using the appropriate install procedures. This is often the easiest type of program for the network supervisor to install. Still others may be programmed to always look on a certain disk drive for their files, for instance on drive C. In this case, the network operating system will typically have some types of commands or functions that can be used to redirect drive letter C of the workstation to the appropriate network directory or location where the files to be executed are located. The programs in this category must be handled very carefully in regard to federal copyright laws. Under almost all software license agreements, one copy of the software must be owned for each user accessing the program.

Network-aware programs have been written to detect and sometimes take advantage of a network. Many programs released in the last few years are designed specifically to detect that they are running on a network and to allow only one user to access them. This prevents users from illegally using more copies of the software than they own. Usually, special multi-user versions of such programs are available that allow five, ten, or some other number of users to access the software simultaneously. The multi-user versions are always more expensive than single-user versions. But they are less expensive than an equal number of single-user copies. Other programs are written to take advantage of the network environment. These programs offer electronic mail, quick messages, easy use of network printers, or network use of a common database.

As can be seen from this discussion, the number of applications that can run on a network are many. However, it is important to be aware of the different types of programs available in the market and how they can interact with the network. Many of the newer applications in the market are network-compatible products. Additionally, companies that produce individual applications for single-user computers also have multi-user and network-compatible versions of their programs.

## LAN Characteristics

Today's local area networks have a number of characteristics that are common among most of the topologies that form their configurations. When a LAN is purchased, the following characteristics should be considered. LANs can provide users with:

1. Flexibility

2. Speed

3. Reliability

4. Hardware and software sharing

5. Transparent interface

6. Adaptability

7. Access to other LANs and WANs

8. Security

9. Centralized management

10. Private ownership of the LAN

## Flexibility

Many different hardware devices such as plotters, printers, and computers can be attached to a local area network. A station or node on a local area network can be a terminal, a microcomputer, a printer, a facsimile machine, or a minicomputer. In addition, individual local area networks can be connected to form a bigger data communication system than the individual LANs by themselves. In most cases, adding or removing one of these devices to or from the LAN is simply a matter of attaching or removing a cable from the device to the transmission medium. Afterwards, software takes care of the rest of the functions required to make the new device available to the system or to remove it from its "inventory."

In addition to the network operating system, which is required, other types of software applications can also reside on file servers on the LAN. In an automated office, as one person is using electronic mail, another can be accessing a database, while another may be manipulating data in a spreadsheet and sending output to a shared laser printer.

Also, local area networks can handle applications with different processing and data transfer capabilities. As an example, some users may be transferring text files through the network at the same time other users are transmitting high-resolution images from a CAD system. This flexibility is inherent on most types of LANs and is one of the reasons for their success.

## Speed

LANS can have high-speed data transfer. This speed is required because of the large number of bytes that must be downloaded when a workstation requests a software application. A good rule of thumb is to have a LAN that downloads files at a speed comparable to the transfer rate from a hard disk to the memory of a microcomputer.

Speeds of local area networks range from a few hundred thousand bits per second for the inexpensive, parallel port-based, local area networks to several million bits per second. The cost and complexity of the local area network tends to increase according to the speed of transmission and the volume of data that it can handle.

# Reliability

A LAN must work continuously and consistently. For a LAN to be considered reliable, all stations must have access to the network according to the privileges established by the network administrator. A single station shouldn't monopolize the capacity of the LAN, since that would inhibit access by other users and increase the response time experienced by network users.

Also, local area networks should be able to recover from a system failure without losing jobs or files located on the server. If a station malfunctions, the rest of the network should continue operating without problems.

# Hardware and Software Sharing

Sometimes there is a specialized device called a server to facilitate sharing. A server is a computer on the LAN that can be accessed by all authorized users of the network. The server contains a resource that it "serves" to the LAN users. The most common type of server is the file server. Using the office automation example, imagine that there is a node located in one of the offices where a file server resides. The file server can contain software applications and data files, and it may have printers, plotters, and other devices attached to it. Other users on the network access the application software and data files stored on the file server. When a user's workstation requests a file, the server "serves" the file to the user's workstation (also called the client).

Servers can provide users other services besides files or programs. Some servers, in addition to being file servers, are also printer servers. These servers have printers, plotters, or some other output device attached to them that can be used by any users on the LAN to send a document for output. In many cases, servers are used as printer servers only, leaving other computers to perform the tasks of file servers. When a document from a user needs to be printed on one of the printers attached to the file server, the document is printed from the user's workstation in much the same manner as if the printer were attached locally. The document reaches the file server and it is transformed into a file that is then "served" to the printer.

Additionally, when software upgrades become available, the upgrades can be placed on the server. When a user requests the software, the user automatically receives the latest release of the product. In this manner, file servers become repositories for software applications.

The software residing on the server consists of software products with a site license for a predetermined number of users. For example, a company may decide that, of their 200 employees, only 50 will be using a word processor at any given time. Therefore, instead of buying 200 copies of the same program, it can purchase one copy with a site license for 50 simultaneous users. The one copy of the software is placed on the file server and downloaded to a user workstation whenever it is requested. This avoids the need to pass diskettes or to keep large inventories of application software and hardware.

## Transparent Interface

Having a transparent interface implies that network access for users should be no more complicated than accessing the same facilities using a different interface. A user should not be expected to learn a series of complicated commands to print a file. Instead, the system should use the same commands or similar commands to the ones that were used when the workstation was not attached to the LAN. For example, if an application is invoked from a local hard disk by typing its name and then pressing the ENTER key, the same procedure should work when requesting the application from a file server.

## Adaptability

A well-designed LAN has the ability to accommodate a variety of hardware and can be reconfigured easily. If a new device such as a plotter or a facsimile machine needs to be added to the network, it should be done without disruption to the users. Additionally, if a node needs to be removed, added, or moved to another location, the network should allow any of these changes without affecting existing users. A LAN should also be capable of expansion without regard to the number of users. That is, the number of users should not inhibit the need for expanding the services of the LAN.

## Access to Other LANs and WANs

In many situations a LAN is just a small component of a much larger network distributed through the corporation facilities. A large corporation may have LANs of different topologies and use different protocols, including packet switching and wide area networks. A LAN should allow user access to the global facilities in the corporation by connecting the local area network to the wide area network facilities using some type of gateway. This connection should also be transparent to the user.

## Security

Connectivity and flexibility of a local area network should not be accomplished at the expense of security. If data and user communication are allowed to be accidentally or intentionally disrupted, then the LAN loses its integrity.

The LAN should have provisions for ID and password security mechanisms. File security should be enforced with the use of read, read-write, execute, and delete attributes. These attributes act on files and directories to prevent the unauthorized copying, deletion, or modification of data. Many operating systems, such as UNIX, already have these types of attributes as part of their security mechanisms. LANs also implement them, and in many cases, take security a few levels higher than the methods employed by the operating system.

Additionally, virus detection mechanisms should always be in place. As users are added to the network and dial-in lines are made available, the potential for the introduction of a computer virus into the network increases. In many cases, the viruses act on the individual workstations and leave the servers alone, mainly because of the protection mechanisms available to the server through the network. However, other viruses replicate themselves through the network, creating an overload of traffic and shutting down practical implementation of the network.

Security should also be extended to hardware devices attached to the network. The LAN should be able to restrict access to hardware devices to only those users who have proper authorization. This can be accomplished through the use of software, mostly the network operating system, and hardware such as call-back units.

## Centralized Management

Most LAN installations are intended to reduce costs and promote ease of use. A LAN should minimize operator intervention and contain several management tools that provide a synopsis of the operation of the network to the network operator. Additionally, the network operator should be able to perform backups of the entire system from a centralized station.

The network operating system has management utilities that enable the local area network operator to obtain a synopsis, at any given time, of the performance of the network and of traffic that flows through it. However, in this case, many LAN administrators find that such monitoring and management utilities are not enough to get a complete "picture" of the network and where some of the problems may be located. For this purpose, many third party vendors offer management and monitoring equipment and software that enhance the software available with the LAN.

## Private Ownership

The hardware, software, and data-carrying medium are normally owned by the corporation or institution that purchased the LAN. This is in contrast to wide area networks in which the hardware is owned by the corporation but the medium belongs to a public carrier. All repairs, maintenance, and new connections are the responsibility of the owner of the LAN.

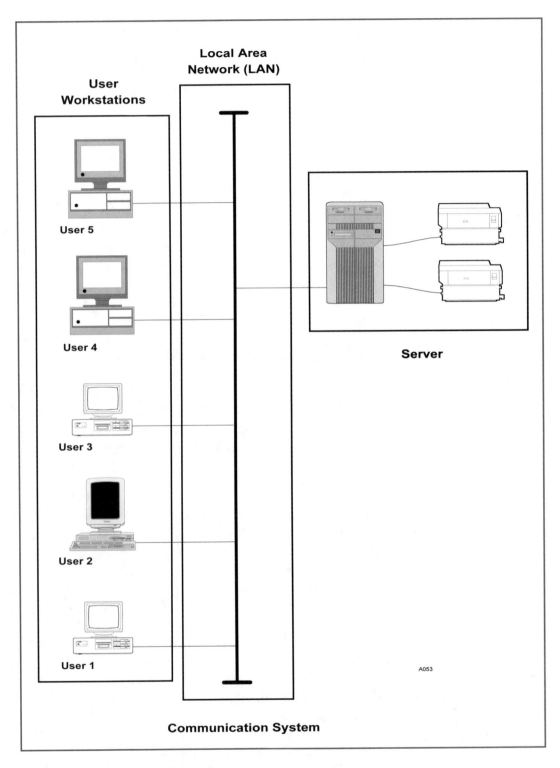

**Figure 6-2.** Primary LAN hardware components.

In conclusion, the above characteristics of local area networks are those that the industry perceives as the qualities of a "good LAN." They can also serve as a comparison list when deciding on the type and configuration of the local area network that needs to be installed at a particular location. However, to obtain a better idea of the involvement required to install a local area network, its components must be understood.

# LAN Components

Two major items must be considered when planning or installing a LAN: the network hardware components and the network software. Three major categories of devices make up the hardware components of a local area network (see Figure 6-2). These are the server, the LAN communication system, and the workstations.

## Servers

As stated before, servers are computers on the network that are accessible to network users. They contain resources that they "serve" to users who request the services. The most common type of server is a file server. Most LANs have at least one file server, and they often have multiple file servers. The **file server** contains software applications and data files that are provided to users upon request. For example, if a user needs a spreadsheet, a request for a specific spreadsheet package is sent to the file server. The server finds the requested application on its disk and downloads a copy of it to the requesting workstation. As far as the user is concerned, the spreadsheet behaves as if it were stored on a local disk.

The file server is simply a computer with one or more large-capacity hard disk drives. Normally it is composed of a fast microcomputer, a fast hard drive, a CD-ROM (or even a CD-ROM tower), and a tape backup. Additional devices such as modems are also often found either internal to or attached externally to the file server. The emphasis must be on speed for the file server since it is the central resource for multiple users. Because of this, it is usually advisable to use SCSI disk subsystems instead of IDE or EIDE, explained later in this chapter.

If a LAN relies on the server for all of its functions, and the server is not also used as a workstation, the server is called a dedicated server. LANs that do not require a distinction between a user workstation and the file server are called peer-to-peer networks. In a peer-to-peer network any microcomputer can function as the file server and workstation at the same time, and is then called a nondedicated server.

Software Stored on Each Server

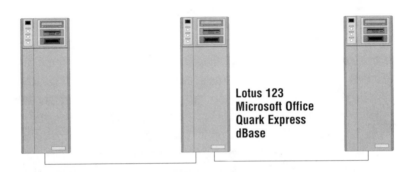

Software Stored on One Server

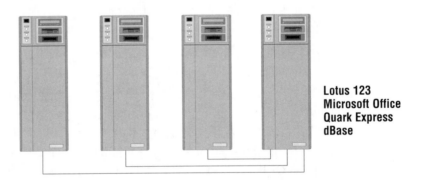

**Figure 6-3.** Possible server configurations.

File servers are not the only type of server that can be present on a network. Any computer that has a sharable resource is considered a server. For example, if users of a LAN need to have access to modems, it is possible to have a computer that contains several modems for user access. This is called a modem server. A gateway is also a type of server, a gateway server. Also, a network can have compact disk (CD) servers. These consist of an array (2 to 14) of CD drives attached to a microcomputer. Users can then access any of the CD disks on the server from their workstations.

As mentioned above, file servers can be nondedicated or dedicated. If a file server is dedicated, it can only be used as a file server and not as a workstation. This is typical when a LAN has many users. For small local area networks, a file server may function in a nondedicated fashion as a file server and as a user workstation.

# Choosing Servers

If the network consists of only one server, the choice of where to install shared software is easy. However, if multiple servers are available, a decision must be made as to which server will hold the shared software.

There are several possibilities for multiple server networks. Assume that a network consists of three servers. One possibility is to purchase three copies of the software and install one on each server. Another possibility is to purchase a fourth server and place all shared software on it. A third option is to install the software on one of the servers and let users of the other servers attach themselves to that one (see Figure 6-3).

Each of these approaches has its pros and cons. If a copy is purchased for each server, the expense of the extra copy may be more than having a network version of the software and a license for all possible users. Additionally, there is the need to keep security and maintenance of the same software product on multiple servers.

Placing all shared software on a single server may prove to be too much for a computer acting as the server. Too many users can slow the response time of the server to unacceptable levels. In addition, hard disk space is quickly consumed by the large amount of software in the server, adding to the degradation of the response time of the system.

Acquiring a fourth server for all shared software and putting the data on the others is probably the most elegant solution. However, in many situations this is not economically feasible.

A final possibility is to spread all shared software among the available servers. This allows the purchase of a single network version of a software product, along with a license for the number of users involved. This method also allows the load created by the shared software to be spread evenly among all available servers (see Figure 6-4).

# Workstations

The typical LAN **workstation** is a microcomputer. For the remainder of this book it is assumed that file servers and workstations consist of some type of microcomputer. Terminals can also be used to communicate on a LAN, but the cost of a personal computer is usually low enough to be justifiable, since a complete computer is obtained.

Once the microcomputer is connected to a LAN, it is used in similar fashion to a microcomputer in stand-alone mode. The LAN just replaces the locations from which files are retrieved. Some LANs, such as those that use Novell NetWare, can have workstations from different vendors, such as IBM and Apple. Users of NetWare can attach an IBM PC or clone and a Macintosh and use their machines the same way they used them in their stand-alone configuration.

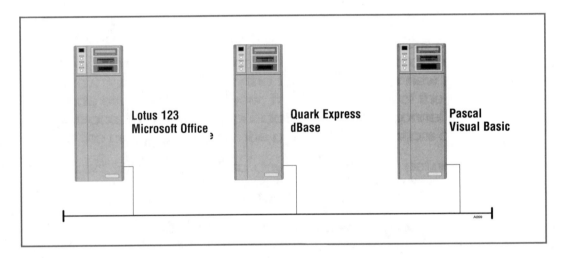

**Figure 6-4.** Distributing software among srvers is an efficient way to maximize the hardware.

The responsibility of the PC workstation is to execute the application served by the LAN file server. On most LANs the workstation typically does the processing. On distributed LAN networks, the file server and the workstation can share the processing duties. This scenario is typically found on LANs dedicated to database functions.

After an application is served to the PC workstation, the application begins execution. During the execution of the program, the user may want to store a file or print a file. At this point the user has two options. To save a copy of the file, the user can save it on a hard disk or floppy disk local to the workstation that he or she is using. The other option is to save it on the file server's hard disk. In the latter case, the file could be made available to all other users on the LAN, or kept for private use by using file security attributes. If the user decides to print the file, it can be sent to a printer attached to the server, or printed locally if the workstation has a printer attached to it.

All workstations and the server must be connected through some type of transmission medium. We call this the local area network communication system, and, as explained in previous chapters, it can consist of twisted pair wire, coaxial cable, optical fiber, and other types of communication media.

# The LAN Communication System

When two or more computers are connected on a network, a network interface board or card (NIC) is required in each computer and server. A special cable is used to connect the network interface board to the LAN transmission medium. Most microcomputers are not equipped with an interface port that can be connected to a second microcomputer for networking purposes (except the Macintosh computer that has a built-in AppleTalk port). Although some networks are implemented through the parallel port or the serial port of personal computers, these networks operate at very low speeds, making them unusable for most companies or situations where large volumes of data need to be transmitted. As a result, a network interface card (NIC) (see Figure 6-5) or network adapter must be installed in the microcomputer. There are many different types and brands of NICs, but each performs the same function. It allows the microcomputer to be connected to a cabling system and transmits data between computers attached to the data transmission media at high speeds.

The speed of transmission will depend on the type of medium, the capabilities of the NIC, and the computer that the NIC is attached to. Typical speed ranges for LANs are from 10 to 100 megabits per second and a few are even higher. However, since the workstations on the LAN are connected by a cable, the geographic range the LAN can cover is limited to buildings or campuses where the cable can be laid.

Data is transmitted from a workstation to a file server and vice versa by packetizing it. When a file is requested from the file server, the NIC translates this file into data packets. Normally, the data packets are of fixed size, although they could be different sizes. Most adapters use packets of 500 to 4202 bytes. The file server's NIC places the data packets on the network data transmission medium, where they are transmitted to the workstation NIC. Here the data packets are reassembled into the original data file and given to the workstation.

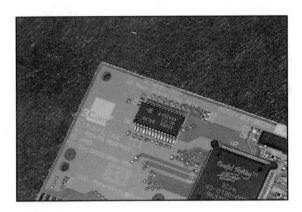

(a) Desktop microcomputer version

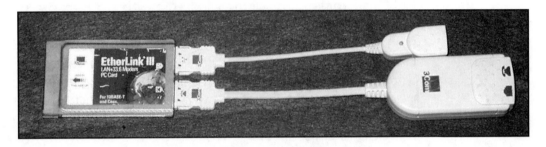

(b) PCMCIA notebook version

**Figure 6-5.** Network interface cards

Each data packet contains the address of the workstation on the network that is to receive the data packet (see Figure 6-6). The address of each node in the LAN is provided by the NIC. This address can be set with switches on the NIC when it is installed, although some NICs already have the address set at the factory before they are shipped to a customer.

Originally, the NIC address used a combination of 8 bits, and therefore could have a value of from 1 to 256. This limited the number of users on the LAN to 256. Large LANs could be created by joining two or more LANs into a single network using one of the network interconnecting devices explained in previous chapters. Newer network adapters, such as 32-bit cards, have larger addresses by using more bytes to form the address. However, many LANs still use the system just outlined.

# LAN Software

The processes that take place on the hardware devices of a LAN must be controlled by software called the **network operating system**. One of the most widely used network operating systems is NetWare by Novell, Inc.

The network operating system controls the operation of the file server, and it makes the network resources accessible and easy to use. It manages server security and provides the network administrators with the tools to control user access to the network and to manage the file structure of the network disks.

The network operating system controls which files a user can access, as well as how the user accesses the files. For example, a user may have access to a word processor file, but only to read it, not modify it. At the same time, another user may have access to the same file and be able to modify it.

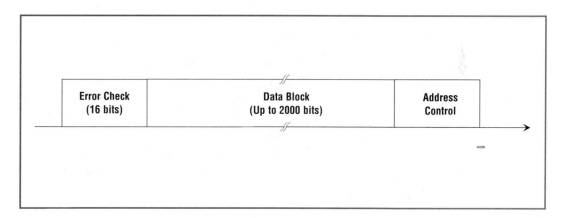

**Figure 6-6.** A network data packet.

In most cases, the network operating system is an extension of the PC workstation operating system. The same commands used to retrieve, store, and print files on the microcomputer are used to perform these functions on the network. The network operating system also provides extensions to the PC operating system to do some functions more efficiently.

# Choosing a Directory for Shared Software

In addition to choosing the server where the shared software is to reside, the directory structure of this server must also be decided. There are several possibilities. One is to place all shared programs under the main or root directory. The other possible solution is to create a directory under the root directory and name this subdirectory SHARESOF,

PROGRAMS, or something that indicates its purpose (see Figure 6-7 for two such subdirectories).

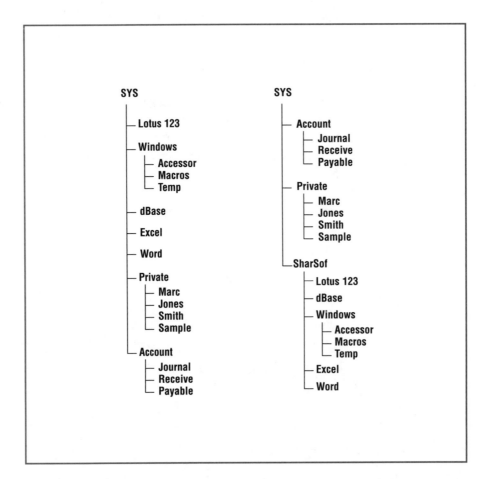

**Figure 6-7.** Possible network subdirectories where applications can reside.

The first solution may not be the best approach. One problem is that the root directory may become cluttered as new programs are added to the server. This makes the task of maintenance and backup more difficult, since each shared program name must be identified during backups.

The second method is the better one. During backup procedures the entire shared software subdirectory can be backed up with a single command. Additionally, establishing security rights over one subdirectory is easier than over multiple subdirectories.

A more complex task is when some software is supposed to be "public domain" and other software is to be secured. The words "public domain" mean that all programs or data in the subdirectory are available to all users for downloading to their workstation, and there are no restrictions imposed on how they use it. Even though such software is shared, it should not share a parent directory with programs and data that require large measures of security.

# LAN Configurations

Network topologies were introduced in Chapter 5. The bus, ring, and star topologies are used extensively in LAN implementations. However, regardless of the topology used in the physical layout of the LAN, most LANs can be divided into baseband and broadband networks.

## Baseband vs. Broadband

Baseband local area networks are capable of carrying only one signal at any given time. The signal is the data that is carried by the media utilized to connect the different nodes in the network. Since only one signal travels through the transmission medium, the entire bandwidth of this medium is used to move the digital bit that is part of the message from one node to another in the LAN.

Broadband networks do not suffer from the limitations of baseband networks. Broadband networks use frequency multiplexing techniques to send data through the transmission medium. The multiplexing techniques allow the network to divide the frequencies available in the cabling medium to create different paths or channels that can be used to deliver the data to the nodes. This allows the network to support many different information paths using the same cabling system.

Although broadband networks provide more capacity and flexibility to organizations, the typical local area network tends to be baseband. The reasons for such decisions are several, but cost, complexity, and the potential for failure are the most commonly cited.

Broadband networks, because of their larger size and the different signals they carry, are more complex to operate and maintain than baseband networks. This complexity also increases their cost. Additionally, assume that data and video signals travel through the same LAN. If the LAN fails, then not only are the data signals lost, but also the video signals. This increases the impact of a failure on the entire organization.

Broadband and baseband are terms used to classify the networks. However, within these two configurations, the physical layout of the network is also used to distinguish one system from another. This physical layout was described in previous chapters when the general network was considered. But, the same physical layout or topology can be applied to local area networks.

## Topologies

### Bus Topology

As mentioned in previous chapters, in the **bus topology** the microcomputer workstations are connected to a single cable that runs the entire length of the network. Data travels through the cable, also called a bus, directly from the sending node to the destination node.

The bus topology is the most widely used of all LAN configurations. The reason for its success is the early popularity of protocols, such as Ethernet, that used this configuration.

### Ring Topology

A ring configuration uses a token passing protocol (see next section). It is the second most popular type of configuration. The **ring topology** connects all nodes with one continuous loop. Data travels in only one direction within the ring, making a complete circle through the loop.

### Star Topology

The third major topology is the **star.** In a star configuration, each node is connected to a central server. Data flows back and forth between the central server and the nodes in the network.

# LAN Protocols

Local area networks have a variety of configurations. However, regardless of the LAN configuration, every message transmitted contains within it the address of the destination node. In addition, each node in the network looks for its address in each message. If the address is present, the station picks up the message. Otherwise the message is allowed to circulate through the transmission medium. But, for this process to take place, the different hardware in the network must communicate under the control of some type of software.

The software that allows the network hardware to communicate is called the **protocol**. The protocol is necessary so that all stations on the system can communicate with each other, whether they are from the same vendor or not. The protocol consists of the set of rules by which two machines talk to each other. It must be present, along with the LAN hardware and the network operating system. Some communication protocols were discussed in previous chapters.

Other common protocols used in LANs are the logical link control (LLC) protocol established by the Institute of Electrical and Electronic Engineers (IEEE) 802 Standards Committee, the carrier sense multiple access/collision detection (CSMA/CD) protocol, and the token passing protocol.

# LLC Protocol

The most important aspect of LAN protocols is the logical link control or LLC. This is a data link protocol that is bit oriented. An LLC's frame, also called a protocol data unit, contains the format shown in Figure 6-8. The destination address identifies the workstation to which the information field is delivered, and the source address identifies the workstation that sent the message. The control field has commands, responses, and number sequences that control the data link. The information field is composed of any combination of bytes.

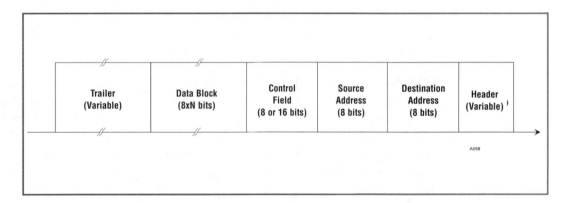

**Figure 6-8.** Format of a logical link control data (LLC) packet.

# CSMA/CD Protocol

The carrier sense multiple access with collision detection (**CSMA/CD**) is a commonly used protocol that anticipates conflicts between nodes trying to use a communication channel at the same time. CSMA/CD was designed to deal with signal collisions inside the transmission media and resolve the conflicts that arise from such collisions. One of the older networking standards, Ethernet, uses this protocol as its controlling standard.

To understand how the CSMA/CD protocol works, let's look at an example of two nodes sending messages through the network transmission medium. If one of the nodes of the network sends a message and no other node is transmitting a signal, then the first node will sense that the communication channel has no "carrier" and that it is free. In this case, the node places the message on the communication media, and the message is allowed to travel through the network to its destination.

If two nodes transmit a signal at the same time, the signals collide, raising the energy level on the communication channel. This signals that the messages or data being transmitted are interfering with each other. In this case, both nodes stop transmission and wait a random amount of time before the transmission starts again. Since each node waits a random period of time, they will begin transmitting at different times, with one of the nodes gaining access to the communication channel before the other node, and therefore sending its message. After the first message is sent, the second node will sense when the communication medium is free and transmit its message.

The CSMA/CD uses frames as its basic data format. The header of the frame, also called the preamble, synchronizes the transmitter and receiver. A control field is used to indicate the type of data being transmitted. In addition, a 32-bit CRC field is used to prevent errors from getting through the system, providing good error detection capability.

Ethernet, AT&T's Saturnalia, and IBM's PC Network are three networking products that use the CSMA/CD protocol. Ethernet was one of the first commercially popular LAN protocols. Ethernet was developed by Xerox Corporation in the early 1970s and has become one of the most widely used networking systems in the design and implementation of LANs. One corporation that uses Ethernet as its main networking solution to connect its terminals and microcomputers to its servers is Digital Equipment Corporation.

## Token Passing Protocol

The token protocol is based on a message (token) being placed on the communication circuit of a LAN. Here it circulates until acquired by a station that wishes to send a message. The station changes the token status from "free" to "busy" and attaches the message to the token.

In the network, the token moves from station to station, with each station examining the address contained in the token. When the message arrives at the receiving station, the station copies it. The receiving station passes an acknowledgment to the sending station. The sending station accepts the acknowledgment and changes the token status from "busy" to "free." At this stage, the other stations or nodes in the network know that they can send messages. The token then continues looping on the circuit until another station places a message in it to be delivered to another node in the network.

# LAN Standards

As in the general discussion of networks, the type of protocol and access method used depends on which LAN standard a specific vendor follows. The standards used in the design of local area networks are set by the Institute of Electrical and Electronic Engineers (IEEE) 802 Standards Committee. These standards have the headings of the subcommittee that created them. As such, the most important of these are as follows:

1. 802.1

2. 802.2: LLC Protocol

3. 802.3: CSMA/CD Baseband Bus

4. 802.4: Token Passing Bus

5. 802.5: Token Passing Ring

6. 802.6: MAN

These standards are used by equipment manufacturers to ensure that their equipment is compatible with any other equipment that is manufactured by other vendors, but follows the standards. In addition, it gives LAN implementers a frame of reference from which to work as they use different vendors to build their networks.

## 802.1

The 802.1 is known as the highest-level interface standard. This specification is the least well defined because it involves a lot of interfacing with other networks and some of the specifications are still under consideration.

## 802.2: LLC Protocol

The 802.2, or LLC Protocol, is equivalent to the second layer of the OSI model and was described previously in this chapter. It provides point-to-point link control between devices at the protocol level. Many of the applications designed for data on LANs use the 802.2 standard so that they can interface with the other layers of the OSI model.

## 802.3: CSMA/CD Baseband Bus

The 802.3 is known as the carrier sense multiple access/collision detection (CSMA/CD) baseband bus. It describes the techniques by which any device on a bus can transmit when the medium interface determines that no other device is already transmitting.

This type of LAN uses coaxial cable or twisted pair wire as the transmission medium. At the physical level, this standard also defines the types of connectors and media that can be used.

The 802.3 standard is based on research originally done by the Xerox Corporation. Xerox called this type of local area network Ethernet. It is among the most popular and is widely used.

## 802.4: Token Passing Bus

The 802.4, or token passing bus, describes a method of operation where each device on a bus topology transmits only when it receives a token. The token is passed in a user-predetermined sequence and guarantees network access to all users. Since the bus topology does not provide a natural sequence of stations, each node is assigned a sequence number, and the token is passed from one station to another following the sequence numbers assigned to the stations.

## 802.5: Token Passing Ring

The 802.5, or token passing ring, is the mechanism utilized on IBM's Token Ring LAN. It uses a token to pass messages between workstations as outlined previously. Several types of cables can be used for token ring LANs, but twisted pair and coaxial cable are the most commonly used.

## 802.6: MAN

The 802.6, or MAN, is the metropolitan area network standard. The specifications were developed to create standards for networks whose stations were more than five kilometers apart. The criteria include standards for transmitting data, voice, and video.

# General Installation of a LAN

Once the topology and vendor of the local area network are selected and the network distribution is designed, the next step in the LAN evolution is the installation. The type and amount of personnel required for the installation of the LAN depend on the size, type, and scope of the LAN itself. However, they all share some common characteristics. Some of these characteristics are as follows:

1. Most LANs use a personal computer as the basic client.

2. Most LANs use one or several fast computers as dedicated servers.

3. All clients have to be provided with an interface card that allows the client computer to become an active member of the network.

4. All hardware in the LAN needs to be protected.

5. Although each LAN operating system is different in how it works and is installed, they all require a network profile to be created and maintained.

6. All users must log in to the network to have access to networking services.

7. All networks have legal issues regarding the use of software that must be dealt with.

These characteristics are the same for all LAN implementations. Therefore, the next section covers the LAN installation process in a general format, in order to be applicable to as many LAN configurations as possible. The student is reminded that although the processes outlined below may seem simplistic, network installation is a complex task that requires thorough preparation prior to installation. Therefore, before installation of the network takes place, the installers will need to follow a system development cycle or approach using systems analysis and design techniques as they are explained in the next chapter. Failure to follow these guidelines will most likely result in a network with poor performance or other anomalies that will make the LAN unsuccessful.

## Installing the LAN Hardware

Most LANs have what is called a LAN kit. It consists of the network interface cards, communication medium cables, and LAN operating system. Assuming that a complete LAN kit is available, the first step is to install the NIC in each microcomputer that is going to be part of the LAN. The NIC is installed in one of the expansion slots inside the machine. The NIC will be responsible for all the network communications between the client computer and the rest of the system. For this purpose, it has a unique address that identifies the client system to any other devices that are part of the LAN.

In many cases the NIC already has a unique address "burned in" by its manufacturer. If the NIC's address was set at the factory, the NIC can be installed as is. Otherwise, a set of dip switches on the NIC must be set to a combination that has not already been used on the LAN. It is suggested that each NIC on the network follow a sequence. Then if something goes wrong during the operation of the network it will be easier to identify problems.

After the NIC is installed, each microcomputer must be connected to other microcomputers on the LAN. The most common way of doing this is to connect each microcomputer in a daisy chain configuration but this will vary according to the type of topology chosen. The first and the last of the microcomputers are given an ending plug called a terminator. This indicates to the network that there are no more nodes in the network beyond these points. The cable used to connect the microcomputers can be optical fiber, coaxial, or twisted pair cable, depending on the requirements of the LAN and anticipated upgrades.

In a general format, that is all the basic hardware installation requirements. Of course, the level of difficulty in performing the above installation will depend on the wiring system layout and the distances involved. But, regardless of the neatness of the cable arrangement, once the NIC is installed properly and each NIC is connected with the right cabling system, the network is ready to accept the software. However, one important aspect that shouldn't be ignored is the protection of the hardware that has just been installed.

## Protecting the Hardware

Electronic equipment is susceptible to power sags, power surges, and electrical noise. As described in previous chapters, a power surge is a sudden increase in power, which in many cases can destroy the microchips that make up the computer circuitry. A power sag is a loss of electrical power, and it can force a computer reset or a network shutdown. Information stored in RAM prior to a power sag is lost, and, in some situations, a network can't automatically rebuild itself to continue operating. Electronic noise is interference from other types of electrical devices such as air conditioners, transformers, lights, and other electrical equipment.

Several devices can protect computers against the problems just outlined. These are power surge protectors, power line conditioners (PLCs), and uninterruptible power supplies (UPSs). The type of device used depends on the equipment to protect, the importance of the data stored in the equipment, and economics.

Power surge protectors are the least expensive of all protecting devices. They range in price from a few dollars to approximately $150 or more. They protect equipment from short duration electrical surges (called transients) and from voltage spikes. Their price depends on the type of materials used to make up the device and how fast these components react to a power surge. Devices with faster reaction times are generally more expensive. Whenever possible, the protector with the fastest reaction time should be purchased. Power surge protectors are normally found at the users' workstations.

Power line conditioners (PLCs) are more expensive than surge protectors. They protect equipment against electrical noise and interference from other equipment. Most PLCs also protect against surges and sags in electrical power. They tend to filter out electrical noise while maintaining power within acceptable levels for the computer to operate. Many user workstations and servers use PLCs to guard against temporary and very short duration power spikes and sags.

Uninterruptible power supplies allow a system to continue functioning for several minutes even when there is a total loss of power. Normally, the additional running time provided by the UPS is enough to safely shut the system or network down; on many occasions, the time is long enough that power is restored without having to shut the system down. They should be used by all servers to protect users' data and the network from a sudden and unexpected loss of power. Additionally, a UPS protects against power surges and electrical noise.

All network servers should be protected by a UPS, and at a minimum, each workstation should have a power surge protector. This will prevent the most common network problems associated with disruptions in the power required to keep the network operational. Once the hardware is installed and properly protected, the next step is to install the LAN software.

## Installing the LAN Software

To install the LAN software, the network operating system must be installed, a station profile for each microcomputer needs to be created, and a profile for each microcomputer logging onto the LAN also needs to be created. The process required to install the network operating system varies according to the type and size of the LAN.

On networks such as Novell's, the network operating system replaces the workstation's native operating system. This involves reformatting the hard disk of the computer that is going to act as the file server. In this case, installing the network operating system consists of following instructions displayed on the screen after placing the network system disk in the drive and turning the computer on. The procedure consists of loading the LAN kit disks in the sequence requested by the installation module. The entire process is normally self-explanatory after the first instructions are displayed on the screen.

On smaller networks, the network operating system is loaded when the user turns on the microcomputer, or it is done automatically by using a batch file that is executed automatically. The network operating system manuals that come with the LAN kit indicate which files must be placed in batch files and which files must reside on the file server.

# The Network Profile

A network profile must be established for each microcomputer on the LAN. The profile indicates the microcomputer's resources that are available for other network users. This profile is set up once when the network is installed, but it can be changed later if necessary.

The profile contains information about user access privileges and password requirements. Additionally, it indicates which devices are printers, which hard disks are shared, and the access mechanisms for these. For example, if a user has a hard disk called C: and it is not included in the network profile, this disk is not accessible to other users.

Also, each user has a profile, which adds security to the LAN. Each device has a name code and each user has a name code. During normal execution of the network operating system, only users with the correct codes and security access can use specific devices.

# Log in to the Network

The last step in installing the local area network software is the login process. Assuming there are no hardware problems, each microcomputer on the LAN has, in its autoexecutable batch file, a copy of the network files required to incorporate the microcomputer into the LAN. When the computer is booted, these files take over the operation of the microcomputer hardware and make a connection to the file server through the NIC and the network cable.

The first network request found by the user is a login ID that is unique to each user, and then a password which may or may not be unique to each user. In some setups, the password may be requested from each user. If the user profile software on the server acknowledges an authorized user, the microcomputer becomes active on the network and can perform any functions authorized for the specific machine.

# Remote LAN Software

Remote software offers microcomputer users the ability to operate programs and access peripherals on a remote system by using a modem. In addition, remote LAN software allows users to have node-to-node communications so users can share networked applications.

This type of software can be used for technical support, group conferencing, and training. Also, network managers can control network functions from locations other than a network station or the file server.

Additionally, technicians at remote locations can access a LAN experiencing problems. This is done to conduct diagnostic tests and software repairs.

## Legal Issues

Software installed on a LAN must comply with licensing and copyright restrictions. Some network administrators wrongly believe that they can place a legally purchased single-user copy of an application on a network and make it available to all users. This practice is a violation of copyright laws and is illegal. It is also called pirating since the software is actually being stolen. An application software program can be used on a LAN only when a volume license exists for the package. Furthermore, the number of users accessing the application program needs to be limited to the number of users stipulated in the licensing agreement. Honesty and integrity are the best paths to follow in this area.

Several management tools are available to aid network managers in enforcing the proper and legal use of software on the network. Among these, metering software is the most widely used. Metering software can be used to monitor the number of users who are running a specific application. The network manager can instruct the software to lock out of the application any users who will create a potential legal conflict. When a user releases the application back into the system, a new user can be added to the total number that have access to the program. Many of the metering programs can perform this process automatically. Additionally, many network-aware programs have this type of capability built in.

# The Network Server

Since most LANs that use PCs as the basic client use some type of server to provide networking functions to users, it is important to discuss some of the characteristics that make a good server. As mentioned before, in many LANs the server is another microcomputer that contains large hard disk storage and a fast CPU. But the configuration of the server shouldn't be left to chance or given low priority. A poorly configured server can slow the response time of the network or require excessive maintenance.

## Server Hardware

The primary function of a server is to provide a service to network users. Servers can provide files to users, printing, and communication services as well as other services. The most important server in a LAN is the file server. Because in most LANs all requests must be processed through the file server, it has a much higher workload than that of a typical stand-alone microcomputer. The stand-alone PC takes care of the needs of a single user. The file server takes care of the needs of all users on the network. Therefore, careful consideration must be given to the hardware that constitutes the file server.

First, a network designer needs to decide whether a dedicated or non-dedicated file server is going to be used. Since a nondedicated server functions as a file server and as a user workstation, a dedicated server will outperform a nondedicated server. For example, assume that an MS-DOS based PC is being considered as the server, and NetWare is the operating system. If the clone is not 100 percent compatible with the IBM PC, interrupts used by NetWare may conflict with the software.

For large networks, the file server should be a dedicated server, and the fastest and most efficient hardware should be considered. Also, to avoid execution problems, a new dedicated server should be compatible with the network software.

Since the file server is just a computer with some added hardware and software, the main components of the server that will affect speed are the central processing unit, the hard disk and controller, RAM caching, hard disk caching, and the random access memory installed on the server.

## The Central Processing Unit (CPU)

The central processing unit performs the calculations and logical operations required of all computers. All programs running on a computer system must be executed by the CPU.

In the personal computer market, the CPU classifies the computer. In the IBM market area, the original IBM PC had a CPU that consisted of 16 bits with a bus consisting of 8 bits. This meant that 16 bits were used to perform the calculations, and data moved inside the computer 8 bits at a time. The processor used in the original IBM PC was the Intel 8088. When the IBM AT was introduced, it had a 32-bit CPU with a bus of 16 bits. Today, the fastest IBM microcomputers and compatibles use a CPU and data bus, both of which process 32 bits. Today, the processors of choice are the Intel Pentium family of microprocessors, but faster processors will change user choices in the future. One good alternative for a server is one where the processor can be upgraded in the future. This provides the best solution for the money at present, but preserves the investment in the hardware by providing an upgrade path.

The main difference between the CPUs in the market is the speed of processing that they are capable of. The size of the data bus and the CPU's clock speed govern the speed of a microcomputer. The bus is the pathway that connects the CPU with the network interface card and other peripherals attached to the microcomputer. The size of the bus determines how much data can be transmitted in each cycle of the CPU's clock. A larger bus size can move data faster and provide better performance.

The CPU's clock speed is the other factor that affects performance. The clock speed determines how frequently cycles occur inside the computer, and therefore how fast data can be transmitted. The clock speed is measured in cycles/second or Hertz (Hz). The original IBM PC had a clock speed of 4.77 MHz. Recently produced microcomputers have clock speeds of 266 MHz and higher.

Whenever installing a new file server, a computer with a faster CPU clock and the largest possible data bus should be utilized. Of course, the computer with the faster CPU and the larger bus is going to be more costly. For small networks, clock speeds of 150 to 200 MHz or more and a data bus of 16 to 32 bits or more should be considered. For large networks, clock speeds of 200 MHz or more and a data bus of 32 bits should be considered. However, with the price of high-end CPUs dropping all the time, even small networks will be able to utilize servers with CPU speeds of 200 MHz at less than the price of yesterday's 33 MHz CPUs.

## The Hard Disk and Controller

A fast computer with a slow hard disk will deteriorate the performance of a LAN. The hard disk is a mechanical device that contains metal platters where data is stored for later retrieval. The hard disk controller is a circuit board that directs the operation of the hard disk.

As data moves inside the server at speeds of 10 million bits per second, for example, data moves to and from the hard disk at speeds of approximately 1/20th of that in the best of situations. This can create a bottleneck that slows the LAN for all of its users. A fast hard disk and controller are essential to the performance of a LAN.

The average time required for the disk to find and read a unit of information is called the access speed. Most drives today have access speeds that range from a low of 9 milliseconds to a high of 80 milliseconds.

Hard disk controllers come in four different categories with varying performance, and they vary in the size of hard disk that can be attached. These are the categories:

1.  ST506. Standard on older IBM ATs and compatibles. This drive controller has a transfer rate of approximately 7 megabits per

second and supports a maximum of two drives, each with a size up to 150 megabytes.

2. ESDI. Enhanced Small Device Interface. This is standard on many older 80386-based computers. The controller has a transfer rate of 10 megabits per second and supports a maximum of four disk drives. Typical drives have 300 megabytes.

3. SCSI. Small Computer System Interface. This controller has data transfers of approximately 10 megabits per second and supports up to 32 disk drives. This type of controller supports large drives having a capacity of 1 gigabyte and more.

4. IDE and Enhanced IDE. Intelligent Drive Electronics. IDE controllers combine features of the other three interfaces and add additional benefits. They are fast like ESDI drives, intelligent like SCSI drives, and look like standard AT ST506 interfaces to the system. With 1 gigabyte and even larger disks common among them, this type of controller is one of the most popular.

In addition to considering the speed of the hard disk and the hard disk controller, drives with enough size to support future upgrades and expansion should be considered.

### Random Access Memory

Random access memory (RAM) is used by the file server to store information for the CPU. The speed of the RAM installed in the CPU determines how fast data is transferred to the CPU when it makes a request from RAM. If the speed of RAM is too slow for the type of CPU in use, problems will arise and LAN deterioration will take place. Care should always be taken to match the speed of RAM to the speed of the CPU clock for optimum performance.

Some network operating systems, such as NetWare, use RAM as buffer areas for print jobs and for disk caching. Disk caching is a method by which the computer will hold in memory the most frequently and recently used portions of files, increasing the efficiency of the input/output process.

If a file server has only the minimum amount of RAM to run the network operating system, performance will deteriorate as users are added to the LAN, due to the increased access to the hard disk by the file server. Adding extra memory will increase the performance of the network by increasing the efficiency of the input/output operations.

## Server Software

To effectively provide file-sharing services, the software that controls the file server must provide security, concurrent access controls, access optimizing, reliability, transparent access to the file server and peripherals attached to the server. and interfaces to other networks.

The file server software should provide user access to those elements necessary to perform job functions, while restricting access to items for which a user does not have access privileges. This means that some users do not know that more files exist. Other users are allowed to read them, and still others are allowed to delete or modify them.

Concurrent access controls allow users to access files in a prioritized fashion using volume, file, and record locking. These controls allow a file to be changed before another user reads the information. Otherwise, a user may be reading data that is no longer current.

Access optimization is achieved by having administrative tools in the LAN that allow for the fine tuning of the network. This provides users with the best possible response time while safeguarding the contents of users' files. Some of these tools are fault tolerance, file recovery, LAN to mainframe communications, disk caching, and multiple disk channels.

The software in the file server and the server itself need to have a continuous and consistent mode of operation if users are to trust the network. In some situations, multiple servers offer each other backup services and increase the reliability of the LAN.

Transparent access means that using the LAN should be a natural extension of the user's knowledge of the individual computer system. LAN users are typically not computer experts. Access to the file server should be no more difficult than accessing a stand-alone computer. This includes accessing peripheral devices such as printers, plotters, and scanners. Additionally, often the LAN needs to interface with other LANs. The server software should have extensions that allow this to take place.

# LAN Security

As the network grows in size and importance, security will become one of the major concerns for the network administrator. The threats that can affect the LAN come from unauthorized users gaining access to sensitive volumes or data files, computer viruses corrupting users' files and programs, accidental erasure of data and programs by authorized users, power failures during an important transaction, breakdown of storage media, and others. Although security mechanisms are explored in other sections of this book, the following is a general overview of some security measures that are common practice for many network administrators.

# Volume Security

One of the most important functions of LAN software is the security of the network against accidental or unauthorized access. One methodology is to split the file server's hard disk into sections, or volumes. Each volume can be given public, private, or shared status. If a volume is made public, then everyone on the network has access to its contents. Private volumes can be accessed only by single users for read or write functions. Finally, shared volumes allow all authorized users to have read and write access to the contents of the volume. This type of security is set up by the network manager using network management tools and then it is enforced by the network operating system or NOS, every time a user logs into the network. Additionally, the use of script or login files can help in establishing better security controls. These types of files are executed every time a user logs into the network. They contain a combination of commands that takes the user to a specific path and locks him or her out of other areas of the network. Some file servers have more sophisticated security levels than the ones mentioned above. Network operating systems, such as Novell's NetWare, allow not only volume security attributes, but extend the security attributes to individual files on any volume.

# Locking

Another type of security employed by LANs is volume, file, and record locking. Volume locking is a technique by which a user can lock all other users out of a volume until he or she is through with the volume. Some networks allow locking to be placed at the file level. Others allow locking at the record level. Record locking is preferred under normal circumstances, since a user can control one record while other users have access to the rest of the records and the rest of the network files.

# Others

Additional types of security that LANs can provide are data encryption, password protection to volumes and files, and physical or electronic keys that must be inserted into a network security device to gain access. Also, antivirus protection software and network management programs provide network managers with additional resources to help protect users and network files.

# Summary

Local area networks are networks that connect devices that are confined to a small geographical area. The actual distance that a LAN spans depends on specific implementations. LANs are implemented in order to transfer data among users in the network or to share resources among users.

A LAN implementation can provide high-speed data transfer capability to all users, without a system operator to facilitate the transmission process. Even when connecting a LAN to a wide area network that covers thousands of miles, data transfer between users of the network is time effective and, in most cases, problem free. The other reason for implementing a LAN is to share hardware and software resources among users of the network.

There are many LAN applications. Some of the more common types of applications are office automation, factory automation, education, computer-aided design, and computer-aided manufacturing.

When a LAN is purchased, the following characteristics should be kept in mind. LANs can provide the user with

1. Flexibility

2. Speed

3. Reliability

4. Hardware and software sharing

5. Transparent interface

6. Adaptability

7. Access to other LANs and WANs

8. Security

9. Centralized management

10. Private ownership of the LAN

Two major items must be considered when planning or installing a LAN: the network hardware components and the network software. There are three major categories of devices that make up the hardware components of a local area network. These are the server, the LAN communication system, and the workstations.

A file server is a computer with some added hardware and software. The main components of the server that will affect speed are the central processing unit, the hard disk and disk controller, and the random access memory installed in the server.

To effectively provide file-sharing services, the software that controls the file server must provide security, concurrent access controls, access optimizing, reliability, transparent access to the file server and peripherals attached to the server, and interfaces to other networks.

LAN servers are computers on the network that are accessible to network users. They contain resources that they "serve" to users who request the service. The most common type of server is the file server. Most LANs have at least one file server, and many have multiple file servers. The file server contains software applications and data files that are provided to users upon request.

When two or more computers are connected on a network, a special cable and a network interface board are required for each computer. Connect the server to the cable and then connect the cable to the board. Most microcomputers are not equipped with an interface port that can be connected to a second microcomputer for networking purposes (except the Macintosh). As a result, a network interface board (NIC) must be installed in the microcomputer.

The processes that take place in the hardware devices of a LAN must be controlled by software. The software comes in the form of the network operating system. One of the most widely used network operating systems is NetWare by Novell, Inc.

The network operating system controls the operation of the file server, and it makes the network resources accessible and easy to use. It manages server security and provides the network administrators with the tools to control user accounts and the network and file structure.

Network topologies come in many different configurations. The bus, ring, and star topologies are used extensively in LAN implementations.

The LAN protocol is the set of rules by which two machines talk to each other. It must be present in addition to the LAN hardware and the network operating system. Some communication protocols used in LANs are the logical link control (LLC) protocol established by the Institute of Electrical and Electronic Engineers (IEEE) 802 Standards Committee, the carrier sense multiple access/collision detection (CSMA/CD) protocol, and the token passing protocol. The type of protocol and access methodology used depends on which LAN standard a specific vendor decides to follow.

# Questions

1. What is a LAN?

2. What types of applications can be found on most LANs?

3. Describe the major characteristics of LANs.

4. What is a file server?

5. What is the function of the network interface card (NIC)?

6. What is the purpose of the network operating system?

7. What are protocols?

8. What is the LAN communication system?

9. Briefly explain two different LAN topologies.

10. What is the 802.2 IEEE standard?

11. What is token passing?

12. Describe three characteristics that affect file server efficiency.

13. Describe four characteristics of server software.

14. Why is it important to have a fast hard disk and controller on a file server?

# Project

## Objective

This project provides hands-on knowledge of software that allows remote access of a personal computer from another personal computer. This type of software is becoming more common in the workplace to provide assistance to users from remote locations. It also helps users run programs that reside in computers located at remote sites. It can also be used to transfer files between computers that have incompatible disk drives.

### Project 1. Remote Access to a PC

There are situations in the workplace in which, for instructional or error-checking needs, it would be desirable to control the functions of one personal computer (host) from another personal computer (remote). The remote computer can be located next to the host computer or miles away in a different geographical location.

To perform the operation, the host and remote computers need to run special software that allows the host to become a "slave" or extension of the remote system. Several commercial programs are available to perform such functions. One of these programs is a shareware program called the TANDEM Remote System (TTRS).

The TANDEM Remote System can be acquired free of charge in most cases from local user groups or dealers who sell public domain software at nominal prices. The software can be tried, and, if found satisfactory, the user is expected to send a contribution back to the author of the program. In return, the author provides, in most cases, program documentation and enhancements to the software.

The main components of TTRS are two programs, TANDEM.EXE and TMODEM.EXE. TANDEM.EXE is the host program and TMODEM.EXE is the remote program. The function of the system varies slightly depending on whether the remote and host systems are connected directly with a null modem or through telephone lines.

**Direct Connection.** Before the remote computer can access the host system, the proper hardware must be connected to both computers using the standard RS-232 port. Follow these steps to see if you have all the required items:

1. Write down the port number (COM 1 or COM2) that you are going to use on the host computer.

2. Write down the port number (COM1 or COM2) that you are going to use on the remote computer.

3. Using a null modem cable, connect the two computers using serial port 1 (COM1).

4. Boot up both systems.

5. Make two copies of the original software. One copy will be used in the remote system and the other in the host computer.

With the TTRS diskettes in the computers' A drives or installed on their hard disks you will need to launch the TMODEM program in the remote computer and TANDEM in the host computer. The command lines are as follows.

For the remote computer the command line is

d:>TMODEM port, baud-rate,,D

d:> is the drive where the program is located

port is the serial port

baud-rate is the baud rate of the serial port

D indicates that the two computers are connected directly.

For the host computer the command line is

d:>TANDEM port, baud-rate,, D

d:> is the drive where the program is located

port is the serial port

baud-rate is the baud rate of the serial port

D indicates that the two computers are connected directly.

6. In the host computer type TANDEM 1, 9600,, D

7. In the remote computer type TMODEM 1, 9600,, D

At this point a password will be required. The passwords available are in a file called PASSWRDS.DAT that is on the original distribution disks.

8. Type any of the passwords provided on the original disk.

**Telephone Line Access.** To access the host computer through the telephone lines, a modem must be present at the host site and at the remote computer. You may want to refer to projects in previous chapters that show you how to connect a modem to a microcomputer.

1. Write down the port number (COM 1 or COM2) that you are going to use on the host computer.

2. Write down the port number (COM 1 or COM2) that you are going to use on the remote computer.

3. Make sure that the host system is attached to a modem set in the "answer" mode, and that the modem is connected to a telephone line.

4. Make sure that the remote system is attached to a modem set in the "originate" mode, and that the modem is connected to a telephone line.

5. Boot up both systems.

6. Make two copies of the original software. One copy will be used on the remote system and the other on the host computer.

With the TTRS diskettes in the computers' A drives or installed on their hard disks, you will need to launch the TMODEM program in the remote computer and TANDEM in the host computer. The command lines are as follows.

For the remote computer the command line is

d:>TMODEM port, baud-rate

d:> is the drive where the program is located

port is the serial port

baud-rate is the baud rate of the serial port

For the host computer the command line is

d:>TANDEM port, baud-rate

d:> is the drive where the program is located

port is the serial port

baud-rate is the baud rate of the serial port

7. Assuming that the host's modem is connected to COM1 and that your modem can transmit with a speed of 1200 baud, in the host computer type **TANDEM 1, 1200.**

8. Assuming that the remote's modem is connected to COM1 and that your modem can transmit with a speed of 1200 baud, in the remote computer type **TMODEM 1, 1200.**

9. The remote modem program will ask you to enter the phone number of the host modem. Type the number correctly without spaces or extra characters. If the connection is successful you will see a CONNECT message on the screen.

At this point a password will be required. The passwords available are in a file called PASSWRDS.DAT that is on the original distribution disks.

10. Type any of the passwords provided on the original disk.

**For Both Cases.** At this point the two computers should be connected. Under the I I KS control several commands can be used to control the host system, run programs on the host from the remote computer, and transfer files. These commands are as follows:

CLS. Clears the screen.

DIR. Displays directories of the host computer. It uses the same specifications as the DOS DIR.

DOS. Takes you to the operating system. This allows the remote computer to run programs that reside on the host computer.

BYE. Hangs up the phone and waits for the next call.

SHUTDOWN. Terminates TANDEM on the host computer from a remote location.

CHAT. Provides a clear screen so that the remote computer can communicate with someone at the host computer.

SEND. Transfers files between the host and the remote computers.

To transfer files between the host and the remote. the command line is as follows:

TANDEM:>SEND direction d:FILE.EXT (d:FILE.EXT)

The direction parameter uses the symbol '~>" to indicate "to" or the symbol "<" to indicate "from." In addition, the words "HOST" and "REMOTE" are used to establish the direction in which the file is to be transmitted. For example, if a file named DATA.DAT resides on the host main directory and it needs to be transferred to the remote computer and placed in a subdirectory C:\DATAFILE., the command line is as follows:

TANDEM:>SEND >REMOTE C:\DATA.DAT C:\DATAFILE\DATA.DAT

This procedure can be used to transfer files between desktop computers and portable computers.

To run a program from the remote computer that resides on the host computer the process is as follows:

Type DOS and press the ENTER key.

You will be taken to DOS and any DOS commands you type will affect the host system but will be displayed on the remote computer.

Type the name of the program that you wish to run and press the ENTER key.

When you are ready to return to the TANDEM environment, exit the program. Type EXIT, and press the ENTER key.

The TANDEM Remote System is useful in many situations in the work environment. It can be used to run demonstrations simultaneously on two computers, to run programs that reside at the office from home, and to provide assistance to users at remote locations.

# 7
# Network Design Fundamentals

## Objectives

After completing this chapter you will

1. Be familiar with the life cycle of network design and implementation.

2. Understand the importance of response time, network modeling, message analysis, and geographic location in network design.

3. Know the different types of security threats to a data communication network.

4. Know some standard controls for unauthorized access to a network by users and by computer viruses.

5. Understand the basic principles for developing a disaster recovery plan.

6. Understand the basic principles for developing a network management plan.

## Key Terms

Life Cycle

Feasibility Study

Response Time

Network Modeling

Network Security

Encryption

Password/ID

Computer Virus

Network Management

# Introduction

Designing or upgrading a network is a complex and time-consuming task that must follow standard system analysis methods. The typical planning methodology includes following the system life cycle and its inherent phases. Although the phases are not always followed in the sequence provided, it is important that network designers follow the life cycle process if the result is to be successful. This chapter describes the different phases of system analysis, network design, and planning. Also, some specialized topics of network design, such as response time and network modeling, are explored.

The introduction of computer processing, centralized storage, and communication networks has increased the need for securing data stored in these systems. This emphasis manifests itself in the increase of available techniques and methods for detecting and deterring intrusions into the network by unauthorized users. Several types of network security enforcement techniques are explained. Additionally, a discussion of viruses is presented.

An additional measure of network security is the implementation of a network disaster recovery plan. The plan must be implemented within the framework of the system analysis approach. Several ideas on how to design a recovery plan are presented in the chapter.

# The Life Cycle of a Network

The life cycle of a network is an important planning consideration because of inevitable technological changes that will have to be dealt with during the development and operation of a network system. Each network is a representation of the technology at the time of its design and implementation. Eventually, the network will become obsolete. New technologies and services will emerge, making it cost effective to replace outdated equipment and software with newer, more powerful, and less expensive technology.

During its **life cycle**, a network passes through the phases outlined in Figure 7-1:

1. The feasibility study involves the activities of problem definition and investigation. The problem definition attempts to find the problems that exist in the organization that caused management to initiate the study. The investigation activity involves gathering input data to develop a precise definition of the present data communication conditions and to uncover problems.

2. The analysis phase uses the data gathered in the feasibility study to identify the requirements that the network must meet in order to have a successful implementation.

3. During the design phase, all components of the network are defined so their acquisition can be made.

4. The implementation phase consists of the installation of the hardware and software that make up the network system. Additionally, during this phase all documentation and training materials are developed.

5. During the maintenance and the upgrade phase, the network is kept operational and fine-tuned by network operations personnel. Further, updates of software and hardware are performed to keep the network operating efficiently and effectively.

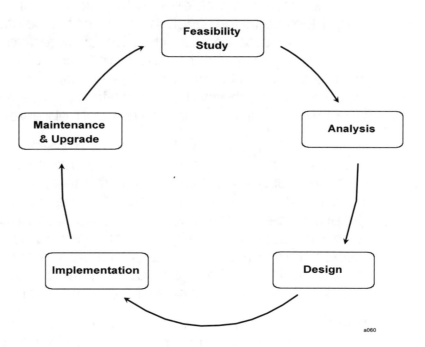

a060

**Figure 7-1.** The network life cycle.

The life cycle concept can be applied to network design as a whole or in part. As a network moves through these phases, the planner becomes more constrained in the alternatives available for increasing data capacity, in the applications available, and in dealing with operational problems that may arise. These restrictions are the result of increased costs and the difficulty in changing the operational procedures of the network. In addition, although the phases of the life cycle are presented here as a series of steps, the designer may have to go back through one or more phases of the design process. This feedback mechanism is important in order to incorporate concepts or ideas that may surface during the design and installation of the network.

# The Feasibility Study

The **feasibility study** is performed in order to define the existing problem clearly and to determine whether a network is operationally feasible for the type of organization that it plans to serve. This is not the place to determine the type of network that may be implemented. Rather, the designer needs to fully understand the problem or problems that are perceived by the management personnel who initiated the request for the study. This phase of the life cycle can be subdivided into problem definition, problem analysis, and solution determination.

Problem definition is the first step in the feasibility study. It is important to distinguish between problems and solutions. If a solution is made part of the problem definition, analysis of alternative solutions becomes handicapped. The problems need to be analyzed to determine whether and how they may point to the formulation of a new network or the upgrade of an existing network. The investigation of the current system takes place by gathering input data from the personnel involved in the use of the network and from the personal observations of the designer.

Interviews with users help to develop a precise definition of current data processing needs and to identify current problems. This process emphasizes only the information that is relevant to the network planning and design process. Additionally, interviews involve personnel in the network design process, therefore facilitating its acceptance when the final product is implemented. This data-gathering process concentrates on terminal or workstation location, the current type of communication facilities and host computer systems, and the future data processing and communication requirements that network users expect.

Aside from the interviews with current or potential network users, technical reports and documents can provide insight into the operation of an existing network. Research can provide exact locations of workstations, multiplexers, gateways, transmission speeds, codes, and current network service and cost. This information complements the interviews of personnel. It is essential in order to determine where potential problems may arise and to provide an effective solution to the corporation.

When extensive on-site interviews and surveys are not economically feasible, questionnaires can be used to gather information. Questionnaires and survey techniques can be combined with follow-up interviews to gather and validate data about the existing network. This helps ensure the success of the final design. Field personnel must always be encouraged to participate fully in developing accurate and complete data and in providing ideas and insights that cannot be provided in questionnaires.

The third aspect of the feasibility study is to examine possible solutions to the problem definition, identify the best solution, and determine if it's realistic based on the gathered data. This analysis provides a "best-scenario" solution, the one that provides the best all-around method for dealing with the problem.

At the end of the feasibility study, a report is produced for management. The report should contain the following items:

1. Findings of the feasibility study

2. Alternative solutions in addition to the best possible solution

3. Reasons for continuing to the next phase of the process

4. If a realistic solution was not found, recommendations for another study and the methodology to follow in order to arrive at a feasible solution

## Analysis

This phase encompasses the analysis of all data gathered during the investigative stage of the feasibility phase. The end result is a set of requirements for the final product. These requirements are approved by management and implemented by the designer or designers of the network.

The formulated requirements must relate computer applications and information systems to the needs for terminals, workstations, communication hardware and software, common-carrier services, data input/output locations, data generation, training, and how the data will be processed and used. As a result, the formulated requirements identify the work activities that will be automated and networked. They relate the activities to the information input/output, the medium of transmission, where and how the data resides, and the geographic location where the information must be generated and processed.

Since data communication networks serve many types of applications, the volume of information for all applications must be combined to determine the final network design. Analyzing the raw data acquired in the investigation section of the feasibility study helps identify the total data volume that must be moved by the network.

The final product of this phase is another document, sometimes called a functional specifications report, which includes the functions that must be performed by the network after it is implemented. The report can include the following sections:

1. Network identification and description
2. Benefits of proposed network
3. Current status of the organization and existing networks
4. Network operational description
5. Data security requirements
6. Applications available for this network
7. Response time
8. Anticipated reliability
9. Data communications load that the network will support
10. Geographic distribution of nodes
11. Documentation
12. Training
13. Network expected life
14. Reference materials used in preparing the report

Many other requirements besides these can be incorporated into the report, but they provide a good basis to work from. The number and complexity of the requirements will vary according to the type and size of network being recommended.

# Design

The design phase of the life cycle is one of the longest phases. The outcome of this phase depends on the expectations of management and the economics of the corporation. At a minimum it will include a set of internal and external specifications. The internal specifications are the "blueprints" of how the network operates, including modules used for building the network. The external specifications are the interfaces that the user will see when using the network. Both of these specifications may include data flow diagrams, logic diagrams, product models, prototypes, and results from network modeling.

At this point, designers should have a detailed description of all network requirements. These requirements should now be prioritized by dividing them into mandatory requirements, desirable requirements, and wish list requirements.

The mandatory requirements are those that must be present if the network is to be operational and effective. The desirable requirements are items that can improve the effectiveness of the network and the work of the users, but can be deferred until later if other priorities warrant it. The wish list requirements are those provided by workers who feel that such items could help them increase their individual productivity. However, when implementing wish list requirements, the network designer needs to be careful. Small increases in productivity might require a large cost, and the money might be expended more effectively in other areas.

The design phase will also indicate how the individual network components will be procured and will outline the procedures for installation and testing of the network. The final document produced during this phase will become the "blueprint" for the remaining phases of the life cycle. Several items that network designers will have to address during this phase are response time, a network model, geographic scope of the network, message analysis, and some software and hardware considerations.

## Response Time

One of the most important requirements in network design is response time. **Response time** is the time that expires between sending an inquiry from a workstation or terminal and receiving the response back at the workstation. The total response time of a network is comprised of delay times that occur at the workstation end when transmitting a message, the time required for the message to get to a host, the host processing time, the transmission back from the host to the workstation, and finally the time required for the workstation to display the information to the user. Usually, a shorter response time requirement will dictate a larger cost of the system. A typical cost versus response time curve is found in Figure 7-2. The graph shows that the cost of a network is exponentially proportional to the average response time required.

To find the response time for a network that has yet to be implemented, the designers should look at statistics from other operating networks with similar workloads, a comparable number of users, and similar applications being run. Although the scenario may be difficult to find, comparing similar networks will provide statistics with approximate average response times and some indication of pitfalls for the network being designed. In situations where a similar network is not available, predicting techniques must be used. These techniques are based on network modeling and simulation methods.

Simulation is a technique for modeling the behavior of the network. Response time is viewed as an average of the time elapsed for certain discrete events, as shown in Figure 7-3.

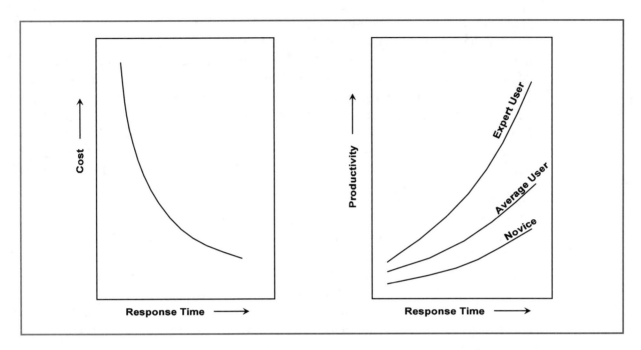

**Figure 7-2.** Cost vs. response time and user benefits of response time improvements

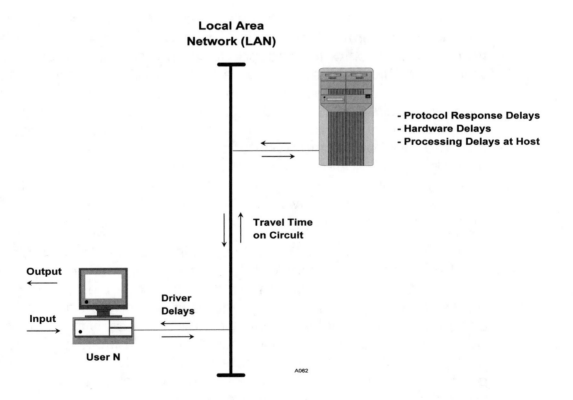

**Figure 7-3.** Reasons for degrading response time.

Simulation programs are written to emulate a series of real-life events, and the elapsed time for each event is added up to provide a measure of the response time and behavior of the network.

## Network Modeling

One of the major uses of the data-gathering process is in developing a network topology. The load (the number of messages that need to be transmitted) and site data are used as input for network modeling programs. **Network modeling** programs use mathematical models that simulate a network.

The network design alternatives are mathematically modeled for performance and then for cost, using public network tariffs and the geographically distributed peak loads found during the investigation step of the feasibility study. The data that makes up the model can be placed in several commercially available software programs to better understand the behavior of the network under certain conditions. The model created, along with the simulation tool, provides an overall performance capacity and cost analysis for each network alternative. However, simulating a network is a complex task that requires a thorough understanding of networks and of the simulation program and its limitations. The advantage of having a model that can be manipulated electronically is that "What if" questions can be asked of the model, and the effect of any changes can be visualized and understood before any money and effort are spent in setting up the network. A good model will allow designers to find weaknesses in the design plan and to anticipate any problems that may appear during installation or operation of the network.

The output from the model is the basis for recommendations of a particular network design to be implemented. All aspects of the network should be included in these recommendations. Some of these factors are least-cost alternative, short response time, technical feasibility, maintainability, and reliability.

Once the overall network topology has been determined, the model is manually fine-tuned to achieve the levels of operational performance required. The modeled network may place hardware in locations where it is not cost effective, due to the time and cost of maintaining such equipment. In this case it would be better to incur the additional cost and place the items in a location where they are more accessible for maintenance purposes.

Network modeling tools are limited in their abilities to analyze the different data communication requirements. They normally model one aspect of the system, such as the speed link between workstations and servers. To model the other aspects of the network, subsequent iterations of the model are performed. The results of each analysis are combined to produce a final network configuration.

## Geographic Scope

To better understand the geographical scope of the network, several maps may need to be generated. The geographic maps of the scope of the network should be prepared after the model is created and tuned. The geographic scope of the network can be local, city-wide, national, or international. Normally, a map is prepared showing the location of individual nodes. The individual items that connect each node, such as gateways and concentrators, do not have to be indicated on the map (see Figure 7-4).

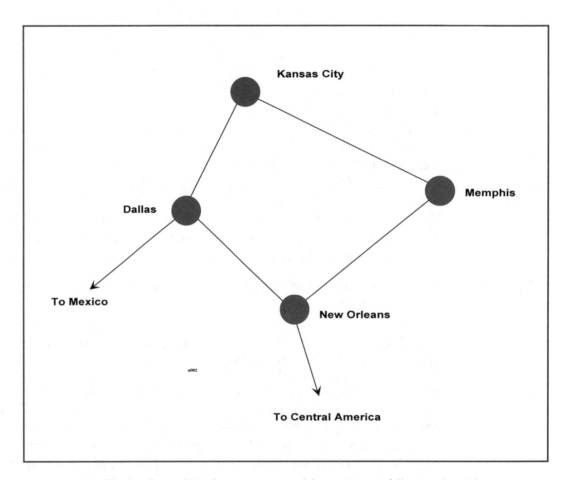

**Figure 7-4.** Illustration showing geographic scope of the network.

The next map to be prepared indicates the location of nodes within the boundaries of the country. It needs to show the different states or provinces that will be connected, and a line must show each connection from state to state.

The third type of map that may be required shows the location of the individual cities that are part of the network. The map should contain lines that connect each city in the network in the same logical fashion that the actual communication lines are distributed.

The last map shows the local facilities and the terminal or workstation location. It can be as wide as the boundaries of a city or as specific as the individual buildings and offices that are part of the network. Individual network connectivity items such as concentrators and multiplexers are not required to be displayed on the map. It is possible that, at this stage, the location of these items is not yet determined.

## Message Analysis

Message analysis involves identifying the message type that will be transmitted or received at each terminal or workstation. The message attributes are also identified, including the number of bytes for each message. Message length and message volume identification are critical to determine the volume of messages that will be transmitted through the network.

The daily traffic volume is sometimes segmented into hourly traffic to provide the designers with the peak traffic hours. This information is used to identify problems with data traffic during peak hours.

It is important to note that most networks are designed based on average traffic volumes instead of traffic volume during peak hours. For most organizations it is not cost effective to purchase a network based solely on volume during peak hours.

## Software/Hardware Considerations

The type of software purchased for the network will determine the operation of the network. It will specify whether the network will perform asynchronous or synchronous communications, full-duplex or half-duplex communications, and the speed of transmissions. Additionally, the software will determine the types of networks that can be accessed by the network being designed.

The network designer should select a protocol that is compatible with the OSI seven-layer model and one that can grow as the network grows within the organization. The protocol is a crucial element of the overall design, since the server architecture must interface with it. If the protocol follows accepted standards, the addition or replacement of multiple platform servers can be accomplished without many difficulties.

The pieces of hardware that are part of a network are

1.  Terminals

2.  Microcomputers and network interface cards

3.  File servers

4.  Terminal controllers

5.  Multiplexers

6.  Concentrators

7.  Line-sharing devices

8.  Protocol converters

9.  Hardware encrypting devices

10. Switches

11. PBX switchboards

12. Communication circuits

13. FEPs

14. Port-sharing devices

15. Host computers

16. Channel extenders

17. Testing equipment

18. Surge protectors, power conditioners, and uninterruptible power supplies

Each of these devices has a unique graphical representation that varies slightly according to the designer (see Figure 7-5). He or she should prepare a graphical representation of the network hardware using the symbols outlined in Figure 7-5 or similar ones.

The final hardware configuration needs to take into account the software protocol and network operating system that are going to be implemented in the network. The results should be the least-cost alternative that meets all the organization's requirements. Additionally, before ordering any hardware, the designers should decide how to handle diagnostics, troubleshooting, and network repair. Most new network hardware has built-in diagnostics and testing capabilities.

Finally, selecting hardware and software involves selecting more than just a system. It involves selecting a vendor. The vendor's ability to maintain, upgrade, and expand the network components will determine the overall success of the network.

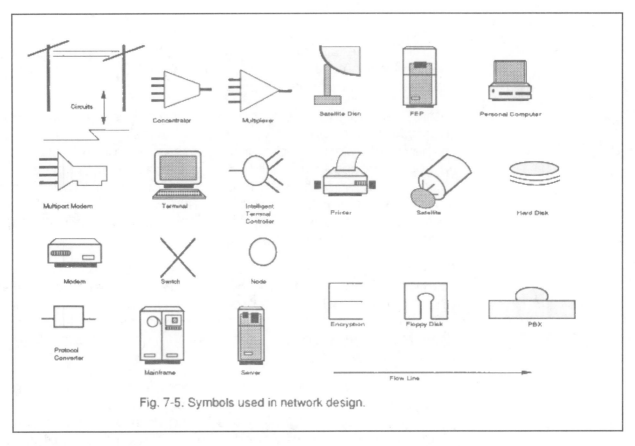

Fig. 7-5. Symbols used in network design.

**Figure 7-5.** Symbols used in network design.

## Implementation

During the implementation phase the individual components of the network are purchased and installed. This phase can be divided into

1. Software acquisition. If a new network is being implemented, the necessary network operating system, application software, managing software, and communication protocols must be procured. A useful tool in software and hardware procurement is a request for proposal (RFP). The RFP is based on the network requirements produced in the investigation step of the feasibility study. Bids come from potential vendors in response to the RFP. The bids are evaluated, using specified criteria, and one is selected.

2. Hardware acquisition. Hardware procurement can be done from the same software vendor or a third party vendor may be used. Some software can run on a multitude of computer hardware configurations (sometimes called platforms). Deciding on

the software first helps narrow the selection of a hardware vendor.

3. Installation. During or after the hardware and software acquisition, the individual components need to be assembled into what will become the network. The final product of this phase is an operational network system.

4. Testing. Testing should be conducted in an integrated fashion. That is, hardware and software should be tested simultaneously as they are implemented, trying to process maximum workloads whenever possible. This will provide statistics that indicate the best and worst possibilities of network efficiency. It will also provide feedback for fine-tuning the network before it becomes fully operational. Integrated testing ensures that all parts of the system will function together properly.

   Testing should be performed using test plans developed during the design phase of the life cycle. There must be a complete and extensive test plan that produces predictable test results reflecting the operation of the network under real-life situations. These results are necessary if management is to trust and accept the network.

5. Documentation. Even though documentation is placed in the life cycle at this stage, it should be an integral part of each phase in network design. Reports that document every aspect of the network, from its conception until final implementation, must be present for audit trail purposes and must always accompany the network. These documents can take the form of reference manuals, maintenance manuals, operational and user manuals, and all the reference materials used in the feasibility study.

6. Switch-over. The switch-over step consists of moving all transactions from the old system to the new system. The final product of this step is the active working network. The switch-over plan must include milestones to be reached during the transition period and contingency plans in case the new system does not meet operational guidelines.

## The Request for Proposals

Once the network has been designed, but before implementation can proceed, the specific vendors must be selected. A formal approach is to send a request for proposal (RFP) to prospective vendors. The RFP is a document that asks each vendor to prepare a price quotation for the configuration described in the RFP. Some RFPs give vendors great latitude in how the proposed system should be implemented. Others are very specific and expect detailed technical data in response from the vendor.

The format of an RFP can vary in terms of specificity. However, as a general rule, an RFP contains the following topics:

1. Title page. This identifies the originating organization and title of the project.

2. Table of contents. Any lengthy document should have a table of contents to provide a quick reference to specific topics.

3. Introduction. This is a brief introduction that includes an overview of the organization for which the final product is intended, the problem to be solved, schedule for the response to the RFP, evaluation and selection criteria, installation schedules, and operation schedules.

4. RFP response guidelines. The RFP guidelines for responding to it establish the schedule for the selection process, the format of the proposal, how proposals are evaluated, the time and place of proposal submission, when presentations are made, and the time for the announcement of the winner or winners.

5. Deadlines. The deadline and place for submitting responses to the RFP must be stated clearly throughout the proposal. The deadlines should also include equipment delivery dates and the date to commence operations.

6. Response format. The format of the response to the RFP depends on the user. Normally, responses come in two separate documents. One document contains the specific technical details of the proposed system. The other document has the financial and contractual details.

7. Evaluation criteria. The RFP needs to describe for the vendors how the responses will be evaluated. It should include a prioritized list indicating the items that are the most important. This allows the vendors to provide further information on these items in their responses.

Typically, vendor responses include the following items:

1. System design

2. System features

3. Upgrade capabilities

4. Installation methods

5. Installation schedule

6. Testing methods

7. Maintenance agreements

8. Cost of items

9. Payment schedule

10. System support

11. Warranty coverage

12. Training options

This is the largest portion of the RFP. It describes the problems that need to be solved. Solutions to these problems should not be included in this section. Rather, the vendors should be allowed to propose their own solutions.

## Maintenance and Upgrade

The last phase in the life cycle of the network is the maintenance and upgrade of the components of the network. During the maintenance and upgrade period the system is kept operational and fine-tuned to keep adequate performance levels and fix system problems.

The products of this phase are change and upgrade requests, updates to existing documentation to reflect changes in the network, and reports and statistics from the monitoring and control functions of the network.

At some point in the life of the system, the new network in its own turn will be replaced or phased out. This final stage in the life cycle leads to the beginning of a new life cycle as the organization goes through the same process to find a replacement or upgrade to the existing system.

# Network Security

An important responsibility of network managers is maintaining control over the security of the network and the data stored and transmitted by it. The major goals of security are to prevent computer crime and data loss.

Detection of **security** problems in a network is compounded by the nature of information processing, storage, and the transmission system in the network. For example:

1. Data is stored on media not easily readable by people.

2. Data can be erased or modified without leaving evidence.

3. Computerized records do not have signatures to verify authenticity or distinguish copies from originals.

4. Data can be accessed and manipulated from remote stations.

5. Transactions are performed at high speeds and often without human monitoring.

The threat of the loss of the data stored in the network is sufficient reason for implementing methods and techniques to detect and prevent loss. It is important to incorporate the security methods during the design phase of the life cycle rather than add them later. Although no system is completely sealed from outside interference, the following methodologies will help in preventing a breach in network security.

# Physical Security

The main emphasis of physical security is to prevent unauthorized access to the communications room, network control center, or communications equipment. This could result in damage to the network equipment or tapping into the circuits by unauthorized personnel.

The room or building that houses network communication equipment should be locked, and access should be restricted by network managers. Terminals should be equipped with locks that deactivate the screen and keyboard switch. In some situations, instead of keys and locks, a programmable plastic card can be used. The locking mechanism that accepts the card may be programmed to accept passwords, in addition to the magnetic code in the card.

# Encryption

With many networks using satellite and microwave relays for transmitting data, anyone with an antenna can pick up the transmission and have access to the data being transmitted. One method to safeguard the information transmitted through the airwaves, and even data transmitted through wires, is called encryption or ciphering.

**Encryption** involves substituting or transposing bits that represent a known data message. The level of encryption can be of any complexity, and it is usually judged by a work factor. A higher work factor indicates a more complex cipher or encryption.

As shown in Figure 7-6, an encrypting system (also called a cryptosystem) between a sender and a receiver consists of the following elements:

1. A message to be transmitted and protected.

2. A large set of invertible cryptographic transformations (ciphers) applied to the message to produce ciphertext and later to recover the original message by applying the inverse of the cipher to the ciphertext.

3. The key of the cryptosystem that selects one specific transformation from the set of possible transformations.

A cryptosystem is effective only if the key is kept secret. Also the set of ciphers must be large enough that the correct key could not be guessed or determined by trial-and-error techniques.

The National Bureau of Standards has set a data encrypting standard (DES). The DES effectiveness derives from its complexity, the large number of possible keys, and the security of the keys used. The DES transformation is an iterative nonlinear block product cipher that uses 64-bit data blocks. It is implemented on special-purpose microcircuits that have been developed for DES and are available commercially. The DES encrypting algorithm is used in reverse for decrypting the ciphertext. The key is also a 64-bit word, 8 of which are parity bits. Therefore, the effective key length is 56 bits.

The suitability of a type of encrypting algorithm for applications in a data network depends on the relevant characteristics of the applications running in the system, the characteristics of the chosen algorithm, and the technical aspects of the network. Even though the purpose of encrypting is to secure data, the effect of the cryptosystem on the network is equally important. A cryptosystem that provides excellent security may deteriorate the performance of the network to unacceptable levels.

The increasing dependence on internet access and the planned interest in electronic commerce transactions across the world-wide-web have precipitated a variety of more complicated cryptographic processes aimed at electronic signatures for secure financial transactions over the internet and authentication of remote users. The initial interest in the additional security provided by these processes was generated by the well publicized break-ins by computer hackers. However, the business interest in secure electronic commerce transcations across the internet probably represents a much larger, more influential and more profitable market for these technologies than hacker prevention.

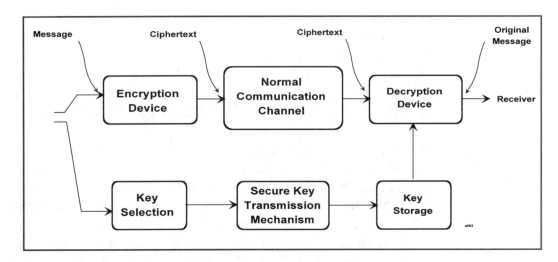

**Figure 7-6.** An encryption system.

# User Identification and Passwords

User identification **(ID)** and **passwords** are the most common security systems employed in networks, and at times the easiest to break. The user ID is provided by the network manager when the user profile is added to the network. The password is normally at the user's discretion. Unfortunately, many users choose passwords that are too simple and that can be easily guessed by trial and error, such as their last name.

Some systems provide the generation of passwords for users. This technique is more effective than allowing users to define their own passwords. The user must keep the password available, but protect it from being accessible by others.

User IDs and passwords by themselves are not an effective security technique. When combined with call-back units (see Chapters 2 and 3), encrypting devices, and network physical security, they provide an effective deterrent to unauthorized users.

# Time and Location Controls

The time and location of user access to the network can be controlled by software and hardware mechanisms. Some users may be allowed to access the system only during specific times of the day and on specified days of the week. Other users may only access the system from specified terminals. Although such measures are an inconvenience to users, they help in managing data flow and in monitoring the network usage.

Time controls are performed on individuals by having a user profile in the network that determines the day and time intervals during which the user can access the system. Location controls are enforced by having a terminal profile. The terminal profile identifies the terminal and sets up specific paths that the terminal can follow to access selected data. No matter who the user is on the terminal, the terminal profile can be given a higher priority to override the user profile.

## Switched Port and Dialing Access

The most vulnerable security point on a network is switched ports that allow dial-in access. They are a security risk because they allow any person with a telephone and terminal to access the system. To enhance the security of switched ports with dial-in access, they should be operational only during the time when transactions are allowed, instead of 24 hours per day. A call-back unit (see Chapter 3) can be used to deter unauthorized calls and to ensure that calls are made only from authorized locations.

The telephone numbers of the switch should be safeguarded and only be available to personnel who must have access to them. User identification and password enforcement take on a higher priority with dial-in access. In systems that contain critical data, a person-to-person authentication as well as application-to-user authentication should he used.

## Audit Logs

Transaction logs are an important aspect of network security. Every login attempt should be logged, including date and time of attempt, user ID and password used, location, and number of unsuccessful attempts. In some situations, after a number of unsuccessful login attempts are made, the data described above may be displayed on an operator console for immediate action.

Many of the above methods can be incorporated into a system including extensive audit trails that collect the necessary information required to determine who is accessing the system. However, audit trails are worthless unless network managers study them and monitor the network.

## Viruses

A **computer virus** is an executable computer program that propagates itself, using other programs as carriers, and sometimes modifies itself during or after replication. It is intended to perform some unwanted function on the computer system attached to the network.

Some viruses perform simple annoying functions such as popping up in the middle of an application to demonstrate they are there. Other viruses are more destructive and erase or modify portions of programs or critical data. They are typically introduced into network computers by floppy disk-based software that was purchased or copied. Many of the known viruses enter networks through programs or data downloaded from electronic bulletin boards. Some are deposited on networks by the creator of the virus. Other viruses migrate from network to network through gateways and other interconnecting hardware.

Viruses can be monitored and eliminated at the user level with the use of antivirus software. This type of application program searches files and looks for known computer viruses, alerting users to their presence. At this point, the user has the option to eliminate the virus or take some other security action. This process can take place on a stand-alone machine before introducing the application in the network. Additionally, the user can also run a virus scanning program from a directory in the network. The program will then scan the user's floppy disk and report any suspicious files.

At the system manager level, virus protection can be accomplished by using a network statistical program with a virus detection component that is designed to run as the network operating system is active. This type of application watches for signs of a virus and alerts the LAN manager at the first symptom. The program warns the LAN manager when application or data files show any change from the original. An example of this type of application is TGR Software's SCUA Plus.

It is important to note that antivirus software does not identify all viruses circulating. This type of software can only work on known viruses and offers little protection against new or unknown viruses. On a regular basis, the makers of antivirus software provide upgrades that contain protection against new computer viruses, introduced since the last release of the virus protection program.

# Disaster Recovery Planning

The increased use of computer systems and data communication networks has expanded the need for a realistic **disaster plan**. The network manager needs to be involved in such planning and should have knowledge in the areas that follow:

1. The need for disaster planning

2. Computer backup approaches

3. Network backup approaches

4. The characteristics of a disaster backup strategy

5. Planning processes of the organization

6. The impact of a data network disaster on the organization

Planning for a disaster is much like planning for a new system. It requires goals, objectives, design, implementation, testing, documentation, and maintenance. Producing a good disaster plan requires significant organizational skills. However, LAN developers and LAN managers should also concentrate on disaster prevention measures. Good prevention measures may mean the disaster recovery plan will not have to be used. Some of the measures below and others will make the recovery process easier and protect users' information.

1. Adequate surge protectors. All computers in the network should be protected with surge protectors that can react to a large voltage spike in as little as one or two nanoseconds. This type of device normally costs about $100, so it can be expensive to outfit a network with many workstations. However, when compared with the cost of a workstation, it is worth the price.

2. Servers must be protected with a UPS. A UPS protects against voltage surges and drops. In many networks, the server contains invaluable data that a company needs to function. Protecting the data is one of the most important functions of the LAN manager. Additionally, the UPS allows the proper shutdown of the network in case of a loss of power.

3. Communication line protectors and filters. Computers connected to modems and telephone lines also need protection from incoming noise and surges that may travel through the phone lines.

4. Protect cables. All cabling must be protected and placed in locations where a user cannot accidentally tamper with the line.

5. Adequate backups. Continuous and comprehensive backups will ensure that all data and programs are safeguarded. If possible, during a period of network inactivity, the backup and recovery plans outlined below should be rehearsed.

# Characteristics of the Disaster Recovery Plan

A disaster plan must meet certain criteria, including:

1. Reliability

2. Operability

3. Response time to activate the plan

4. Cost effectiveness

## Reliability

Whatever the strategy taken to safeguard the network and the data stored on it, the organization must be confident that, in case of a disaster, the plan will work. Confidence can be achieved by using proven techniques to replace network media in case of a failure.

The best plans are those that are kept simple. The plan needs to be tested in order to ensure that the information in the system is secured. Any disaster plan is suspect without proper testing.

## Operability

The methods used for recovering from a disaster should be consistent with the normal methods of backup and restoration that are used in the routine management of the network. This ensures that, in case of failure, trained personnel will be able to restore the system quickly and without errors. Additionally, the plan should be well documented and distributed to appropriate personnel.

## Response Time to Activate the Plan

The recovery plan must be capable of being activated within the time constraints imposed by the network. In some cases, backup networks are activated on a temporary basis until the stricken facility is restored to an acceptable operational level. The network design must be flexible to allow for time-sensitive considerations.

## Cost Effectiveness

The recovery plan must be cost effective since it will be idle for most of the network life. However, in a disaster, the backup system must also be flexible enough for long-term use, if necessary.

## Disaster Recovery Methodologies

Extensive planning and research are required to produce an effective disaster recovery plan. Some of the concerns that a manager may want to address in preparing a recovery plan follow:

1. Create a list of the critical applications. This will require involvement from top management. The items on the list should be prioritized, and their impact on the firm should be analyzed.

2. Determine the required recovery time for the organization.

3. Determine the critical nodes in the network.

4. Analyze the critical workload for each node, and create a transaction profile for it.

5. Analyze the use of shared communication facilities and alternate methods of information transfer.

6. Obtain best vendor and carrier lead-time estimates for a backup network.

7. Identify facilities that exceed the recovery time. These facilities are critical and the recovery time exceeds the allowable down time. These must be restored first.

8. Determine costs.

9. Have the vendor develop a plan to connect users with planned backup networks.

10. List all cable and front end requirements.

11. Make a list of equipment that can be shared, such as modems.

12. List all facilities that can be provided at the recovery site in case of a prolonged down time.

13. List all support personnel available for recovery.

14. List all dial-up facilities at the recovery site.

## The Planning Process

The disaster recovery plan may be divided into strategic and implementation sections. The strategic section lists the goals, design objectives, and strategies for network recovery. The implementation section describes the steps to take during the recovery process. Some of the major items to be included in the plan are provided below.

1. List all assumptions, objectives, and the methodology for implementing the objectives.

2. List all tasks to be performed before, during, and after a disaster.

3. Put together a technical description of any backup networks.

4. List all personnel involved in the recovery phase and their responsibilities.

5. Describe how the recovery site will be employed.

6. Make a list of critical nodes and their profiles.

7. Make a list of vendors and carriers who will supply facilities and backup.

8. Make a list of alternate sources of equipment and supplies.

9.  Create all necessary network diagrams.

10. Make a list of all required software, manuals, testing, and operational procedures of backup networks.

11. Diagram all backup circuits.

12. Describe procedures for updating the recovery plan.

A commitment to an effective disaster recovery plan must have the support of top management. They must be aware of the consequences of the failure of such a plan. A team consisting of a coordinator and representatives from management is required to continually upgrade the plan as facilities are added and modified, if the firm is to be protected.

# Network Management

For a network to be effective and efficient over a long period of time, a good **network management** plan must be created. The network management plan must have two goals:

1.  The plan should prevent problems where possible.

2.  The plan should prepare for problems that will most likely occur.

A comprehensive plan needs to include the following duties:

1.  Monitor and control hard disk space.

2.  Monitor network workload and performance.

3.  Add to and maintain user login information and workstation information.

4.  Monitor and reset network devices.

5.  Perform regular maintenance on software and data files stored in the servers.

6.  Make regular backups of data and programs stored in the servers.

## Managing Hard Disk Space

The server's hard disk is one of the network's primary commodities. Files for network-based programs are stored on the hard disk. Print jobs that are sent from workstations to network printers are stored on the hard disk in a queue before they are printed. And in some networks, personal files and data are stored on the network hard disk.

If the hard disk space fills up, then print jobs can't be printed and users can't save their data files. Data files may also be corrupted since data manipulation can't be accomplished.

Disk space must be available at all times for legitimate users of the network. The hard disk space must be checked every day. Growth of users' files should be controlled to ensure that a single user doesn't monopolize the hard disk. Unwanted files must be deleted, and when heavy disk fragmentation occurs, all files could be backed up and the disk reformatted. This will allow defragmentation of files on the hard disk and provide for more efficient access to data on the server's hard disk. Some networks allow the use of software to repack files on the hard disk and eliminate file fragmentation. When possible, such tools should be used. However, all files should be backed up before using a defragmentation software application, in case something goes wrong.

## Monitoring Server Performance

The performance of the LAN's server will determine how quickly the server can deliver data to the user. The servers must be monitored to ensure that they are performing at their peak.

Several factors determine the response of a server. One of these factors is the number of users that are attached to the system. Working with more users will slow the server response time. If a specific application has a large number of users, the server that contains the application could be dedicated to serve only such a program. Other servers could be used to distribute the load of other programs on the system.

Additionally, the server's main memory (RAM) should be monitored to make sure that it is used efficiently. Many servers use RAM as disk buffers. These buffers cannot function if there isn't sufficient memory to run the network operating system and the buffers. If a server has to reduce the number of buffers required for I/O, the overall performance of the network will suffer.

Most networks provide tools that show statistical data about the use of the network and outline potential problems. An experienced network administrator uses these statistics to ensure that the network operates at its peak level at all times.

## Maintaining User and Workstation Information

Network users have network identification numbers that can be used to monitor security and the growth of the network. A network manager must keep a log of information about the network users such as login

ID, node address, network address, and some personal information such as phone, name, and address. Also, network cabling, workstation type, configuration, and purpose of use should be kept in records. This information can be stored in a database. It can be used to detect problems with data delivery, make changes to users' profiles, workstation profiles, and accounts, and support other tasks.

# Monitoring and Resetting Network Devices

A network consists not only of servers and workstations but also of printers, input devices such as scanners, and other machines. Some devices may need to be reset daily (such as some types of gateways), while other devices require periodic maintenance. Some types of electronic mail routers may need to be monitored hourly to make sure they are working properly. In any case, all devices should be monitored periodically, and a schedule of reset and maintenance should be created to ensure that all network devices work when a user requests them.

# Maintaining Software

Software applications, especially database applications, need regular maintenance to rebuild files and reclaim space left empty by deleted records. Space not used must be made available to the system, and in many cases index files will have to be rebuilt.

Additionally, as new software upgrades become available, they need to be placed in the network. After an upgrade is placed in the network, file cleanup may have to be done. Also, any incompatibilities between the new software and the network will need to be resolved.

Old e-mail messages will have to be deleted and the space they occupy made available to the system. The same type of procedure will have to be performed as users are added to or deleted from the network.

# Making Regular Backups

Backups of user information and data must be made on a periodic basis. If a server's hard disk fails, a major problem could occur if backups are inadequate.

Backups of server information are normally placed on tapes or cartridges. Tapes and cartridges offer an inexpensive solution to backup needs and can hold large amounts of information. Their capacity ranges from 20 megabytes to as much as 8 gigabytes or more.

Writing information from the server's hard disk to a tape or cartridge is a slow process. Network managers should have automated backup procedures and a tape system that offers at least 3 megabytes of transfer speed per minute.

# Summary

The life cycle of a network is an important planning consideration. One significant aspect is the technological changes that will have to be dealt with during the useful life of the network. Each network is a representation of the technology at the time of its design and implementation.

During the course of its life cycle, a network passes through the following phases:

1. The feasibility study involves the activities of problem definition and investigation. The problem definition attempts to find the problems that exist in the organization that caused management to initiate the study. The investigation activity involves gathering input data to develop a precise definition of the present data communication conditions and to uncover problems.

2. The analysis phase uses the data gathered in step 1 to identify the requirements that the network must meet if it is to be a successful implementation.

3. During the design phase, all the components that will comprise the network are developed.

4. The implementation phase consists of the installation of the hardware and software that make up the network system. Also, during this phase, all training and documentation materials are developed.

5. During the maintenance and upgrade phase the network is kept operational and fine-tuned by network operations personnel. Further, updates of software and hardware are performed to keep the network operating efficiently and effectively.

One of the most important requirements in network design is response time. Response time is the total time that expires between sending an inquiry from a workstation or terminal and receiving the response back at the workstation.

One of the major uses of the data gathering process is in developing a network topology. The load and site data collected are used as input for network modeling programs. These programs use mathematical models to simulate a network.

The network operating system and the protocols that the host can handle limit the number and types of application software programs that can be used on a network. These limitations can be overcome with the acquisition of protocol converters and FEPs.

The type of software purchased for the network will determine whether the network uses asynchronous or synchronous communication, full-duplex or half-duplex communication, and the speed of transmission. Additionally, the limitations imposed by the software will determine the types of other networks that can be interfaced with. The network designer should select a protocol that is compatible with the ISO seven-layer model and one that can grow as the network grows. The protocol is a crucial element of the overall design, since the server architecture must interface with it.

Once the network has been designed, the specific vendors must be selected. A formal approach is to send a request for proposal (RFP) to prospective vendors. The RFP is a document that asks each vendor to prepare specifications and a price quotation for the configuration described in the RFP.

An important responsibility of network managers is maintaining control over the security of the network and the data on it. The major goals of security measures are to prevent computer crime and data loss. Some of the data losses can be the result of computer viruses. A computer virus is an executable computer program that propagates itself, using other programs as carriers, and sometimes modifies itself during or after replication. It is intended to perform some unwanted function on the computer system attached to the network. Viruses can be monitored and eliminated with the use of antivirus software.

Another method to safeguard the information transmitted is called encrypting or ciphering. User IDs and passwords by themselves are not an effective security technique. When combined with call-back units, encrypting devices, and network physical security, they provide an effective deterrent to unauthorized users.

The time and location of user access to the network can be controlled by software and hardware mechanisms. Although such measures are an inconvenience to users, they help in providing access to data by monitoring communication sessions and access during critical times. The most vulnerable security point on a network is switched ports that allow dial-in access. To enhance the security of switched ports with dial-in access, they should be operational only during the time when transactions are allowed. A call-back unit can be used to ensure that calls are made only from authorized locations.

The increasing use of computer systems and data communication networks requires managers to have a realistic disaster plan. The network manager needs to be involved in the planning and should have knowledge of

1. The need for disaster planning

2. Computer backup approaches

3. Network backup approaches

4. The characteristics of a disaster backup strategy

5. Planning processes of the organization

6. The impact of a data network disaster on the organization

Planning a disaster recovery system requires goals, objectives, design, implementation, testing, documentation, and maintenance. A disaster plan must meet certain criteria:

1. Reliability

2. Operability

3. Response time to activate the plan

4. Cost-effectiveness

For networks to be effective and efficient over a long period of time, a good network management plan is needed. The network management plan must have two goals:

1. The plan should prevent problems where possible.

2. The plan should prepare for problems that will most likely occur.

A comprehensive plan needs to address the following tasks:

1. Monitor and control hard disk space.

2. Monitor network workload and performance.

3. Add to and maintain user login information and workstation information.

4. Monitor and reset network devices.

5. Perform regular maintenance on software and data files stored on the servers.

6. Make regular backups of data and programs stored on the servers.

# Questions

1. Briefly describe the life cycle phases for network design.

2. Name four items that should be included in the report produced at the end of the feasibility study.

3. Why is network response time important?

4. What is network modeling?

5. What is the purpose of message analysis?

6. Name ten hardware items that are part of a network.

7. What are the steps of the implementation phase?

8. What are the major sections of an RFP?

9. Briefly describe encryption.

10. Why are passwords and user IDs not enough security for a network?

11. What is a virus? How can it be detected?

12. Why should there be a disaster recovery plan for a data communications network?

13. Name four characteristics of a disaster recovery plan.

14. Name four major items that should be included in the recovery plan.

# Projects

## Objective

There are two different projects in this section. The first project provides some general guidelines for troubleshooting a small local area network. Before expensive testing methods are used to find problems with LANs, the guidelines provided below may find and correct a problem in a more efficient manner. The second project is the study of the design and installation of a local area network for the computer laboratory.

### Project 1. Troubleshooting a LAN

Troubleshooting a LAN is accomplished by using an established methodology of problem determination and recovery through event login and report techniques. Some troubleshooting techniques will be explained in later chapters in this book. However, sometimes the best planned approach does not work. The following suggestions may accomplish what the scientific methods can't do. Try to follow them in the order they are listed.

1. If the problem appears to be on the network, try turning the power to network devices off and on in a systematic manner. Turn off the power to routers, gateways, and network modems. After turning the power off, wait approximately 30 seconds and turn the power back on. Sometimes a device gets "hung up" because of an electrical malfunction or an instruction that it cannot execute.

2. If the problem appears to be in your workstation, turn the machine off and reboot the computer.

3. Check for viruses on the file server and your workstation.

4. Reload the network software and any other software that controls devices such as gateways.

5. Swap out devices, cables, connectors, and network interface cards on your machine and then across the network.

6. Reconfigure the user profile in the network server.

7. Add more memory to the file server.

If the above suggestions do not work and the LAN manuals do not offer any other possibilities, call the LAN vendor.

## Project 2. Study of a Local Area Network

Go to the school's data processing center or any other site where a local area network may be in operation. Carefully document the following topics by questioning network managers and by observing the LAN in operation.

1. Describe the hardware that constitutes the LAN. Use the following checklist as a guide.

   a. Is the network a peer-to-peer network or a dedicated file server network?

   b. What models of server(s) are available?

   c. What is the internal configuration of the server(s) (i.e., amount of RAM, disk space, processor speed, coprocessor speed, number of floppy drives and types, etc.)?

   d. What models of workstations are available?

e. What is the internal configuration of the workstations (i.e., amount of RAM, disk space, processor speed, coprocessor speed, number of floppy drives and types, etc.)?

f. What make, model, and type of network interface card is being used?

g. What is the network configuration? Why was this type chosen?

h. What models and types of printers are available to network users?

i. Are there any gateways to other networks? If yes, what type and models are available?

j. What are the physical limitations of the network (i.e., number of users, maximum distance of transmission)?

k. What type of transmission medium is being used? Why was this type chosen?

2. What network operating system is in place? Why was this type chosen?

3. How do the users interact with the software stored on the network?

4. What type of work is normally accomplished by the workstations?

5. How do users perform network operations such as printing, copying files, and so forth?

6. What are the maintenance policies?

7. Are there any support fees? If yes, what type and amount?

8. What is the cost of adding stations?

9. What is the cost of adding a server?

10. What are the system management procedures in place and their cost?

11. How are software licensing agreements handled?

12. What types of upgrades or modifications are planned for the next three years?

After all the material is compiled, create a report indicating your findings about the status of the local area network. The report should consist of at least five pages, but it will probably be much longer.

After completing the report on the actual LAN, provide suggestions for improving the system without increasing the current costs. For each suggestion, provide evidence in the form of interviews, data compiled from magazines, or vendor specification sheets. Is there a way to provide a better service and lower the costs? What problems do you anticipate with this network during the next three years? How can a solution be put in place before serious interruption of LAN services occurs?

# 8
# Introduction to Novell NetWare 4

## Objectives

After completing this chapter you will

1. Understand the history of Novell NetWare and the important features of NetWare 4.

2. Understand the basic hardware components required to install NetWare 4.

3. Obtain an overview of the software components of NetWare 4.

4. Understand the concepts of volumes and drive mappings.

5. Understand the concept of trustee and trustee rights for both the file system and Novell Directory Services.

## Key Terms

Novell NetWare

Server Computer

Client Computer

Network Interface Card

Volume

Drive Mapping

Search Drive

Trustee

File System Rights

Novell Directory Services Rights

# Introduction

This chapter introduces a network operating system known as **Novell NetWare** and begins to explain the importance of Novell NetWare version 4, specifically version 4.11. It will introduce concepts that will be more thoroughly discussed in later chapters.

Originally designed for computers running the CP/M operating system, NetWare was quickly adapted by Novell for use on the IBM PC when the PC was introduced in the early 1980s. This adaptation was a key strategic move that helps account for the large market share currently enjoyed by Novell in the local area network arena.

NetWare's software and hardware components are:

1. Software:

   a. Novell NetWare 4.11 Operating System running on shared computers called **servers.**

   b. The Novell NetWare client software that runs on the **client computer** which is alternately referred to as a node or workstation.

   c. The software, known as drivers, that controls the network card for both the server and the client workstation and the hard disk of the file server.

2. Hardware

   a. 386 or faster Intel-based PC with at least 20 MB RAM and at least 115 MB of hard disk space to hold the DOS partition (15 MB) and for the SYS volume (100 MB minimum) for the server.

   b. 386 or faster workstation.

   c. Network interface card in all nodes and in the file server.

   d. Cable (and hubs if needed) to connect these network interface cards.

The NetWare 4.11 Operating System is installed on the servers. The servers under NetWare 4.11 are connected by Novell Directory Services (NDS), which allows multiple servers to be linked in an enterprise network. NetWare 4.11 allows the servers to act as "traffic cops" which manage access by clients to the files stored on the servers' hard disks and the printers controlled by the servers.

The NetWare client software, called the NetWare DOS Requester or Client 32, allows the user to treat the servers as though they were disk drives attached to the user's client computer. Ordinary activities on the client computer can access disk drives on the servers just as though the servers' disks were on the local client computer. Additionally, the data and programs on the servers can be protected by assigning the proper file system trustee rights to users on the network. Client software is introduced later in this chapter, and its installation is discussed in Chapter 9. File system trustee assignments are discussed in Chapter 12, and Novell Directory Services trustee assignments are discussed in Chapter 14.

# Overview of NetWare

Little remains constant in the world of networking. Network operating systems, hardware components, and topologies have changed rapidly over the last several years to keep pace with advancing technology and consumer demand. Novell, Inc. has performed better than most at maintaining a salable product and a share of the market. Novell's original network product, however, did not do well. The system was a file server and network operating system software, with serial cables to connect to client computers running the CP/M operating system. The product line was expanded somewhat, but the company went bankrupt. Novell's reorganization, however, took place at an opportune point in history. The introduction of the IBM PC gave Novell an entirely new market. Novell's operating system was eventually rewritten to allow the IBM PC to be used as both the file server and the client. Novell has introduced many software and hardware products since then. It now controls the largest single share of the local area networking market with Novell NetWare. "NetWare" refers to all of Novell's network operating system products. The term IntranetWare refers to Novell's latest release of NetWare, version 4.11, bundled with the Novell Web Server, the FTP Server, the Multi Protocol Router, and the IPX/IP gateway products.

Novell NetWare was originally designed around hardware using a star topology to communicate with a single file server. The file server simply allowed client computers to store and share files. This structure has influenced all of Novell's products to date although NetWare 4.11 is not strictly server-centric. NetWare has become largely hardware independent, allowing many topologies and file servers to be used simultaneously, but communication on the network is still handled almost entirely through a primary file server. Two client computers may be connected directly to each other by a network cable, but for a file to be transferred from one to the other, that file must first be sent to a file server, then to the target client computer. Of course, the network provides many other functions, but they are generally centered around the idea of a client computer connected to one or more file servers.

NetWare 4, as an enterprise network operating system, goes beyond the strictly server-centric model. It can represent a whole company in a single location or a whole global company with multiple file servers and thousands of users. This concept is supported by Novell Directory Services, a topic which will be discussed in Chapter 10. However, even though NetWare 4 has a more global focus, many operations are still server-centric. These functions will be pointed out when we come to them in later chapters.

## Novell Client Software

By far, the most common client on a Novell network is an IBM PC or PC-compatible computer running DOS or Windows 95. Macintosh, OS/2, and Windows NT clients are also now used, but their numbers are not yet large. DOS or Windows 95 handles all of the low-level functions of the computer such as reading and writing to the disk drives, loading and executing application programs, and handling input from the keyboard. When running an application program such as a word processor, DOS or Windows 95 allocates memory, reads the program from the disk drive and then allows the program to begin. The application program can then use the resources of the computer through what are known as DOS or Windows 95 function calls.

For instance, there are many different types of printers and dozens of companies manufacturing them. To the application program, this is irrelevant. It will simply make a DOS or Windows 95 function call to write data to the printer, and DOS or Windows 95 will handle the output to the device. Since even DOS can't "know" the details of every peripheral device one might attach to a computer, including a network, programs known as drivers are often used to help the local operating system provide a common environment for application programs to work in.

Attaching a Novell network to a computer is a good example of this. It essentially involves two components: the **network interface card** or NIC and the network driver programs. Novell offers a variety of programs that serve as the drivers depending on the configuration of the workstation. The NIC is the hardware that is physically connected to the network, much as a telephone is the piece of hardware that is physically connected to the telephone network. It generates the proper electrical signal to communicate on the particular type of network being used. It may use pulses of light or radio waves to send signals across the network. The network drivers used on a particular workstation must consist of an appropriate combination of the programs needed to perform three functions: provide a hardware dependent driver for the network card, provide the appropriate communications protocol to be used on the network, and provide an interface for the user.

# IPX.COM and NETX.COM

Historically, Novell's long-used system of providing the hardware-dependent driver and the communications protocol was to use a program called IPX.COM. It was generated at the time NetWare was installed because it is actually built out of two components. One component is the hardware-dependent NIC driver and the other is the IPX protocol driver. (IPX stands for Internetwork Packet eXchange.) The resulting IPX.COM program was then unique to the type of NIC it ran on.

IPX.COM together with NET#.COM formed an early version of the NetWare client shell program which allowed the client to connect to a server. Note that the # in NET# represents the version of DOS running on the client workstation when the NET# is executed. NET# was later replaced by NETX which runs with all versions of DOS. This basic NetWare shell supported only one communications protocol, IPX.

# Open Data-Link Interface

Later, Novell changed the focus of its efforts to a standard called Open Data-Link Interface. The purpose was to create client software that would support multiple communications protocols, such as IPX and TCPIP, running simultaneously over the same network interface card. ODI also provided a modular approach to client software creation. The two functions of the NIC driver and IPX protocol driver were spread out over three programs:

LSL.COM

MLID (LAN driver)

IPXODI

The first program is called LSL.COM (LSL stands for Link Support Layer). It allows multiple communications protocols, which are loaded later, to be run on the same NIC.

The second program is strictly an ODI-compliant NIC driver program called the Multiple Link Interface Driver (MLID) and is given a name that indicates which brand of NIC it supports. Intel EtherExpress 16 cards, for instance, use a program called EXP16ODI.COM. A network card called the SMC EtherCard PLUS Elite10T/A uses a program called SMCPLUS.COM. These driver programs are packaged with the NIC, and

Novell also provides them on their distribution media for major brands of network interface cards.

The third program is the communications protocol driver, IPXODI.COM. As its name indicates, it is an Internetwork Packet Exchange protocol driver that conforms to the Open Data-Link Interface standard and is specific to Novell. Other communications protocols such as TCPIP may also be loaded so that a given workstation can communicate simultaneously with a TCPIP network and with a Novell IPX network.

Note that LSL, the MLID, and IPXODI do not have to be compiled together; they are complete programs on their own. They obtain the configuration parameters for the network interface card from a file called NET.CFG. NET.CFG will be discussed further in a later chapter.

Prior to the introduction of NetWare 3.12 and NetWare 4, the fourth function, that of a user interface, was provided by one of three different versions of essentially the same program: NETX.COM, XMSNETX.EXE, or EMSNETX.EXE. The three different versions of this program were needed to take advantage of different memory configurations of the workstation. NETX.COM uses conventional memory, XMSNETX.EXE uses extended memory, and EMSNETX.EXE uses expanded memory. The letter "X" appears before the extension (.EXE or .COM) in each of these names to indicate that they can be used with any DOS version. Prior to the release of DOS version 5.0, Novell supplied the rather cumbersome collection of NET2, NET3, NET4, XMSNET2, XMSNET3, XMSNET4, EMSNET2, EMSNET3, and EMSNET4 for use with DOS 2.x, DOS 3.x, and DOS 4.x respectively. Using the ODI approach for IPX, one must merely include the following in one's AUTOEXEC.BAT:

> LSL
>
> NIC driver such as SMCPLUS
>
> IPXODI
>
> NETX (or XMSNETX or EMSNETX)

## NetWare DOS Requester

Although the NETX version of workstation software will still allow the user to connect to a NetWare 3.12 network, NetWare 3.12 and NetWare version 4.0 and later have provided a new version of workstation software called the NetWare DOS Requester. The NetWare DOS Requester version of workstation software is ODI-compliant and still requires the use of LSL, the NIC driver, and IPXODI. However, NETX has been replaced with the workstation VLM (Virtual Loadable Module) manager which coexists with DOS and uses DOS tables. VLMs will be addressed further in Chapter 9.

## Client 32

With NetWare 4.11 came an even newer and more efficient type of client software setup called Client 32. Client 32 together with the network drivers make up the NetWare client software which provides a complete interface between DOS/Windows 3.1, Windows 95, or Windows NT and NetWare. The NetWare client software provides an interface that allows users to interact with the computer in a transparent or natural manner. This shields users from the complex low-level operations of the computer and the network. Therefore, the NetWare client software protects the user from having to know how to interact directly with the network.

# The User Environment

## Network Volumes and Network Drives

The highest level in the NetWare directory structure is the NetWare **volume**. All file servers must have a volume called SYS:, and a NetWare file server may have a total of up to 64 volumes. A single NetWare file server can support up to 32 physical disk drives and 32 TB (terabytes, or trillion bytes) of physical hard disk space. Volumes may span physical disk drives, or they may divide a physical disk drive. In either case, volumes are specified during installation.

Volumes are divided into directories. The NetWare client software allows DOS or Windows 95 and the user to treat the file server as a disk drive attached to the client computer. DOS assigns a drive letter to each of the disk drives physically attached to the computer. In general, A and B designate floppy disk drives while C, D, and E usually represent hard disk drives local to the user. On a typical system, with two floppy disk drives and a hard disk drive, DOS would assign A, B, and C to the those disk drives.

When the NetWare client software programs are loaded, another drive letter is made available to the user. Typically, F is used to designate the first network drive and is often used to designate the SYS: volume. In this textbook, all references to the F: drive assume that F designates the entire SYS: volume. Ordinary DOS commands like DIR (which displays a list of the files on the disk) and CHDIR (which moves access to a different area of the disk) can be used on the network drive F. In addition, application programs can make ordinary DOS function calls to carry out their functions on the network drive as if it were a hard disk attached to the computer. The network drive is the hard disk on the file server, the same hard disk accessed by every other user on the network. Figure 8-1 shows three computers, a file server and two client computers. The first client has local disk drives A, B, and C. It also has access to drive F, which is actually on the file server. The second client has only one local disk drive, but can also access drive F.

## DOS Directories

In DOS you can create directories to organize the data on a disk. A directory contains files grouped together on the disk. Every disk has what is called the root directory even though it is not referred to as "root" in any DOS command. Since a "\" (a backslash) is used to separate directory names, a backslash with no name is considered the root directory.

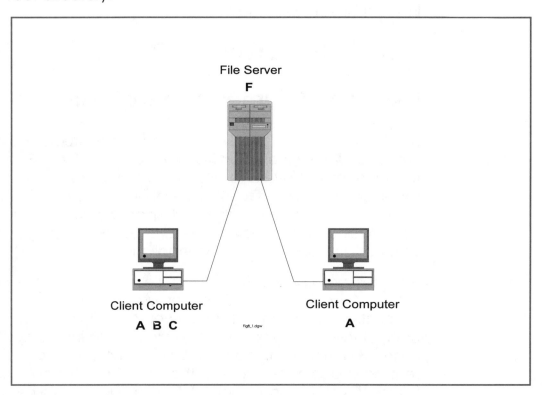

**Figure 8-1.** Client computers networked to a server.

Figure 8-2 shows how a hard disk might be organized. The files in the root directory could be listed by typing the DIR command. The DIR command lists the files in the current directory. In this case DIR C: would list the files COMMAND.COM, LSL.COM, SMCPLUS.COM, IPXODI.COM,VLM.EXE and a directory called WORD. The files in the directory WORD could be displayed by typing DIR C:\WORD and pressing the ENTER key. WORD.EXE and LETTER.DOC would be listed. Another way to view the list of files in the WORD directory would be to use the CHDIR command. CHDIR stands for change directory and can be abbreviated further by using only CD. If you were to type CD

C:\WORD, the current directory would be changed to the WORD directory and DIR C: would list the files WORD.EXE and LETTER.DOC. In this way the drive letter C moves around the disk drive pointing to different areas. Just as the root directory contains a directory called WORD, the WORD directory could contain another directory and so on. The same commands can be used on the network drive F.

In Figure 8-1 the first computer could create a directory called F:\HISFILES by using the MKDIR command. MKDIR stands for make directory and can be abbreviated further by using only MD. By typing the command MD F:\HISFILES, the first user can create a place to store files on the file server. The user at the second computer could type MD F:\HERFILES. Now, if either computer user typed DIR F:, both directory names would be listed.

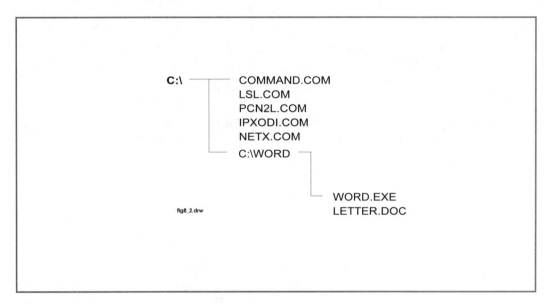

**Figure 8-2.** Possible hard disk organization.

## Drive Mappings

With directories containing directories and every user on the network creating directories, the directory structure can become quite complex. Suppose a user on the network needed quick and easy access to files in both the F:\HISFILES directory and the F:\HERFILES directory. Rather than constantly using the CHDIR command to move drive F to the other area, he could use the NetWare MAP command to create a drive letter for one of the directories. Figure 8-3 shows the result of the first user typing MAP G:=F:\HERFILES. This creates drive letter G, which points to the HERFILES directory on the same physical drive as F:\HISFILES. This arrangement does not affect the second user. **Drive mappings** pertain only to the client computer where the MAP command was issued. Each user still has access to the HERFILES directory through drive letter F. The first user simply has the choice of using drive letter F or drive letter G.

## Paths and Search Drives

Drive mappings allow users to access data easily without worrying about the directory names. The DOS PATH statement allows the user to completely ignore the current directory when running programs. NetWare combines these functions in the **search drive**. Ordinarily, to execute a program, it must reside in the current directory or the full path must be used when referring to the program. The "path" is the complete directory name where the program resides. Referring to Figure 8-3, the first user may have a program in the HISFILES directory called WORD.EXE. If the current directory is F:\HERFILES, he would have to type F:\HISFILES\WORD to execute the WORD program. DOS provides a way to eliminate the need to precede a command with the directory location. The PATH command tells the computer where to look for a program if it can't be found in the current directory. If the first user types PATH F:\HISFILES he can use all the programs in the HISFILES directory without typing the entire path. He could simply type WORD and the computer would look in the current directory first, then look in the HISFILES directory and find, and then execute, the program. Multiple directories can be included in the PATH command to instruct the computer to search several areas for the program.

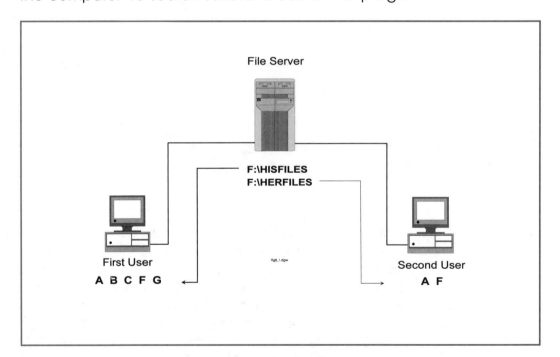

**Figure 8-3.** Paths for different network users.

The command PATH F:\HERFILES;F:\HISFILES would tell the computer to search the current directory first (as it always does), then the F:\HERFILES directory, and lastly the F:\HISFILES directory. A NetWare search drive is a drive mapping that is automatically inserted in the PATH. In Figure 8-4, the second user has typed the command MAP

S1:=F:\HISFILES. This NetWare command automatically chooses a drive letter starting from the end of the alphabet and maps it to the directory indicated. But the drive letter is more than the pointer used in the other drive letters, it is also a PATH to the directory. The second user can use drive letter Z as she would any other drive letter, but if she is using drive A, for instance, she needs only to type WORD to run the program contained in the F:\HISFILES directory. A user may have up to 16 search drives mapped at a given time.

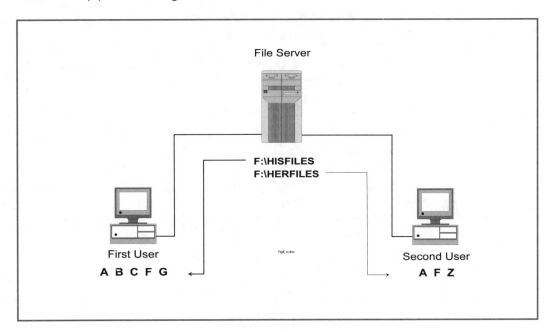

**Figure 8-4.** New paths of users after MAP command.

## File System Trustee Rights

NetWare allows users to share data or to restrict access to data. **Trustee rights** allow access to specific directories on the file server. Without trustee rights to a certain directory, a user cannot access the data in that directory. Trustee rights are composed of several permissions a user may have to a specific directory or file. These permissions include Supervisory, Read, Write, Create, Erase, Modify, File Scan and Access Control. Each of these permissions may be granted or denied to a user. The meanings of these permissions or rights with respect to a directory are listed below:

1. **Supervisory.** The user has all other rights in the directory even if the directory does not allow certain rights.

2. **Read**. The user can open and read files in the directory. The File Scan right is usually also given with the Read right so that the user can see the directory's directory listing.

3. **Write**. The user can write to existing files in the directory.

4. **Create**. The user can create new files in the directory.

5. **Erase**. The user can erase files in the directory.

6. **Modify**. The user can modify the attribute flags of the files in the directory. The attribute of a file indicates what access all users have to a file.

7. **File Scan**. The user can see what files and subdirectories are listed in the directory.

8. **Access Control**. The user can grant rights to other users in the directory.

Figure 8-5 shows the trustee rights each of the users has to the file server using the first letter of the above listed rights. The first user has all rights except Supervisory and Access Control to the F:\HISFILES directory. He can use all of the files there any way he wants, but he cannot grant those rights to any other users. He only has Read and File Scan rights in the F:\HERFILES directory. This means he can only read from the data there, not change it or add to it. The second user has all rights to the F:\HERFILES directory. She could even grant additional rights in that directory to the first user. Her access to the F:\HISFILES directory is restricted to Create and File Scan. This allows her to create new files in the directory but not to read or change the files already there.

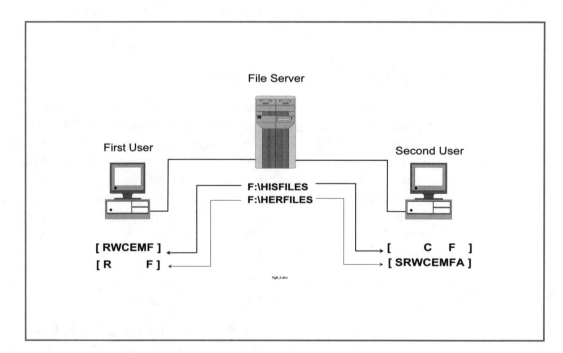

**Figure 8-5.** Trustee rights for users.

## Novell Directory Services Trustee Rights

NetWare 4.11 allows a user to have a single login ID and obtain access to multiple servers and resources within the enterprise network system. Novell NetWare 4.11 utilizes Novell Directory Services to link servers, users, and resources such as printer and print queues into an enterprise network system. Access to resources in the enterprise network system is controlled by **NDS** object and property **rights**. Every resource in the enterprise network is an object. Users, printers, print queues, etc. are all objects, and each object has characteristics called properties. NDS object rights determine what level of access a user has to an NDS object, while NDS property rights control the ability to manipulate the specific properties or characteristics of an NDS object. The NDS object and property trustee rights are listed below and discussed further in Chapter 14.

### NDS Object Trustee Rights

**Supervisor:** The trustee with this right has all object privileges and has access to all properties.

**Browse:** The trustee with this right has visibility of all objects in an NDS tree.

**Create:** The trustee with this right can create a new object beneath this object in the NDS tree. Only available on container objects.

**Delete:** The trustee with this right can delete this object from the NDS tree.

**Rename:** The trustee with this right can change the name of the object.

### NDS Property Rights

**Supervisor:** The trustee with this right has all rights to the property.

**Compare:** The trustee with this right can compare a value of the property to any other value.

**Read:** The trustee with this right can read the values of the property, and this right implies that the trustee also has the compare right.

**Write:** The trustee with this right can add, change, or delete any of the values of the property, and this right implies that the trustee also has the Add Self property right.

**Add Self:** The trustee with this right can add or delete itself as a value of the property.

# Novell Network Example

As outlined before, a local area network links two or more computers and other peripherals together for the purpose of sharing data and equipment. A Novell NetWare 4.11-based local area network normally consists of multiple file servers linked together to form an enterprise network. Each of these file servers is considered to be a dedicated file server. In its simplest configuration, a NetWare 4.11 network can be composed of a single NetWare 4.11 file server. Novell networks can consist of one or more file servers, each with dozens of workstations, multiple shared printers, and other devices that can be attached to the file server or workstations. A small office network or a teaching laboratory can be established easily by creating one for the first time or by using existing networks.

The basic components of a LAN are as follows:

1. A file server (an IBM PC or compatible computer with a 80836 or faster processor) with at least 20 megabytes of RAM and a hard disk (with a minimum of 115 megabytes of free storage).

2. Network interface cards (NICs), at least one for the server and one for each of the workstations.

3. Transmission media (twisted pair, coaxial, or other type according to the type of NICs used).

4. Novell NetWare 4.11.

5. A printer should also be added to the network (preferably more than one).

If a Novell NetWare-based network is not already available, the process for installing one is outlined in Chapter 9. The following list provides a general review of the process.

1. Find a location for the server.

2. Find locations for the workstations.

3. Configure each NIC to contain a unique node address if not already preconfigured from the factory.

4. Install the NIC in each of the workstations and servers that will make up the nodes of the network.

5. Connect each node with the medium chosen.

6. Document all the hardware used as well as the specific configuration settings for all hardware that makes up the network.

7. Install the NetWare network operating system and use the data from item 6 to answer NetWare's requests.

8. Install workstation software.

Figure 8-6 displays a possible configuration for such a laboratory or work environment. If the network is used to provide instructions   on the use of commands and network management, a program   called LANSKOOL from Intel, Inc. may  be a good  addition to the system. This program allows the instructor to  project his or her workstation screen on the  screen of  other users  for the  purpose of answering questions or for instructional needs.

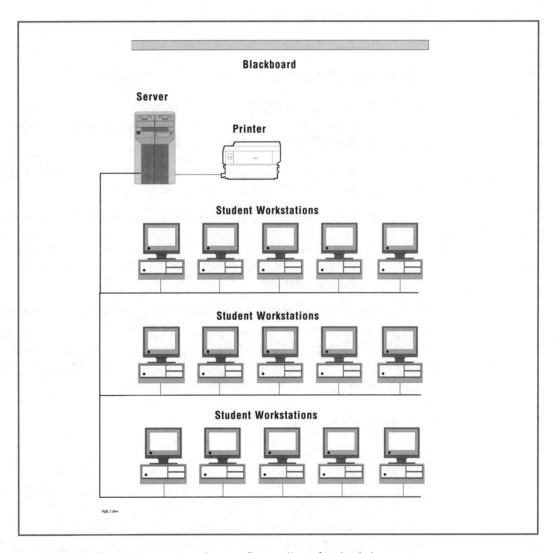

**Figure 8-6.** Possible network configuration for training users.

The other scenario consists of a Novell network that already exists. It is costly to purchase additional workstations, materials,  and space if all that is required is a laboratory or room for providing training to  users. If a current network is in place with users' workstations available, all that is needed is an additional server that can function as a training server for the users. This server can be connected to the existing wiring and, after NetWare is installed in it, training can be conducted using existing workstations. Figure 8-7 depicts this type of network.

The equipment required for this situation is as follows:

1. A file server (an IBM-PC or compatible computer with an 80386 or faster processor) with at least 20 megabytes of RAM and a hard disk (with a minimum of 115 megabytes of free storage).

2. A network interface card (NIC) for the server.

3. Novell NetWare 4.11.

4. A cable to connect the new server to existing network cable.

The process for installing the server is as follows:

1. Find a location for the server. If it is going to be used for training, then probably the classroom or a secluded area near the classroom is a good place.

2. Install the NIC in the server and, if required, provide a unique node address for the board.

3. Connect the server to existing network transmission media.

4. Install NetWare on the server, installing this new server into the already existing NetWare 4.11 tree which was created for the first file server.

The process of installing NetWare 4.11 is provided in the next chapter in this book. After the server goes on line, users who need training will simply attach their workstation to the tree which contains both servers and obtain access to the files and directories of either server based on rights assigned by the network administrator.

## Summary

NetWare 4.11 provides access to multiple file servers by many client computers through the hardware and software on each computer. The hardware consists of a network interface card, or NIC. Under DOS, using the ODI concept, the NIC is controlled by LSL.COM, a program named to represent the brand of NIC being used, and a program called IPXODI.COM. Another program, NETX or the newer VLM.EXE VLM manager, provides the interface to DOS and to the file server.

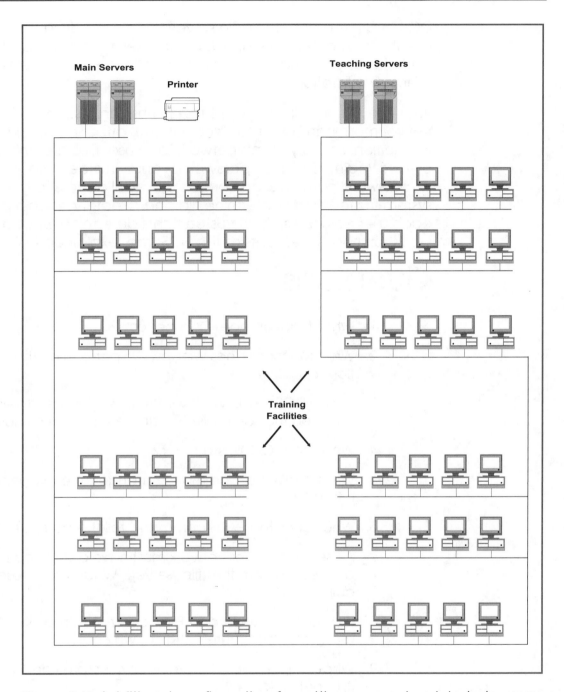

**Figure 8-7.** Additional configuration for setting up a network to train users.

With these programs loaded, the file servers of the NetWare 4.11 network appear to the client computer as a disk drive attached to the client computer. DOS commands can be used to create and access directories on the file server.

The four programs make up the NetWare VLM version client software that serves as the interface between the computer operating system and the network operating system. Alternatively, the newer Client 32 workstation software can be used. The NetWare client software allows

DOS and the user to treat file servers as a disk drive attached to the client computer. This protects the user from having to learn new commands and makes using the network a natural extension of the user's workstation.

With the use of drive mappings, paths, and search drives, a user's environment can be customized without affecting other network users. In addition, security of the network and user files are enhanced by the use of login IDs and passwords and trustee rights. The login ID/password combination controls physical access to the network. File system trustee rights determine file and directory access privileges that each user possesses. NDS trustee rights determine what a user can do with the various elements of the NDS tree, explained in Chapter 14.

# Questions

1. What function does DOS perform?

2. What functions does Windows 95 perform on the client workstation?

3. Under DOS and Windows 95, files may be stored in different areas on the same disk. What are these areas called?

4. What does CHDIR stand for?

5. What NetWare command changes the assignment of drive letters?

6. What does the PATH command tell the computer?

7. A user on a Novell network must have a set of permissions to use a directory on the file server. What are these permissions called?

8. If a user has Read and File Scan rights in a directory, can the user store data there? Why or why not?

9. What does Novell Directory Services provide for the NetWare 4.11 network?

10. What is controlled by NDS object trustee rights?

11. What is controlled by NDS property trustee rights?

12. What is an enterprise network system, and how does NetWare 4.11 support this concept?

# PROJECT

## Objective

Before NetWare 4.11 can be installed on a system, a listing of hardware, prospective users, and other resources must be recorded. Also, all steps taken during the installation process must be recorded in case something goes wrong and the process has to be repeated.

Additionally, knowing the applications, directories, users, and workstations on the network will help in maintaining the network and in performing future upgrades or expansions that may be required.

### Creating a Novell NetWare Log Book

A typical log book contains the information outlined below. One should be created for each server that is part of a NetWare 4 tree. Additionally, information about the overall tree should also be documented.

Name of the server.

Type of hardware.

Date of installation.

Name of installer.

Name and version of the operating system in use.

Installation date of the operating system.

Name of the operating system installer.

Server name.

Purchase date of the server.

Server's network address(es).

Location of the server.

Volume name(s) in the server.

Volume disk number.

Volume size(s).

Users' workstations.

Users' names.

Users' locations.

Users' network addresses.

Users' workstation types.

Users' workstation RAM.

Users' workstation disk options.

Users' workstation graphics boards and monitors.

Users' workstation hardware options and configuration.

## Applications:

For each application in use:

Name of the applications in use.

Application's vendor.

Application's purchase date.

Application's version number.

Serial number.

Type of license (single user/network).

Number of simultaneous user licenses purchased.

Application's memory requirements.

Application's disk space requirements.

Additional log information. Using a word processor and the preceding list as a guide, create an application log book and fill in the information requested for the network that you will be installing during the hands-on portion of this class. Make sure that all information is correct because once the network is set up, it is difficult and time consuming to correct major errors or omissions in the setup process.

# 9
# NetWare 4 Installation

## Objectives

After completing this chapter you will

1. Understand the hardware and software requirements for installing NetWare 4.11.

2. Know the steps to install NetWare 4.11 on a file server.

3. Be able to install appropriate NetWare client software on a DOS/Windows 3.1 client computer.

4. Be able to install appropriate NetWare client software on a Windows 95 client computer.

5. Understand the difference between upgrading a 3.12 NetWare server to a 4.11 and performing a NetWare 4.11 new installation.

6. Have installed a NetWare 4.11 server.

7. Have installed Client 32 for Windows 3.1 and/or Windows 95.

## Key Terms

Client 32

Client computer

Server Computer

Bootable partition

DOS

CD-ROM

Drivers

File Server

IPX Internal Network Number

Network Number

AUTOEXEC.BAT

STARTUP.NCF

AUTOEXEC.NCF

Disk Drivers

LAN Drivers

Interrupt

Memory Address

Port Address

CD-ROM drivers

# Introduction

As NetWare 4 has matured, the installation process for both server and client software has been simplified. As an enterprise system, the installation of earlier versions of NetWare 4 were cryptic at best and often seemingly impossible. NetWare 4.11, however, is a major improvement and even has a version once again dedicated to the small business owner.

This chapter will compare and contrast various methods for installing the NetWare 4.11 file server and will provide hands-on practice in performing a simple NetWare 4.11 installation. Additionally, the chapter will explore various choices for client software ranging from a historical perspective on how client software has been done up to a detailed discussion and hands-on practice for installing Novell's latest client software, **Client 32**.

At the end of this section, you will get the opportunity to install a NetWare 4.11 server and a NetWare 4.11 client. You will then test the installation by a simple login process. Details about login and other functions will be discussed in later chapters.

## Installing NetWare 4 on the File Server

Traditionally, NetWare has focused on a server-centric architecture for its network operating systems. **Clients** share resources by first attaching and then logging into a central **server**. NetWare 4.11 goes beyond the strictly server-centric design to combine multiple servers into an enterprise network tree which contains and organizes the users, file servers, printing resources, etc. of the overall network. But, although version 4.11 goes beyond the single server, each file server must itself be installed into the network tree.

The first server to be installed for a given tree actually defines the tree during its installation. Succeeding servers are installed into an existing tree. With respect to the server, the focus of this chapter is to detail the steps needed to prepare for and to install the first NetWare 4.11 server in a given tree. The chapter will then give an overview of design considerations that must be weighed when installing successive servers into the tree.

## Installation Preparation

If you were installing a complicated home appliance that you had never installed before, you would want to pay special attention to the installation instructions, making sure that you had all the required materials and equipment to accomplish the installation. In addition, you would want to make sure that you fully understood the steps needed for installation. Installing the first NetWare 4.11 server is a similar process. It is a process that functions very well when required materials and equipment are obtained and when a complete understanding of the installation steps is obtained prior to beginning the installation process. If installation preparation is shortchanged, the installation process can become unnecessarily complicated. This section details the steps needed for proper installation preparation.

The high-level requirements for installation are detailed in Figure 9-1.

**Hardware Required:**

- 386 (faster is highly recommended) PC or PC compatible with

  - 20 MB RAM memory

  - 115 MB minimum hard disk

  - VGA monitor (color optional)

  - ODI-compliant network interface card and cable

  - CD-ROM preferred but not absolutely required

**Software Required:**

- NetWare 4.11 Original Operating System CD-ROM disk or access to same over a network connection

- DOS 3 or higher for creating the bootable DOS partition

- DOS drivers for the CD-ROM on the machine which will become the new file server

- Drivers for the hard disk drives in the computer which will become the file server (obtained on the NetWare 4.11 CD or from the hard disk drive manufacturer)

- Drivers for the network interface card(s) in the computer which will become the file server (obtained on the NetWare 4.11 CD or from the NIC manufacturer with the latter preferred).

**Figure 9-1.** Hardware, software, and equipment required for a NetWare File Server Installation

# 4.11 Installation

## Installation Overview

A NetWare 4.11 server must have a **bootable** DOS **partition** with server boot files to be able to bring up the file server. The server boot files directory is created by using the NetWare 4.11 Operating System installation CD either directly on a CD-ROM attached to the file server or by connecting to the installation files over the network.  After the server boot files are copied to the DOS partition, the installation can then proceed to create and configure the NetWare partition on the first and succeeding hard drives.

## Creating the Bootable DOS partition

As mentioned, the first step in installing a Novell server is to create a bootable DOS partition on the first drive of the NetWare server.  This generally requires the computer to be booted with a previously created DOS diskette with the **DOS** operating system on it.

The simplest method for creating a bootable DOS diskette is to utilize an already existing DOS machine and

> Bring up the already existing DOS machine to the C:> prompt

> Put a blank formatted diskette in the diskette drive

> Enter

> **FORMAT A:/S**

By formatting the diskette with the /S parameter, the diskette becomes a system diskette, able to boot a computer on its own.

Before leaving the already existing DOS machine, some additional DOS system files must be copied to the diskette.  These files are

> **FDISK.COM**

> **FORMAT.COM**

The FDISK command will be used to create the DOS partition on the first hard drive on the server, and the FORMAT command will be used to make that blank partition into a bootable DOS partition.

Note that if the new file server has a **CD-ROM**, the **drivers** for the CD-ROM must be copied to the boot diskette as well so that they can be copied to the DOS partition of the new server.  Refer to CD-ROM documentation for instructions for these drivers or copy them from a

DOS machine already running the same type of CD-ROM drive as is in the new file server.

Once the bootable DOS diskette has been made, it is used to boot the new server. Once the server has been booted, the FDISK command from the diskette is used to create a DOS partition of at least 15 MB on the new hard drive. If space is not at a premium, it is a good idea to create a larger DOS partition to store client boot files, etc.

Once the primary DOS partition has been created on the new hard drive, the system reboots, still with the DOS diskette in the diskette drive. Then, the DOS partition is formatted using

**FORMAT C:/S**

This operation formats the DOS partition and transfers the system files necessary for the new hard drive to boot to the DOS operating system itself.

At this point, the DOS diskette must be removed, and the new file server must be booted on its own to verify that the new DOS system partition functions. Before moving on, the CD-ROM drivers must be copied from the DOS diskette to the DOS partition on the new server so that the new CD-ROM can be "seen" from DOS. Once these drivers have been installed, it is imperative that they be tested by booting the new server without the DOS diskette and then accessing files on the CD-ROM by doing a simple directory listing. If the CD-ROM drive cannot be accessed, these problems must be resolved before proceeding with a CD-ROM installation.

# Background Information Needed Before Proceeding with Server Installation

Before we proceed with the actual installation, several terms and files must be discussed. They are as follows:

**File Server Name**

**IPX Internal Network Number**

**Network Number (or External IPX Network Number)**

**SERVER.EXE**

**AUTOEXEC.BAT**

**STARTUP.NCF**

**AUTOEXEC.NCF**

**Disk Drivers**

**LAN Drivers**

**Interrupt**

**Memory Address**

**Port or I/O Address**

## File Server Name

The name of the **file server** is one of the first pieces of information required in setting up a new file server. It must uniquely identify the server among other servers connected over the same cabling system. It must be 2 to 47 characters in length and can contain letters, numbers, and the underscore character. It should be descriptive of the server while not being unnecessarily long.

## IPX Internal Network Number

This is a hexadecimal number of up to 8 hexadecimal numbers, not 00000000 and not FFFFFFFF. This number uniquely identifies the server from a systems viewpoint. The number cannot be the same as any other server's internal IPX network number, and it cannot be the same as another network number on a connected network. An example of a legal **IPX Internal Network Number** is 3D2AA153.

## External Network Number

This is a hexadecimal number of up to 8 hexadecimal numbers, not 00000000 and not FFFFFFFF. This number uniquely identifies the cable segment to which it is assigned. It cannot be the same as any other **network number** on the connected network, and it cannot be the same as any other server's internal IPX network number. It is often called the "wire" number even though the cabling system may contain wireless segments. It must be the same for all servers on a segment.

## SERVER.EXE

SERVER.EXE is the core portion of the network operating system. It is stored in a directory on the DOS partition of the server and is the program which, when executed, utilizes multiple configuration files to bring up the server.

## AUTOEXEC.BAT

**AUTOEXEC.BAT** on the DOS partition usually contains only the SERVER.EXE command so that the server can automatically boot itself when it is turned on. If the AUTOEXEC.BAT is not present, one would have to actually enter SERVER on the console to get the server to boot.

## STARTUP.NCF

The **STARTUP.NCF** file is a startup configuration file which is stored on the DOS partition on the file server. It is used by SERVER.EXE to, at minimum, provide hard disk drives so that SERVER.EXE can recognize the hard disk of the server. STARTUP.NCF then calls AUTOEXEC.NCF, explained below. A sample STARTUP.NCF file is shown in Figure 9-2.

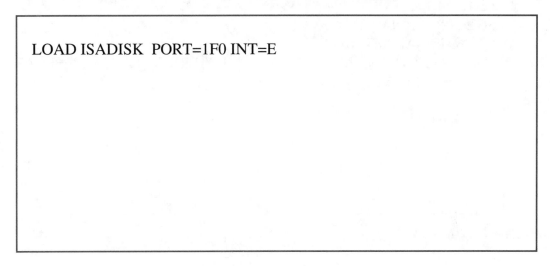

```
LOAD ISADISK  PORT=1F0 INT=E
```

**Figure 9-2**. A sample STARTUP.NCF file.

## AUTOEXEC.NCF

The **AUTOEXEC.NCF** file is to NetWare 4.11 much as the AUTOEXEC.BAT file is to DOS. It provides environment and configuration information for bringing up the server. Just like the AUTOEXEC.BAT file, it could techni-cally be omitted. But, if it is omitted, the person bringing up the file server must know the file server's name, the IPX Internal Network Number, the drivers for the network interface cards and the hardware specifications for these cards, etc. In other words, omission of the AUTOEXEC.NCF file is not a practical option. A sample AUTOEXEC.NCF file is shown in Figure 9-3.

### Disk Drivers

The hard disk(s) of a file server are not recognizable without the use of a software program, which is a NetWare 4.11-compliant **disk driver**. The hard disk driver is loaded in the STARTUP.NCF file so that the server can recognize its hard disk. The disk driver is a NetWare Loadable Module (NLM), which may itself be a driver that ends in .DSK, .HAM, or .CDM. The disk driver requires that the installer provide the disk drive's

```
SET TIME ZONE = CST8CDT
SET DAYLIGHT SAVINGS TIME OFFSET = 1:00:00
SET START OF DAYLIGHT SAVINGS TIME = (APRIL SUNDAY FIRST 2:00:00 AM)
SET END OF DAYLIGHT SAVINGS TIME = (OCTOBER SUNDAY LAST 2:00:00 AM)
SET DEFAULT TIME SERVER TYPE=SINGLE

SET BINDERY CONTEXT = O=MAINCO
FILE SERVER NAME MAINCO
IPX INTERNAL NET 1011ABD1
LOAD NE2000 INT=3 PORT=300 FRAME=EHTERNET_802.2 NAME=BOARD2
BIND IPX TO BOARD2 NET=80724155
```

**Figure 9-3.** A sample AUTOEXEC.NCF file.

interrupt number and other configuration parameters, discussed later in the chapter. The disk driver is activated by loading it in the STARTUP.NCF file as shown in Figure 9-2.

## LAN Drivers

The network interface card(s) of a file server are recognized through loading a software program, which is a NetWare 4.11-compliant network interface card (NIC) driver. Just like the hard disk, the network interface card is recognized by loading the **LAN driver** NetWare Loadable Module (NLM), which is a driver that ends in .LAN. The LAN driver requires the installer to provide the NIC's interrupt number, memory address, and port (I/O) address. The LAN driver is activated by loading it in the AUTOEXEC.NCF file as shown in Figure 9-3.

## Interrupt Number

An IBM PC or PC compatible utilizes **interrupt** numbers for communication with the various devices attached to the PC. In general, only one device can utilize a given interrupt number, 0 to 15, and many of these interrupt numbers are already assigned to such things as the keyboard and mouse. The IDE hard disk generally utilizes interrupt 14, which is represented by the hexadecimal number E, and NICs utilize unused interrupt numbers such as 3, 5, and 10. One must refer to the documentation and usually to the setup diskette that comes with a given NIC to determine how to configure a NIC card to a given interrupt number. This interrupt number must then be entered in the AUTOEXEC.NCF file as shown in Figure 9-3.

## Memory Address

Each network interface card utilized in a PC usually uses at least some portion of the RAM memory of the PC itself for normal operation. The **memory address** defined with the NIC in the AUTOEXEC.NCF must correspond to the memory address set on the NIC during setup, and it must not conflict with the memory address for any other device in the PC. Note that some NICs, notably the NE2000 board, do not require a memory address. This can be very important when one is trying to add an NIC to a machine that already has many additional devices installed.

## Port Address

The **port address** or I/O address is the location within the RAM of the PC that the board utilizes for communicating with the CPU of the PC. This address also cannot conflict with the memory or I/O addresses of other devices in the PC.

# Choices for Server Installation

In general, NetWare 4.11 can be installed using either

**Simple Installation**

or

**Custom Installation**.

Simple Installation requires far less effort on the part of the installer and can be used if all of the following conditions are met:

- DOS is already installed on a 15MB DOS partition

- The DOS partition is already bootable

- The remaining free hard disk space is at least 90 MB and is available solely for NetWare to use

- Each hard disk in the system is to contain one and only one volume

- A simple NDS directory with a single container can be used

- Randomly generated internal IPX addresses can be used

- IPX is the only communications protocol to be used

- It will not be necessary to mirror or duplex the hard drives on the system

- The AUTOEXEC.NCF and the STARTUP.NCF files do not have to have custom entries

Custom installation must be used when any of the above conditions is not met, or, at the installer's discretion, custom installation can be used simply so that the installer has an opportunity to view exactly what configuration parameters are being used.

# Hands-On Simple Installation

1. Create the bootable DOS partition on the PC that will be the new server following the sets listed earlier in this chapter. Be sure to include the DOS **CD-ROM drivers** so that the CD-ROM can be recognized by DOS.

2. Boot the new server to make sure that the DOS partition is bootable. If it is not, repeat the process of creating the bootable DOS partition before you proceed.

3. Place the NetWare 4.11 Operating System CD in the CD-ROM drive and close it.

4. Assuming that the new CD-ROM's drive letter is D:, enter

   **D:**

   **INSTALL**

   This process activates the installation process.

5. Select

   **English Language** and press <Enter>.

6. Select

   **NetWare 4.11** and press <Enter>.

7. Select

   **Simple Installation of NetWare 4.11** and press <Enter>.

8. Enter the name of the server, for example, enter the word SERVERXXX where XXX is your three initials. Remember that the server name must be unique among servers on the same cabling system.

   Enter

   **SERVERXXX** and press <Enter>.

9. Select

   **Copy the server boot files to the DOS partition**

   (When this operation completes, the server boot files are in the directory C:\NWSERVER on the DOS partition.)

10. **SERVER.EXE** is automatically started once the server boot files have been copied.

11. The installation process will attempt to identify server drivers for the hard disk drive and the network interface card. If the drivers are automatically detected, the drivers selected will be displayed on a Summary Screen. If these drivers are correct, select

    **Continue Installation** and press <Enter>.

    If the drivers are not automatically detected or if you wish to use different drivers, select the appropriate disk driver and the appropriate network interface card driver for your server following the screen prompts; otherwise skip to step 12.

12. The simple installation process automatically selects a random IPX Internal Network Number.

13. When asked whether or not to continue accessing the CD-ROM from DOS, or to try to mount the CD-ROM as a NetWare volume, select

    **Continue accessing the CD-ROM via DOS** and press <Enter>.

14. Note that the SYS: volume (the main NetWare volume is automatically mounted at this point during the Simple Installation.

15. Wait while the system files are automatically copied to the hard drive of the server.

16. When the system files have been copied, the server will attempt to locate an existing Novell Directory Services tree. If one or more is found, it will be displayed for you to choose whether or not to install into an existing tree or to select another tree after noting the names of these trees. For purposes of this simple installation, select

    Select another tree and press <Enter>.

    Press <INS>.

    Press <Enter> to confirm that you want to create a new tree.

17. Select

    **YES** and press <Enter> to create a new tree.

18. Select the **time zone for your server** and press <Enter>.

19. Type in your directory tree name, remembering that it must be unique from all other trees visible on this network (you saw the other tree names displayed in step 16).

Enter

**TREEXXX** where XXX is your initials and press <Enter>.

20. Enter **the network administrator's password** and press <Enter>.

(Note: It would be a good idea to use something like PASSWORDXXX where XXX is replaced with your initials. Of course, in a live network, this password would be unacceptable, but in a teaching environment it is more important to have a memorable password than it is to enforce security.)

21. **Confirm the network administrator's password by reentering it** and press <Enter>.

22. When prompted, **insert the license diskette into the A: drive** and press <Enter>.

23. Wait while the **System and Public files are copied to the server**.

24. Select

**Continue the installation** and press <Enter>.

25. After reading the closing screen, press <Enter> to return to the server prompt.

26. Bring the server down by entering

**DOWN** and press <Enter>.

**EXIT** and press <Enter>.

## To verify that the server is properly installed:

27. **Reboot the server** by pressing CTRL/ALT/DEL keys simultaneously.

28. Enter

**CD \NWSERVER** and press <Enter>.

**SERVER** and press <Enter>.

Wait for the server to "come up"

29. When the server is up, enter

**MODULES** to see what Netware Loadable Modules are loaded.

**CONFIG** to check that the server's name, IPX Internal Network Number, and network interface card are properly configured.

### When the new server is operational

1. From a NetWare 4.11 client station, reboot the workstation using either VLM or Client 32 software.

2. Enter

   **F:** (or your first network drive as given to you by your instructor).

3. Enter **LOGIN SERVERXXX\.ADMIN.TREEXXX** and press <Enter> if using the VLM client.

4. Enter your password.

5. Wait until the system logs in.

# Creating Workstation Installation Diskette Sets for NetWare 4.11 Clients

To ease the need for having CD-ROMs on all machines in a classroom, it is a good idea to create an installation diskette set for each of the clients supported with NetWare 4.11. Instructions for creating diskettes for the VLM client, the DOS/Windows 3.1 Client 32, and for the Windows 95 Client 32 are given here. While Client32 is the client of choice for NetWare 4.11, the VLM client also works and is sometimes needed, especially when there is a need for a small client that can easily fit on a diskette. Creation of the VLM client is presented here for use in these situations, and for use with previous versions of NetWare 4 and NetWare 3.12.

### To create an installation diskette set for the VLM client

1. Boot a computer containing a CD-ROM with a DOS diskette with drivers for the CD-ROM.

2. Enter the drive letter of the CD-ROM, D: for example, and press <Enter>.

3. Enter

   INSTALL and press <Enter>. Figure 9-4 is displayed.

4. Select

   Select this line to install in English and press <Enter>.

5. **Press any key 4 times** after reading each of the 4 license agreement screens.

6. Select

   Diskette Creation and press <Enter>.

7. Select type of client, **NetWare DOS/WINDOWS Client (VLM)** in this case as shown in Figure 9-5, and press <Enter>.

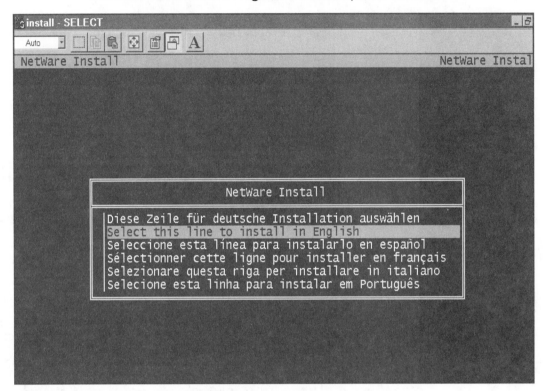

**Figure 9-4.** An initial server installation screen.

8. Enter the drive letter for the diskette drive as

   **A: and press <Enter>**.

9. Following the prompt, insert a blank formatted disk into the drive letter you entered and press any key to continue.

10. Wait while the first diskette is created. Label it as prompted as

    **NetWare Client for DOS and MS Windows Disk 1**

11. Insert a blank formatted disk into the drive letter you entered and press any key to continue.

12. Wait while the second diskette is created. Label it as prompted as

    **NetWare Client for DOS and MS Windows Disk 2**

13. Insert a blank formatted disk into the drive letter you entered and press any key to continue.

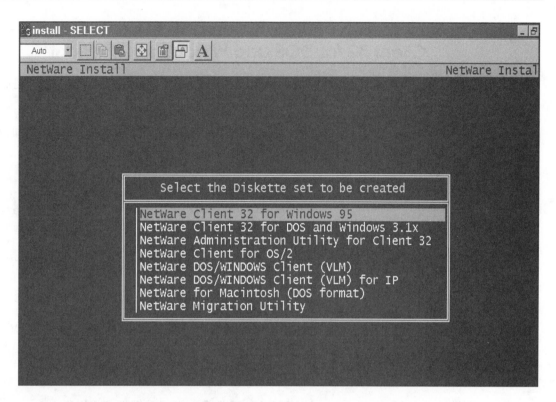

**Figure 9-5.** NetWare client diskette selection screen

14. Wait while the third diskette is created. Label it as prompted as

**NetWare Client for DOS and MS Windows Disk 3**

15. Insert a blank formatted disk into the drive letter you entered and press any key to continue.

16. Wait while the fourth diskette is created. Label it as prompted as

**NetWare Client for DOS and MS Windows Disk 4**

17. Insert a blank formatted disk into the drive letter you entered and press any key to continue.

18. Wait while the fifth diskette is created. Label it as prompted as

**NetWare Client for DOS and MS Windows Disk 5**

19. Insert a blank formatted disk into the drive letter you entered and press any key to continue.

20. Wait while the sixth diskette is created. Label it as prompted as

**NetWare Client for DOS and MS Windows ODI LAN Drivers**

Press any key to continue.

283

## To create an installation diskette set for the NetWare Client 32 for DOS and Windows 3.1x client

1. Boot a computer with a CD-ROM with a DOS diskette with drivers for the CD-ROM.

2. Enter the drive letter of the CD-ROM, D: for example, and press <Enter>.

3. Enter

   **INSTALL** and press <Enter>.

   Figure 9-4 is displayed.

4. Select

   **Select this line to install in English** and press <Enter>.

5. **Press any key 4 times** after reading each of the 4 license agreement screens.

6. Select

   **Diskette Creation** and press <Enter>.

7. Select

   **NetWare Client 32 for DOS and WINDOWS 3.1x** and press <Enter>.

8. Select

   **English diskettes** and press <Enter>.

   Note that you are prompted that you will need 8 diskettes.

9. Enter the drive letter for the diskette drive such as

   **A:** and press <Enter>.

10. Following the prompt, insert a blank formatted disk into the drive letter you entered and press any key to continue.

11. Wait while the first diskette is created. Label it as prompted as

    **NetWare Client 32 for DOS and Windows 3.1x Disk 1 DOS**

12. Repeat steps 10 and 11 noting the appropriate diskette label to write on each diskette until all diskettes have been created.

13. Press any key to quit the diskette creation process.

14. Press <Esc> to exit the installation program.

## To create an installation diskette set for the NetWare Client 32 for Windows 95 client

1. Boot a computer with a CD-ROM with a DOS diskette with drivers for the CD-ROM.

2. Enter the drive letter of the CD-ROM, D: for example, and press <Enter>.

3. Enter

   **INSTALL** and press <Enter>.

   Figure 9-4 is displayed.

4. Select

   **Select this line to install in English** and press <Enter>.

5. **Press any key 4 times** after reading each of the 4 license agreement screens.

6. Select

   **Diskette Creation** and press <Enter>.

7. Select

   **NetWare Client 32 for windows 95** and press <Enter>.

8. Select

   **English diskettes** and press <Enter>.

   Note that you are prompted that you will need 8 diskettes.

9. Enter the drive letter for the diskette drive such as

   **A:** and press <Enter>.

10. Following the prompt, insert a blank formatted disk into the drive letter you entered and press any key to continue.

11. Wait while the first diskette is created. Label it as prompted as

    **NetWare Client 32 for Windows 95 Disk 1**

12. Repeat steps 9 and 10 noting the appropriate diskette label to write on each diskette until all diskettes have been created.

13. Press any key to quit the diskette creation process.

14. Press <Esc> to exit the installation program.

# Installing the Workstation Boot Disk Using NetWare DOS Requester

## Introduction to the NetWare DOS Requester

The NetWare DOS Requester is usually installed on the hard drive of the workstation rather than on a floppy diskette. NetWare 4.11 utilizes several Windows-based utilities including its on-line documentation, Dynatext, and the NetWare DOS Requester must modify several Windows configuration files to allow Windows to function properly with these utilities. Additionally, the workstation hard drive must be prepared so that it is a bootable DOS device prior to loading the NetWare DOS Requester.

The NetWare DOS Requester utilizes the LSL (Link Support Layer), the ODI-compliant LAN driver, and IPXODI just as the DOS redirector workstation setup did. However, instead of utilizing NETX to connect the user to the network, it uses a VLM manager, often called the DOS requester, to load modular workstation routines much like NLMs that are used on the file server itself. Additionally, instead of keeping two sets of system tables as NETX did, the NetWare DOS Requester utilizes the same tables as DOS. This makes the operation of the client more efficient.

Note that the command

LASTDRIVE=Z:

must be placed in the CONFIG SYS file of the workstation so that VLMs can recognize all 26 drives and thereby make drives available to NetWare.

## Installing the NetWare DOS Requester

Reminder: Before attempting to install the NetWare DOS Requester, it is a good idea to create the diskette set for VLMs from the NetWare 4.11 Operating System Installation CD. Creation of these diskettes from a machine with a CD-ROM alleviates the need for having a CD-ROM drive on all machines in the classroom.

1. On the machine that will become the NetWare client, install DOS (version 3.3 or later) and WINDOWS 3.1. Boot the workstation by pressing Ctrl Alt Del.

2. Insert the diskette labeled Disk 1 into the diskette drive, change to the A: drive, enter INSTALL, and press ENTER.

3. The client installation screen will appear.

4. Enter **C:\NWCLIENT** for the directory in which the NetWare Client software is to be installed and **press <ENTER>**.

5. Answer **Yes** to allow for changes to the CONFIG.SYS and AUTOEXEC.BAT files for automatic loading of the workstation software and press ENTER.  Note that the previous CONFIG.SYS and AUTOEXEC.BAT files will be stored in files called CONFIG.BNW and AUTOEXEC.BNW respectively so that reclamation of these files will be possible if the client install does not go smoothly.

6. Enter **Yes** and **press <Enter>** to allow for Windows Support.

7. Enter **the name of the directory in which WINDOWS is installed**, usually C:\WINDOWS on the hard drive and press ENTER.

8. Enter **the name of the appropriate LAN driver for the network board** which is installed in the workstation.  (Note: You may need to have the driver diskette which was included with the LAN card when it was purchased or an updated driver diskette as part of this process.)

9. If the "Insert the Driver Disk" message appears, put the Disk 2 diskette indicated into the floppy diskette drive.

10. Press **<Enter>** to begin copying files to the workstation hard drive, changing diskettes as prompted.

The installation, when complete, will have inserted the LASTDRIVE=Z: command into the CONFIG.SYS file, and it will have inserted a call to a file called STARTNET.BAT in the NWCLIENT directory.  STARTNET.BAT will then set the language for NetWare and load LSL, the LAN driver, IPXODI, and will execute VLM to load the VLMs.  Remember that configuration information for the workstation is stored in NET.CFG and may need to be edited for specific equipment configuration information.

# Testing the New Boot Process

1. With the workstation cable to the network firmly installed, press the CTRL/ALT/DEL keys simultaneously to boot your workstation. Wait for LSL, the NIC driver, IPXODI, and VLM to run from the default NWCLIENT directory.

2. Type **F:** (or the first network drive) and press <ENTER>.

3. Type **LOGIN SERVERXXX\.ADMIN.TREEXXX** where SERVERXXX is the name of the file server you wish to log in and press <ENTER>.

4. Type the network administrator's password, if one has been assigned.

Note that the boot files copied to the hard disk can be copied to a diskette if desired. If desired, copy the CONFIG.SYS, AUTOEXEC.BAT, and the entire NWCLIENT directory to the diskette for backup purposes.

# Installing Client 32

## Installing Client 32 for DOS/Windows 3.1

Reminder: Before attempting to install Client 32 for DOS/Windows, it is a good idea to create the diskette set for Client 32 for DOS/Windows from the NetWare 4.11 Operating System Installation CD. Creation of these diskettes from a machine with a CD-ROM alleviates the need for having a CD-ROM drive on all machines in the classroom.

1. On the machine that will become the NetWare client, install DOS (version 3.3 or later) and WINDOWS 3.1. Boot the workstation by pressing Ctrl Alt Del.

2. Activate Windows by entering **WIN** and pressing <Enter>.

3. Insert the diskette labeled Disk 1 into the diskette drive, change to the A: drive, choose **Run A:SETUP** from the File selection on the main Windows menu bar, and click the OK button.

4. Select **English Language** and click OK.

5. Click the **Continue** button on the introductory screen.

6. After reading the license agreement, click the **Yes** button.

7. Click the **Next** button on the Directory locations box.

8. Select the appropriate 32-bit network interface card (LAN) driver for your network board. Note that the board's interrupt number, memory address, and port address must already have been configured using software from the board's manufacturer.

9. Click the **Next** button this time and the next time it is presented.

10. Wait for the installation process to finish and then select

    **Restart Computer (Recommended)** and click the OK button

11.  Wait for the station to boot and run Windows by entering **WIN.**

12.  Select **NetWare User Tools for Windows**

13.  Click the **NetWare Settings** button and click the **Startup tab**

14.  Click **Launch at startup.**

15.  Click the **Login tab**

16.  Click the following selections:

> **Display Connection Page**
>
> **Display Script Page**
>
> **Run login scripts**
>
> **Close on exit**
>
> **Display Variables Page**
>
> **Restore Permanent Connections**

17.  Click the OK button

18.  Click the **Exit Door (upper left button on screen)** to exit NetWare User Tools for Windows

19.  Reboot the computer.

# Testing the New Boot Process with Client 32 for Windows 3.1

1.  With the workstation cable to the network firmly installed, press the CTRL/ALT/DEL keys simultaneously to boot your workstation. Wait for the station to boot and for the client software to run.

2.  When prompted, enter .ADMIN.TREEXXX for the user ID on the login tab and the password in the password box. Click on the Connections tab to make sure that the desired server is entered in the connections box as shown in Figure 9-6.

3.  Click the OK button to complete the login process. NetWare drives should now be accessible through the File Manager in Windows 3.1.

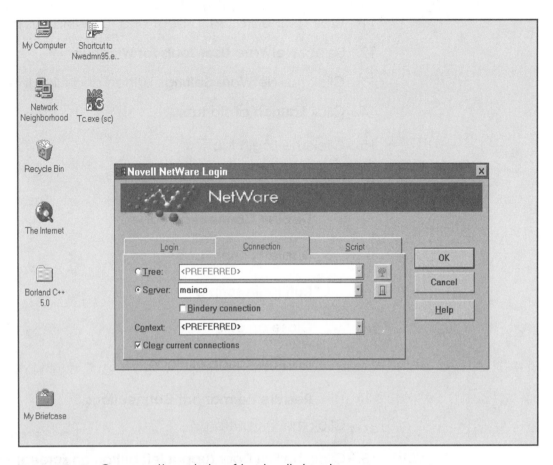

**Figure 9-6.** Connections tab of login dialog box

# Installing the Client 32 for Windows 95

Reminder: Before attempting to install Client 32 for Windows 95, it is a good idea to create the diskette set for Client 32 for Windows 95 from the NetWare 4.11 Operating System Installation CD. Creation of these diskettes from a machine with a CD-ROM alleviates the need for having a CD-ROM drive on all machines in the classroom.

1. On the machine that will become the NetWare client, install Windows 95. Boot the workstation by turning it on or by clicking on Shut Down and then Restart Computer.

2. Insert the diskette labeled Disk 1 into the diskette drive, change to the A: drive, and choose **Run A:SETUP** from the Start Menu Run selection.

3. After reading the license agreement, click the **Yes** button as shown in Figure 9-7.

4. Click **Do not upgrade your NDIS drives to ODI automatically**.

5. Click the Start button to begin installation as shown in Figure 9-8. Installation will automatically proceed without intervention.

6. When the installation is complete, click on the Customize button.

7. Select Novell NetWare Client 32 and then Properties.

8. Enter the name of the preferred server. Set the first network drive to the appropriate letter, probably F:.

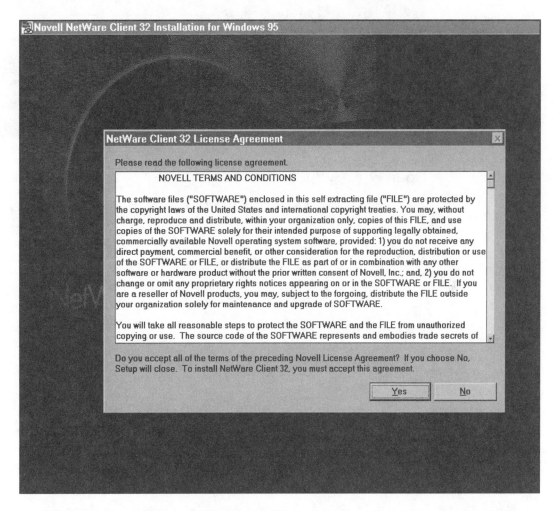

**Figure 9-7.** Windows 95 Client 32 installation license agreement.

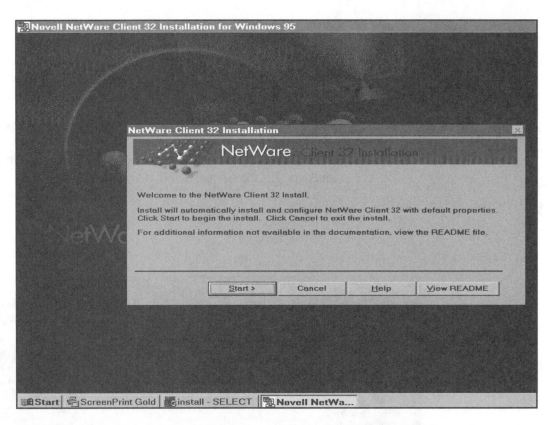

**Figure 9-8.** Actual start of Windows 95 Client32 installation

9. Click **Login** and make sure that the following selections are chosen:

>   **Display Connection Page**
>
>   **Display Script Page**
>
>   **Run login scripts**
>
>   **Close on exit**
>
>   **Save settings when exiting Login**

10. Click the **OK** button and then click the **OK** button again.

11. Click the **YES** button to reboot your computer.

## Testing the New Boot Process with Client 32 for Windows 95

1. Boot your Windows 95 station by either turning it on if it is off or by clicking on Shut Down and then Restart Computer if Windows 95 is already active.

2. When prompted, enter .**ADMIN.TREEXXX** for the user ID on the login tab and the password in the password box. Click on the Connections tab to make sure that the desired server is entered in the connections box.

3. Click the OK button to complete the login process. NetWare drives should now be accessible through the Explorer and through My Computer on Windows 95.

# Summary

The installation process for the NetWare 4 server gets easier with each new edition of NetWare. In this chapter you learned that NetWare 4 can be installed by either the simple or the custom installation method, and you learned the strict requirements for performing a simple installation. You learned the background information needed for a successful installation, and you performed the installation.

NetWare 4.11 supports a variety of clients. Using the installation CD-ROM disk, diskette sets can be created for the VLM client, as well as the Client 32 clients for DOS/Windows and Windows 95. You also learned how to install and test each of these clients.

# Questions

1. What is an enterprise-wide network and how does it differ from a single-server network?

2. What are the minimum hardware requirements for installing NetWare 4.11?

3. What are the minimum software requirements for installing NetWare 4.11?

4. What is SERVER.EXE? How can is be customized for a particular server?

5. What is the Internal IPX Network Number?

6. What is the network number (External IPX number)? How must this number be unique?

7. What are the requirements for a simple NetWare 4.11 install?

8. Why is it necessary to install a bootable DOS partition on the NetWare 4.11 server?

9. What is held in the NWSERVER directory after NetWare 4.11 is installed?

10. What is the difference between IPX.COM/NET#.COM and the VLM client?

11. What is the difference between the VLM client and Client 32 for DOS/Windows 3.1?

12. Is it necessary to have a CD-ROM on every workstation in a NetWare 4.11 network? Why or why not?

13. What is the purpose of the Open Data Link Interface model?

14. How can you determine that a NetWare 4.11 server has been properly installed?

15. How are the interrupt number, memory address, and port address used for interfacing a network interface card with a NetWare 4.11 server?

# Project

## Objective

There are usually multiple servers in a NetWare 4.11 network. The purpose of this project is to install a second server on top of half of the NDS directory trees created in the Hands-On section of this chapter. This exercise requires more thought than many of the projects in this book.

Outline:

1. For every second server in the classroom, go to the server console and enter

   **DOWN** and press <Enter>

   Wait for the server to go down and then enter

   **EXIT** and press <enter>

2. On the "downed" server, boot the machine with the DOS bootable diskette, and use FDISK to remove all the partitions on the hard drive.

3. Repeat the simple installation process, including the creation of the DOS bootable partition, and when prompted for the tree name into which to install, select the tree name of your partner's NDS tree. After this project, each tree will contain two servers.

# 10
# Novell Directory Services

## Objectives

After completing this chapter you will

1. Understand the architecture of Novell Directory Services.

2. Be able to describe the major feature and benefits of Novell Directory Services in an enterprise networking environment.

3. Understand the major components of NDS.

4. Understand NDS naming conventions.

5. Be able to create a Windows 3.1x or Windows 95 icon for NetWare Administrator utility.

## Key Terms

Objects

Properties

Single Login

Enterprise Network

Values

Container

Country Object

Organization Object

Organizational Unit Object

Leaf Object

Common Name

Distinguished Name

Relative Distinguished Name

NetWare Administrator

NETADMIN

CX

# Introduction

Although Novell NetWare version 4 can be used to serve the needs of the small company using a single file server, NetWare 4 was actually created to serve the needs of a large company or even a global company utilizing multiple file servers connected by both local area and wide area networking media.  As such, NetWare 4 is described as an enterprise system.  With NetWare 3 and earlier versions of NetWare, companies could utilize multiple file servers, but each user had to be set up with a unique user account for each file server.  Thus, network administration in this multiple file server environment was difficult, to say the least.

With NetWare 4 came the advent of the enterprise-wide single log in for each user through the use of Novell Directory Services and the Novell Directory Services tree concept.  The purpose of this chapter is to explain the architecture of NDS and how it is used to support an enterprise-wide network.  The chapter also explains the naming conventions for objects in the NDS tree and will examine several utilities used with NDS.  Finally, it will present hands-on exercises on how to create an icon for NetWare Administrator on both Windows 3.1 and Windows 95.

## Overview of NDS

Novell Directory Services (NDS) is a directory naming service provided by Novell as a part of all Novell NetWare 4 network operating systems. NDS keeps a directory of all network components ranging from users to file servers to printers.  Each of the network components is called an **object** in NDS, and each object has **properties** or characteristics specific to the type of object.  The entire database of network components and their values is organized into a hierarchical configuration, which is  referred to as the NDS tree.

All users on all NetWare 4 servers in a single NDS database or tree have access to all the network resources in the tree, depending on NDS object trustee assignments, which are assigned to the user. This means that a user can have a **single login** ID and be granted rights to any NDS object in the tree and to the file system on any of the file servers that are a part of the tree.

NDS is a single global database that supports centralized management of network resources for an **enterprise network**.  Additionally, it provides for a logical organization of network resources, which is independent of the physical location of network resources. NetWare 4 provides a series of utilities to view the components of the NDS tree for ease of maintenance. Most importantly, though, NDS allows a single user log in to provide access to all the network resources that the user needs.

NDS consists of several types of architectural components that are generically called objects. Each of these objects has characteristics called properties, and each property can then have one or more **values**. In general, objects are such things as users, printers, file servers, etc., which have characteristics or properties that are particular to the type of object. For example, a user would have a name, a password, etc., while a printer would have a name, a print queue assignment, etc. The value of a property is the actual current worth of a specific characteristic. For example, a user might be named John, and thus, the value of the name property for that user would be John. Refer to Figure 10-1 for an example of the properties and values assigned to the user John as compared to the properties and values assigned to the file server SERVER1.

**USER OBJECT - John**

| Property | Value |
|----------|-------|
| Name | John |
| Title | Manager Accountant |
| Password | novell |

**Server Object - SERVER1**

| Property | Object |
|----------|--------|
| Name | SERVER1 |
| Location | First Floor Computer Room |
| Net Address | 332C4603: 000000000001: 0451 |

**Figure 10-1.** Properties and values of a user object and a server object.

# NDS Architecture Overview

An NDS tree consists of various types of objects originating from an object called (ROOT). Additionally, an NDS tree can consist of various container and leaf objects as shown in Figure 10-2.

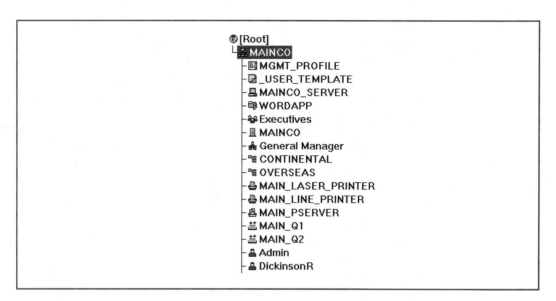

**Figure 10-2.** A sample NDS tree.

# (ROOT)

The (ROOT) object is the highest level in the NDS tree and ultimately provides access to all other objects in the tree. There is only one (ROOT) in any NDS tree, and it cannot be moved, deleted, or renamed. It can contain only Country, Organization, and Alias objects pointing to Country or Organization objects. These objects are explained below.

# Container Objects

A **container** object is a grouping object that exists for the purpose of organizing other objects in the NDS directory tree. There are three types of container objects besides the (ROOT), which is the ultimate container object, containing everything in the NDS tree.

The three types of containers are:

**Country Object**

**Organization Object**

**Organizational Unit Object**

Each of these objects is explained below.

## Country Object

The Country object is used to indicate the country where the network resides. The object is used to organize other NDS directory objects within the country. When used, this object must be a valid two-character country code. However, since use of the object is optional and since over time it has become apparent that many companies do not organize along country boundaries, the use of the Country code is not widespread. In fact, this object is rarely used in NetWare 4 designs.

## Organization

Every NDS directory tree must have at least one **organization object**. This object represents the highest level in the NDS directory tree beneath (ROOT) and can represent the entire company. Alternately, a company may have multiple divisions or organizations at the top and therefore would have multiple organization objects at the top of the tree. This object can contain leaf objects or Organizational Units. It can also contain alias objects, which point to other Organizational Units or leaf objects.

## Organizational Unit

An **organizational unit** represents a subdivision of the company, perhaps a division, a department, or a workgroup. It can be contained in an Organization or in another Organizational Unit. It can also contain leaf objects and alias objects pointing to other leaf objects or Organizational Units. The purpose of the Organizational Unit is to subdivide the company from an organizational viewpoint.

## Leaf Objects

The actual resources in a network are called **leaf objects**. These include such things as users, printers, computers, servers, volumes on servers, print queues, etc.

A list of the available container and leaf objects and their definition is shown in Figure 10-3.

## Putting the Objects Together

Using the object definitions and rules given earlier in this chapter a particular NDS directory tree might look like the tree in Figure 10-4. In this tree, the company has

One Organization Object called MAINCO.

Main divisions called CONTINENTAL and OVERSEAS represented by Organizational Units.

The CONTINENTAL Organization Unit is further subdivided into NY, SANFRAN, and DALLAS Organizational Units. OVERSEAS is further subdivided into LONDON and FRANKFURT organizational units. Each Organizational Unit contains leaf objects appropriate to the workings of the company.

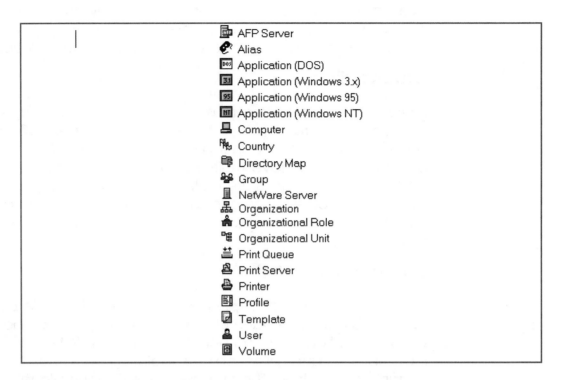

**Figure 10-3.** Container and Leaf Objects

# Naming Conventions

Just as one must understand the directory naming conventions of DOS in order to handle DOS operations, the network administrator must understand the NDS directory object naming conventions in order to successfully work with objects in an NDS tree. In order to understand the naming conventions themselves, we must first discuss the concepts of context, current context, common name, distinguished name, and relative distinguished name.

## Context

The context of an object is the NDS name of the container containing the object. It lists the containers from the container in question back to the (ROOT). The context of an object does not change regardless of who is viewing the NDS directory tree or what container is currently being viewed.

The context of the user MannS is the Accounting container, and the Accounting container's distinguished name is

**Accounting.DALLAS.CONTINENTAL.MAINCO**

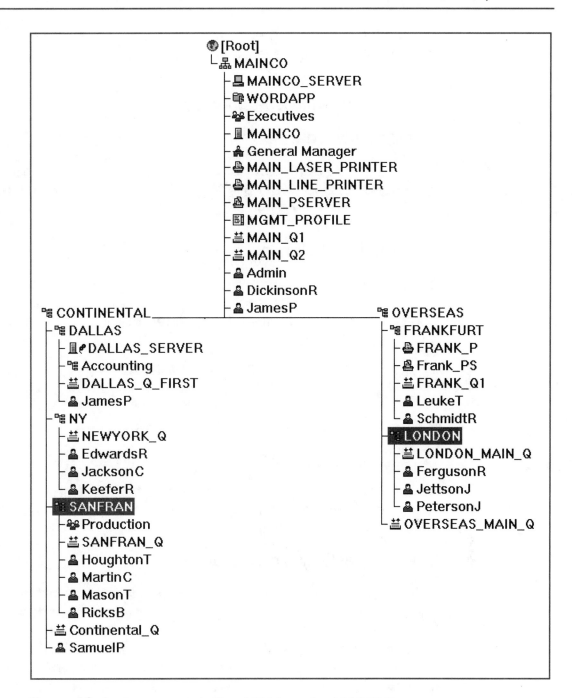

**Figure 10-4.** A representative NDS tree for MAINCO

## Current Context

Current context is the name of the container that the person logged in and viewing the NDS directory tree is currently viewing. The current context varies by what portion of the NDS directory tree is being viewed. It lists the containers from the current container being viewed back to the (ROOT). To determine the current context, one can enter CX from the command line through either DOS or Windows 95.

For example, if the user's current context were the DALLAS container, the following would be displayed when the CX command is entered at the command prompt:

**.DALLAS.CONTINENTAL.MAINCO**

## Common Name

A leaf object's **common name** is simply the name of the object. The common name for MannS in the Accounting container is just

**MannS**

## Distinguished Name

The **distinguished name** for an object begins with a period and contains the common name of the object and the name of the object's context.  For example, the distinguished name of JamesP in Figure 10-4 is

**.JamesP.DALLAS.CONTINENTAL.MAINCO**

The distinguished name of the Accounting container in Figure 10-4 is

**.Accounting.DALLAS.CONTINENTAL.MAINCO**

Note that each distinguished name must begin with a period.  The distinguished name for an object fully and uniquely identifies the NDS object in the NDS tree.

## Relative Distinguished Name

An object's **relative distinguished name** varies with the current context. It lists the name of the object and the containers from the object's context, which when combined with the fully distinguished name of the current context yields the fully distinguished name of the object.  For example, if the current context were O=CONTINENTAL, the relative distinguished name for SamuelP, a user object in the CONTINENTAL Organization, is merely SamuelP.  The relative distinguished name for Mason, a user in the SANFRAN Organizational Unit, is MASON.SANFRAN, given the current context is O=CONTINENTAL.

The rules for forming a relative distinguished name are:

A relative distinguished name never begins with a period.

A relative distinguished name, when appended with the distinguished name of the current context and when preceded by a period, forms the distinguished name of the original object.

Each trailing period on the right of a relative distinguished name removes one container from the left of the current context.

For example, the relative distinguished name for MannS considering the current context is the DALLAS container is determined as follows:

First determine the distinguished name for MannS:

**.MannS.Accounting.DALLAS.CONTINENTAL.MAINCO**

Then, determine the distinguished name for the current context:

**.DALLAS.CONTINENTAL.MAINCO**

The relative distinguished name is determined by calculating the part of the distinguished name for MannS not contained in the current context:

**MannS.Accounting**

The relative distinguished name for PetersonJ in the LONDON container, assuming the current context is the LONDON container, is determined the same way:

First, the distinguished name for PetersonJ is

**.PetersonJ.LONDON.OVERSEAS.MAINCO**

Then, the distinguished name for the LONDON container is determined:

**.LONDON.OVERSEAS.MAINCO**

The relative distinguished name for PetersonJ is therefore just

**PetersonJ**

Now consider determining a somewhat more difficult relative distinguished name. Consider PetersonJ's relative distinguished name considering the current context is the DALLAS container.

First, the distinguished name for Peterson J is

**.PetersonJ.LONDON.OVERSEAS.MAINCO**

The distinguished name for DALLAS is

**.DALLAS.CONTINENTAL.MAINCO**

Therefore, the relative distinguished name for PetersonJ is

**PetersonJ.LONDON.OVERSEAS..**

Note that the two periods at the right of the relative distinguished name remove two containers from the left of the distinguished name of the current context.

# Utilities For Managing and Manipulating NDS

Novell provides three main utilities for managing and manipulating NDS. They are

**NetWare Administrator**

**NETADMIN**

**CX**

**NetWare Administrator** is a graphical user interface that runs under Windows 3.1s and Windows 95. There is also a version of NetWare Administrator for Windows NT. This textbook will focus on Windows 3.1 and Windows 95 because of their wide popularity as clients in NetWare 4 networks. Figure 10-5 shows NetWare Administrator's view of the NDS tree for the MAINCO company.

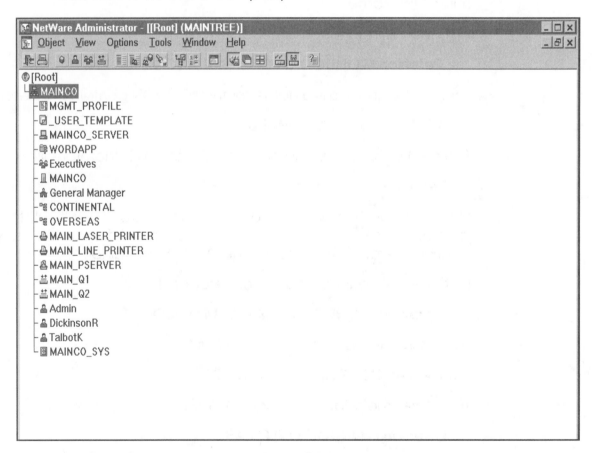

**Figure 10-5.** NetWare Administrator view of MAINCO NDS tree.

**NETADMIN** is a DOS text-base menu type utility that provides many of the same functions as NetWare Administrator. It was popular during the earlier days of NetWare 4 because of the general lack of widespread use of Windows. Figure 10-6 shows NETADMIN's view of the NDS tree for the MAINCO company. NETADMIN is no longer popular and will not be covered further in this textbook.

**CX** is a command line utility that can be used to display the user's current context and to navigate NDS. CX will be used throughout the text from time to time for convenience. If the user's current context were .DALLAS.MAINCO, the following would be displayed when the user enters the command CX at the command prompt:

**.DALLAS.MAINCO**

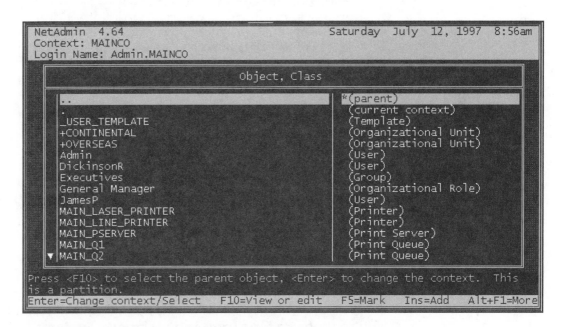

**Figure 10-6.** NetADMIN view of MAINCO NDS tree.

# NetWare Administrator

As previously mentioned, versions of NetWare Administrator are available for both Windows 3.1 and Windows 95. The following hands-on exercises will illustrate how to create an icon for NetWare Administrator.

# Hands-On Creating an Icon for NetWare Administrator in Windows 3.1

1. Boot the computer. (Consult your instructor for specifics about booting your computer. In general, this is accomplished by simultaneously pressing the Ctrl, Alt, and Del keys.)

2.  Log into your NetWare 4 server with your user ID and password, which were assigned by your instructor.

3.  Activate Windows.  (Again consult your instructor for specific instructions.  Generally, Windows 3.1 can be activated by entering WIN and pressing the <Enter> key.)

4.  Click on the **Windows** selection on the main Windows menu bar and then highlight the   **NetWare Window** to bring this window into focus.

5.  Click on the **Name box**  and enter **NetWare Administrator.**

6.  Click on the **Command box** and then click on the **Browse button** and locate **NWADM3X.EXE** in the PUBLIC directory on the SYS volume of the server.  (This is likely to be on drive letter Z: but it may be in another location.  Consult your instructor.)

7.  Click on the **OK button** to complete the function,

The NetWare Administrator Icon should now appear on the screen.

## Hands-On Creating an Icon for NetWare Administrator on the Desktop  in Windows 95

1.  Bring up the computer in Windows 95.  (Consult your instructor for specifics for brining up Windows 95.  In general, it is merely necessary to turn on the computer, but different lab setups may require different use interaction.)

2.  Log into your NetWare 4 server with your user ID and password, which were assigned by your instructor.

3.  Activate Windows Explorer  by clicking on the **Start button**, then the **Program icon**, and then **Windows Explorer**.

4.  Locate **the drive that is mapped to the SYS volume of your file server**.  Click it open.

5.  Locate **the PUBLIC** directory and click it open.

6.  Locate **the NWADMN95.EXE** program and **drag and drop it onto the desktop**.

A shortcut to  NetWare Adminstrator is now shown on the desktop.

# Summary

NetWare 4 is described as an enterprise system, providing a single log on for each user, which can be configured to grant the user access to resources on multiple servers and to NDS itself. The NDS tree structure is the architectural component that makes the single log on possible.

NDS is a series of containers and leaf objects that represent the functional network. The naming convention for NDS relies on two types of names: the distinguished name and the relative distinguished name. Each of these names requires a knowledge of context and current context in order to form or interpret NDS names.

This chapter explained the architecture of NDS and how it is used to support an enterprise-wide network. The chapter also explained the NDS naming conventions for objects in the NDS tree. It also presented an exercise in which you created an icon on the desktop for NetWare Administrator, the NetWare 4.11 account and resource administration tool.

# Questions

1. Identify the components of an NDS directory.

2. How does the NDS directory support a single user log in?

3. What is an object? What are examples of objects?

4. What are properties of objects? What are values of properties? Give an example of properties and values of properties for a user named Peter Jensen and a print queue named MAIN-CO_Q.

5. What is a country object and why is it not often used?

6. What is an organization object and what kinds of objects can it contain?

7. What is an organizational unit object and what kinds of objects can it contain?

8. What is a leaf object? List and explain at least five types of leaf objects.

9. What is an NDS tree?

10. What is the (ROOT) of an NDS tree?

11. What is the distinguished name for MartinC in Figure 10-4?

12. What is the distinguished name for JamesP in Figure 10-4?

13. What is the relative distinguished name for JamesP in Figure 10-4, assuming current context is the CONTINENTAL container?

14. What is the relative distinguished name for MartinC in Figure 10-4 assuming current context is the Accounting container?

15. What is the relative distinguished name for the DALLAS container in Figure 10-4 assuming current context is the OVERSEAS container?

# Project

## Objective

The purpose of this project is to give the student more practice in determining distinguished and relative distinguished names. The exercise utilizes the Directory tree in Figure 10-4:

### Part I:

Give the distinguished name for each of the following:

1. FergusonR in the FRANKFURT container.

2. JettsonJ in the LONDON container.

3. RicksB in the SANFRAN container.

4. NEWYORK_Q in the NY container.

5. MAIN_PSERVER in the MAINCO container.

6. FRANK_PS in the FRANKFURT container.

7. MartinC in the SANFRAN container.

8. EDWARDSR in the NY container.

9. The Accounting container in the Dallas container.

10. MAIN_Q in the MAINCO container.

## Part II:

Give the relative distinguished name for each of the following assuming the current context indicated.

| Object | Current Context |
|---|---|
| FergusonR | OVERSEAS |
| KeeferR | LONDON |
| EdwardsR | CONTINENTAL |
| MAIN_PSERVER | LONDON |
| Continental_Q | LONDON |
| FRANK_Q1 | OVERSEAS |
| FRANK_Q1 | SANFRAN |
| DALLAS | LONDON |
| LeukeT | LONDON |
| MasonT | FRANKFURT |

# 11

# Creating the User Account, Mappings and Login Scripts

## Objectives

After completing this chapter you will

1. Understand how to use NetWare Administrator to create user accounts.

2. Understand the functions of each of the main option buttons for a user object.

3. Be able to define and understand the purpose of each of the four types of login scripts.

4. Understand login script commands.

5. Understand how to use login script variables.

6. Understand how to map network and search drives.

7. Be able to log in and log out of a file server.

## Key Terms

File Server

Login Restrictions

Password Restrictions

Login Time Restrictions

Network Address Restrictions

Intruder Lockout

Group

Security Equal To

Postal Address

Login Script

Container Login Script

Profile Login Script

User Login Script

# Introduction

In the last chapter, Novell NetWare was installed on the **file server** and the workstation was booted with the network workstation software. That arrangement allowed the user Admin, the administrator for the network, to log in to the file server and view the files listed there. Now the file server must be set up to allow other users to log in and easily manage their files and directories.

NetWare 4.11's major system configuration utility is NetWare Administrator. Using this utility, the Admin can begin to create user accounts, groups of user accounts, and other types of objects introduced in the last chapter. Each account or group can have different access rights, legal login times, and other attributes. Many of the controls used to set up the user's environment are executed when the user logs in through the use of a login script. It can set the user's drive mappings, check various conditions at the time the user logs in, and write messages to the screen.

# NetWare Administrator

## Introduction

NetWare Administrator, NWAdmin, allows the network administrators to create, change, and delete users and groups of users in addition to enabling many other functions. It is by far the most important utility Novell provides with NetWare 4.11 since it used to set up the most fundamental aspects of the network. As with many NetWare utilities, some menu options only appear for the Admin. Users can choose other limited menu options themselves to view and change their own accounts. Figure 11-1 shows NetWare Administrator's main screen.

## Creation of a User Account

To create a user one would

1. Click on the container to contain the user. You should create for yourself an Administrator equivalent account that you can use throughout the course.

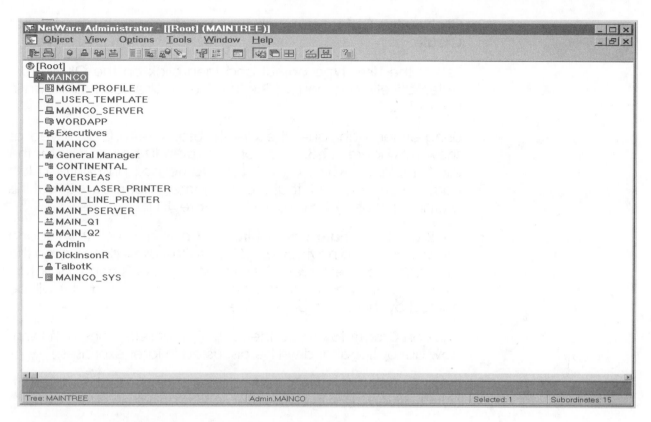

Figure 11-1. NetWare Administrator main screen.

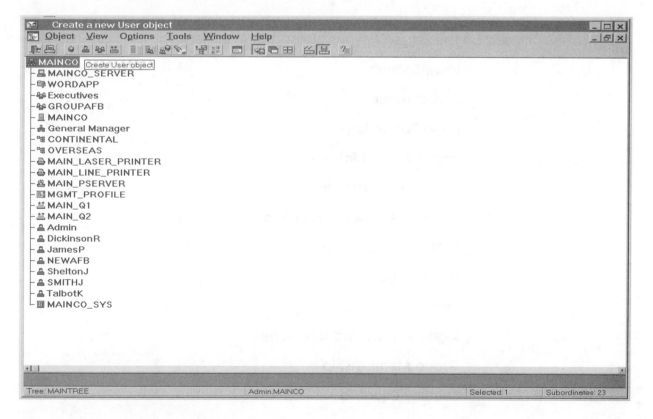

Figure 11-2. Selecting the Create User icon.

2. Click on the **Object** selection from the top menu bar and select **Create**.

3. Select the **User type object** and then click on the **OK** button. (Alternatively, one could click the Create User icon as shown in Figure 11-2.)

4. Using either technique, the Create User screen is displayed as shown in Figure 11-3. Click on the **Login ID box** and enter the user's login ID. Click on the **Last Name** box and enter a last name. You may think that the last name is not required, but it is a critical property for a user in NetWare 4.11.

5. Click on the **Create Home Directory** box and use the second browse button to navigate and locate the Users directory on the SYS volume of the server. By default, the user's home directory will be created beneath the directory indicated, and it will be named by the user's login name.

6. Click on **Create** to create the user. (Other selections in this window are optional and will be discussed in later exercises.)

7. Locate the new user just created and double click it. (Alternatively, right click the user object and then select details.)

8. A screen such as the one shown in Figure 11-4 is displayed.

The selection buttons on the right-hand side of the screen can vary based on the Page Options chosen, but, in general, they are as follows:

**Identification**

**Environment**

**Login Restrictions**

**Password Restrictions**

**Login Time Restrictions**

**Network Address Restriction**

**Print Job Configuration**

**Login Script**

**Intruder Lockout**

**Rights to Files and Directories**

**Group Membership**

**Security Equal To**

**Postal Address**

**Account Balance***

**See Also***

**Applications***

**Launcher Configuration***

**NetWare Registry Editor***

Note that the starred items will not be discussed as part of this introductory course. Each of the other topics will be explained before a hands-on session.

Each of the pertinent buttons listed above will be discussed as preparation for a hands-on exercise to allow the student to create his or her own user account.

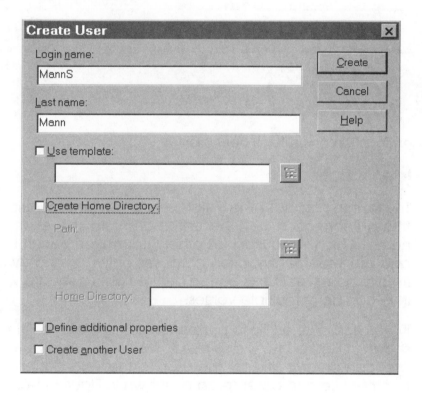

**Figure 11-3.** Create a new user screen.

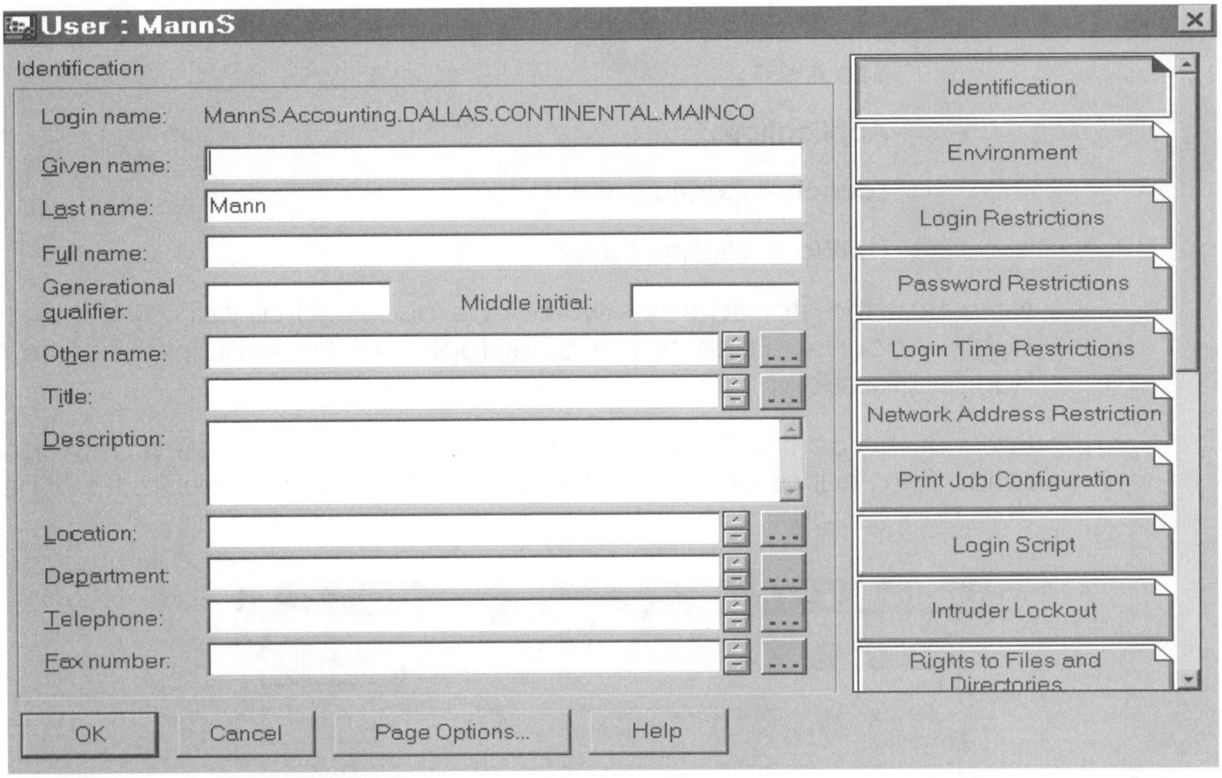

**Figure 11-4.** Identification page for a new user.

### Identification

This button produces the initial user screen where various types of identifying information can be entered. With the exception of the last name, which is required, all other information on this screen is optional and used for identification purposes only. It is noteworthy that each item that has an Ellipsis button on the right (a square with three periods in it) can have multiple values.

If we click on the Ellipsis button to the right of the Title line, the screen shown in Figure 11-5 is displayed. When the Add button is clicked, the user can enter a title for the user. If the Add button is clicked again, another title can be entered as shown in Figure 11-6. Then, when the OK button is clicked, the main identification screen is once again displayed. The two titles can alternately be displayed by clicking the up or the down arrow to the right of the title field.

### Environment

The Environment page shows particulars about the user's operating environment as shown in Figure 11-7. Most notable for the beginning student is the specification for the user's home directory, a designation that can be changed from this screen if necessary.

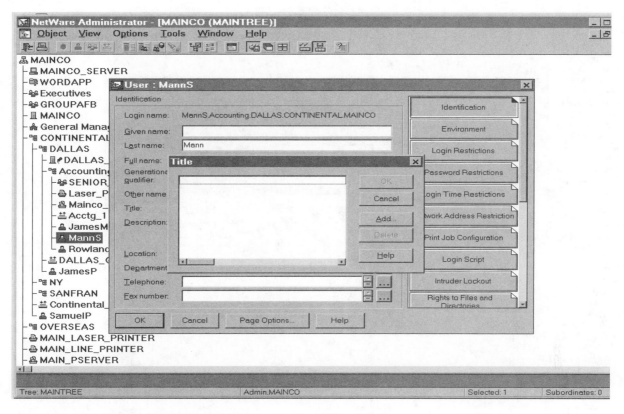

**Figure 11-5.** Using the Ellipsis button on the Title field.

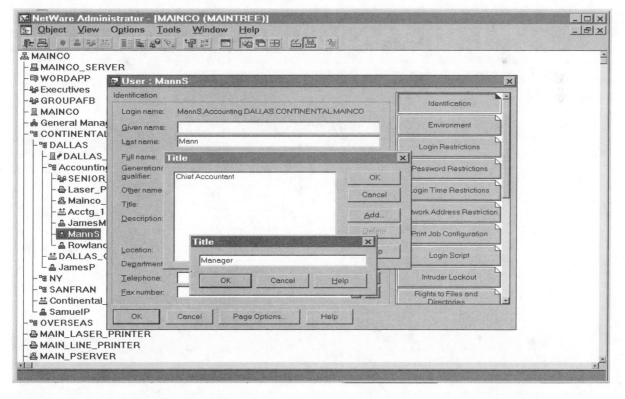

**Figure 11-6.** Adding a new title.

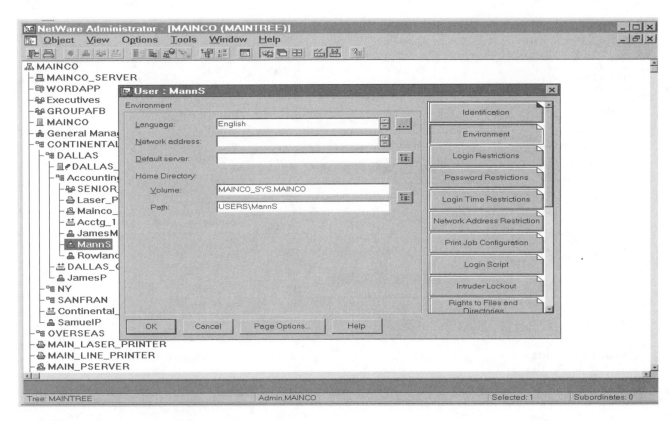

**Figure 11-7.** The Environment page for a user.

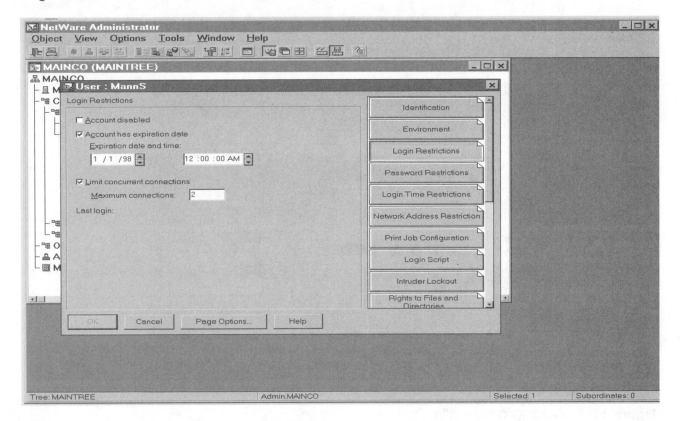

**Figure 11-8.** The Login Restrictions page.

## Login Restrictions

The **login restrictions** page is shown in Figure 11-8. This page allows the administrator to disable the account, to set an expiration date for the account, and to limit concurrent connections.

The Account Disabled option is most often used to disable an account for a person who no longer works for the company. In most cases, it is important that the account merely be disabled rather than being deleted so that the structure and access rights that the person was using can be retained until someone else can take his or her job. Additionally, this feature can be used to allow the Administrator to create an account for a new employee but to leave it deactivated until the employee reports for work.

The Account expiration date should be set for temporary or contract employees so that the Administrator does not have to remember to deactivate these users' accounts when the user no longer works for the company. If the user's contract is extended, all the Administrator need do is to change the expiration date so that the user can once again use the account.

The Limit Concurrent Connections option is used to keep a user from using the same login ID in many places throughout the company simultaneously. There are several reasons for wanting to limit a user's simultaneous connections. Most important is that several applications utilize the user's login name to identify temporary files the application has to create in normal processing. If the user is logged in from multiple stations, there is a good chance that duplicate temporary files may be created and that they may collide. Additionally, many usage statistics are kept by user ID. Therefore, if a single user is using his or her ID at multiple stations on a regular basis, these statistics will be skewed. If the user really needs additional accounts for business reasons, the administrator can easily create additional separate accounts for the user, thus avoiding clashes.

## Password Restrictions

The **Password Restrictions** page is shown in Figure 11-9. The information on this page is fully discussed in the next chapter and will therefore be omitted here.

## Login Time Restrictions

The **Login Time Restrictions** page is shown in Figure 11-10. It can be used to block the user from logging in by boxing the desired block-out time with the mouse and then clicking the OK button. The Login Time

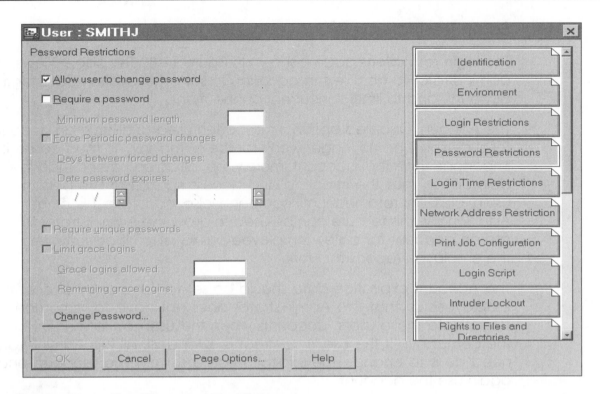

**Figure 11-9.** The Password Restrictions page.

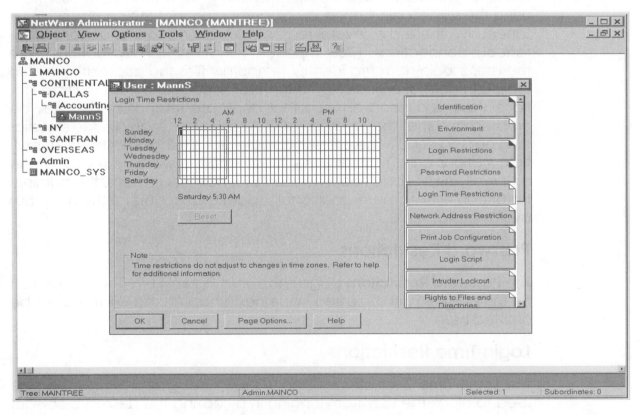

**Figure 11-10.** The Login Time Restrictions page.

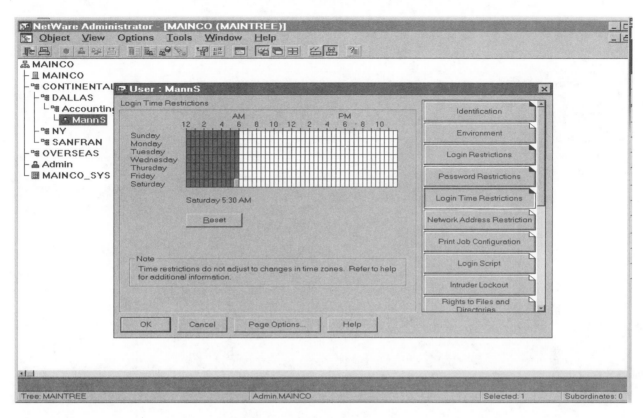

**Figure 11-11.** The Login Time Restrictions page with midnight to 6 a.m. excluded.

Restrictions screen is shown in 30 minute increments, 24 hours per day, 7 days per week. Figure 11-11 shows the login restrictions being set for user MannS who cannot log in from 12 midnight until 6 a.m. seven days per week.

## Network Address Restriction

The **Network Address Restriction** page is shown in Figure 11-12. This page can be used to limit the physical stations that a user can use for logging in and to limit the protocols that the user can use from the station. Except in highly secure organizations, implementation of this restriction can cause more harm than good because it makes it impossible for a user to automatically use another station within the company if his or her station is inoperable.

## Print Job Configuration

This page is discussed in Chapter 13 and will not be discussed here.

## Login Script

This page contains information about the user's login script, and it allows the administrator to cause a profile login script to be executed

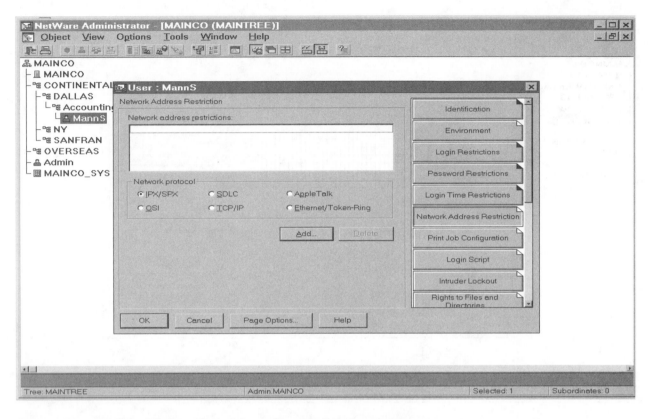

**Figure 11-12.** The Network Address Restrictions page.

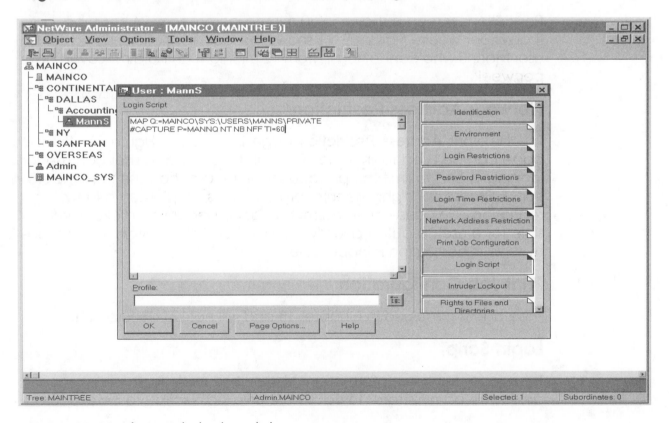

**Figure 11-13.** A sample login script.

for the user. A sample user login script is shown in Figure 11-13. A more complete discussion of login scripts and their usages is contained in the latter part of this chapter.

## Intruder Lockout

This screen reports whether or not the user's account is locked out. The administrator can unlock the account by deselecting the Account locked box on the screen.

**Intruder lockout** parameters are set by container and pertain to all users in a given container. For example, a user's account can be locked if he or she uses a correct login name but an incorrect password for a particular number of times during a particular period of time. Then the account will be locked for the time indicated. All these parameters can be set for the container. In general, intruder detection is meant to keep illegal users from hacking into a system.

## Rights to Files and Directories

This page, shown in Figure 11-14, is used to grant and see trustee rights assigned to a user. This page is fully discussed in Chapter 12 and is therefore omitted here.

## Group Membership

Users are generally not totally unique although they usually think they are. Their needs often can be grouped according to their job functions. Therefore, rights can be assigned to a **group** and users can be placed in the group instead of assigning individual users specific directory and file system rights to each area of the server they need to access. The group membership screen shows which groups the user is a member of and allows the administrator to assign the user to additional groups by utilizing the Add button function. Figure 11-15 shows the Group Membership page.

## Security Equal To

The **security equal to** page shows which users and groups that this user is security equivalent to. This means that this user can do the same things and have the same rights and privileges as all those to which the user is security equivalent. Using security equivalence is not something that should be widely done. If the user to which this user is security equivalent is deleted, and if that user were providing the new user with necessary rights, the new user would be nonfunctional.

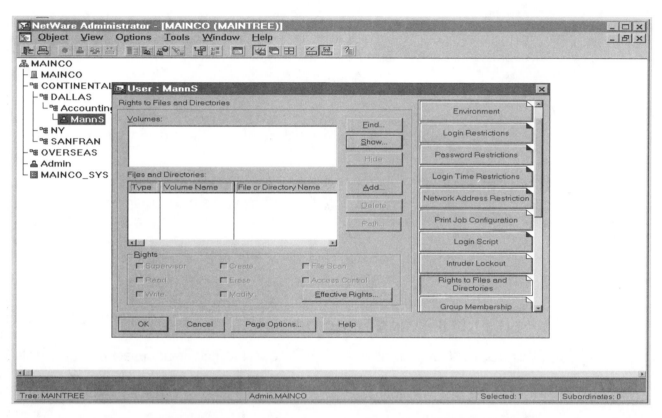

**Figure 11-14.** The Rights to Files and Directories page.

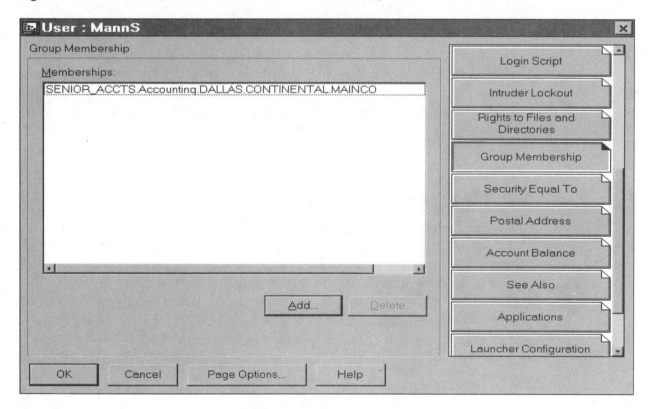

**Figure 11-15.** The Group Membership page.

### Postal Address

The **Postal Address** page contains name and address information that can be used for mailing lists, etc.

### Login Scripts

NetWare 4.11 allows each user name to have a **login script** that establishes much of the user's environment each time he or she logs in. Figure 11-16 shows the login script editor within NetWare Administrator for the user's login script. Netware Administrator provides the Admin with a simple editor similar to a text editor for creating and modifying login scripts. This login script performs several mapping operations such as mapping the \SOFTWARE\DATA directory to appear as the root directory of drive I. A message is displayed to the user, and finally the EXIT command sends a command to DOS to display a directory listing. All of these commands are executed each time the user GUEST logs in.

NetWare 4.11 does not require each user to have a login script since the Admin can set a container-wide login script in a container object, which acts as a type of system login script every time a user in the container logs in.

# Login Scripts

As mentioned earlier, every time a user logs in, NetWare is capable of running one to three login scripts for the user. The function of these login scripts is to issue all the commands needed to set up the user's environment. The environment, in this case, refers primarily to the drive mappings created for the user, but there are many other commands available in login scripts for customizing the log in.

NetWare 4.11 provides 4 types of login scripts:

**Container login script**

**Profile login script**

**User login script**

**Default login script**

# Container Login Script

The **container login script** is used to set up the environment for all users in a given container. The container login script runs first for all users in a container. This login script is set up by accessing the details for the container object, clicking the Login Script button, and then entering the appropriate login script commands. It is important to remember that all the commands placed in the container login script are executed for all users in the container.

# Profile Login Script

Netware 4.11 provides a **profile** or group type **login script** through a profile object. The profile object has a login script property like the login script property for the user. Login script commands meant to be used by users in a particular functional category or group can be entered for the profile object. Then, the profile object's login script can be tied to execute for the user just after the container login script by entering the name of the profile object on the Login Script Properties page of the user. For example, user JamesM is set to execute the profile login script from the profile object Executives because the name of the profile object is entered into the appropriate box in Figure 11-16. The profile login script, if one exists, is executed immediately after the container login script.

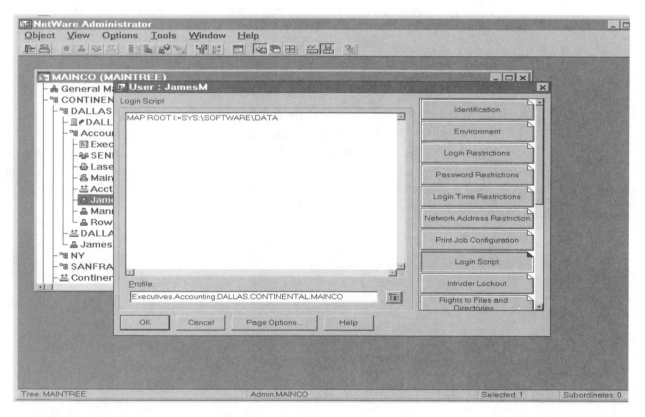

**Figure 11-16.** Assigning a profile login script.

# User Login Script

The **user login script** is used to set up the environment for a given user. This login script is entered through NetWare Administrator by using the Login Script page for the user as shown in Figure 11-16. The user login script executes after the profile login script if there is a profile login script or after the container login script if there is no profile login script.

# Default Login Script

This login script provides commands to set up a user to at least be able to do some minimal tasks within the network. If there is a user login script, the default login script does not run. Further, if the NO DEFAULT command appears in the container or profile login script, the default login script does not run. The default login script is hard-coded within the NetWare 4.11 operating system and cannot be changed.

A user might log in as user JamesM. The LOGIN program checks the user name given and executes the container login script set up by the Admin using NetWare Administrator, then executes the profile login script from the profile object Executives, and then executes the user's login script.

Many of the commands that can be used in a login script can also be used from the command line. In other words, if the appropriate PATHs have been established, a user can issue several of the commands by typing the name of the command at the F> prompt. The MAP command is a good example. The MAP command can be used in a login script or at the command prompt to map a network or search drive (explained later in this chapter).

The following is a partial list of login script commands and their uses.

1. BREAK ON | OFF

2. COMSPEC = drive:(\)file name

    COMSPEC = *n:(\)file name

    COMSPEC = Sn:(\)file name

3. DISPLAY file name

    FDISPLAY file name

4. DOS BREAK ON | OFF

5. (DOS) SET name="value"

6. DOS VERIFY ON | OFF

7. DRIVE drive letter:

   DRIVE *drive number:

8. EXIT ("file name")

9. #program name with command line options

10. FIRE PHASERS number TIMES

11. IF condition (AND condition) THEN command

    IF condition (AND condition) THEN BEGIN

    commands

    END

12. INCLUDE file name

13. MAP

14. PAUSE

    WAIT

15. REMARK remark statement

    REM, *, or ; are all remark statements

16. WRITE "comment to be displayed"

# Commands

## BREAK

The BREAK command controls how the keyboard responds during execution of the login script. If the command BREAK ON is used, the login script can be halted by holding down the CONTROL key and pressing BREAK. The BREAK key may also be labeled SCROLL LOCK. If the command is in the form BREAK OFF, the execution of the login script cannot be stopped with CONTROL-BREAK. Note that this command affects only the execution of the Login Script.

## COMSPEC

The COMSPEC command can be very important to the proper operation of the workstation. DOS always keeps a pointer (called the COMSPEC environment variable) to the file containing the command processor program. The command processor provided with every version of DOS is a program called COMMAND.COM. DOS must be told where this file is located because it must often be reloaded into memory after the execution of a program. Ordinarily when a computer is booted the COMSPEC variable is set to point to the COMMAND.COM that was used to boot the computer. If the computer was booted from floppy disk drive A:, the COMSPEC variable would probably read

COMSPEC=A:\COMMAND.COM.

But if the boot disk was then removed, COMMAND.COM would no longer reside where the COMSPEC variable points to. If this computer were on a network, the COMSPEC variable could be set to point to a copy of COMMAND.COM on a network drive where it cannot be removed.

The COMSPEC login script command allows the variable to be set automatically when the user logs in. In its simplest form, the command COMSPEC = drive:(\)file name sets the COMSPEC variable to a value such as

COMSPEC = F:COMMAND.COM

where F: has already been mapped to a directory containing a copy of COMMAND.COM. The drive option can indicate any drive letter that exists at the time the COMSPEC command is executed.

The two other forms of the command allow the COMSPEC variable to be set to a value that is indicated at the time the login script is executed. An "*n:" indicates a drive number that might be used in the login script. The command might read

COMSPEC = *2:COMMAND.COM

The result is to set the COMSPEC variable to point to a copy of COMMAND.COM in a directory on the second network drive, already mapped to whatever the drive letter may be.

The "Sn:" in the third form of the command indicates a search drive number. Under NetWare, a special type of drive mapping called a search drive can be made to allow the computer to automatically search a directory for a program that is not in the current directory. When mapping such a search drive, the user maps a search drive number such as S1: or S2:. NetWare designates the associated drive letter by starting at the end of the alphabet, so S1: becomes drive letter Z: and S2: becomes Y: unless those letters are already in use. By using a command such as

COMSPEC = S1:COMMAND.COM

the Admin can ensure that the COMSPEC variable points to the first search drive already assigned, without knowing what drive letter it is using.

In any of the three forms of this command, the drive letter used should point to the directory containing the COMMAND.COM program, because the command accepts only twelve characters after the drive specification. With this restriction a command such as

COMSPEC = S1:\DOS\COMMAND.COM

would not be legal. The path \DOS\COMMAND.COM is too long.

## DISPLAY

Using the DISPLAY command, a message can be displayed on the screen each time a user logs in. The message is contained in a file represented by the file name option in the command. The file name can include a complete directory path such as

DISPLAY F:\PUBLIC\MESSAGE.TXT

DISPLAY is used when the file contains only the ASCII characters that are to be displayed. FDISPLAY is used when the file contains control characters placed there by a word processing program that are not intended to be displayed. FDISPLAY will filter out these characters before printing the message on the screen.

## (DOS)BREAK

DOS also has a BREAK command. This login script command sets the DOS environment variable to BREAK ON or BREAK OFF.

## (DOS)SET

The SET command is used to set any DOS environment variable to any value. These values can be checked later by other login script commands, batch file commands, or other programs. This command is identical in function to the DOS command SET. The only differences are the optional word DOS and the use of quotation marks around the value in the login script command. Some examples are

DOS SET USER="JANE"

SET ROOM="D229"

SET PROMPT="$P$G"

Several login script variables can be used to place special values in an environment variable. These variables will be discussed later.

## DOS VERIFY

The DOS VERIFY flag can be set so that each time a file is copied DOS will read the newly created copy and compare it with the original to ensure it is correct. The login script command DOS VERIFY can be used to turn this feature on or off.

## DRIVE

The drive command is used to set the default drive. Normally the default drive is the first network drive, usually drive F. With the DRIVE drive letter: command it can be set to any valid local or network drive letter. The DRIVE *drive number: form of the command is used to set the default drive to a number indicating the order in which the drive was mapped. For instance, the command

> DRIVE *1:

would set the default drive to the first network drive letter, which might be F.

> The command

> DRIVE C:

could be used to set the default drive to be the local hard disk drive C:.

## EXIT

The EXIT command is used to terminate a login script and to start another program. It is often necessary to start another program, usually a menu program, at the conclusion of the login script. When the login program finishes processing the login script, it can pass control on to any executable program named in the parameter "file name" or if there is no parameter in quotes, control passes to the client operating system. For example, if a user needed a menu program called MENU.EXE executed each time she logged in, the last line in his login script might be

> EXIT "F:MENU"

The item in quotes can actually be any operating system command as long as it is fourteen characters or less in length. Therefore, in addition to any executable program, any batch file or DOS internal command can be used. For example, suppose a user simply needed a directory listing each time he logged in. The last line in the login script would be

> EXIT "DIR /W"

When the EXIT command is used in a login script, no further login scripts run. Programs that terminate and stay resident should not be used.

## #Program name with command line options

The "#" symbol is known as the External Program Execution command. This command tells the LOGIN program to temporarily suspend its operations to load and run the program named. When the program is finished, control is returned to the LOGIN program and the login script resumes execution at the next line. The program called by the External Program Execution command must have either an .EXE or .COM extension, but it can be called from any directory with any command line options it needs. The login script command

### #F:\APPS\LOTUS\LOTUS COLOR.SET

loads and executes a program called LOTUS from the F:\APPS\LOTUS directory and passes the command line parameter COLOR.SET to it. As with the EXIT command, terminate and stay resident programs are excluded.

The example above, however, would be a very unusual case since after the user exited the LOTUS program, control would return to the LOGIN program and the rest of the login script would be executed.

## FIRE PHASERS

The FIRE PHASERS command is used to catch the user's attention by generating a science fiction-like sound. The "number" parameter tells the login script how many times to make the sound. The command

### FIRE PHASERS 3 TIMES

would cause the alarm to sound three times. This command should be used judiciously, especially if it is placed in the system login script, which is executed by all users. Execution of this command must complete prior to the login script's continuing. An alternate construction is FIRE 3.

## IF Statement

This command structure allows the login script to test conditions and execute different commands based on the result. The command executed as a result of the comparison can be any valid login script command. In the diagram of the IF THEN structure, the "condition" represents a true or false comparison of two items. The comparison will always be in the form

ITEM OPERATOR ITEM

where the operator tests the relationship between the two items. In the first form of the command, a single command is executed as the result of any number of comparisons, if they are all true. In the second form of the command, the key word BEGIN is used to start a list of commands to be executed. The key word END is used to indicate the end of the list of commands. Between the BEGIN and END may be any number of commands that will be executed only if all the conditions are true. It is important to note that the IF THEN statement must be allowed to wrap naturally when it extends beyond one line of the screen. Also, the IF THEN with the BEGIN and END option must be allowed to wrap naturally until the BEGIN has been entered. Then, each additional command should wrap naturally with the ENTER key being pressed at the end of each command.

The IF THEN command will accept many different operators in the testing of the two items, as shown below:

| To represent equal | To represent not equal |
|---|---|
| IS | IS NOT |
| = | != |
| == | <> |
| EQUALS | # |
| | DOES NOT EQUAL |
| | NOT EQUAL TO |

Four more relationships can be tested using the following operators. Either the symbols on the right or the words on the left may be used in the IF THEN command.

| | |
|---|---|
| IS  GREATER  THAN | > |
| IS  LESS  THAN | < |
| IS  GREATER  THAN  OR  EQUAL  TO | >= |
| IS  LESS  THAN  OR  EQUAL  TO | <= |

Several pairs of items can be compared using the AND operator. Also, the AND operator may be replaced with a comma. Comparisons such as these are possible:

```
IF DAY_OF_WEEK IS "Monday" AND HOUR >= "09" THEN SET
NOW="*"
```

This command tests whether a variable DAY_OF_WEEK is equal to Monday and checks whether a variable HOUR is greater than or equal to 9. If both conditions are true a DOS environment variable NOW is given a value of "*".

IF DAY > THAN "15", DAY_OF_WEEK IS NOT "Sunday" THEN BEGIN

    FIRE PHASERS 2 TIMES

DOS SET REMIND="Pay the bills today!"

END

This command checks to see if the day of the month is greater than 15 and makes sure the day of the week is not Sunday. If those conditions are met, the alarm will sound two times and a DOS environment variable is set to the string "Pay the bills today!"

The variables DAY, DAY_OF_WEEK, and HOUR are login script variables that are set before execution of the login script. Many more such variables are available for use in the IF THEN command as well as other commands. The following is a complete list of the login script identifier variables available. (Note that all are character variables and, as such, must be compared to constant values in double quotes.)

| Variable | Possible Values |
|---|---|
| AM_PM | (a.m. or p.m.) |
| DAY | (01 - 31) |
| DAY_OF_WEEK | (Sunday - Saturday) |
| ERROR_LEVEL | (0 - 255) |
| FULL_NAME | (The user's full name recorded in SYSCON) |
| GREETING_TIME | (Morning, afternoon, evening) |
| HOUR | (1 - 12) |
| HOUR24 | (00 - 24) |
| LOGIN_NAME | (The user's login name) |
| MACHINE | (The name of the workstation type of computer) |
| MEMBER OF | (The MEMBER OF variable is a special case in that it is not used with a comparison operator. It is used to check if the user is a member of a given group.) |
| MINUTE | (00 - 59) |
| MONTH | (01 - 12) |
| MONTH_NAME | (January - December) |

| | |
|---|---|
| NDAY_OF_WEEK | (1 - 7 where Sunday is 1 and Saturday is 7) |
| NEW_MAIL | (YES or NO indicating whether new mail is waiting for the user) |
| OS | (The operating system running on the user's workstation) |
| OS_VERSION | (The version number of a DOS workstation) |
| P_STATION | (The physical node number of the workstation) |
| SECOND | (00 - 59) |
| SHELL_TYPE | (A code number indicating the type of network shell running on the user's workstation) |
| SHORT_YEAR | (The last two digits of the year) |
| SMACHINE | (A shortened name for the workstation type) |
| STATION | (The connection number assigned to the workstation) |
| YEAR | (The year) |

## INCLUDE

This login script command tells the login script to pull in a second file as a part of the currently executing login script. When the commands are finished executing in the second login script, control is returned to the calling login script. Each script file can call other script files to a maximum of ten login scripts.

Nesting login scripts in this way can be very helpful if many different users need a section of their login script to be the same, but heavy nesting is not recommended because it makes documenting a user's actual login script unnecessarily difficult.

## MAP

The MAP command is used to display or set the drive mappings of the workstation. It assigns drive letters to directories on the file server or to drives on the local workstation.  It can also be used to display those assignments. There are fourteen separate forms of this command, each requiring a complete description. This command is another in which the login script variables can be used. Directory names used in the MAP command can contain login script variables preceded by a "%".

Suppose that F: is mapped to volume SYS:\ and that a subdirectory under a directory called \USERS has been created for each user with the user's name being the name of the directory. For user SMANN the directory would be F:\USERS\SMANN. A directory for each user is usually referred to as a user's home directory. Each user might need a drive letter assigned to his or her home directory in the login script. To do this a MAP command could be placed in each user's login script that includes the login script variable LOGIN_NAME.

**MAP H:=F:\USERS\%LOGIN_NAME**

When the login program executes this command it will replace the %LOGIN_NAME with the individual user's name and, in the case of user SMANN, the result would be

**MAP H:=F:\USERS\SMANN**

giving the user a new drive letter H: that points to the F:\USERS\SMANN directory.

In its simplest form, the MAP command alone displays all drive letter assignments, including the drive letters assigned to local disk drives. The command

**MAP drive:**

displays the directory or local drive that the drive letter listed points to.

**MAP drive:=directory**

sets the drive letter listed to point to the directory listed. The directory may contain the volume name.

**MAP drive:=directory ; drive:=directory ; ...**

shows that multiple drive letter assignments may be made following a single MAP command. Each assignment is separated by a semicolon.

**MAP directory**

changes the current drive letter to point to the directory listed. The directory may contain a volume name.

**MAP drive:=**

assigns the drive letter listed to point to the current directory.

**MAP drive:=drive:**

assigns the drive letter on the left to point to the directory pointed to by the drive letter on the right.

**MAP INSERT search drive:=directory**

creates a new search drive pointing to the directory listed.

### MAP DEL drive:

deletes the drive letter assignment.

### MAP REM drive:

removes the drive letter assignment, exactly the same as the MAP DEL command.

### MAP DISPLAY OFF

instructs the login program  not to display the drive mappings made when the user logs in. Ordinarily the drive mappings are displayed.

### MAP DISPLAY ON

explicitly tells the login program to display the drive mappings when the user logs in.

### MAP ERRORS OFF

instructs the login program not to display any error messages that may be generated as a result of an incorrect MAP command in the login script. Ordinarily all errors would be displayed.

### MAP ERRORS ON

explicitly tells the login program to display all error messages concerning MAP commands in the login script.

## PAUSE

The login script command PAUSE works exactly the same as the DOS batch file command of the same name. It halts execution of the login script and displays the message "Strike a key when ready..." After the user presses a key the login script is resumed at the next command. The word WAIT may be used for the same function.

## REMARK

Often the Admin will wish to place remarks or comments in the text of the login script that are not intended to be executed. These might include explanations of a particularly complex IF THEN structure, the need for various drive mappings, or a message for future administrators. Either of the four forms of the REMARK command will prevent the login program from attempting to execute the remark statement following it.

## WRITE

The WRITE command is roughly equivalent to the PRINT command in the BASIC programming language or the ECHO command in a batch file. It displays the text following it on the user's screen at the time it is executed. The easiest way to use the WRITE command is to simply put a message in quotes.

> WRITE "Welcome to file server FS_ONE."

The WRITE command above would tell the user which file server he or she just logged in to. But WRITE commands can be much more flexible. The text to be displayed can use the same login script variables that the IF THEN command can use. As in the MAP command the variable is preceded by a "%" to tell the login program to convert it to the value it represents. In the command

> WRITE "Welcome %LOGIN_NAME, to file server FS_ONE."

the %LOGIN_NAME would be converted to the user name. In the case of user JSMITH, the message displayed would read:

> Welcome JSMITH, to file server FS_ONE.

The login script variables can also be used outside the quotes without the preceding "%". The command

> WRITE "Welcome ";LOGIN_NAME;", to file server FS_ONE."

is exactly equivalent to the write command above. Notice that a semicolon is used to separate the components of the text when a variable is used outside the quotes and without the "%". Also note that identifier variables must be in uppercase in most instances, so it is a good idea to use uppercase all the time.

In addition to the login script variables, there are four special symbols that may be used within the quotes to control the format of the text printed on the screen. They appear in Table 11-1.

| Symbol | Description |
| --- | --- |
| \r | Carriage return. Causes the cursor to return to column one on the same line of the screen. |
| \n | New line. Causes the cursor to go to the first column of the next line. The cursor will automatically go to a new line at the end of a WRITE command. |
| \" | Embedded quotation mark. Must be used to display a quotation. |

\7              ASCII character seven. Causes a beep sound

to be generated.

Table 11-1. Format symbols.

The WRITE command below shows the effects of some of these symbols.

WRITE "HAPPY\n     \"BIRTHDAY\"\n      ";LOGIN_NAME

For user JSMITH, the output on the screen would look like this:

HAPPY

"BIRTHDAY"

JSMITH

The login script commands listed above give the Administrator a very powerful language to meet the user's needs. With them a user's environment can be constructed to allow him or her to use the network freely or to take the user directly into an application. The possibilities are endless.

In the next section of this chapter, NetWare Administrator will be used to create users, assign them various characteristics or properties, and create login scripts.

# Hands-on NetWare

In the previous chapter, Novell NetWare was completely installed on a file server, and Novell client software was installed on a workstation. However, the installation of the NetWare software was only a small part of creating a usable network. The structure of the directories, the creation of user accounts, the setting up of network printers, and many other tasks will require much more work and thought. A network's administrator is the one who must consider how the network will be used and determine how best to serve each user, while maintaining overall system continuity and security.

When NetWare is installed, a user account called Admin is automatically created. It has complete trustee rights over the entire server at least initially and permission to use all options in each of the NetWare utilities. Originally the account has only the password assigned during installation.

In this section you will prepare the server and workstation for operation, log in to the network as the network Admin, start the Netware Administrator utility, and create for yourself an Administrator-equivalent account. All commands shown here are written in uppercase characters for clarity. However, they can be entered as either uppercase or lowercase.

# Preparing the Network for Operation

1. Prepare the server for operation by simply turning it on. A message saying that the LAN is initializing and the volumes are being mounted should appear, assuming that you have inserted the command SERVER.EXE into the AUTOEXEC.BAT file on the server.

2. At a network workstation, boot the workstation and activate the client software. A login screen similar to Figure 11-17 should appear.

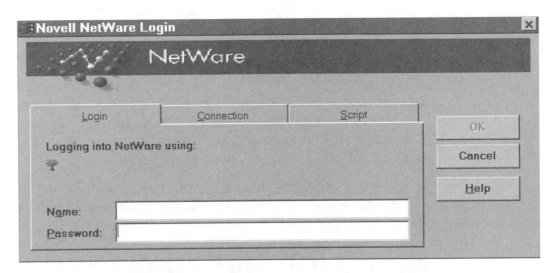

**Figure 11-17.** Login dialog box.

# Logging In

Once the screen shown in Figure 11-17 is displayed, we know that the network drivers have been loaded, and the workstation is attached to the file server. However, no one is logged in. Logging in tells NDS who the user is and how much access that user has.

1. Click in the Name box and type in the name of the Admin. The name of the Admin account for the MAINCO company is .ADMIN.MAINCO.

2. Click in the Password box and type in the password. Notice that the password is encrypted as is should be.

3. Click the OK button to log in. The Login Results box is displayed because that is how the client was configured in the previous chapter.

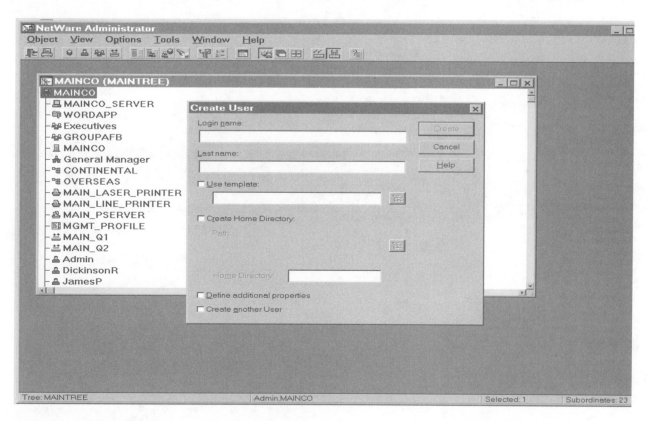

**Figure 11-18.** Creating a user dialog box.

## Starting the NetWare Administrator Utility

If you are running Windows 3.1, locate the NetWare program group by clicking on the Windows selection in the main menu bar and selecting the NetWare program group.

1. Double-click on the NetWare Administrator icon to activate the program.

2. A screen similar to Figure 11-18 should appear.

## Creating a User

1. Click on the MAINCO container.

2. Click on the Create User icon on the menu bar. (Or, alternatively, click on Object on the menu bar and then Create. Select User Object and then click the OK button.)

3. The screen depicted in Figure 11-18 appears.

4. Click in the Login Name box and enter ADMINXXX where XXX is your three initials.

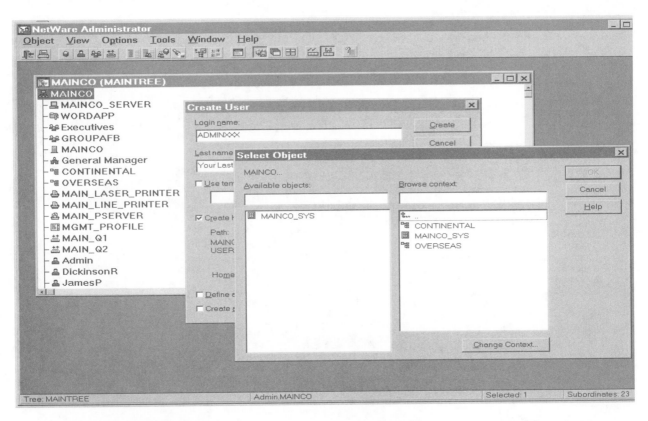

**Figure 11-19.** Selecting a path to the user's home directory.

5. Attempt to click the Create button at this point. This action is not possible since the Create button is dimmed. The Create button is dimmed because a critical property of the user has not been entered, the last name.

6. Click in the Last Name box and enter your last name.

7. Click the box to the left of the Create Home Directory line to indicate that you wish to create a home directory. Again, attempt to click the Create button. The Create button is now dimmed because you have indicated that you wish the user to have a home directory, but you have not specified the location of that directory.

8. Click the Browse button. (This button is the second square button in the current window.)

9. A screen similar to Figure 11-19 is displayed.

10. Double-click the MAINCO_SYS directory in the Browse context side of the screen.

11. Click the Users directory on the left side of the screen, and then click the OK button.

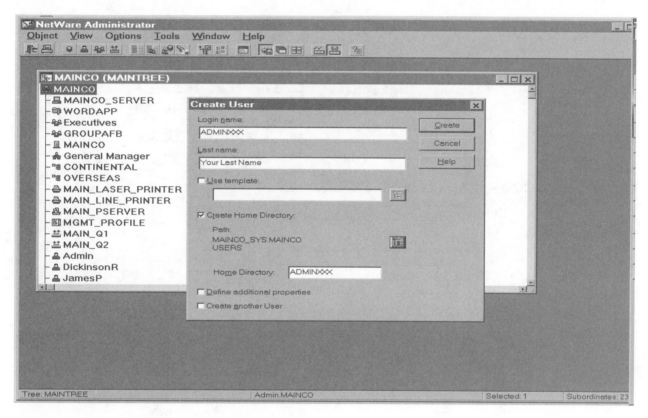

**Figure 11-20.** User's home directory.

12. Notice that the path to the user's home directory has been filled in, and the actual home directory name is shown in Figure 11-20.

13. Click the Create button to create the user.

## Making the New User Admin Equivalent

1. Double click the ADMINXXX user you just created.

2. The screen shown in Figure 11-21 appears.

3. Arrow down until the Security Equal To button appears on the right of the screen as shown in Figure 11-22.

4. Click the Security Equal To button to display the screen in Figure 11-23.

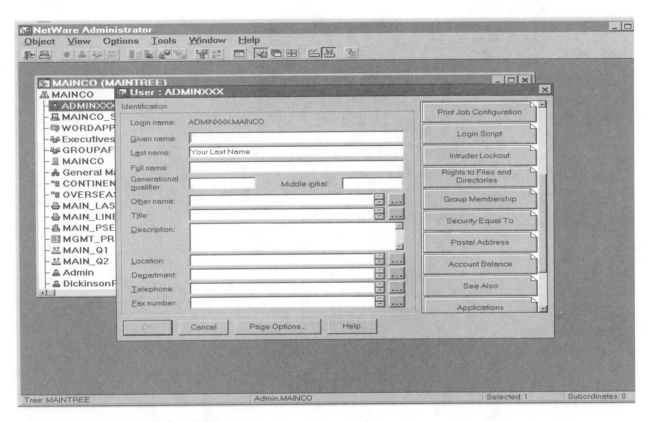

**Figure 11-21.** User ADMINXXX main screen.

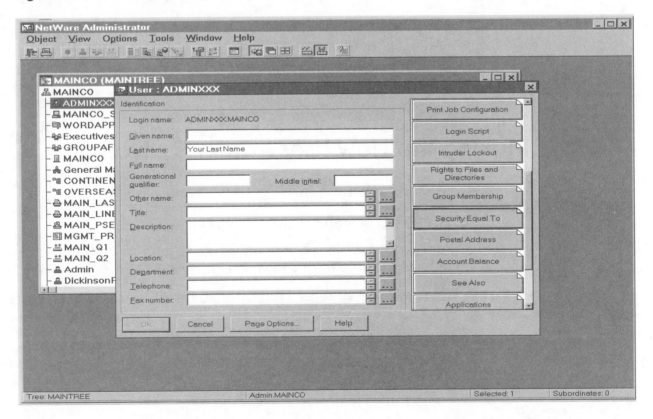

**Figure 11-22.** User ADMINXXX main screen showing Security Equal To button.

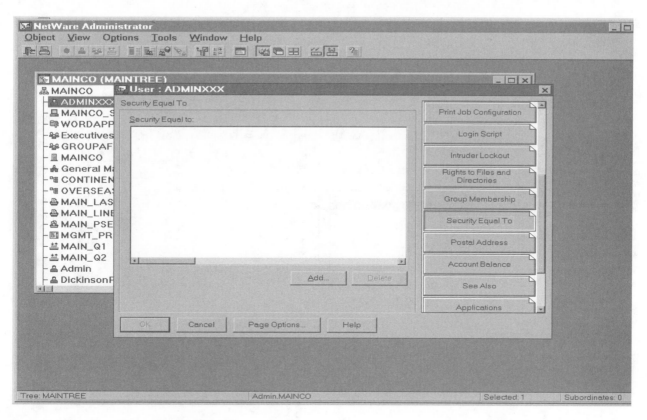

**Figure 11-23.** Security Equal To page.

5. Click the Add button, click the real Admin user in the left side of the screen displayed, then click the OK button in the Add screen, and then the OK button in the Security Equal To screen. Refer to Figures 11-24 and 11-25.

6. Click the Password Restrictions button on the right of the screen.

7. Click the Change Password button and enter the password FIRST in both the New and Retype password boxes as shown in Figure 11-26.

## Logging in as the Admin Equivalent New User and Creating Another User

1. Log in as the new ADMINXXX user that you just created.

2. Following the above procedure, create a new user call USERXXX who has a home directory called SYS:\USERS\USERXXX where XXX is your initials. Set the password for this account to your last name.

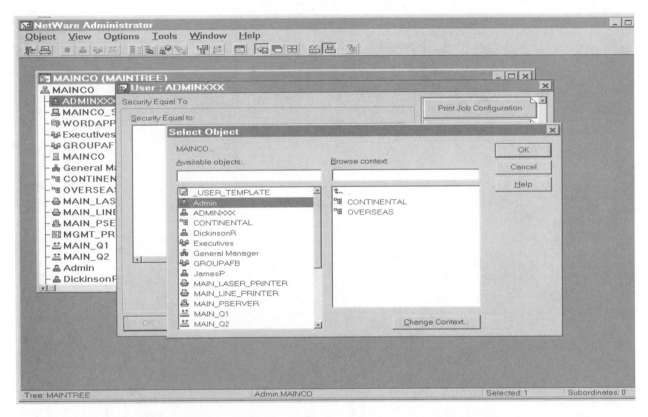

**Figure 11-24.** Selecting a security equivalent.

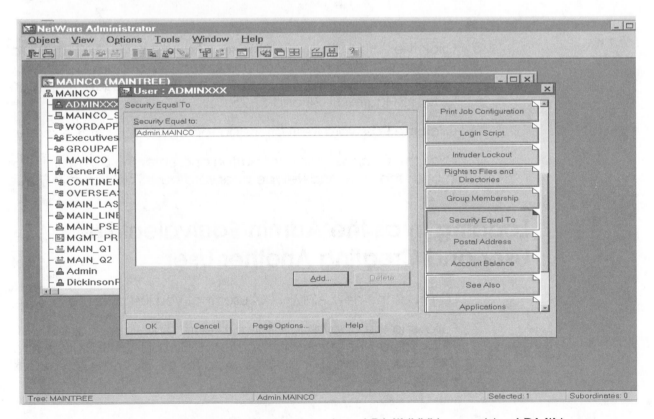

**Figure 11-25.** Security Equal To page showing ADMINXXX equal to ADMIN.

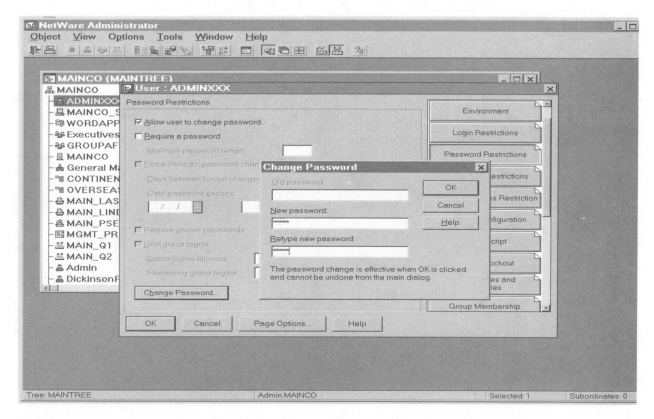

**Figure 11-26.** Changing the user's password.

3. Double-click the user icon.

4. Click the Login Time Restrictions button to display Figure 11-27.

5. Click in the upper left of the Time Restrictions box by Sunday and underneath the 12. While holding down the left mouse button, drag down to Saturday until you reach 1 hour AFTER the present time that you are attempting this Hands-On exercise. Release the left mouse button and click OK. Your windows should be as shown in Figure 11-28 if the current time is 3 p.m.

6. Click the OK button. The dark area of the screen indicates the times during which the user CANNOT log in.

7. Attempt to log in as USERXXX. You should receive a message as in Figure 11-29 if you have set the login time restrictions properly.

## Creating a User Login Script for USERXXX

1. Log in as your ADMINXXX user.

2. Double-click the USERXXX user to expose the Details screen.

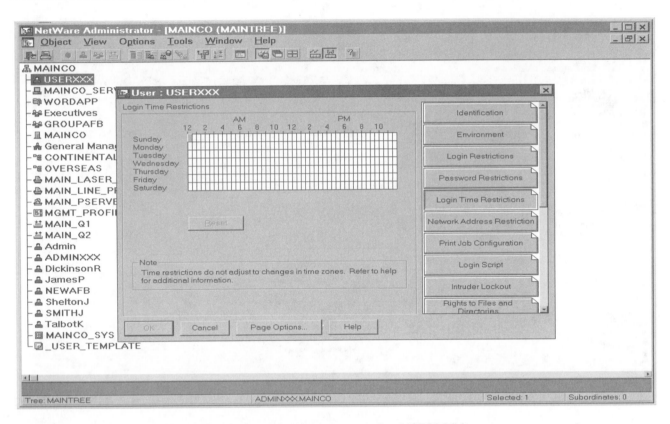

**Figure 11-27.** The Login Time Restriction screen for USERXXX.

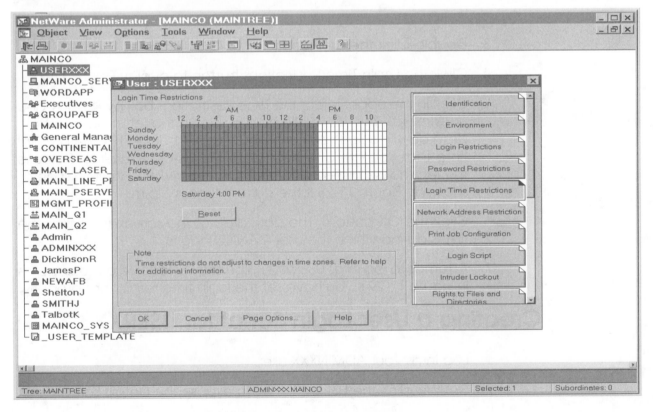

**Figure 11-28.** USERXXX with login time restricted midnight to 4 p.m.

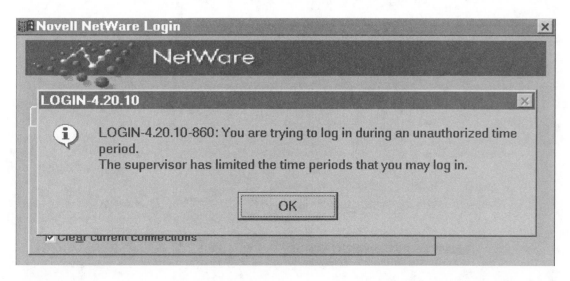

**Figure 11-29.** Error message USERXXX receives when trying to log in during a restricted time.

3. Reset the login time restrictions so that the user cannot log in from 12 midnight until 6 a.m. every day of the week. Be sure to click OK to save the change.

4. Click the Login Script button to display the Login Script screen as shown in Figure 11-30.

5. Click in the Login Script box and type in the following commands:

```
WRITE "Good %GREETING_TIME  %LOGIN_NAME"
PAUSE
IF HOUR24="12" then
        WRITE "TIME FOR LUNCH!"
        PAUSE
ELSE
        WRITE "TIME FOR WORK!"
        PAUSE
ENDIF
MAP ROOT H:=SYS:\USERS\%LOGIN_NAME
MAP
PAUSE
```

Your screen should look something like Figure 11-31.

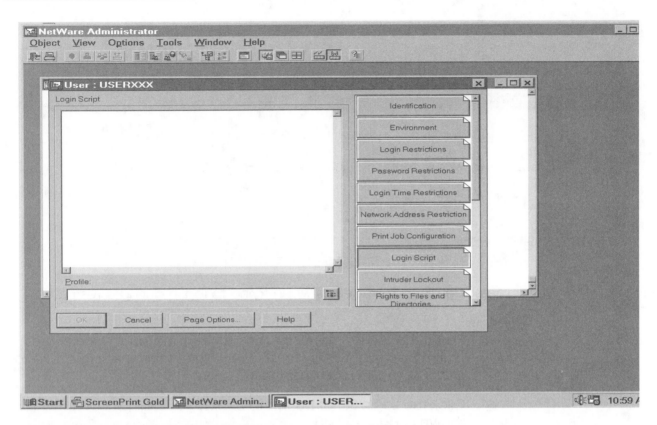

**Figure 11-30.** USERXXX Login Script page.

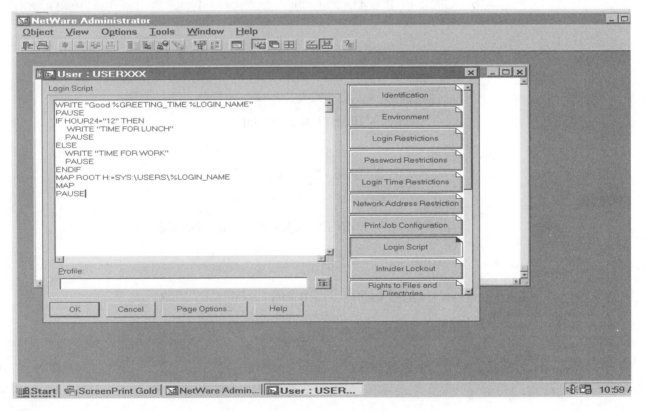

**Figure 11-31.** USERXXX Login Script page with login script entered.

6. Click the OK button to save the login script changes.

7. Log in as USERXXX. What messages appeared? You should see something like the screen in Figure 11-32 if the hour of the day is not 12, and something like Figure 11-33 if the hour of the day is 12.

# Summary

One of the most important aspects of managing a network involves the creation of user accounts. These accounts control how and when the user will be able to use the network. With the NetWare Administrator utility, the Admin can create accounts that allow users to do the work they need to do and provide them with login scripts that set up helpful environments. The login script commands and variables available allow the Admin to create very complex programs that can take different actions based on who the user is, the time of day, and other factors.

When creating a user, the Admin can specify security equivalencies. The new user can be given security equivalence to any user or group already on the server, including the Admin. Additionally, the Admin can specify login time restrictions, login scripts, and a host of other characteristics for the user's account. All of these characteristics are aimed at making the network easier to user for the user while preserving the integrity of the network. The next chapter will examine file system security, assignments that are also made with Netware Administrator.

# Questions

1. What is the purpose of a login script?

2 What are the four types of login scripts within NetWare 4,11, and how can they be used together to accomplish setting up the user's environment?

3. Which login script(s) would the Administrator use to affect the user's environment each time the user logs in?

4. What can the Admin do if a user forgets his or her password?

5. What should the Administrator do to ensure the security of the ADMIN account?

6. Explain the function of the following lines in a login script:

   IF DAY IS EQUAL TO "29" AND MONTH = "02" THEN BEGIN

   WRITE "Today is special!"

   END.

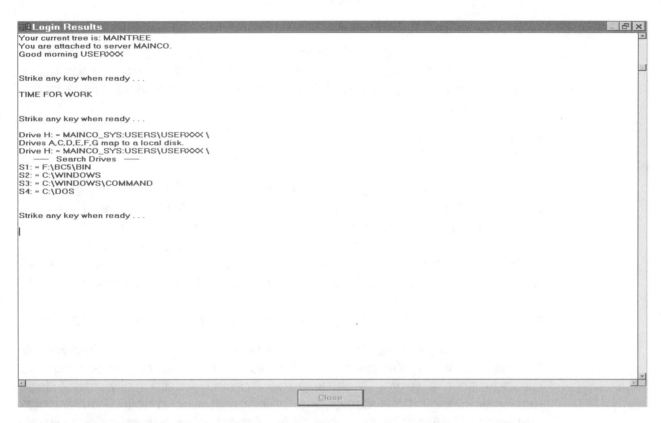

**Figure 11-32.** USERXXX dialog box when logging in other than with Hour=12.

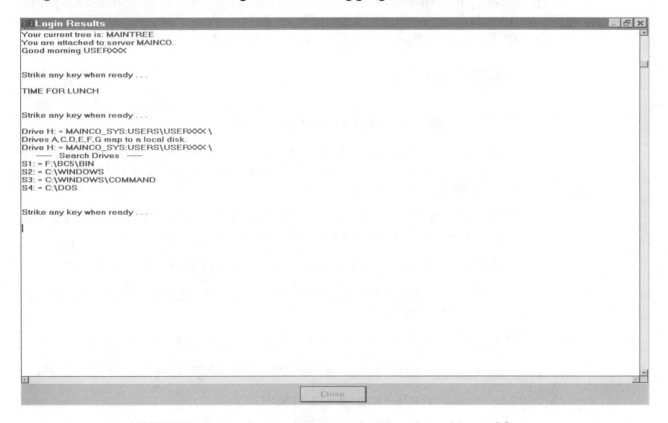

**Figure 11-33.** USERXXX dialog box when logging in when Hour=12.

# Projects

## Objective

The following projects will provide additional practice on how to create a user and login scripts. Login scripts provide a mechanism by which the system manager can customize the network and thereby make using the system easier for users.

## Project 1. Using the NetWare Administrator Utility

1. Use the NetWare Administrator utility to create a new user. Use your initials as the name of the user.

2. Create a login script for the user that maps the drive letters F:, G:, and H: to the SYS:\LOGIN, SYS:\SYSTEM, and SYS:\PUBLIC, respectively.

3. Add statements to the login script that print the message "Today is the first day of the rest of your life" only if the user logs in on today's date.

4. Using SHIFT/PRINT SCREEN, print the login script just created.

5. Log in as the new user. Use the SHIFT/PRINT SCREEN keys to record the results of the login script.

6. While still logged in as the new user, start the NetWare Administrator utility and attempt to create another user. Were you successful? Why or why not?

7. Exit the NetWare Administrator utility and log in under your Admin equivalent account, ADMINXXX.

8. Start the NetWare Administrator utility and delete the new user just created.

9. Exit the NetWare Administrator utility.

## Project 2. More Login Scripts

1. Using the NetWare Administrator utility, create another new user USXXX, where XXX is your initials.

2. Turn off the map display.

3. Type the basic login script commands. (MAP a search drive to the PUBLIC directory, and set up COMSPEC.)

4. Type all mappings to the basic applications installed on your file server.

5. Make sure that everyone's first network drive is mapped to his or her home directory.

6. Type a greeting to be displayed when a user logs in.

7. Type the commands necessary to display the current date and time of day.

8. Type the commands necessary to remind all users of a meeting that begins at 12:00 noon every day of the week.

9. Turn the map display on and display the mappings at the end of the script.

10. Print the new user's login script.

11. Log in as the new user and test the login script.

# 12
# File System Security and Organization

## Objectives

After completing this chapter you will

1. Know the advantages of organizing users into groups.

2. Recognize the available directory and file trustee rights.

3. Understand the available directory and file attributes.

4. Be familiar with the five levels of security.

5. Know how to assign restrictions to a user's account.

## Key Terms

Levels of Security

Passwords

Password Restrictions

Directory Trustee Rights

File Trustee Rights

File Attributes

Directory Attributes

Groups

## Introduction

A network may have many functions. It may have electronic mail, shared printers, or shared modems. All of these functions are usually secondary to providing users with shared disk space for programs and data. In addition to the shared space, most users will need to be able to store data in a private area.

Creating a structure in which users can access the shared data they need and protect their private data is the Administrator's task. Usually programs and data must be placed in different areas with different access rights. Different users will have many different needs, and normally several groups of users will have similar needs. Under NetWare, the Administrator can grant trustee rights to these groups and still be able to customize the accounts of each user. Additionally, with NetWare 4.11, the Administrator can grant rights to the container(s) holding the user object, to organizational roles that the user occupies, to users to which the user is security equivalent, and even to a special object (PUBLIC), which supplies rights to all users connected to a file server in a NetWare 4.11 network whether or not the user is logged in.

The principle of allowing some users access to data while restricting other users is known as network file system security. NetWare 4.11 establishes system security at five levels, through passwords, trustee directory and file rights, directory attributes, file attributes, and through NDS Object and Property rights, which will be covered in Chapter 14. This multilevel approach allows the Administrator to customize the security requirements to fit any need.

# Levels of Security

There are four main **levels of security**:

1. Passwords

2. Trustee Directory and File rights

3. File attributes

4. Directory attributes

5. NDS Object and Property rights

## Passwords

Each NetWare account can be given a **password**. The password is a string of characters that the user types in when he or she logs in. The appropriate login program compares the login name and password to those stored by NDS. If they match, the user is allowed access to the account and the resources to which NDS provides access for that account. The login name is intended to be known by everyone while the password is kept secret by the user.

The Administrator can give the user a password or allow the user to choose one the first time he or she logs in. After it has been entered, neither the user nor the Administrator can view it. If it is forgotten, the only way to access the account is for the Administrator to change the password. Using NetWare Administrator, the Administrator can set defaults concerning passwords for all new accounts. See Figure 12-1 for the **password restrictions** available on a user account. You can also create a user template object with password restrictions and then use the template to create new users, transferring the password restrictions to the new user.

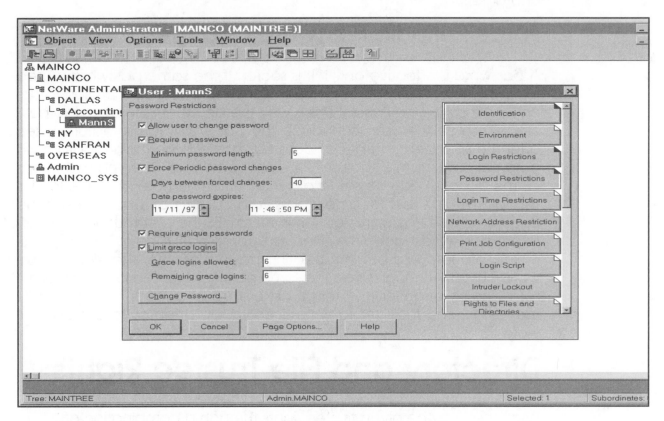

**Figure 12-1.** Password restrictions available under NDS.

# Allowing the User to Change the Password

The user may or may not be allowed to change his or her password. In general, it is a good idea to allow the user to change his or her password; otherwise, the Administrator must take responsibility for changing users' passwords in order to help maintain security. If passwords are never changed, security is eventually diminished as users tell their peers their passwords and as passwords are written on notes taped to the users' monitors, etc. In fact, the user can be forced to change his or her password regularly as explained below.

## Minimum Password Length

Each account can be required to have a password or not. If it does have a password, a minimum length can be set. The default minimum password length is 5 characters; the maximum is 128 characters. Popular and effective password lengths generally range from 5 to 10 characters.

## Force Periodic Password Changes

A password is effective only if it is secret. If the same password is used for a very long time, the opportunity for an unauthorized person to discover it may be increased. This is why the account can be set to periodically force the user to change the password. If this feature is set, after the specified number of days has passed, the login program will automatically prompt the user for a new password when he or she logs in. The account can be set to allow a certain number of grace log ins that prompt the user for a new password but do not require one. If the Require Unique Passwords option is set to YES the user must enter a different password each time. NetWare remembers the last eight passwords so one could begin repeating passwords after the eighth password is used. Although using the same password for too long may allow someone to discover it, forcing the user to change it too frequently may also force the user to write it down too often or to use obvious words.

# Directory and File Trustee Rights

Each user may be given trustee rights through a combination of:

1.  His or her individual account

2.  Each group to which the user belongs

3.  Each organizational role the users occupies

4.  The container(s) containing the user

5.  Through being security equivalent to another user

6.  Through rights given to (PUBLIC)

In NetWare 4.11, as with previous versions of NetWare, both Trustee Directory and Trustee File assignments are possible. When a user is given some access to a directory, he or she is said to be a trustee of that directory. A user's effective rights are the combination of rights at each directory obtained from any of the six sources listed above.

Figure 12-2 shows the **directory trustee rights** for user MannS in his home directory called SYS:USERS\MannS. The only directory trustee right not given to user MannS is the S or Supervisor right to the directory. If the Administrator were to grant MannS the S right, the Admin would merely have to click the white box in front of the Supervisor right.

The rights that can be given are:

1. **Read**.

> Directory Right: The user can open and read files in the directory. The File Scan right is also needed to view the directory listing for the given directory.

> File Right: The user can see the information in a closed file to use it or to execute it even if the directory does not allow the Read permission.

2. **Write**.

> Directory Right: The user can change the contents of existing files in the directory.

> File Right: The user can change the contents of the given file even if the directory does not allow the Write permission.

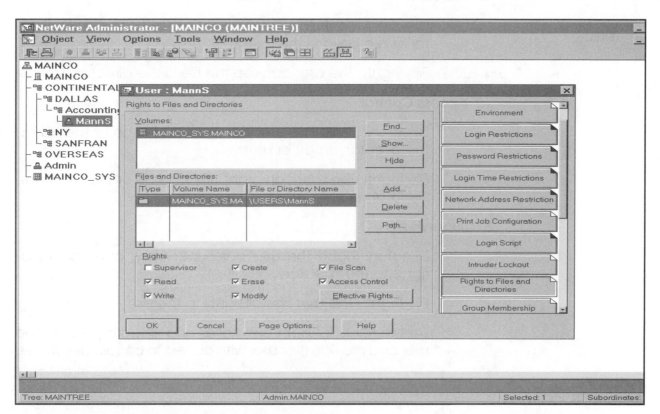

**Figure 12-2.** Trustee rights for user MannS.

3. **Create**.

   Directory Right: The user can create files and subdirectories in the directory.

   File Right: The user can salvage a file if it has been deleted.

4. **Erase**.

   Directory Right: The user can erase files and subdirectories of the directory.

   File Right: The user can delete a file even if the directory does not allow the Delete permission.

5. **Modify**.

   Directory Right: The user can modify the Attributes and names of the files and subdirectories in the directory. The Attribute of a file indicates what access anyone has to the file.

   File Right: The user can modify the attributes and the name of the file.

6. **File Scan**.

   Directory Right: The user can see what files and subdirectories are listed in the directory.

   File Right: The user can see the file in the directory listing.

7. **Access Control.**

   Directory Right: The user can grant rights he or she has to the directory to other users.

   File Right: The user can grant any right he or she has to the file to other users.

8. **Supervisor.**

   Directory Right: The user has Supervisory, and hence, all rights to the directory.

   File Right: The user has all rights to the file.

   Trustee rights for both directories and files are given to the user and provide that user with access to certain directories.

# Directory Inherited Rights Filter

Normally, if a user has specific trustee rights to a given directory, the user inherits these rights for all subdirectories of the original directory. When a directory is created, it has the same rights as the full set of trustee rights. These directory rights, called the inherited rights filter, are attached to the directory. The inherited rights filter for a directory may be altered using NetWare Administrator and other utilities to limit any user's inherited rights to that directory, except for the Supervisor right. The Supervisor file and directory right cannot be eliminated from the Inherited Rights Filter.

Suppose a user is given Read, File Scan, Create, and Erase rights to a directory called PROGRAMS. This means that the user will also inherit the same rights for all subdirectories of the directory PROGRAMS unless the inherited rights mask for a subdirectory limits these rights. Suppose that the subdirectory called COBOL under the PROGRAMS directory has the limited inherited rights filter of Read, File Scan, and Modify. This would mean that the user's effective rights for the directory \PROGRAMS\COBOL would be only Read and File Scan because these rights are the only rights the user had to the parent directory (PROGRAMS) that are also present in the inherited rights filter of the subdirectory (\PROGRAMS\COBOL).

|  | Jacob's Rights |
|---|---|
| ACCTG (directory) |  |
| IRF | -- |
| Inherited Rights | -- |
| Trustee Assign. | ( RWCEMFA) |
| Effective Rights | ( RWCEMFA) |
| SPREADSHEET (directory) |  |
| IRF | (SRW EF A) |
| Inherited Rights | ( RW EF A) |
| Trustee Assign. | -- |
| Effective Rights | ( RW EF A) |
| MAIN.WK1 (file) |  |
| IRF | (SR    F   ) |
| Inherited Rights | ( R    F   ) |
| Trustee Assign. | -- |
| Effective Rights | ( R    F   ) |

Note that the above analysis depends on Jacob's having been given the trustee assignment of all but the Supervisor right in the ACCTG directory and the Inherited Rights Filter of ( RW EF A) for the SPREADSHEET directory.

**Figure 12-3.** Sample effective rights calculations.

| | Ralph as a user | Ralph as a member of the Accounting Group | Rights granted to the container containing Ralph | All Ralph's rights considered together |
|---|---|---|---|---|
| ACCOUNTING (directory) | | | | |
| IRF | -- | -- | -- | |
| Inherited Rights | -- | -- | -- | |
| Trustee Assign. | ( R CE F ) | -- | ( R      FA) | |
| Effective Rights | | -- | | |
| DATABASE (directory) | | | | |
| IRF | (SR      F ) | (SR      F ) | (SR      F ) | ( R      F ) |
| Inherited Rights | | | | |
| Trustee Assign. | | ( RWCEMFA) | | |
| Effective Rights | | | | |
| MAIN.DBF (file) | | | | |
| IRF | (SRWCEMFA) | (SRWCEMFA) | (SRWCEMFA) | |
| Inherited Rights | | | | |
| Trustee Assign. | -- | -- | -- | |
| Effective Rights | | | | |

The above trustee assignments and inherited rights filters have been assigned. The effective rights at each directory and file are calculated and then added together to form the overall effective rights as shown below.

| | Ralph as a user | Ralph as a member of the Accounting Group | Rights granted to the container containing Ralph | All Ralph's rights considered together |
|---|---|---|---|---|
| ACCOUNTING (directory) | | | | |
| IRF | -- | -- | -- | |
| Inherited Rights | -- | -- | -- | |
| Trustee Assign. | ( R CE F ) | -- | ( R      FA) | |
| Effective Rights | ( R CE F ) | -- | ( R      FA) | ( R CE   FA) |
| DATABASE (directory) | | | | |
| IRF | (SR      F ) | (SR      F ) | (SR      F ) | ( R      F ) |
| Inherited Rights | ( R      F ) | -- | ( R      F ) | |
| Trustee Assign. | | ( RWCEMFA) | | |
| Effective Rights | ( R      F ) | ( RWCEMFA) | ( R      F ) | ( RWCEMFA) |
| MAIN.DBF (file) | | | | |
| IRF | (SRWCEMFA) | (SRWCEMFA) | (SRWCEMFA) | |
| Inherited Rights | ( R      F ) | (SRWCEMFA) | ( R      F ) | |
| Trustee Assign. | -- | -- | -- | |
| Effective Rights | ( R      F ) | (SRWCEMFA) | ( R      F ) | (SRWCEMFA) |

**Figure 12-4.** Sample effective rights calculations.

Note also that when a user is given explicit trustee rights to a directory, these rights override any limitation indicated by the inherited rights filter for the directory. The inherited rights filter affects only those rights that would normally be inherited in a directory.

Trustee file rights are the same as the trustee directory rights except that they are assigned to a file, not to a directory. When specific file system rights are given, they override any directory trustee rights explicitly assigned or directory trustee rights that are inherited.

Refer to Figures 12-3 and 12-4 for sample effective rights calculations for given scenarios. The Directory structure is \ACCTG\SPREADSHEET, and the file MAIN.WK1 is in the \ACCTG\SPREADSHEET directory.

The Directory Structure for Figure 12-4 is \ACCOUNTING\DATABASE with MAIN.DBF in the \ACCOUNTING\DATABASE driectory.

# File Attributes

Information stored on the file server is stored in files. These files can have several different **file attributes** that may further control the user's access or track the use of the file. Attributes limit what a user can do with a file in much the same way that directory rights limit what can be done with the files in a directory. For instance, a file can have a Read Only attribute, which means the user cannot write to it or delete it. The file is said to be "flagged" Read Only. If the user has the Modify File Name/Flags right, he or she can remove the Read Only flag from the file using either the DOS ATTRIB command or NetWare Administrator. This allows the Administrator or the user to safeguard certain files against such actions as accidental changes or deletions, while still being able to make those changes if necessary. If the user does not have the Modify File Name/Flags right, he or she cannot remove the Read Only attribute. This would give the Administrator the ability to protect individual files in a directory. The file attributes available in NetWare are as follows:

1. **A** - Archive Needed. Identifies files modified after last backup. It is assigned automatically.

2. **Cc** -Can't Compress. The file cannot be compressed.

3. **Co** -Compressed. The file is compressed.

4. **Ci** - Copy Inhibit. The file, which must have an .EXE or .COM extension, can be executed only. The program cannot be copied. This attribute cannot be removed once set.

5. **Di** - Delete Inhibited. The file cannot be deleted.

6. **Dc** - Don't Compress. This file cannot be compressed even when compression is activated for the volume.

7. **Dm** - Don't Migrate. This attribute keeps this file from being migrated to nearline storage. (This assumes that the system has been set up to migrate files from online storage to nearline storage.)

8. **Ds** - Don't Suballocate. Do not allow this file to use the system's suballocated blocks left over when a file does not use all of the block to which it is assigned.

9.  **X** - Execute Only. The file can only be executed.

10. **H** - Hidden. The file name is hidden from directory searches so it is not listed in the DOS DIR command. Unlike the DOS file attribute Hidden, a program file flagged Hidden cannot be executed.

11. **Ic** - Immediate Compress. This file will be immediately compressed when it is stored.

12. **M** -Migrated.  This file has been migrated to nearline storage. (This assumes that the system has been set up to migrate files from online storage to nearline storage.)

13. **N** - Normal

14. **P** - Purge. This attribute indicates that the file will be purged from the file system after it has been deleted. It will not be possible to undelete this file later.

15. **Ro** - Read Only.  This attribute indicates that the file can only be read.  It cannot be deleted or updated without first resetting this attribute.

16. **Rw** - Read/Write.  This file can be read, its contents can be updated, and it can be erased with this attribute set.

17. **Ri** - Rename Inhibit.  The file cannot be renamed.

18. **Sh** - Shareable. The file can be read by several users simultaneously.

19. **Sy** - System. The file is one of the operating system files. It cannot be deleted or changed by the user.

20. **T** - Transactional. This attribute is a safety feature that is usually applied to a database file. NetWare ensures that changes to the file are either completed or not made at all in case of an interruption during the process.

NetWare Administrator can be used to set file attributes as shown in Figure 12-5.

## Directory Attributes

Just as there are file attributes, there are **directory attributes**. Attributes assigned to the directory are inherited by the files in the directory. These attributes and their meanings are:

1.  **Di** - Delete Inhibited. The directory and the files in it cannot be deleted.

2.  **Dc** - Don't Compress. The files in this directory  cannot be com-

pressed even when compression is activated for the volume.

3. **Dm** - Don't Migrate. This attribute keeps this files in this directory from being migrated to nearline storage. (This assumes that the system has been set up to migrate files from online storage to nearline storage.)

4. **H** - Hidden. The file names in this directory and the directory name itself is hidden from directory searches so it is not listed in the DOS DIR command. Unlike the DOS file attribute Hidden, a program file flagged Hidden cannot be executed.

5. **Ic** - Immediate Compress. Files in this directory are to be immediately compressed when they are stored.

6. **N** - Normal.

7. **P** - Purge. This attribute indicates that the files in this directory will be purged from the file system after they have been deleted. It will not be possible to undelete this file later.

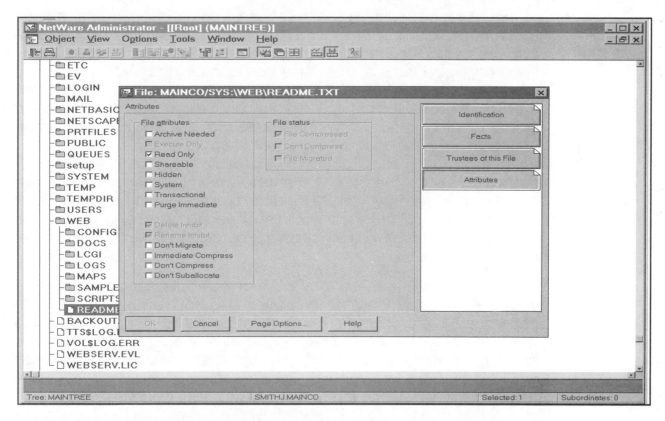

**Figure 12-5.** Setting file attributes through Netware Administrator.

8. **Ri** - Rename Inhibit. The files in this directory cannot be renamed.

9. **Sy** - System. The files in this directory are operating system files. They cannot be deleted or changed by the user.

NetWare Administrator can be used to set directory attributes similar to the way it is used to set file attributes.

# Organization

## Types of Users

When NetWare was installed, it automatically created a user account called Admin representing the Administrator. The person who assumes the role of Admin is responsible for the smooth operation of a single container up to operation of the entire network. It is the Admin's job to ensure easy and productive access to the network. As a network grows, there will likely be more than one Administrator account with each Administrator account having administration responsibility for a part of the NDS tree. For simplicity in this textbook, though, we will refer to the Admin account. A user must be given an account with access to the necessary directories and files. Most users will need drive mappings to particular directories. A typist in an office, for example, may need only read access to the directory containing a word processing program and write access to a document directory. A casual user or a user whose uses of the network are not very well defined may also need limited program groups in Windows and may not be given permission to alter his or her account. A more sophisticated user may want to control as much of his or her account as possible; the Admin may or may not want to allow the user the rights to control his or her account. In addition, this user may want to be able to configure the software he or she is using. A typist probably would not need to be able to change the configuration of the word processing program, but the office manager might.

If it is a large office there may be many people needing the same access rights and menus. One solution is to have all the typists log in under the same user name. An account called TYPIST could be set up that allows several users to be logged in at the same time. This one account could have everything a typist might want, and all the typists would share the same directory space, software, and data. This situation could work well as long as the typists could agree on how their directory space was to be handled. Having everyone log in using the same login name can be inconvenient, however. Individual typists may need a more customized environment to work with. Electronic mail and other messages could not be sent to individuals.

# Groups

With various users needing different attributes to their accounts, individual accounts would have to be created. But since many users may need the same access rights, it is possible to create **groups** of users that can be given the same rights. A group could be created called TYPIST rather than an individual account. The group would be given the rights, and then each member of the group TYPIST in the office would be made a user in that group. Each typist in the office could have his or her own login name, login scripts, passwords, and other attributes. Each member of the group TYPIST, for example, may have programs he or she wants in addition to the word processing software provided by the company. If the Administrator sets up the accounts properly, the users could have private areas on the file server to store their programs. Some of the members of the group TYPIST may wish to share some of their private directory space with only certain other individuals, not everyone in the group TYPIST. Users can make these modifications themselves assuming the Administrator has set up their accounts correctly and they know how.

## Group Hierarchy

NetWare does not explicitly provide for groups of groups, but the same thing can be accomplished logically. Suppose there were several office managers overseeing the network users. They would need access to everything the members of the group TYPIST have plus additional space for confidential employee information. A group called MANAGER could be created that has only the additional rights needed. A manager would then belong to both groups, MANAGER and TYPIST. A member of the board might need even more information available. That position might need access to pending contracts, for instance. A group called BOARD would give those members access to very critical data only, but since a member of the board might not need to see the work in progress by the members of the group TYPIST, he or she might be a member of the group BOARD and MANAGER and not TYPIST. In this way a hierarchy of users can be established so changes can be made to each group according to the functions they require.

# Data Organization

The way data is organized on the file server hard disk can greatly influence the efficiency of the network. Since the Admin is responsible for providing the users with a convenient working environment, he or she must arrange the items stored on the server in a way that will make it easy for the user to access them. This implies that it must be easy for the Admin to assign the proper rights in order to maintain security. The items on the server would need to be arranged by function, as much as possible, with data, application software, operating system software, NetWare public utilities, and NetWare system software in separate areas.

## Types of Data

All of the above items may be referred to as data. However, in this context, data is the information created and stored by the user. Application software is the set of programs used to create the data. The operating system consists of DOS and its program utilities such as FORMAT.COM and CHKDSK.COM. NetWare has several public utilities that are intended to be used by any user who knows how, since they cannot harm the accounts of anyone else. Other utilities, software, and data used only by NetWare itself or the Administrator is known as system software.

Suppose a company had the same types of users as above with members of the groups TYPIST, MANAGERS, and BOARD MEMBERS. Since each user has his or her own account, the Administrator might be tempted to arrange the directories something like the way shown in Figure 12-6.

In Figure 12-6 user JACK is a member of the group TYPIST who needs access to a word processing program and a database program. JACK stores only low security letters and bills in his data directory. JILL, on the other hand, is a manager and needs to use the same type of software but must store very sensitive data such as employee evaluations and contract bids. JACK could be made a trustee with full rights in the F:\JACK\DATA directory and only read rights in the F:\JACK\APPS directory. JILL would then need similar rights in the directories under F:\JILL, but she would also need full access to JACK's data directory.

Since there are usually more members of the group TYPIST than managers supervising them, JILL would need full rights to all the members of the group TYPIST.

The network Admin would have to list each of the members of the group TYPIST data directories under JILL's trustee assignments. Also, the software that each of these users needs is being duplicated, wasting space and installation time. A more efficient approach would be to put all the software under one directory and all the data under another.

Figure 12-7 shows a better directory structure. Under this structure the group called MANAGER would have read and write access to the entire F:\DATA directory and read access to the F:\APPS directory. The group TYPIST would have read and write access to only the F:\DATA\TYPIST directory, and it would also have read access to the F:\APPS directory.With these groups created, there could be as many members of the group TYPIST and as many managers as necessary. JACK may not have any explicit trustee rights but instead belongs to the group TYPIST. JILL also might have no trustee assignments listed in her account but her membership in the MANAGER group would give her all the rights she needs.

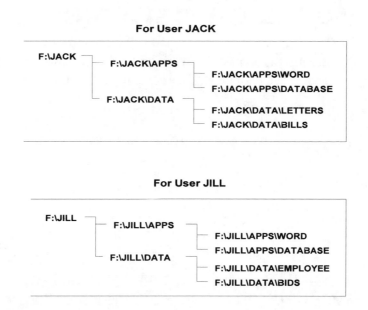

Figure 12-6. Directory arrangement.

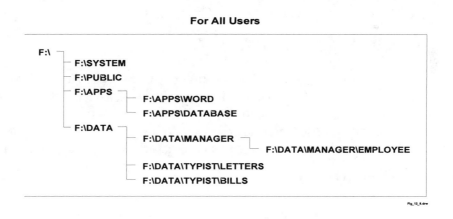

Figure 12-7. A more efficient directory arrangement.

Assigning rights to groups, in general, makes a networking system easier to maintain. For example, let's say that Jack's work doubles, and the comp-any hires an additional typist named Paula. Assuming that Jack receives all of his rights through the group TYPIST, Paula's account can be created and added to the TYPIST group rather than forcing the administrator to assign rights directly to Paula's user account.

# Hands-on NetWare

In order to complete the hands-on section of this chapter, the file server and a workstation should be ready to use.

1. The file server must be on.

2. A workstation must be booted and the appropriate network drivers must be loaded.

3. Network Drive F: should be the default first network drive at the workstation.

4. The user account created in the previous chapter must still be available, and the user must be logged in.

In the example below, **TYPE THE NAME OF YOUR ACCOUNT WHERE SMITHJ IS USED**. For instance, if the instructions read "LOG IN as SMITHJ", you should LOG IN as your user account with Admin capabilities.

Each numbered set of instructions can be completed at different times, as long as they are finished in order. For instance, the exercise on Minimum Password Length must be completed before the exercise on Force Periodic Password Changes.

## Levels of Security

As discussed earlier NetWare provides the Administrator with five levels of security. With these five levels, a blanket can be woven around the data providing just the right amount of access for each user. The following instructions will demonstrate the properties of the first four levels of security. The fifth level of security will be discussed in Chapter 14.

## Passwords

Passwords are the "first line" of defense against intentional attempts to break network security. Two restrictions that can be placed on the password are Minimum Password Length and Force Periodic Password Changes as shown in Figure 12-8.

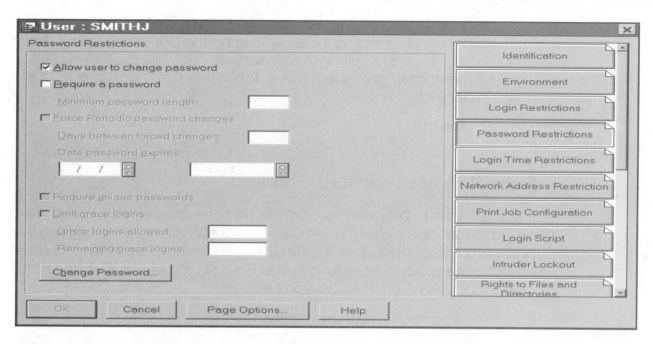

**Figure 12-8.** NetWare Administrator Password Restrictions screen.

## Changing the Password and Minimum Password Length

If a user is allowed to change the password, he or she may be tempted to use very short words to make memorizing it easier. Unfortunately, it also becomes easier to guess. For this reason a minimum length can be set on the password. A program called SETPASS can be run at the command prompt. This program requires the user to enter the old password and then to enter the new password two times to verify its accuracy. The SETPASS program is self-explanatory and is not discussed further here.

The password can also be changed by using NetWare Administrator.

1. Log in with **your user name**.

2. Activate Windows 3.1 if necessary. If you are logging in from Windows 95, Windows 95 is already activated.

3. Double-click on the **NetWare Administrator** icon previously created.

4. Double-click on the **MAINCO container** and open other containers until your user ID is visible.

5. Right-click on **your user ID** and choose **Details.**

6. Click on the **Change Password button**. Figure 12-9 appears.

7. Enter **the old password and the new password** in both new password boxes and click OK. The password is changed.

8. If you are not going to do further work, close NetWare Administrator by double-clicking on the box at the upper left of the NetWare Administrator screen. (In Windows 95, you can alternately click the X box in the upper right-hand corner of the screen.)

9. **Log out**.

## Force Periodic Password Changes

Forcing a user to periodically change his or her password is considered an important component of password security. However, changing the password too often makes it difficult to remember. The following steps illustrate the process of setting Force Periodic Password Changes and what happens when the password expires.

1. Log in with **your user name**.

2. Activate Windows 3.1 if necessary. If you are logging in from Windows 95, Windows 95 is already activated.

3. Double-click on the **NetWare Administrator icon** previously created.

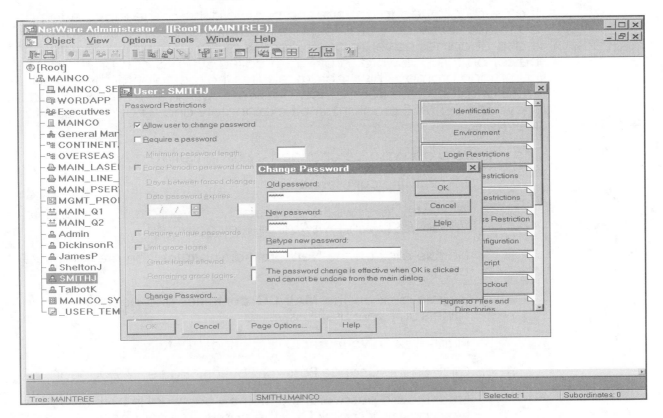

**Figure 12-9.** Change Password dialog in NetWare Administrator.

4. Double-click on the **MAINCO container** and open other containers until your user ID is visible.

5. Right-click on **your user ID** and choose Details.

6. Click on the **Password Restrictions button.**

7. Refer to Figure 12-8 to require a password and to force period password changes every 30 days starting today a minute or two from now. Be sure to click **OK** to save the changes.

8. If you are not going to do further work, close NetWare Administrator by double-clicking on the box at the upper left of the NetWare Administrator screen. (In Windows 95, you can alternately click the X box in the upper right-hand corner of the screen.)

9. **Log out.**

10. Wait a few minutes (long enough for the expiration date and time to take effect) and **log in** again. What happened?

# Trustee Rights

The second level of security, trustee rights, requires the most work on the part of the Administrator. NetWare Administrator is used to identify each directory the user or group has trustee rights in. In the following steps you will use your account to give yourself trustee rights in a new directory. Depending on how NetWare 4 is installed, the ADMIN is usually given the Supervisor right to the root of each volume of each server. However, since NetWare 4 is usually an enterprise network with many subadministrators, the Admin customarily will need to grant rights to subadministartors as well as users in a manner similar to what is shown below.

1. Log in with **your user name**.

2. Activate Windows 3.1 if necessary. If you are logging in from Windows 95, Windows 95 is already activated.

3. Double-click on the **NetWare Administrator icon** previously created.

4. Double-click on the **MAINCO container** and open other containers until your user ID is visible.

5. Right-click on **your user ID** and choose **Details.**

6. Click on the **Rights to Files and Directories button** on the right side of the screen.

7. Figure 12-10 is displayed. Don't be misled into thinking that the user has no rights. Click on the **Show button** and then navigate until you find the SYS volume listed on the Available Objects list as shown in Figure 12-11.

8. Click on MAINCO_SYS and click OK. (Click on your SYS volume whatever its name happens to be.)

9. The existing file and directory rights on this volume are displayed as in Figure 12-12.

10. Click on each File or Directory to see what rights are assigned to that selection as shown in Figure 12-12.

11. Add a trustee assignment to the WEB directory that gives your user rights to read and update files in that directory. To do this, first click on Add. Then double-click on the SYS volume, MAINCO_SYS in this case, in the right side of the screen.

12. Click on the WEB directory in the left window of the screen as shown in Figure 12-13. Then click the OK button.

13. Click on the Write right, and then click the OK button. See Figure 12-14.

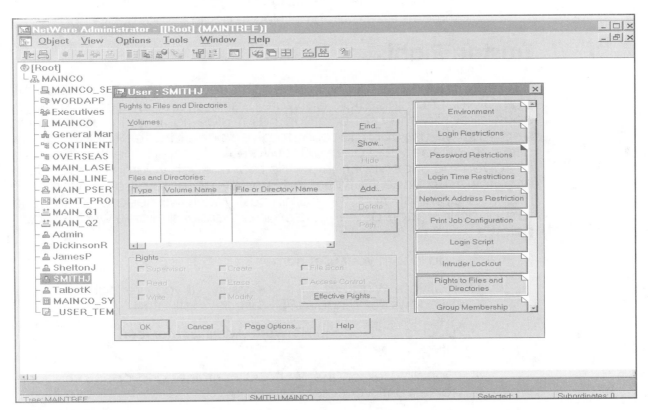

Figure 12-10. Rights to Files and Directories screen.

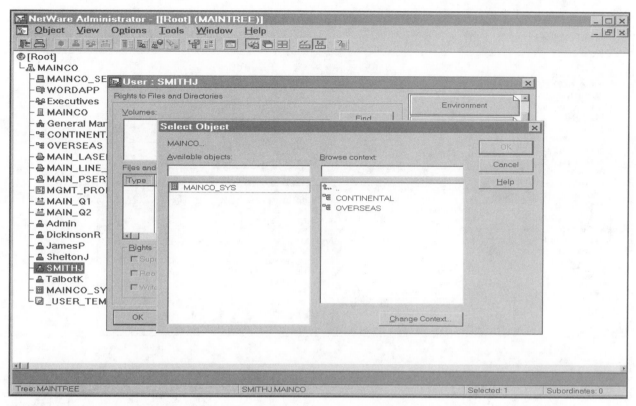

**Figure 12-11.** Available Objects screen.

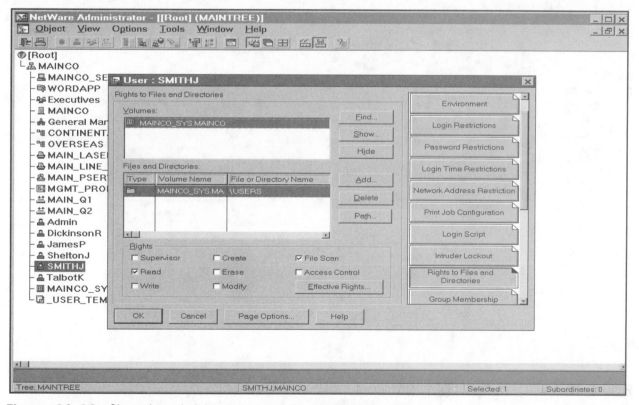

**Figure 12-12.** Showing rights assigned on MAINCO_SYS.

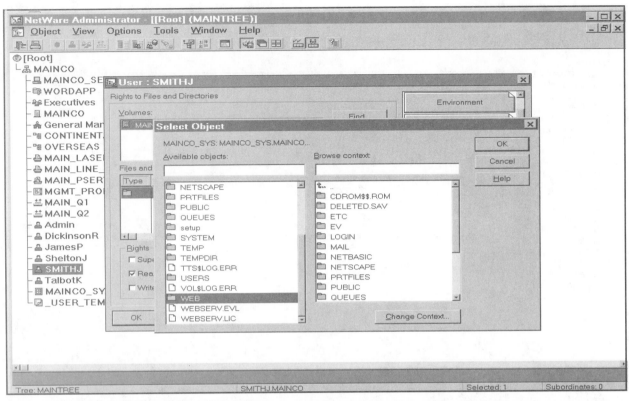

**Figure 12-13.** Selecting the directory for which rights are to be assigned.

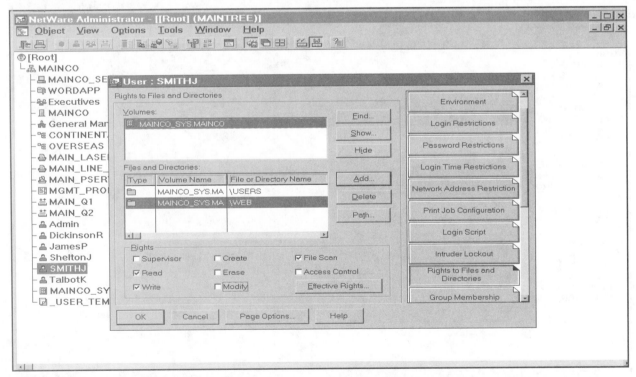

**Figure 12-14.** Directory rights granted for the WEB directory.

14. If you are not going to do further work, close NetWare Administrator by double-clicking on the box at the upper left of the NetWare Administrator screen. (In Windows 95, you can alternately click the X box in the upper right-hand corner of the screen.)

15. Log out.

# Directory Attributes

The Administrator can set each user's access rights to particular values in particular directories. The user automatically has the same rights in any subdirectory. For instance, user SMITHJ in the preceding example was given complete rights to the MAIL directory. If any directories are created below the MAIL directory, user SMITHJ will have complete rights to those as well.

Often, in a large directory structure, one or two directories may need to be restricted so that users have rights to these directories only when they are explicitly given by granting Trustee Directory Rights. Inherited Rights can be restricted by creating an inherited rights filter that restricts all users except those with Supervisor file system authority. The following directions illustrate how the NetWare Administrator program is used to make the directory rights changes.

1. Log in with **your user name**.

2. Activate Windows 3.1 if necessary. If you are logging in from Windows 95, Windows 95 is already activated.

3. Double-click on the **NetWare Administrator icon** previously created.

4. Double-click on **the MAINCO container** and open other containers until the MAINCO_SYS volume to display its contents.

5. Right-click on **the WEB directory** and choose **Details.**

6. Click on **the Attributes button** on the right of the screen.

7. Click **the directory attributes desired** and click the **OK button**.

# File Attributes

File attributes could be said to be the last line of defense in security since often they are used to prevent accidental erasure or changes to files. With a file flagged as Read Only, no user, including the Administrator, can change or delete the file. If the user has the Modify File Names/Flags right in the directory, the Read Only attribute can be set to Read Write, which then allows changes. The following short exercise demonstrates this point.

1. Log in with **your user name.**

2. Activate Windows 3.1 if necessary. If you are logging in from Windows 95, Windows 95 is already activated.

3. Double-click on the **NetWare Administrator** icon previously created.

4. Double-click on **the MAINCO container** and open other containers until the MAINCO_SYS volume to display its contents.

5. Position on **the Readme.txt file under the WEB directory.** Right-click and select **details.** Figure 12-15 is displayed.

6. Click on **Attributes.** The file is already set to Read Only. Click **Cancel** to leave this screen.

7. To prove that the read-only attribute keeps the file from being erased, click on **the Readme.txt file** and the press the **Del key**. Click on the **Yes button** to confirm the delete. The message shown in Figure 12-16 shows that the file cannot be deleted.

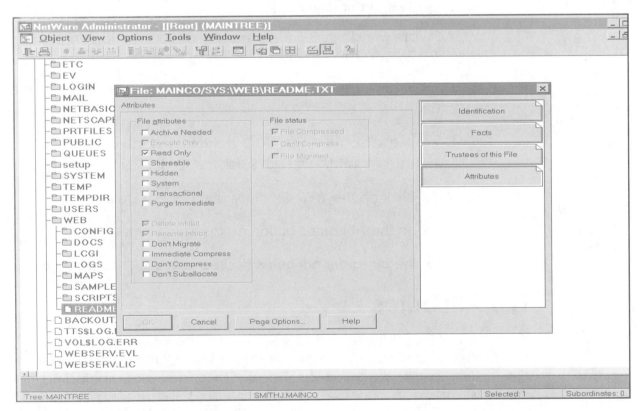

**Figure 12-15.** Directory attributes.

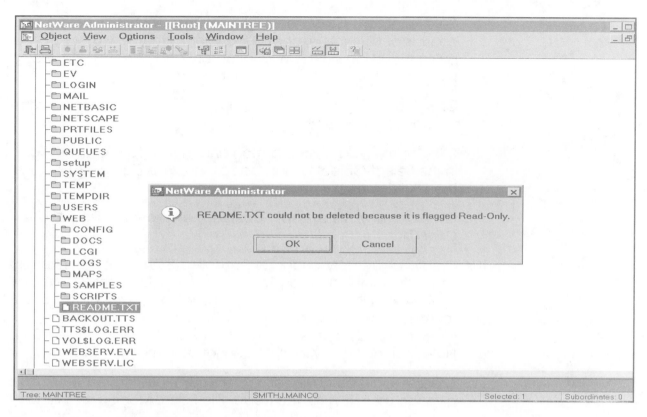

**Figure 12-16.** README.TXT cannot be deleted.

## Effective Rights

The combination of trustee rights and directory rights is called a user's effective rights. The effective rights are those rights that are granted specifically in the user trustee assignments and/or inherited by a combination of rights inherited from the parent directory which are not limited by the inherited rights mask. To show this, a user account that is non-Administrator-equivalent is needed. The following steps create such a user.

1. Log in with your user name.

2. Activate Windows 3.1 if necessary. If you are logging in from Windows 95, Windows 95 is already activated.

3. Double-click on the NetWare Administrator icon previously created.

4. Create a new user. This user should be called NEWxxx where XXX is your initials.

5. Create a directory under SYS: called DIRxxx where xxx is your initials.

6. Give directory file system rights at the DIRAFB directory that consists of all rights except Supervisor to the new user. Do this by right-clicking on the new directory and selecting details. A figure similar to Figure 12-17 is displayed.

7. Click the Trustees of this Directory button to obtain the screen shown in Figure 12-18.

8. Click on the Add Trustee button and then locate your new user in the Select Object dialog box as shown in Figure 12-19. Click the OK button.

9. Click on all rights except Supervisor as shown in Figure 12-20. Click OK.

10. Create a directory under DIRxxx called SUB1. Set the inherited rights filter for this directory to Read and File Scan only. Do this by right-clicking the directory name, clicking on trustees of this directory and then removing the checks from all but the Read, Create, File Scan, and Access Control boxes as shown in Figure 12-21. Note that the Supervisor right cannot be removed. Click OK.

11. Create a directory under SYS:\DIRxxx\SUB1 called SUB2 and give the user NEWxxx the Read, File Scan, Modify, and Access Control trustee assignments.

12. Log in as the new user you just created. Position on the new directory called DIRxxx. Right-click, select details, and click on trustees of this directory. Click on the Effective Rights button. Browse to find the user NEWxxx to show the effective rights of the user in the new directory DIRxxx. Note that the rights are the same as the trustee rights that you specifically granted to the new user NEWxxx.

13. Click the Close button and then the Cancel button.

14. Double-click the DIRxxx directory to display the \DIRxxx\SUB1 directory. Right-click on the SUB1 directory and select details. Click on the trustee list of this object. What user(s) have explicit rights to \DIRxxx\SUB1?

15. Click the Effective Rights button to display the user's effective rights in \DIRxxx\SUB1. Observe that the effective rights are (RCFA). The rights have been limited by the inherited rights filter on the SUB1 directory.

16. Click the Close button, and click the Cancel button.

17. Double-click the SUB1 directory to expose the SUB2 directory. Right-click on the SUB2 directory and select details. Click on Trustees of this Directory. Click the Effective Rights button to display the new user's effective rights to the directory.

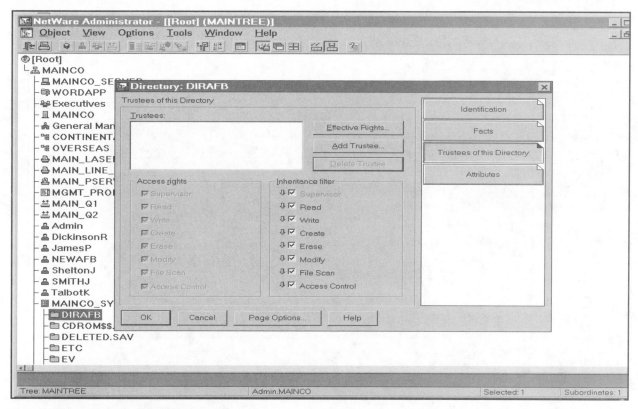

Figure 12-17. Details of DIRAFB.

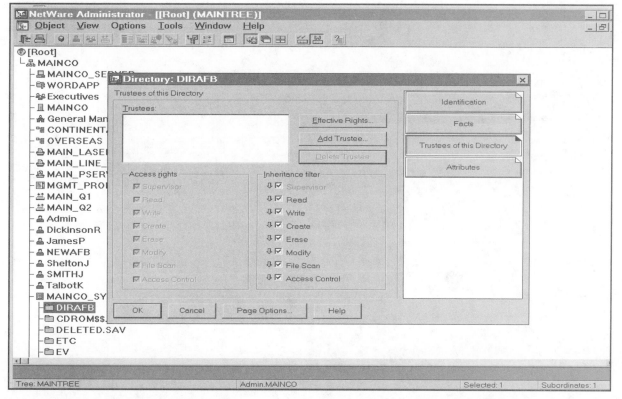

Figure 12-18. Trustees of DIRAFB.

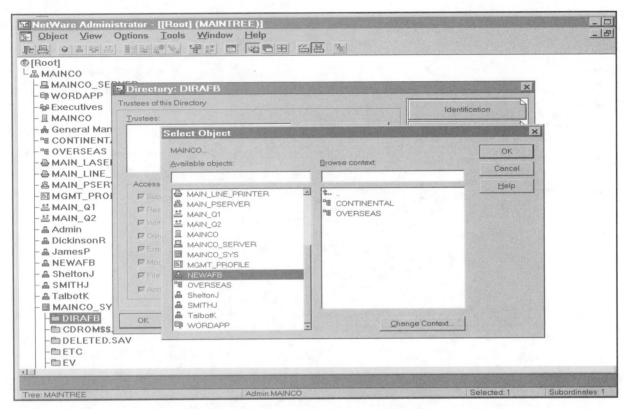

**Figure 12-19.** Selecting NEWAFB to be a trustee of DIRAFB.

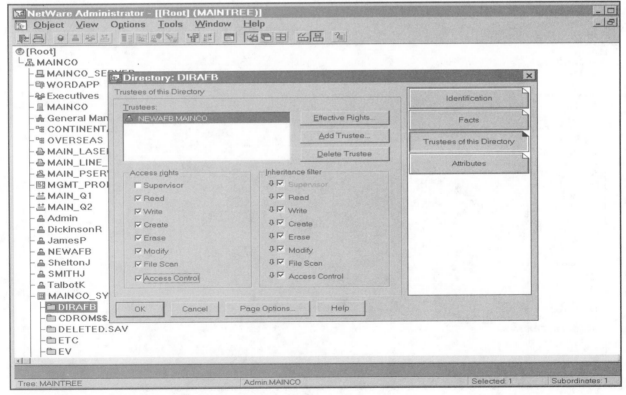

**Figure 12-20.** Rights to DIRAFB given to NEWAFB.

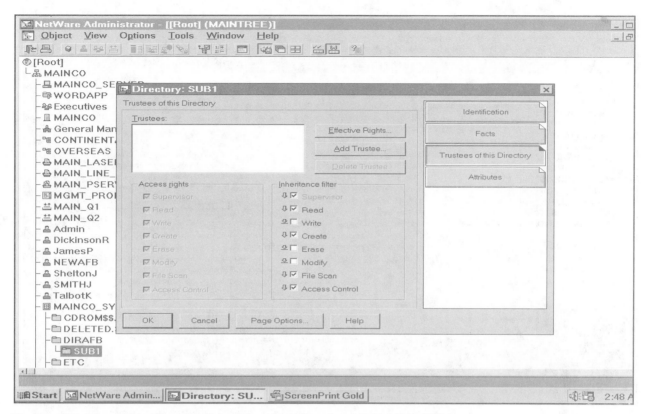

**Figure 12-21.** Inherited Rights Filter setting for \DIRAFB\SUB1.

# Groups

The new account created in the previous section was not given Administrator equivalence. Therefore, the only rights available were those granted in the Trustee Assignments list. Since it can become tedious to maintain many users' accounts when new directories are added, NetWare provides the ability to assign users to a group, and then simply grant the group trustee rights. The following example illustrates the use of groups when assigning trustee rights.

1. Log in with **your user name**.

2. Activate Windows 3.1 if necessary. If you are logging in from Windows 95, Windows 95 is already activated.

3. Double-click on the **NetWare Administrator icon** previously created.

4. Create **a group under MAINCO called GROUPXXX** where xxx is your initials. Place your new user in the group by clicking the Members button as in Figure 12-22.

5. Click on the **Add button** and select the new user as a member. Click **OK** as in Figure 12-23.

385

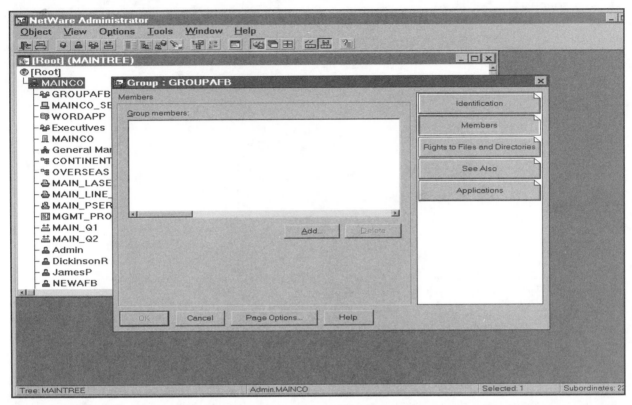

**Figure 12-22.** GROUPAFB initial group membership screen.

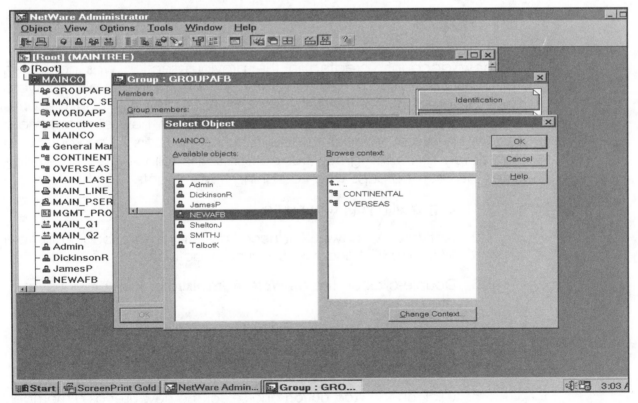

**Figure 12-23.** Adding NEWAFB to GROUPAFB.

6. Click on **Rights to Files and Directories** and then click on the **Add button**. Navigate on the right of the screen until you can select the \DIRxxx\SUB directory on the left of the screen and click **OK**.

7. Click on **all rights including the Supervisor right** and click the **OK button.**

8. Repeat the above process, logging in as the new user and checking rights to directories

   DIRxxx

   \DIRxxx\SUB1

   \DIRxxx\SUB1\SUB2

   Note that the group rights from the new group were combined with the user's rights to form the effective rights.

# Summary

Network security is broken down into five levels; passwords, trustee rights, directory attributes, file attributes, and NDS Object and Property rights. The first four levels were covered in this chapter, and NDS rights will be covered in Chapter 14. The Administrator can place certain restrictions on the password that are intended to force the user to maintain a secure password. The only rights a user has in a given directory are those granted by the Administrator. These rights will be listed in the user's trustee assignments.

Additionally, the user could obtain rights from groups to which he or she belongs, Organizational Roles he occupies, other users to which he is security equivalent, the container(s) that contain the user, and from the special object (PUBLIC). Rights from each of these sources are filtered by the inherited rights filter to filter out unwanted inherited rights, and then they are combined together on a directory by directory basis to form the user's effective rights. The inherited rights for all users except the Administrator are restricted by the inherited rights filter placed on a directory. File attributes are primarily used to prevent accidental damage to files because the attributes apply to the Administrator as well as the other users. With the proper rights in a directory, the file attributes can be changed. The combination of all the rights and restrictions a user has in a given directory is known as the effective rights.

Users usually fall into categories that require different rights and restrictions. NetWare provides the ability to put these users into groups that can be given the same rights as the users. The groups can then be structured to allow the Administrator to make changes easily to many user accounts by changing only the group account. Additionally, a user can receive rights from being an occupant of an organizational role, from being security equivalent to another user, from rights assigned to the container(s) that hold the user and from rights assigned to the special object (PUBLIC).

Information on the server must be organized as well. Programs and operating system software should be placed in one region and data created by the users in another. This structure has several advantages. The software and data can be more easily shared. The trustee assignments can be more easily standardized, and the Administrator can more easily isolate the data that must be backed up on a regular basis.

# Questions

1. Describe the four levels of security discussed in this chapter.

2. What is the fifth level of security?

3. Can any user change his or her password?

4. What trustee rights are automatically granted to any user?

5. A user has all trustee rights in a directory but still cannot access the files in it. What could be preventing him from using the files?

6. A user checks her own Trustee Assignments list and finds that the only directory listed is her MAIL directory, yet she is able to use many different programs on the server. How can this be?

7. What are the six ways that a user can obtain directory and/or file trustee rights?

8. What are the minimal directory trustee assignments given when a user is made a trustee of a directory?

9. What directory rights are needed to change the contents of a file?

10. What is the effect of the Ic Directory Attribute?

# Projects

## Objective

The following projects provide additional practice in establishing security and trustee rights.

### Project 1: Practicing the Login Script Commands

1. Given the following directory structure, write the MAP commands needed to map the drive letters H:, I:, J:, and K: to the numbered directories. Do not attempt to perform these operations on the computer unless appropriate directories have been established.

```
F:\___ |
        |-ACCOUNTS
        |    |
        |    |-RECEIVE (1)
        |    |-PAY (2)
        | - APPS
        |-PERSONEL
        |    |
        |    |-ARCHIVE
        |    |    |
        |    |    |-FULLTIME (3)
        |    |    |-PARTTIME
        |    |
        |    |-CURRENT
        |         |-FULLTIME
        |         |-PARTTIME (4)
```

2. Write the MAP command needed to give a search drive to the APPS directory.

3. Create a new user. Give the new user a login script that prints "Happy Birthday" on your birthday.

4. Using the network, create a directory structure similar to the following:

F:\___ |

     | -(Your User Name)

        |

     | -SECURE

        |

     | -DATA

Using the NetWare Administrator create a new user with all trustee rights to the directory (your user name) except Supervisor and Access Control. Use NetWare Administrator to make the contents of the SECURE directory inaccessible to the user. Use the SHIFT/PRINT SCREEN keys at each step and remove the directories and the user when you are finished.

5. Test your activities. How do you know that what you have done actually works?

## Project 2: More Practice with Effective Rights

All questions in this project are based on the following file system directory structure:

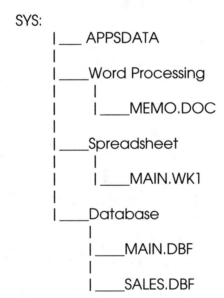

```
SYS:
    |___ APPSDATA
    |
    |___Word Processing
    |       |
    |       |___MEMO.DOC
    |
    |___Spreadsheet
    |       |
    |       |___MAIN.WK1
    |
    |___Database
            |
            |___MAIN.DBF
            |
            |___SALES.DBF
```

A.   Sam is given all rights except the Supervisor directory right to the APPSDATA directory. The Spreadsheet directory has an Inherited Rights Filter of (R C FM}

What are Sam's effective rights to the MAIN.WK1 directory? Can he update the file?

B.   Jackie is given (R C MF) to the APPSDATA directory. She also belongs to the Accounting group, which is given (RWF) to the Database directory. The Inherited Rights Filter on the Database directory is (RF). What are Jackie's effective rights within the Database directory?

C.   Determine the effective rights at each level for Jackie and for the group Accounting. Then add the effective rights together at each level to determine Jackie's overall effective rights.

# 13
# Network Printing

## Objectives

After completing this chapter you will

1. Understand the concepts of network printing.

2. Know how network printers can be attached to the network.

3. Know how to install and configure a print queue, printer, and print server.

4. Know how to activate and control a print server.

5. Be able to send data to a network printer.

## Key Terms

Print Queue

PCONSOLE

Print Server

Printer

Auto Load

PSERVER

Manual Load

NPRINTER.NLM

Remote Printing

NPRINTER.EXE

CAPTURE

# Introduction

Often an important function of a network is printer sharing. Printing across a network involves loading special software on the workstation that remains resident along with the other network drivers. The software intercepts output that a normal application such as a word processor sends to the workstation's printer port. That data is then sent across the network to a printer attached to another computer, which is either the file server running the print server software, another file server running remote printer software, or a workstation running remote printer software. With a network, many users can send output to the same printer. Also, for different purposes, users may wish to select among different types of printers available on the network.

NetWare has supported network printing since its earliest versions, but earlier printing support lacked many important features. Several third-party products offered capabilities that made network printing a much more valuable resource. With later versions of NetWare, however, some of these features have been introduced as separate utilities.

Printers can be attached to the network in several ways:

**Attached to the file server that is the print server**

**Attached to another file server in the enterprise**

**Attached to a workstation**

In addition, several third party vendors have produced products that allow even more flexibility in printing. Only the first three methods will be discussed here.

To accommodate the many users and printers that might be on a network, NetWare 4.11 has three main printing objects with various properties attached to each one. These are:

**Print Queue**

**Printer**

**Print Server**

These three objects are linked together to provide the printing function, and each of these objects has properties or characteristics that are defined to customize network printing for the entire enterprise.

# Print Queue

Obviously, if everyone on the network sent data to a printer at once, problems would arise. A system had to be created to allow the data from each user to be stored and printed when the printer becomes available. Print queues provide this function and more. Essentially, a **print queue** is a file on one of the volumes of a server that holds a print job until it can be serviced by a print server to be sent to an appropriate printer. The NetWare Administrator utility and the DOS text-based printing utility, **PCONSOLE**, can be used to create and configure a print queue. The following steps will create a print queue named Acctg_1 in the Accounting container.

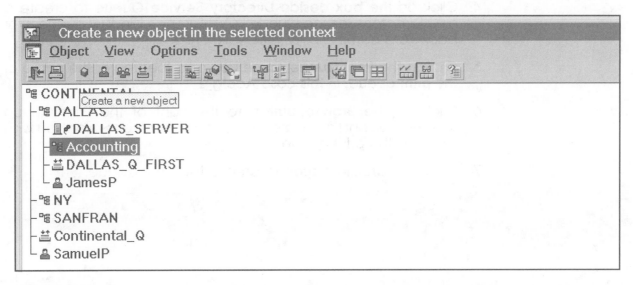

**Figure 13-1.** Create a new object.

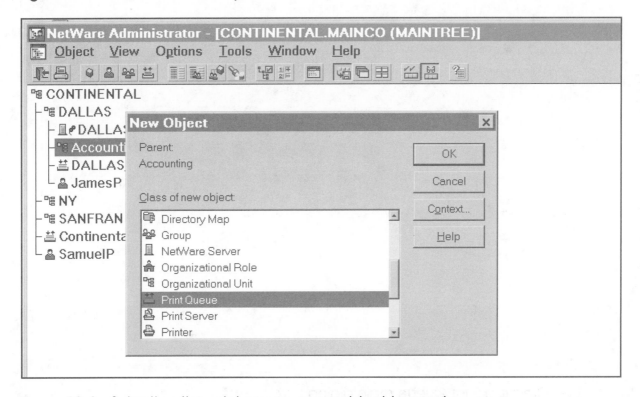

**Figure 13-2.** Selecting the print queue as an object to create.

1. Click on **the container in which the print queue is to be created**, and then click on the **Create a New Object icon** on the menu bar at the top of the screen as shown in Figure 13-1.

2. Select the **Print Queue object** and click the **OK button** as in Figure 13-2.

3. The Create a Print Queue main dialog box appears as in Figure 13-3.

4. Click on **the box beside Directory Service Queue** to create a new Directory Service Queue. (A reference bindery queue is for backward compatibility with NetWare 3.x.)

5. Click in **the Print Queue name box** and then enter **the name of the print queue, in this case Acctg_1.**

6. Click on the **Browse button** to the right of the Print Queue Volume box and navigate to find the volume on which you wish to place the print queue.

7. Click the **Create button** to create the print queue.

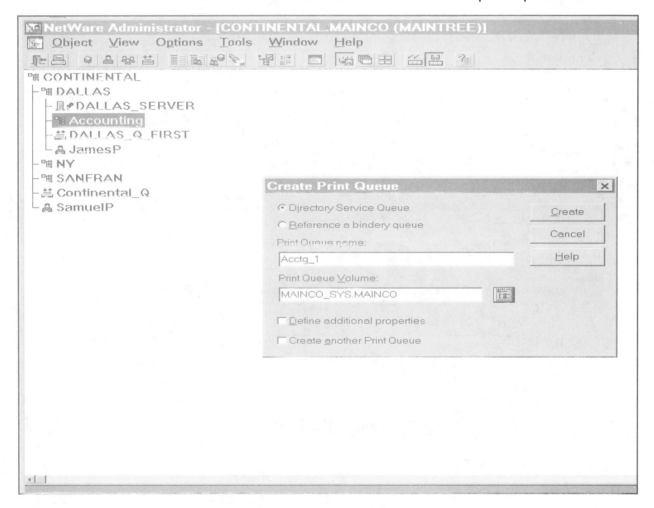

**Figure 13-3.** Create a Print Queue main dialog box.

# Print Server

A **print server** in NetWare 4.11 is a program that runs on a file server in the form of an NLM. This program monitors the queues and printers assigned to it and directs each completed job in each print queue to the appropriate printer. The following steps will create a print server object called Acctg_PS in the Accounting Container.

1. Repeat the steps used above to create an object, except this time, create a print server object.

2. The Create Print Server dialog box appears as in Figure 13-4.

3. Click in t**he Print Server Name box** and then enter **the name of the print server, in this case Acctg_PS**.

4. Click the **Create button** to complete the creation of the Print Server Object.

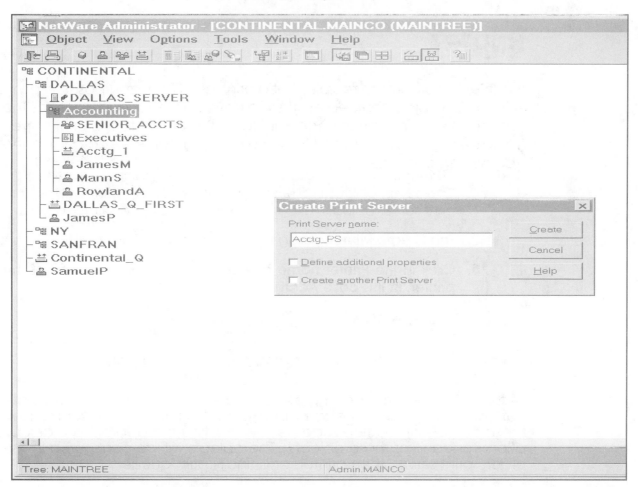

**Figure 13-4.** Create a Print Server.

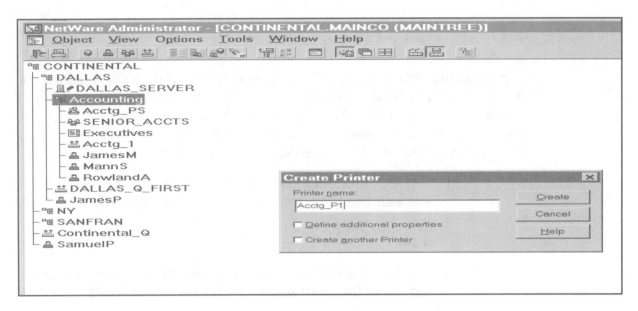

**Figure 13-5.** Create a Printer.

# Printer

A **printer** is the ultimate recipient of a print job. For our purposes, a printer is an NDS object that represents the physical printer and contains the configuration information necessary to tie the printer to the print server. The following steps are used to create a printer named Acctg_P1 in the Accounting container.

1. Create an object in the same manner as the print queue and print server objects, except be sure to create a printer object.

2. The Create Printer dialog box appears as in Figure 13-5.

3. Click in **the Printer name box** and then enter **the name of the printer, in this case Acctg_P1**.

# Tying the Print Queue, Print Server, and Printer Together

At this point, the three printing objects have been created, but they are not yet associated with each other so that printing can occur. Now, these objects will be tied together by creating the appropriate associations for each of these objects. The objects will be configured in the order: print server, then printer, and finally print queue.

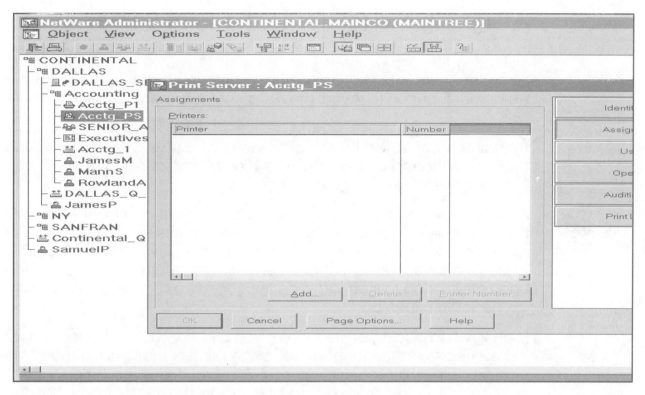

**Figure 13-6.** Assignments page for a print server.

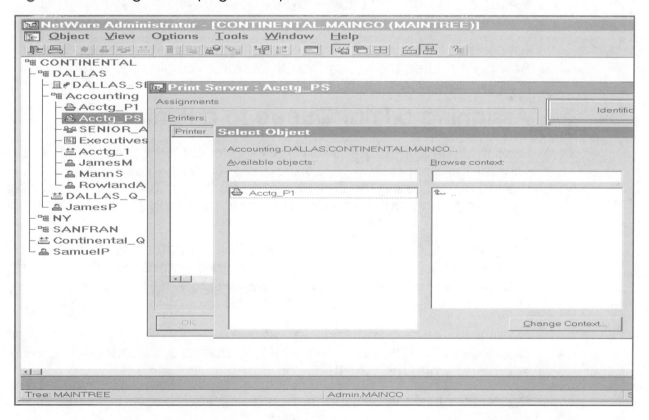

**Figure 13-7.** Adding a Printer to a Print Server.

## Assigning the Printer to the Print Server

First, using the details screen for the print server, (double-click on the Print Server object to access the details screen), click on the Assignments button to reveal the Assignments screen as shown in Figure 13-6.

The printers controlled by this print server must be added by clicking the Add button to access the Add dialog box for each printer to be controlled as shown in Figure 13-7.

A single print server can control up to 256 printers, numbered 0 to 255, but only one printer can occupy a given printer port number. For example, it would be wrong to attempt to place two printers at port 1. In fact, if this were done, the print server would return an error condition upon attempting to start, advising you that two or more printers occupy the same printer port.

Further, when adding printers to a given print server, it is simpler and far more effective in the long run to assign printers that exist in the same context as the print server. Figure 13-7, in fact, first gives the opportunity of selecting the Acctg_P1 printer created earlier. Note that the Acctg_P1 printer and the Acctg_PS print server both exist in the Accounting container.

To assign the Acctg_P1 printer to the Acctg_PS printer, click the Acctg_P1 printer, then click the OK button to display the screen shown in Figure 13-8. Click OK to save the configuration.

## Assigning a Print Queue to a Printer

Now that the printer has been assigned to the print server, it is necessary for the print queue to be assigned to the printer. This is accomplished by accessing the Details screen for the printer and then clicking the Assignments button to display the Assignments page as shown in Figure 13-9.

Assigning the Acctg_1 print queue to this printer is accomplished by clicking the Add button, clicking the Acctg_1 printer, and then clicking OK. The result of these actions is shown in Figure 13-10. Additional print queues can be assigned to this printer by repeating the Add process.

Note that the first print queue assigned becomes the default print queue for this printer. The default queue's importance will be explained when the CAPTURE command is discussed.

Remember that the OK button must be clicked to save this assignment.

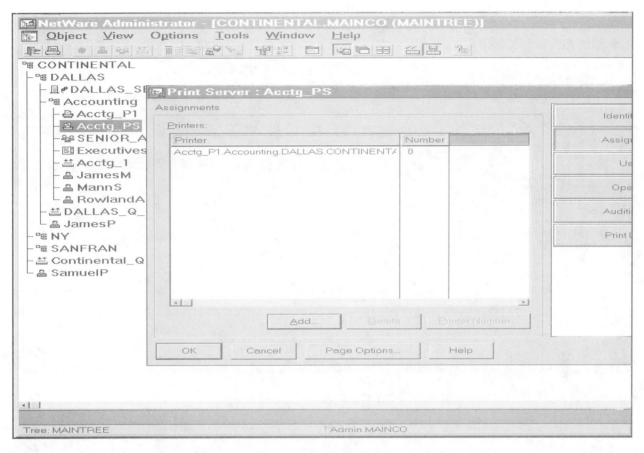

Figure 13-8. Acctg_PS with the Acctg_P1 printer assigned.

At this point, the three printing objects are now linked together. A few more steps are necessary, though, before actual printing can begin.

## Configuring the Printer

The printer object itself must be configured to match the physical usage of the printer. This is accomplished by accessing the Configuration button under the Details option for the printer object. To access this screen, double-click the printer object, then click the Configuration button to display the Configuration page as shown in Figure 13-11.

Most of the parameters on this page can be left in their default modes for beginning students. However, it is very important that the printer type match the actual interface of the printer. Usually, the interface is parallel, but this fact must be verified. Also, the communications for the printer must be specified by clicking the Communications button to display the Communications page as shown in Figure 13-12.

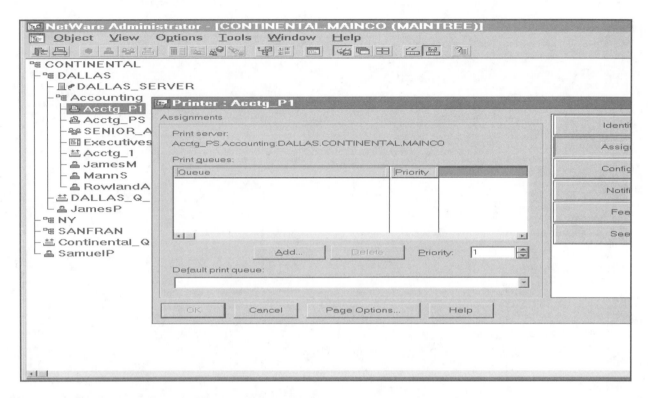

Figure 13-9. The Printer Assignments page.

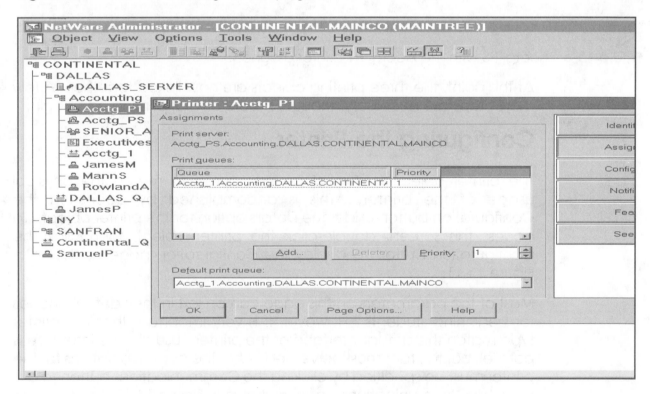

Figure 13-10. Acctg_1 Print Queue assigned to the Acctg_P1 printer.

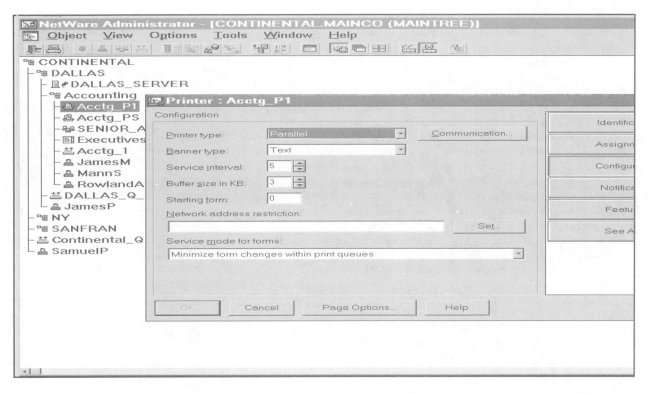

Figure 13-11. Printer Configuration page.

For a printer attached to the computer on LPT1, the normal method of communication is to use interrupt 7, and for LPT2, usually interrupt 5 is used. However, if there is no interrupt available because all interrupts are used for other devices, the printer can be operated in polled mode. Using polling, the computer to which the printer and any other polled devices are attached periodically checks with the devices to see if they need attention. The polled method is slow but it does function when an interrupt is not available. For purposes of discussion, though, interrupt 7 has been chosen.

The next item that must be specified is the connection type for the printer. Very simply, if the printer is to be directly attached to the file server running the PSERVER.NLM software controlling the print server, then the print should be specified as an **Auto Load** printer by clicking the box to the left of the Auto Load selection. If the printer is to be attached to another file server that is not running **PSERVER** or it is attached to a workstation, the printer must be specified as a **Manual Load** printer. Figure 13-13 shows a printer set up on LPT1 of the file server running PSERVER.

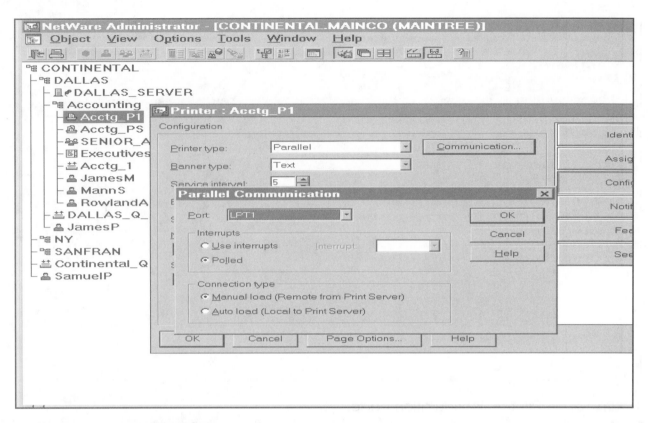

**Figure 13-12.** Parallel Communication page for printer Acctg_P1.

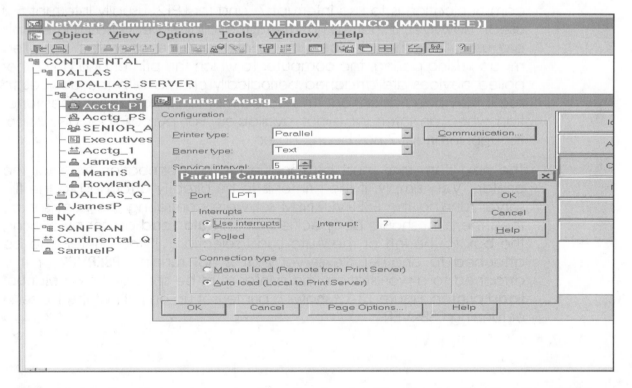

**Figure 13-13.** Parallel communications for Acctg_P1 attached to the file server running PSERVER.

## Checking the Print Queue Assignments

Now that the printer has been assigned to the print server and the print queue has been assigned to the printer, it is time to check the assignments page for the print queue. The assignments for print queue Acctg_1 are shown in Figure 13-14.

Note that by assigning the printer to the print server and the print queue to the printer that the Acctg_1 queue is automatically assigned to the print server Acctg_PS. A further check can be done by examining the print layout button under details of the print server. This screen, shown in Figure 13-15, shows that there is a queue called Acctg_1 that is assigned to a printer called Acctg_P1, which is then serviced by Acctg_PS. The exclamation point by the print server indicates that the print server is not functioning.

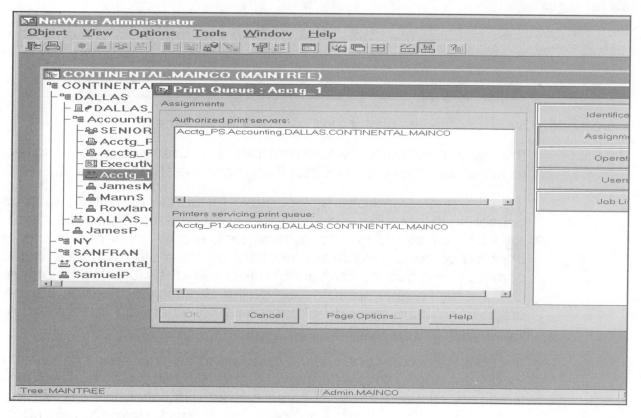

**Figure 13-14.** Print queue Acctg_1 assignments.

## Print Queue Operators and Users

By default, the print queue operator is the user that created the queue, and the print queue users are the users in the container containing the queue and print queue creator as shown in Figures 13-16 and 13-17.

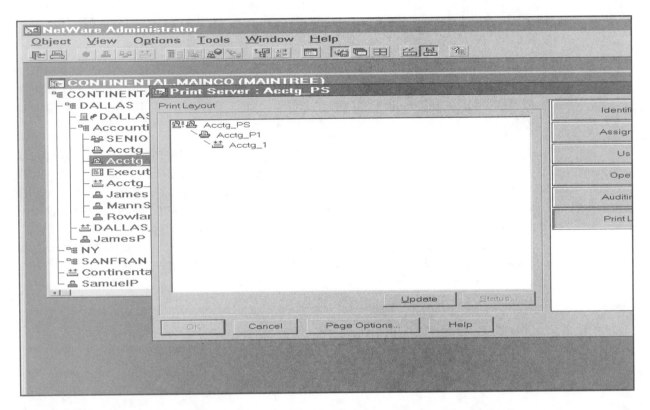

**Figure 13-15.** Overall print server, printer, and print queue assignments.

This assignment is usually sufficient because users are usually placed together with the resources that they use in the same container.

The print queue operator is responsible for queue operations such as controlling the jobs in the queue by changing their priority order, deleting jobs that should not have been sent, etc. A print queue user is capable of performing these functions on his or her own jobs, but a common print queue user cannot affect the jobs submitted by others. Only the print queue operator can do this. Additional operators can be assigned by using the Add dialog similar to other Add dialogs examined earlier in this chapter.

The print queue user can use the queue and can access his or her own jobs in the queue to delete them. Generally, all users in a given container are allowed to use a given printer. However, if this is not the desired situation, users can be added and deleted using the Add/Delete dialog discussed earlier in the chapter.

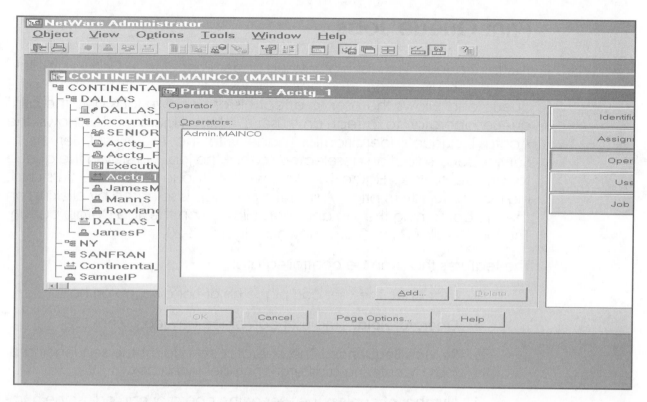

Figure 13-16. Print queue operator for print queue Acctg_1.

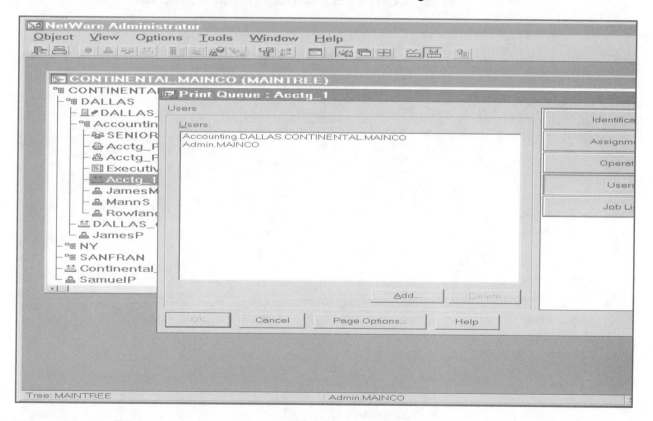

Figure 13-17. Print queue users for print queue Acctg_1.

## Print Queue Jobs

The print queue's job list is accessed under Print Queue Details by clicking the Job List button. This page shows the current status of the print queue and allows the user to affect his or her own jobs and the print queue operator to affect any user's jobs. Figure 13-18 shows the Acctg_1 queue's identification page with the Allow Print Servers to Service Jobs selection deselected so that the jobs will stay in the queue for us to examine. Figure 13-19 shows the queue with three outstanding jobs, all ready to print. A specific print job is selected by clicking on the line containing the job and then clicking on the Job Details button. The job details for job 3 are shown in Figure 13-20.

The features that can be controlled are:

1. **User Hold:** The user can place his or her own job on hold.

2. **Operator Hold:** The user can place any job on hold.

3. **Service Sequence:** The operator can adjust the sequencing of jobs by entering a different number in this box.

4. **Number of copies:** The user or the operator can adjust the number of copies for a job that has not started printing.

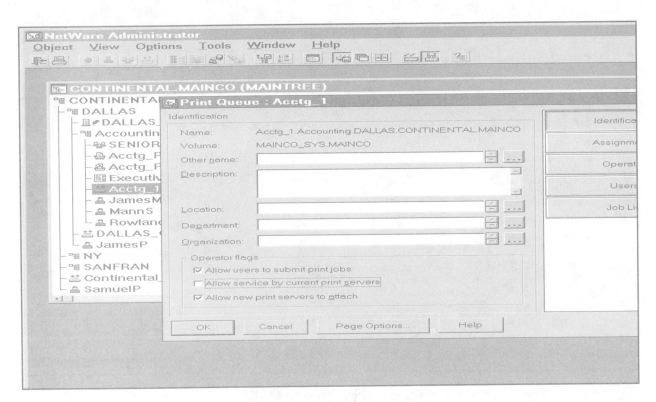

Figure 13-18. Print Queue identification page.

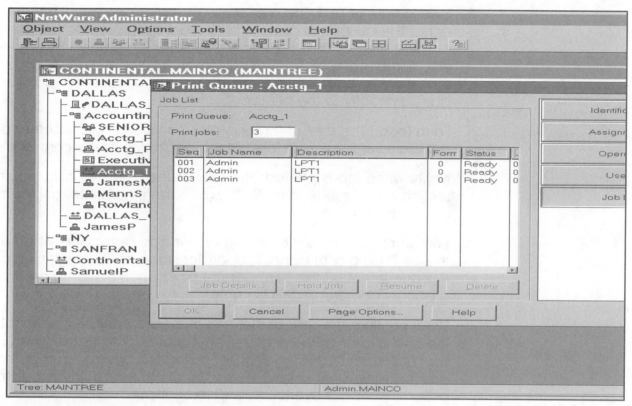

**Figure 13-19.** Print queue Job List page.

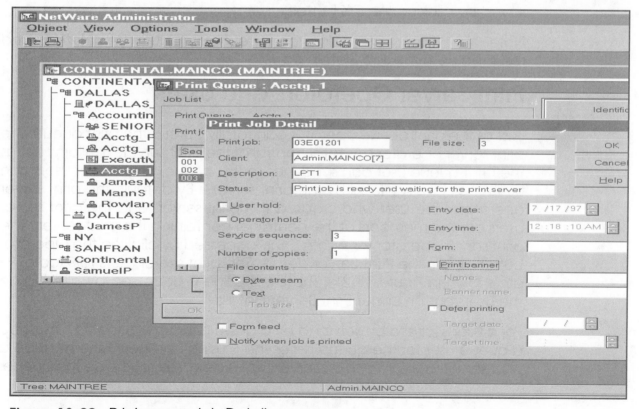

**Figure 13-20.** Print queue Job Details page.

5. **Byte Stream or Text:** The user or the operator can select whether or not the job passes all control characters through to the printer (byte stream) or if each tab character is replaced by a specific number of spaces. The customary choice is byte stream so that control characters inserted by the application can be passed directly to the printer.

6. **Form feed:** The user or the operator can determine whether or not there will be a form feed at the beginning of the print job.

7. **Notify when job is printed:** The user or the operator can adjust the job in the queue to notify the user when the printer begins to service the job.

8. **Print banner:** The user or the operator can determine whether there will be a print banner separator page at the beginning of the document. If the print banner box is marked, a name and a banner name can also be entered.

9. **Defer printing:** The user or the operator can defer printing of this job until a later date and time. This is especially useful when a user has submitted a lengthy job during the busiest hours of the day and the print output needs to be deferred so as not to adversely impact overall printing throughput.

When the desired flags and entries have been made, the changes are saved by clicking the OK button.

Note also that a given job can be held (paused), deleted, and resumed from the Job Details page.

## Print Server Operators and Users

Just as the print queue operator can totally control the print queue, the print server operator has total control of the print server. Similarly, just as the print queue user can send jobs to the queue, print server users can have their jobs serviced by the print server. By default, the print server operator is the user who created the print server, and the print server users are the members of the container containing the print server. The print server operator for Acctg_PS is accessed by clicking the Operator button under the Print Server details. The print server users for Acctg_PS are shown in Figure 13-21. The Users page is accessed by clicking on the Users button under Print Server Details.

For a user's jobs to be serviced by a given print server, the user must be a queue user for the queue he or she is using and he or she must be a print server user for the print server that is assigned to service the queue.

# Activating the Print Server

To activate the print server, enter

**LOAD PSERVER printservername**

on the file server console. This action will autoload **NRINTER.NLM** for all printers configured as directly attached to the file server (configured as Auto Load). There can be a maximum of 7 printers directly attached to the file server.

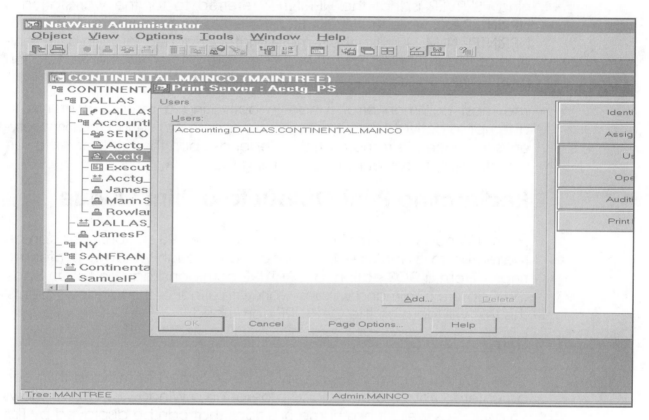

Figure 13-21. Print server users for Acctg_PS.

To activate **remote printing** for a printer attached to another file server that is not the print server, the print server itself must first be running, and then on the remote file server, the following command must be entered:

**LOAD NPRINTER printservername printerport**

where printservername is the name of the print server that is to control this printer and printerport is the port number assigned to this printer in the port assignments under the print server. The printer that is being configured in this manner must have been set up as a Manual Load printer.

To unload a print server, enter:

**UNLOAD PSERVER**

To activate remote printing for a printer attached to a workstation, it is easiest to log in and then go to the command prompt and enter

**NPRINTER printservername printerport.**

The only difference between activating the remote printer on a workstation and activating a remote printer on a file server that is not running PSERVER is that the NPRINTER referred to for the workstation is **NPRINTER.EXE** while the NPRINTER referred to for the remote file server is NPRINTER.NLM. Just like the remote printer attached through a file server that is not running PSERVER, the remote printer for the workstation must have been configured for Manual Load.

The most common error made in activating a remote printer is to attempt to activate the remote printer prior to activating the print server itself. Since the remote printer depends upon the print server to service it, the print server must be running first.

# Redirecting Print Output to a Print Queue

From a Windows 3.1 station or from a Windows 95 station, print can be redirected to a NetWare 4.11 print queue through Windows printer settings. From a DOS station, a CAPTURE command can be used. Since the Capture command will also work with either of the Windows clients, this text will focus on the CAPTURE command.

## Redirecting Print Output Using the CAPTURE command

The CAPTURE command is a very old DOS-based command that can be entered from the command prompt on a Windows 3.1 or Windows 95 station as well. It has numerous flags that can be displayed by first going to the command prompt and then entering:

**CAPTURE /?**

This command causes the various options for the CAPTURE command to be displayed as shown in Figure 13-22 through 13-24. Only a few of these flags are customarily used and will therefore be discussed here.Almost any application can be used with network printers using the CAPTURE program. It is a memory-resident program that intercepts data that the workstation sends to its printer ports, and redirects that data to a print queue. The CAPTURE program can be used in three different ways: in conjunction with the CAPTURE /ENDCAP program, with the AUTO ENDCAP feature, or with the TIMEOUT feature.

The CAPTURE /ENDCAP program is used to turn off redirection of the printer data. It essentially unloads the CAPTURE program from memory and places the data in the print queue. Notice that the data is only stored, not put in the queue, until the CAPTURE /ENDCAP program is run. This way a user may send data to the network printer in many separate pieces. When the CAPTURE /ENDCAP command is given, all the data is placed in the queue.

With the AUTO ENDCAP feature of the CAPTURE program enabled, the printer output data is sent on to the print queue when the application that created the print job terminates. For instance, if a user wants to send data to a network printer using a word processor, he or she would first run the CAPTURE program, then start the word processing program. Any printing that is done from the word processing program is stored until the user exits the word processing program. It is only then that the data is placed in the print queue.

Using the TIMEOUT feature (TI=XX) allows the user's data to be sent to the print queue while the user is still in the application program. A timeout period is given in seconds and tells the CAPTURE program when to send the data that it has captured on to the print queue. The CAPTURE program waits the time specified after the last output has been captured before placing the data in the print queue.

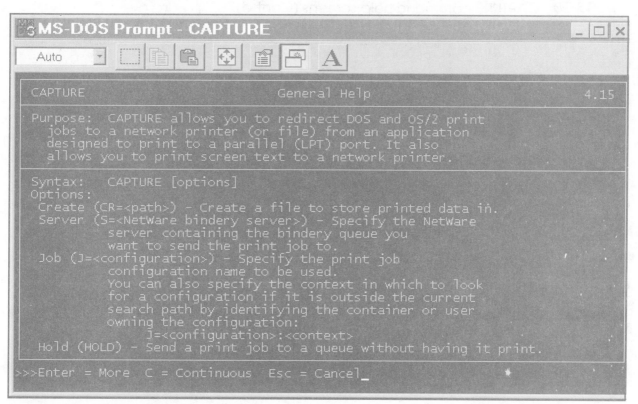

**Figure 13-22.** CAPTURE command help screens.

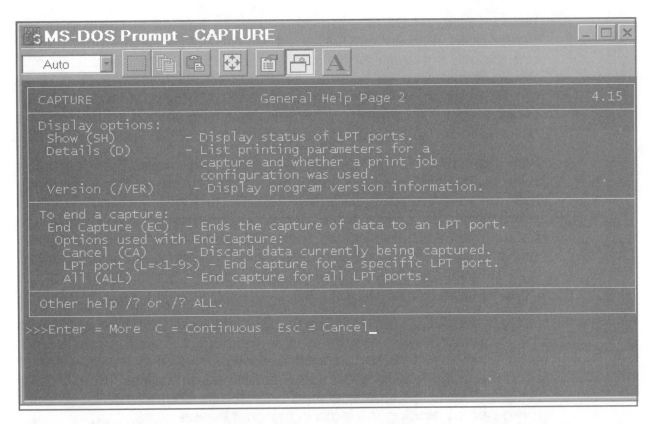

**Figure 13-23.** CAPTURE command help screens (Cont'd).

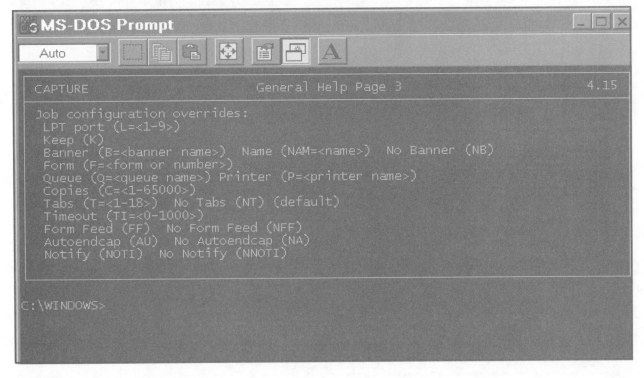

**Figure 13-24.** CAPTURE command help screens (Cont'd).

Suppose a spreadsheet program is being used with the TIMEOUT feature set to 15 seconds. When the user requests a chart to be printed, the output is stored, and a timer starts counting after the last byte is captured. If the user prints another chart less than 15 seconds later, the data will continue to be stored. The data will be sent to the print queue only when a time longer than 15 seconds passes between print requests.

Making the timeout period too short may break up data that should be printed together. For instance, it may take longer than 15 seconds for the second chart in a single report to be calculated. Someone else's data could be placed in the queue between the first and second charts.

Making the period too long may cause data that the user intended to be printed separately to be printed together instead. If the user wanted the charts to be printed separately, he or she would have to watch the clock until the 15 seconds had passed before printing the second chart. This is not usually a problem since most applications would advance to the next page before printing the second time. A period longer than a few seconds may also be a source of frustration for the user. Even when only one person is sending data to be printed, he or she must wait for the data to be captured, wait the timeout period, then wait for the print server to start processing the data in the queue. These delays can add up to a long enough time that the user may wonder if there is a problem with the printer.

The last and easiest way to send data to a network printer is to use an application program that is designed to send its output to a print queue on a NetWare network. While both Windows 3.1 and Windows 95 can be configured in this manner, the discussion of procedures used to accomplish this type of redirection are too lengthy for an introductory textbook.

A sample CAPTURE command might be:

**CAPTURE  Q=.Acctg_1.Accounting.DALLAS.CONTINENTAL.MAINCO NT NB NFF TI=120**

The effect of this capture would be to redirect output normally intended for LPT1 to the Acctg_1 queue in Byte Stream format (NT) with No Banner (NB), No initial Form Feed (NFF), and with printing starting after 120 seconds of inactivity in the print queue.

# Hands-on NetWare

In order to complete the following exercises, the file server and at least two workstations should be ready to use.

1. The file server should be on.

2. Your station must be logged into the server using your ADMINXXX account following procedures previously explained.

3. The accounts and objects created earlier should be available.

## Configuring the Print Server and Print Queue

The long list of steps below creates a new print server, new printer, and new print queue. These operations can be carried out at any workstation that is logged into the network using your ADMINXXX user created earlier. Since only one print server can be running on a file server at a time, it might be a good idea for students to work in teams to perform this hands-on exercise and the projects at the end of the chapter.

1. After logging in, start NetWare Administrator and position on the MAINCO container as shown in Figure 13-25.

2. Create a print queue called PQXXX where XXX are your initials. Use the **Browse button** to select the appropriate volume on your classroom server and then click the **Create button.**

3. Create a print server called PSXXX where XXX are your initials. Click the **Create button** after entering the name **PSXXX.**

4. Create a printer called PTRXXX where XXX are your initials. Click the **Create button** after entering the name PTRXXX.

5. Double-click the **printer object** just created, and click the **Assignments button.** Click the **Add button**, click **PQXXX**, and then click the **OK button**. This action associates the print queue with a given printer. Note that if you desire, you could add additional printers to the list of queues serviced by this printer. Your screen should look similar to Figure 13-26.

6. Click the **Configuration button** to display the configuration page for the printer, and then click the **Communication button** to set up the physical communications for the printer. Consult your instructor to determine the actual physical setup of the printer attached to your file server. In most cases, it will be running on LPT1 port with Interrupt 7, and the printer will be configured for Auto Load since it is attached to the file server. Click the **OK button** to save the configuration. Your screen should look similar to

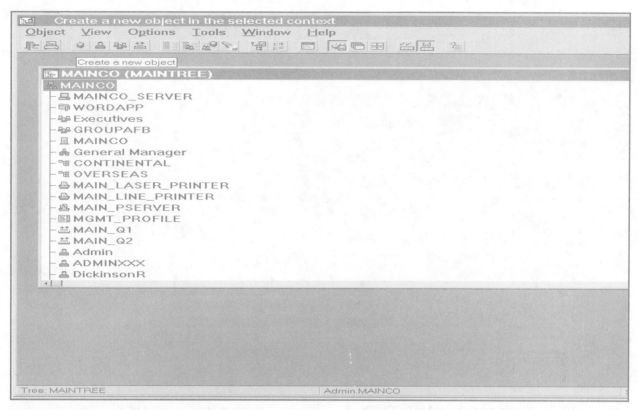

**Figure 13-25.** Position on MAINCO to create a print queue.

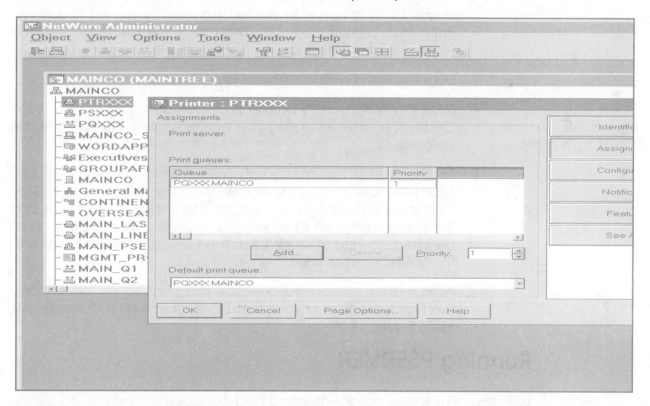

**Figure 13-26.** PQ_XXX assigned to printer PTRXXX.

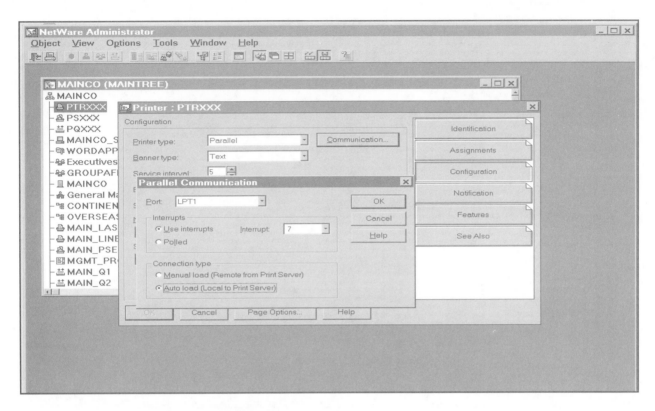

Figure 13-27.  Configuration for PTRXXX.

Figure 13-27 unless your printer is physically configured differently than described here.  Then click the OK button on the
Printer Assignments page.

7. Double-click the PSXXX object just created.

8. Click the Assignments button and then add PTRXXX.  Click the
OK button after selecting the printer.  Click OK to save the
assignment.

9. To check that the configuration is entered correctly, double-
click the PQXXX object and then click the Assignments button
to display the print server assigned to service the queue and
the printer assigned to service the queue.  Your screen should
be similar to Figure 13-28. Click the Cancel button to return to
the MAINCO container.

10. As a further check, double-click the print server object and
then click the Print Layout button.  Your screen should be similar to Figure 13-29.

## Running PSERVER

With the print server object created and configured and the print server software loaded onto the file server hard disk using the NetWare
Administrator program, the print server can be started by loading the

PSERVER program on the file server. Note that only one student at a time can load his or her print server and test it; therefore, it might be a good idea for students to work in pairs.

1.  On the file server console enter

    **LOAD PSERVER PSXXX**

2.  Wait for the print server to load.

# Sending Output to the Print Server

The Print Server is up and running. All that remains is to test it. Leave the print server software running. Use a workstation logged in as your ADMINXXX to perform these operations.

1.  Get to the Command Prompt and enter:

    **CAPTURE Q=.PQXXX.MAINCO NT NB NFF TI=120**

2.  Enter

    **COPY C:\AUTOEXEC.BAT   LPT1:**

    to copy a file to the new print queue.

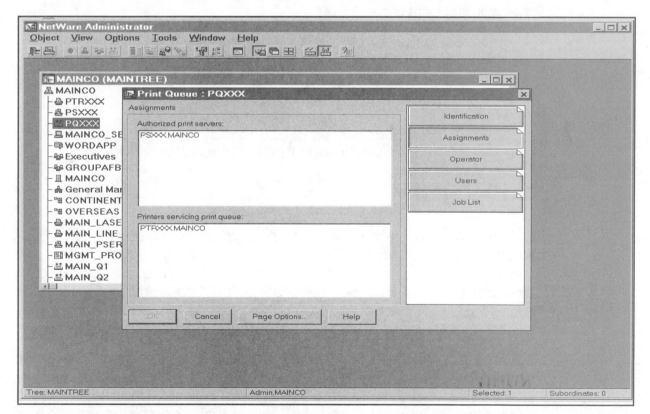

**Figure 13-28.**  Print Queue assignments for print queue PQXXX.

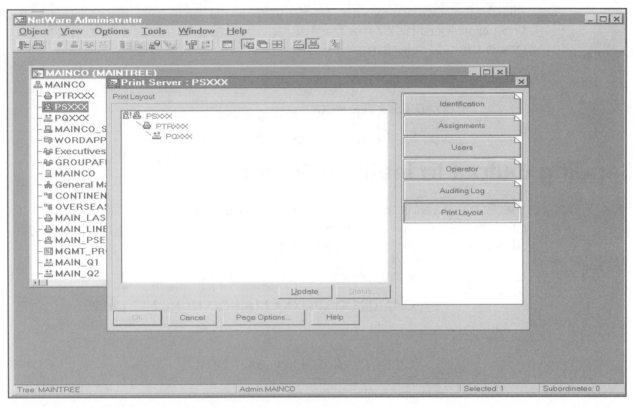

**Figure 13-29.** Print layout for print server PSXXX.

3. Go to the print server and watch the screens for the print job to get to the printer. Wait for it to print.

4. Enter CAPTURE /ENDCAP. This ends the redirection of LPT1 to the queue named PQXXX.

5. Reattempt step 2. What happened? You should have received an error message since the queue is no longer active.

# Summary

One of the most often used features of a network is sharing printers. A Novell network allows printers located on the file server that is the print server, on another file server, or on a workstation to be accessed by any user or group with authorization. NetWare Administrator can be used to redirect print output to a given queue, which is then serviced by the print server to send the output to the appropriate printer.

It is important to note that there are many other Novell printer setup options as well as printing options from third party vendors such as Hewlett-Packard than have been discussed in this chapter. Students are referred to Novell's product documentation and to the various third party printing vendors for further information.

# Questions

1. In what ways can a printer be attached to a network using NetWare 4's printer control software?

2. How many printers can be attached to file server that is running the PSERVER software?

3. If a print server has only one printer port, but two printers are attached, where are the two other places the second printer can reside?

4. Can a single print queue feed data to more than one printer?

5. What is the syntax for loading and activating a print server called MYPSERVER on a NetWare 4 file server?

6. What are the steps for creating a print queue, printer, and print server and then tying them together?

7. How can you determine whether or not you have associated the print queue, printer, and print server properly?

8. What is the CAPTURE command to redirect print from LPT1 to a print queue under the MAINCO container named MAIN_Q2?

9. What is the syntax for ending a CAPTURE command redirection?

10. What is the meaning of TI=0 for the CAPTURE command? What is the meaning of TI=120?

# Projects

## Objective

The following projects provide additional practice with the basic networking printing facilities of NetWare. Additionally, the second project provides more hands-on training in creating print queues and sending print jobs across the network.

### Project 1. Basic Network Printing

1. Create another print queue on the print server you created during the Hands-On exercise. This print queue should also be serviced by PSXXX and redirected to PTRXXXNEW.

2. Enter a CAPTURE statement that redirects print from LPT1 to the first PQXXX and print a text file from your C: drive.

3. Enter a CAPTURE statement which redirects print from LPT1 to the second print queue PQXXXNEW.

What happened? Why?

## Project 2. Advanced Network Printing

1. Create a print queue with a unique name on an existing print server. Be sure to include your user name as a print queue operator.

2. Set the printer to OFF LINE. Send a file to the print queue. Then use the NetWare Administrator utility to remove the file from the queue. Put the printer back on line.

3. Try the same operation as above, but send your data to a classmate's print queue. You should not be able to remove the print job.

## Project 3. Setting Up a Print Server with One Locally Attached Printer and One Remote Printer

1. Following instructions given in the Hands-On section of this chapter, modify your print server to have one remote printer.

2. Assign a new queue to this printer and test its operation. You will need to run NPRINTER on a workstation with a printer attached to fully test this exercise.

# 14
# NDS Security

## Objectives

After completing this chapter you will

1.  Understand the meaning of NDS object and property rights.

2.  Know how to assign NDS object and property rights to trustees to provide access to the tree.

3.  Recognize default object and property rights assigned to various users and groups by NetWare 4.11.

4.  Be able to list the ways a user obtains NDS rights.

5.  Calculate a user's effective rights.

6.  Understand the general considerations that must be made in assigning NDS object and property trustee rights.

## Key Terms

Selected Property Rights

Inherited Rights

Object Rights

Property Rights

Inherited Rights Filter

Effective Rights

## Introduction

NDS object and property rights control access to the NDS tree itself, much as directory and file system rights control access to the file system on the server(s) in the network. NDS rights, though, consist of two sets of rights:

423

**Object Rights that determine what a user can do with the objects in the tree.**

**Property Rights that determine what a user can do with the properties or characteristics of the objects in the tree.**

Just as directory and file system rights are assigned to an object called a trustee, NDS object and property rights are also assigned to an object called a trustee. Only trustees can use objects, and the rights either explicitly granted to or inherited by a trustee determine the kinds of actions the trustee can perform with an object. Except for one very small exception, NDS object and property rights have absolutely nothing to do with directory and file system rights. This one exception will be explained later in the chapter.

The purpose of this chapter is to explain the various NDS object and property rights and their meanings, to show the student how to assign these object and property rights, to explain default object and property rights automatically assigned by NetWare 4.11, to delineate the ways that a user can obtain object and property rights, to explain how to calculate effective rights, and finally to discuss considerations that should be made in designing an NDS rights structure for an NDS tree.

# NDS Object and Property Rights

## A Broad Overview of NDS Trustee Rights

A user can obtain NDS Object and Property Rights from the same sources the user could obtain file system rights from trustee assignments and inherited rights for:

**The user account.**

**The group(s) to which the user belongs,**

**The container(s) to which the user belongs,**

**The organizational roles that the user occupies,**

**The users to which this user is security equivalent,**

**The special object (PUBLIC) that supplies rights to all users connected to a file server in a NetWare 4.11 network whether or not the user is logged in.**

For a user or other object to be granted object and property rights to a given NDS object, the user must be placed on that object's Access Control List (ACL). The ACL is a property is available for every object in the NDS tree. Thus, the name of each trustee for an object must be placed in the object's Access Control List.

Like file system rights, NDS object rights can be inherited. NDS property rights are broken into two classifications: All properties, and Selected properties. Rights assigned through All Properties can be inherited just like NDS object rights. Rights assigned through the **Selected Properties** feature cannot be inherited.

Additionally, there are **Inherited Rights Filters** or IRFs that can be assigned to NDS objects and NDS properties. These IRFs work like the file system IRFs except that the Supervisor right for NDS Objects and Properties can be blocked, unlike the Supervisor right for the file system, which cannot be blocked.

# NDS Object Rights

**Object rights** determine what a trustee can do with an object. There are five NDS Object Rights:

1. **Supervisor.** This trustee assignment gives the user all access rights to both the object and to all properties of the object. This right, though, can be blocked with an IRF in NetWare 4.11.

2. **Browse**. This trustee assignment gives the users the right to see the objects in the NDS tree. Without this right, the user cannot even see the objects in the tree.

3. **Create**. This trustee assignments gives the user the right to create another object beneath this object. The Create right applies only to container objects since objects cannot be created beneath a leaf.

4. **Delete.** This trustee assignment gives the user the right to delete this object from the NDS tree.

5. **Rename.** This trustee assignment gives the user the right to rename the object.

Some students find it helpful to utilize a phrase (though not in order) such as Black Cats Do Run Swiftly to assist in remembering these five object rights.

# NDS Property Rights

NDS **Property Rights** determine what a trustee can do with the characteristics or properties of an object. NDS Property Rights are:

1. **Supervisor**. This trustee assignment gives the trustee all rights to the property. Remember, though, that the Supervisor property right can be blocked by an IRF.

2. **Compare.** This trustee assignment gives the trustee the right to compare the value of the property with other known values to

determine whether the property value is greater than, less than, or equal to the external value in question. A comparison returns a simple true or false. With this property right, the trustee cannot see the value of the property.

3. **Read**. This trustee assignment gives the trustee the right to read the value of a property of an object. This property right also implies that the trustee has the Compare right.

4. **Write**. This trustee assignment gives the trustee the right to change the value of a property of an object. This property right also implies that the trustee has the Add Self right.

5. **Add Self**. This trustee assignment gives the trustee the right to add or remove himself to a property. This property only applies to properties that have lists of values such as group membership, etc. One must be careful with this property, as it allows the trustee to place himself on the Access Control List of the object and therefore grant himself more rights to the object.

A phrase (though again not in order) to help you remember the five property rights is Red Cats Walk Away Slowly.

As mentioned earlier, property rights can be assigned through two ways:

**All Properties option**

**Selected Properties option**

The All Properties option allows trustee rights to just what it says - All properties - at the same time. Trustee rights granted through the All Properties option can be inherited.

The Selected Properties option allows trustee rights to be set for specific properties. All assignments through the Selected Properties option override assignments for the same property through the All Properties option, yet trustee assignments through Selected Properties are not inherited.

# Default NDS Object and Property Trustee Assignments

Through the normal setup of the system, the following default NDS Object and Property trustee assignments are shown in Figure 14-1.

| Trustee | Default Object or Property Right | Purpose of Default Right |
|---|---|---|
| (PUBLIC) | Browse Object Right to the (ROOT) object | Lets users see the NDS tree and the objects within it |
| (PUBLIC) | Read property right to the messaging property of the server object | Lets clients on the network identify the messaging server assigned to this server, if any. |
| (PUBLIC) | Read property right to the Default Server property for every user | Identifies the default server for each user. |
| Admin | Supervisor Object Right to the (ROOT) | Lets the Admin (the first user object) administer the NDS tree |
| Server | Supervisor Object Right to itself | Lets the server change its own parameters. This is needed for normal server operation. |
| (ROOT) | Read property right to the Network Address and Group Membership Properties for every user | Lets all users in the tree identify the network address and group membership of a user. |
| User | Read right to All Properties of his own user object | Lets the user see all his properties |
| User | Read and Write selected property to the Login script Property of his own user object | Allows the user to change and execute his of her own login script |
| User | Read and Write selected property rights to the Print Job Configuration Property of his own user object | Allows the user to create a print job configuration and use it |
| Container Object when it is created | Browse Object Right to the (ROOT) object | Lets users in the container read (and execute) the container's login script and read (and use) the container's print job configuration. |
| Users in a Container | Inherit object and rights assigned through All Properties option from the containers above the user object | Lets object and property rights be assigned more easily |
| Creator of an object | Receives the Supervisor Object Right to the Object | Creator user can reasonably control the object. Allows for administrators for new container to be given only the Create Object right. |

**Figure 14-1.** Default NDS Object and Property Rights.

# Inheritance and Effective Rights

Generally, object and property rights assigned through the All Properties option are **inherited** just like file system rights. Just as with file system rights, unwanted inheritance can be limited by placing an Inherited Rights Filter for Object Rights and/or an Inherited Rights Filter for Property Rights at a lower level in the NDS tree. Only the rights specifically listed in the Inherited Rights Filters can be inherited from above. Remember, though, that the Supervisor right for NDS objects and the Supervisor right for the All Properties option can be filtered out by an IRF. The Supervisor file system right cannot be filtered.

Inheritance can also be limited by the application of another specific trustee assignment for the same user, group, organizational role, etc. at a lower level. Explicit trustee assignments always override inherited rights.

**Effective rights** are the sum of all the explicit and inherited rights that an object has at a given level in the NDS tree. Remember that rights can be obtained in the six ways listed earlier in the chapter.

In a very simple example, suppose that Sam, a user in the MAINCO container, is given NDS object rights of ( BCDR) to the CONTINENTAL container. This means that Sam can see the objects in the tree under the CONTINENTAL container, he can create objects under the CONTINENTAL container, he can delete the CONTINENTAL container, and he can rename the CONTINENTAL container. Assuming there are no IRFs assigned, he will have the same object trustee rights through inheritance to all containers below the CONTINENTAL container.

What happens, though, if there is an IRF at the DALLAS container that allows only ( B D )? Simply put, the IRF limits Sam's inherited rights in the DALLAS container to Browse and Delete. Further, the only rights that Sam can inherit in lower containers such as Accounting are Browse and Delete since the rights that can be inherited from above are based on the actual rights that an object has to the container above.

In chart form, the determination of these rights is shown in Figure 14-2.

Now, let's examine a slightly different scenario by granting Sam an additional explicit object trustee assignment at the DALLAS container of ( BCD ). This additional assignment overrides any inherited rights he may have had. This is shown in Figure 14-3.

| | Sam as a user |
|---|---|
| .CONTINENTAL.MAINCO | |
| IRF | (SBCDR) |
| Inherited Rights | -- |
| Trustee Assign. | ( BCDR) |
| Effective Rights | ( BCDR) |
| .DALLAS.CONTINENTAL.MAINCO | |
| IRF | ( B D ) |
| Inherited Rights | ( B D ) |
| Trustee Assign. | -- |
| Effective Rights | ( B D ) |
| .Accounting.DALLAS.CONTINENTAL.MAINCO | |
| IRF | (SBCDR) |
| Inherited Rights | ( B D ) |
| Trustee Assign. | -- |
| Effective Rights | ( B D ) |

**Figure 14-2.** Determining inheritance and effective rights with NDS.

| | Sam as a user |
|---|---|
| .CONTINENTAL.MAINCO | |
| IRF | (SBCDR) |
| Inherited Rights | -- |
| Trustee Assign. | ( BCDR) |
| Effective Rights | ( BCDR) |
| .DALLAS.CONTINENTAL.MAINCO | |
| IRF | ( B D ) |
| Inherited Rights | ( B D ) |
| Trustee Assign. | ( BCD ) |
| Effective Rights | ( BCD ) |
| .Accounting.DALLAS.CONTINENTAL.MAINCO | |
| IRF | (SBCDR) |
| Inherited Rights | ( BCD ) |
| Trustee Assign. | -- |
| Effective Rights | ( BCD ) |

**Figure 14-3.** Determining effective rights with additional trustee assignments.

Further, let's consider Sam's effective rights assuming that the special object (PUBLIC) had the Browse right to the (ROOT); Sam is a member of a group called .MAINGRP.MAINCO, which has an explicit object trustee assignment to .DALLAS.CONTINENTAL.MAINCO of ( BC R); and Sam's container, MAINCO, has (SBCDR) to the Accounting container. To figure Sam's effective rights at each container, each method for obtaining rights must be considered and calculated separately. Then, the effective rights at each container are added together to determine Sam's ultimate effective rights at that container. These calculations are shown in Figure 14-4.

The effective property rights a user obtains from explicit assignments to the All Properties and from inheritance and IRFs for All Properties are calculated the same as the object rights above except that selected property rights at a given level in the tree override All Property rights assignments, and selected property rights are not inherited.

# Considerations for Proper Assignment of NDS Object and Property Rights

NDS Object and Property Rights should be assigned sparingly, giving users only the rights necessary for them to do their jobs using the system.

As a rule, the best place to start is to consider what rights are assigned by default. These rights are generally sufficient for users to complete their tasks. Then, as with file system rights, rights should be assigned first to group type objects and then to specific users as appropriate.

### (PUBLIC)

Rights needed for all users attached to a NetWare 4.11 server whether they are logged in or not (generally just ( B )) should be assigned to (PUBLIC). Care should be taken in assigning any additional rights to this object since these rights are available to users whether or not they are authenticated to NDS.

### Container Rights

Rights needed by all users in a given container should be assigned to the container so that they can be inherited by the users in the container. Don't forget that some rights are automatically assigned to the container by default upon creation of objects in the container. Refer to Figure 14-1.

### Groups

Groups are objects that contain users for members. All object and property rights assigned to a group also belong to each user of the

| | Sam | (PUBLIC) | MAINGRP | MAINCO | Sam as a user |
|---|---|---|---|---|---|
| **(ROOT)** | | | | | |
| IRF | (SBCDR) | (SBCDR) | (SBCDR) | (SBCDR) | (SBCDR) |
| Inherited Rights | -- | -- | -- | -- | |
| Trustee Assign. | -- | ( B    ) | -- | -- | |
| Effective Rights | -- | ( B    ) | -- | -- | ( B    ) |
| **.MAINCO** | | | | | |
| IRF | (SBCDR) | (SBCDR) | (SBCDR) | (SBCDR) | (SBCDR) |
| Inherited Rights | -- | ( B    ) | -- | -- | |
| Trustee Assign. | -- | -- | -- | -- | |
| Effective Rights | -- | ( B    ) | -- | -- | ( B    ) |
| **.CONTINENTAL.MAINCO** | | | | | |
| IRF | (SBCDR) | (SBCDR) | (SBCDR) | (SBCDR) | (SBCDR) |
| Inherited Rights | -- | ( B    ) | -- | -- | |
| Trustee Assign. | ( BCDR) | -- | -- | -- | |
| Effective Rights | ( BCDR) | ( B    ) | -- | --- | ( BCDR) |
| **.DALLAS.CONTINENTAL.MAINCO** | | | | | |
| IRF | ( B D ) | ( B D ) | ( B D ) | ( B D ) | ( B D ) |
| Inherited Rights | ( B D ) | ( B    ) | -- | -- | |
| Trustee Assign. | -- | -- | ( BCR ) | -- | |
| Effective Rights | ( B D ) | ( B    ) | ( BCR ) | ( B D ) | ( BCDR ) |
| **.Accounting.DALLAS. CONTINENTAL.MAINCO** | | | | | |
| IRF | (SBCDR) | (SBCDR) | (SBCDR) | (SBCDR) | (SBCDR) |
| Inherited Rights | ( B D ) | ( B    ) | ( BCR ) | ( B D ) | |
| Trustee Assign. | -- | -- | -- | (SBCDR) | |
| Effective Rights | ( B D ) | ( B    ) | ( BCR ) | (SBCDR) | (SBCDR) |

**Figure 14-4.** Complex calculation of NDS effective rights.

group. Groups should be used to organize users with similar needs so that rights can be granted to the single group object rather than to users individually.

## Organizational Role Rights

Many times, object and property rights are needed based on the job function that an individual performs. In this case, it is a good idea to create an organizational role object, assign rights to the organizational role object and then make the subject user an occupant of the organizational role. In this way, the user obtains rights based on his or her function rather than individually. When the user transfers to another job, a new person or persons can be made occupants of the organizational role and the person transferring can be removed as an occupant from the former organizational role.

## Security Equivalence

A user can be made security equivalent to another user and thereby obtain the object and All Properties rights assigned to the other user. This method for granting rights should be used on a temporary basis only, perhaps for a user who is visiting a given office and helping out on a project. If the user is to have these rights permanently, they should be assigned by other means. If they are not, when the person to which the user is made security equivalent is deleted from the tree, our user will not have the rights necessary to perform his job.

## Pitfalls to Avoid

Because of inheritance and other basic NDS principles, the following cautions should be heeded:

1. Avoid granting NDS rights higher in the tree than necessary.

2. Avoid granting the Supervisor object right to the server object to more than a limited number of users since granting this NDS right also grants the user the Supervisory file system right to all volumes on the given server.

3. Remember that granting the Supervisor object right also grants by default the Supervisor right to All Properties. Most notably, this means that the user has the Supervisory right to the Access Control List property (ACL) and can grant rights to others. One method for avoid the latter situation is to grant a further limited Read and Compare Access Control List property right through the Selected Properties option. Also remember, though, that the Selected Property assignment limits the user only at this level of the tree.

4. Granting the Write right to an object through the All Properties option also grants the user the right to place himself on the Access Control List for the object.

5. Be careful when setting Inherited Rights Filters for an object or for the properties of the object. Generally, if NDS object and property rights are prudently assigned, an IRF is unnecessary. When an IRF is used, the consequences can be more than intended. For example, initially, to remove the S object right from the IRF for a container, there must be at least one user with an explicit object trustee assignment of Supervisor for that container. The problem comes when that user is removed from the tree. Because the Supervisor right is blocked in the IRF and because the user who had the explicit Supervisor object right has been removed from the tree, that portion of the tree can be non-maintainable. The only choice at this state is to consult Novell

Consulting to reestablish a user with the Supervisor object right to the container.

# Hands-On Netware

## Assigning Object Rights

Assigning object rights is accomplished through NetWare Administrator. The user assigning object rights to another user, group, etc. must have control over the object to which rights are assigned as well as the object receiving the rights. Therefore, the administrative account is usually used.

The steps for assigning your NEWXXX user the ( BCDR) rights to the DALLAS container are as follows:

1. Log in as your ADMINXXX user where XXX is your initials.

2. Activate NetWare Administrator.

3. Right-click on the USERXXX user. You should see a small menu as shown in Figure 14-5.

4. Select Rights to Other Objects.

5. The Search Context box is displayed as in Figure 14-6.

6. Press the Delete key to begin searching from the (ROOT) and select the Search Entire Subtree option. Then click OK. Note that you could use the Browse button to begin searching from any place in the tree. The Rights to Other Objects box is displayed as in Figure 14-7.

7. Note that the selections for Object and Property Rights are dimmed until you click on the USERXXX object. Then the screen will appear as in Figure 14-8 showing that the user has the Read right to all of his or her own properties. Note in this screen that the user indicated on the top is the object having rights and the object to which the user has rights is listed in the Assigned Objects box. This is a little confusing since the user is the same in both cases so far.

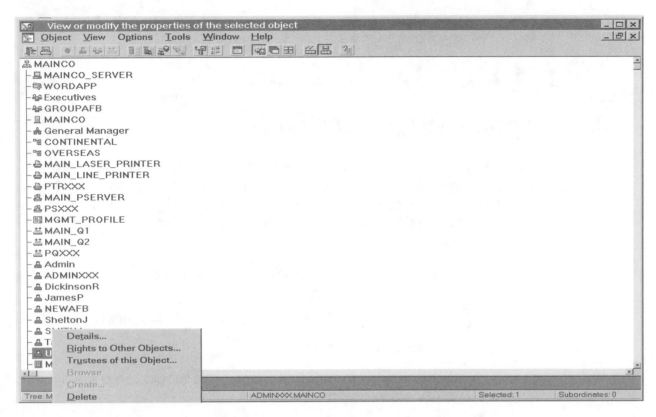

**Figure 14-5.** Small menu of NWAdmin options.

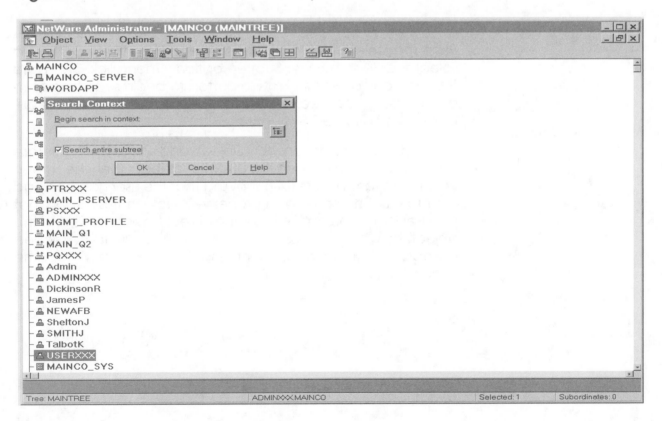

**Figure 14-6.** Search Context box.

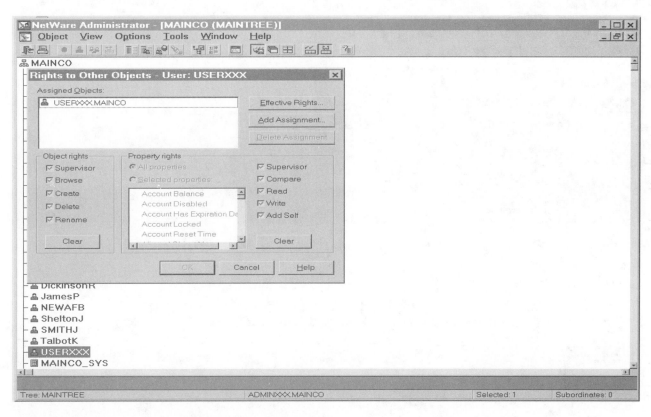

**Figure 14-7.** Rights to Other Objects box.

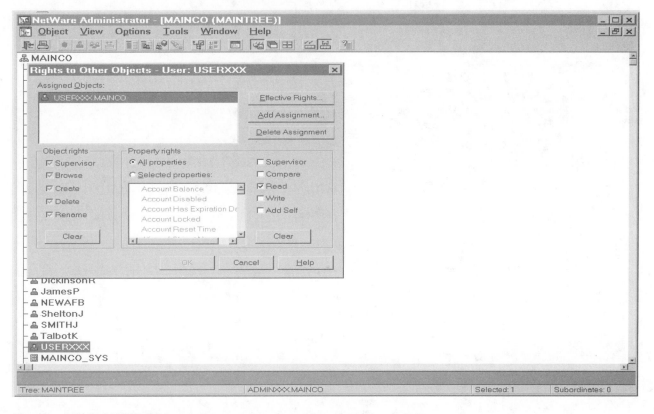

**Figure 14-8.** USERXXX existing object and property rights.

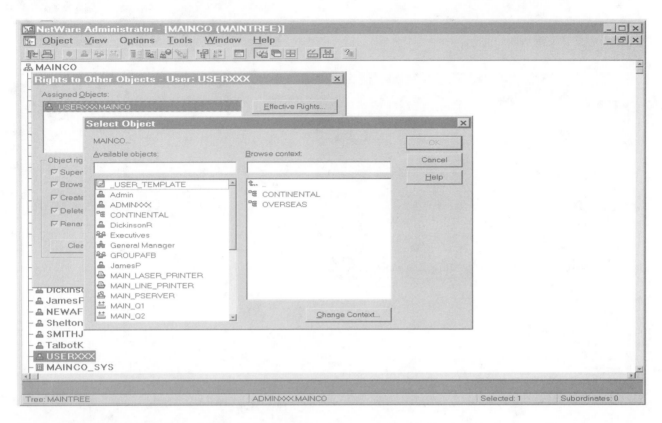

**Figure 14-9.** Add assignment dialog box.

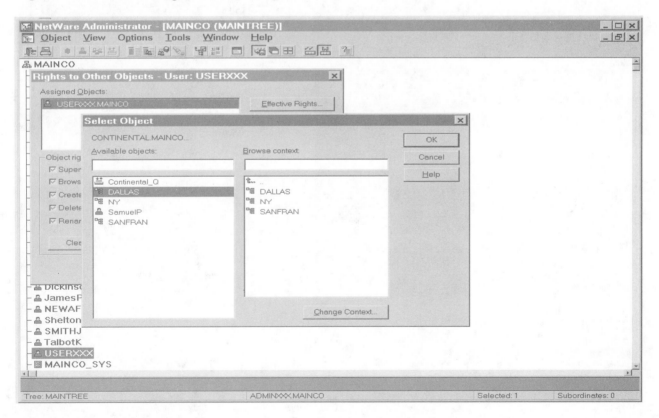

**Figure 14-10.** Available objects to which rights can be granted.

8. Click the **Add Assignments button** to obtain the screen shown in Figure 14-9.

9. Navigate on the right until the container DALLAS is available as an object to be chosen in the left box. (Double-click **the CONTINENTAL Organizational Unit** to expose the DALLAS container.)

10. Click **the Dallas container** in the Available Objects Box and then click the **OK button** as shown in Figure 14-10.

11. Note that by default USERXXX obtains the Browse Object Right and the Read and Compare property rights to All Properties of the Dallas container object as shown in Figure 14-11.

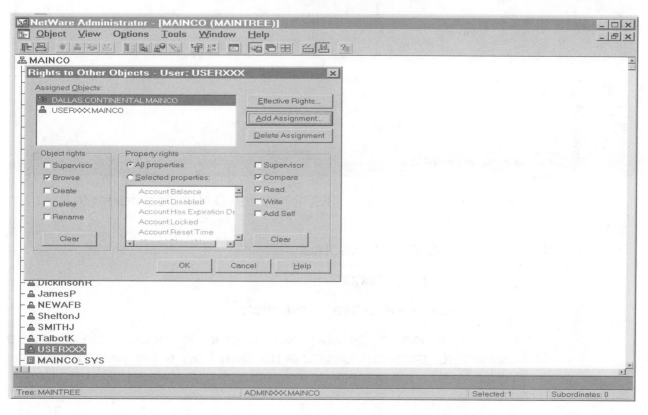

**Figure 14-11.** Default object rights for Dallas container for USERXXX.

12. Click **the box next to the Create, Delete, and Rename object rights** as shown in Figure 14-12, and then click the **OK button**.

## Exercising the NDS Rights Assigned

Log in as USERXXX and create a user object called PETERXXX in the Dallas container to prove that USERXXX has the Create right to the DALLAS container.

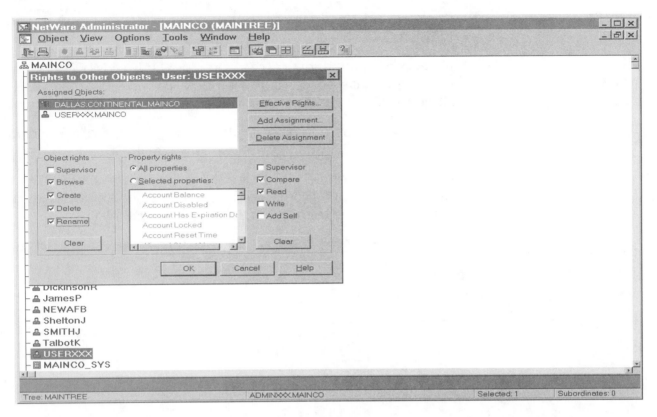

**Figure 14-12.** Assigning Object Rights of (BCDR ) for the DALLAS container to USERXXX.

Now that your USERXXX is created,

1. Log in as **USERXXX**.

2. Activate **NetWare Administrator**.

What happened? USERXXX was unable to access the NetWare Administrator program because he didn't have file system rights on MAINCO\SYS:. This underlines the separation between NDS and file system rights.

## Giving USERXXX File System Rights

Log in as ADMINXXX and give USERXXX file system rights to MAINCO\SYS: of ( RWCEMF ) as follows:

1. Log in as **ADMINXXX.**

2. Activate **NetWare Administrator**.

3. Locate **the USERXXX** and double-click it to display the details about USERXXX.

4. Click the **Rights to Files and Directories button** to display the Rights to Files and Directories page.

5. For good measure, display existing file system rights on MAIN-CO_SYS first by clicking the **Show button**, then clicking **the MAIN-CO_SYS object**, and then clicking the **OK button**. Click the **Files and Directory assignment** shown. The file system rights already assigned to USERXXX are only to his home directory as shown in Figure 14-13.

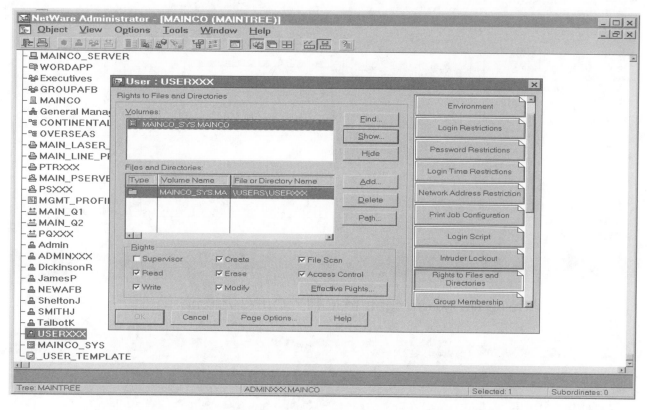

**Figure 14-13.** Rights granted to files and directories.

6. Click the **Add button** to add file system rights. Select **MAIN-CO_SYS** and click the **OK button** to add rights to the entire volume as shown in Figure 14-14. Note that we might not want the rights at the root of the SYS volume if this were a live system.

7. Note that USERXXX by default receives only the Read and File Scan file system rights as shown in Figure 14-15. Click **the boxes by Write, Create, Erase, and Modify,** and then click the **OK button**.

## Reattempt the Hands-On Activity: Exercising NDS Object Rights Assigned

1. Log in as **USERXXX**.

2. Activate **NetWare Administrator**.

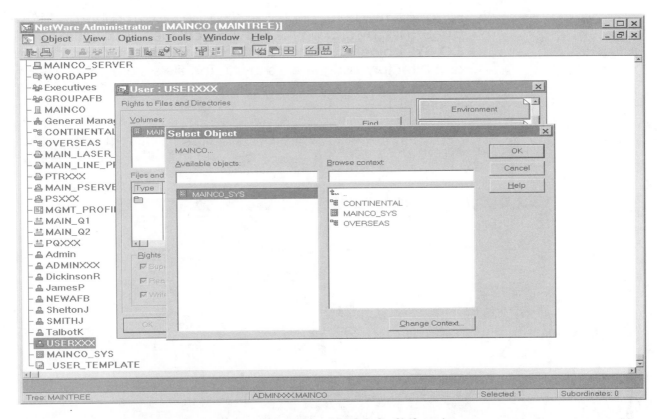

**Figure 14-14.** Adding file system rights to MAINCO_SYS volume.

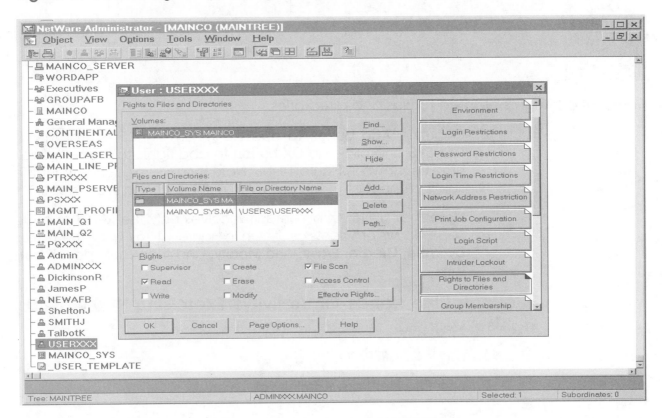

**Figure 14-15.** Default file system rights for trustee USERXXX.

The process has again failed. Do you have any idea why it has failed? (Hint: Examine the shortcut or the program item for NetWare Administrator, and then examine the Login script for USERXXX. If you completed the login script exercise, USERXXX has a MAP ROOT drive to SYS:\USERS\USERXXX. Therefore, he cannot use the H: drive mapping to get to NetWare Administrator.)

Change the USERXXX login script to MAP ROOT J: to the user's home directory.

1. Log in as **ADMINXXX**.

2. Activate **NetWare Administrator**.

3. Double-click on **USERXXX**.

4. Click on the **Login Script button** to display the current login script.

5. Change the H: drive mapping to a J: drive mapping and click the **OK button.**

6. Close **NetWare Administrator**.

7. Log in as **USERXXX**.

8. Activate **NetWare Administrator**.

9. Double-click **the CONTINENTAL container** to expose the DALLAS container.

10. Right-click **the Dallas container** and select **Create** as shown in Figure 14-16.

11. Create a user called **PETERXXX** with a home directory under SYS:\USERS called PETERXXX. Refer to the details about creating a user in Chapter 11 if you don't remember how to create the home directory. Your screen should look like Figure 14-17 before you click the Create button.

12. Double-click **the DALLAS container** to expose PETERXXX.

13. Right click on **PETERXXX** and select Trustees of this object.

14. Click on the **USERXXX.MAINCO** user, the user you used to create PETERXXX. Notice that USERXXX has the Supervisor right to PETERXXX as shown in Figure 14-18 because USERXXX created PETERXXX.

15. Click **the (PUBLIC)** object and notice that all rights are dimmed.

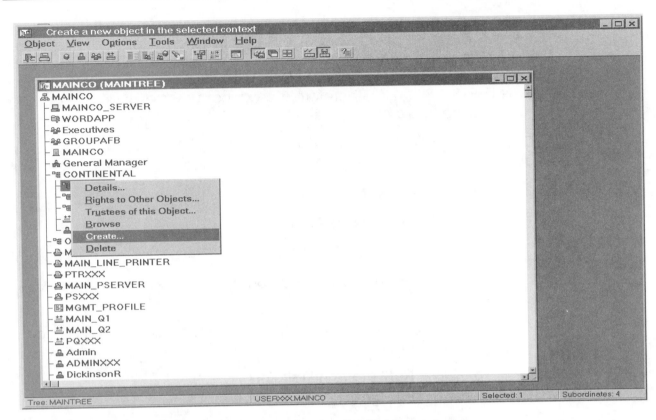

**Figure 14-16.** Creating an object under the DALLAS container.

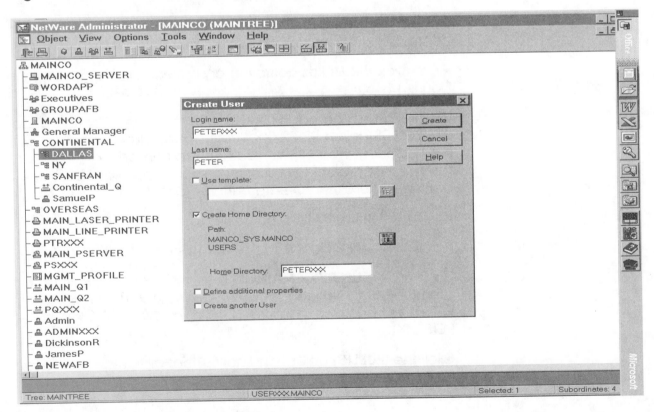

**Figure 14-17.** Creating user PETERXXX.

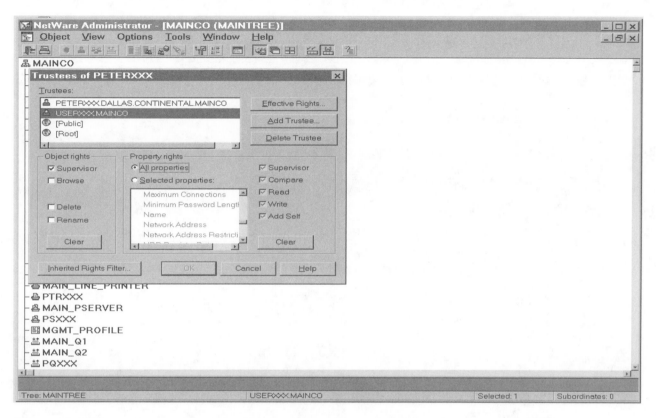

**Figure 14-18.** USERXXX, the creator, has Supervisor object right to PETERXXX.

16. Click the Selected Properties button under Property Rights and then use the up and down arrows to determine what selected properties are assigned to (PUBLIC). Notice that the Default Server property is checked. Click on this property to determine the rights that (PUBLIC} has. This means that all users can read the default server assigned to PETERXXX.

17. Check out the same information for (ROOT). Note that (ROOT) has Read rights to the Network Address property.

18. Do not log out. Continue with the next exercise.

## Setting an Inherited Rights Filter and Determining Its Effect

1. Continuing on from the previous exercise, click **the Inherited Rights Filter button** for PETERXXX to display Figure 14-19.

2. Deselect **the Supervisor, Delete, and Rename rights by clicking in the box** to the left of each right. Then click the **OK button**.

3. Close **Netware Administrator**.

4. Log in as your **ADMINXXX** object.

5. Activate **NetWare Administrator**.

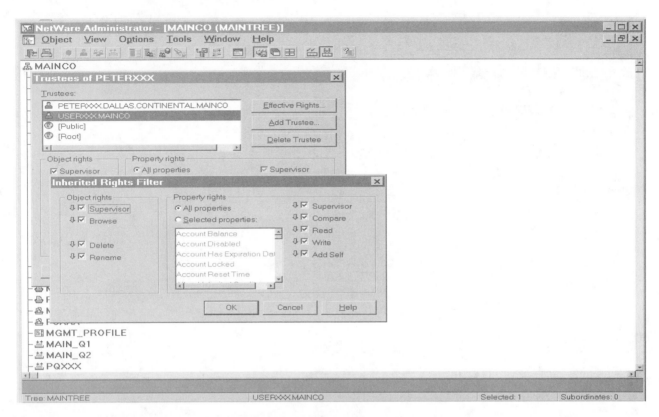

**Figure 14-19.** Inherited Rights Filter for PETERXXX.

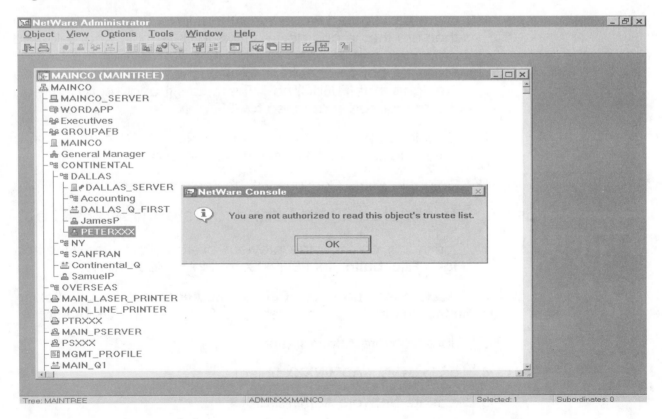

**Figure 14-20.** Access failure message.

6. Double-click **the CONTINENTAL container** and then double-click **the DALLAS container** to expose PETERXXX.

7. Right-click on **PETERXXX**. A screen like Figure 14-20 is displayed. Why can't ADMINXXX access PETERXXX's object trustee list? ADMINXXX cannot read PETERXXX's object trustee list because the inherited rights filter you set blocked ADMINXXX's Supervisor Object Right from the above containers.

# Summary

NetWare 4 provides an additional level of security through NDS Object and Property Rights. NDS Object rights determine what a given object can do with other objects while Property rights determine what a given object can do with the properties of another object. NDS Object and Property Rights granted through the All Properties option are inherited by lower containers in the tree. An explicit trustee assignment overrides inherited rights for both objects and properties.

A user can obtain object and property rights in six ways:

The user account,

The group(s) to which the user belongs,

The container(s) to which the user belongs,

The organizational roles that the user occupies,

The users to which this user is security equivalent,

The special object (PUBLIC) that supplies rights to all users connected to a file server in a NetWare 4.11 network whether or not the user is logged in.

Inherited Rights Filters exist for both NDS Object rights and NDS Property rights. The IRFs limit rights that can be inherited for an object. A user's effective rights are determined by calculating all six ways that a user can obtain rights, limiting those rights by the appropriate IRFs, and then adding the effective rights together.

# Questions

1. What do NDS Object rights control?

2. What are the NDS Object rights, and what is the meaning of each right?

3. What do Property Rights govern?

4. What are the NDS Property Rights and what is the meaning of each right?

5. What is the difference between rights granted using the All Properties option and rights granted using the Selected Properties option?

6. What is an Inherited Rights Filter? How is it used?

7. What are effective rights?

8. In what ways can a given user obtain NDS object and property rights?

9. Can rights granted to selected properties be inherited?

10. Can rights granted to selected properties override rights granted using the All Properties option?

11. What is the problem with giving all users the Supervisor object right to the server? What can they do with the server object, and what rights do they have to the file system on the server?

12. What NDS object and property rights does a user receive for objects he or she created?

13. What is the ACL property? Why is it important?

14. What can a user do with the Add Self property right to all properties?

15. (True/False) The Supervisor NDS Object Right cannot be blocked.

16. What can happen if the Supervisor right is removed from the IRF for a container object?

17. (True/False) NDS object rights control file system rights.

18. Why does special care need to be taken when assigning object and file rights to the (PUBLIC) object?

# Projects

## Objective

The following projects provide reinforcement for NDS Object and Property Right principles discussed in this chapter.

### Project 1:

Using the NDS tree structure for the class and paper and pencil, determine the effective NDS Object rights for your user USERXXX, assuming the following:

   a. USERXXX has an explicit NDS trustee assignment to the OVERSEAS container granting him (SBCDR) rights, and there is an IRF of ( BCDR) at the FRANKFURT container. What are USERXXX's effective rights to the FRANKFURT container? Can USERXXX create an Organizational Unit under FRANKFURT called CARS? If so, what object rights would USERXXX have to the CARS container?

   b. Consider that USERXXX is also a member of a group called MAINGROUP which has ( B ) rights to the MAINCO container. What are USERXXX's effective rights in the MAINCO container, the OVERSEAS Container, and the FRANKFURT container assuming that the rights specified in Project 1-a. are also still in effect?

   c. Discarding all rights granted above, what are USERXXX's effective rights at each container in the tree assuming that USERXXX has the ( BC ) rights to MAINCO; USERXXX belongs to a group that has the ( BCR ) rights to the LONDON container; USERXXX is in an organizational role called Managers in the MAINCO container which has the (S ) right to the CONTINENTAL container; and the following IRFs exist:

   | | |
   |---|---|
   | CONTINENTAL | ( BCDR) |
   | FRANKFURT | (S     ) |
   | LONDON | ( BC R  ) |
   | DALLAS | ( B     ) |

### Project 2:

Repeat each of the exercises in Project 1 on the system, examining the effective rights at each container indicated.

# 15
# Backing Up NetWare 4.11

## Objectives

After completing this chapter, the student will

1. Understand the importance of regular backups.

2. Be able to explain common backup methodologies and be able to select the appropriate backup methodology for a given case study company.

3. Understand the components of the SBACKUP backup utility for NetWare 4.11.

4. Understand practical considerations for restoring a server after failure.

## Key Terms

Backup

Full Backup

Incremental Backup

Differential Backup

SBACKUP

## Introduction

Making regular backups is probably the most important but least glamorous job that befalls a network administrator. It is a thankless job but a very necessary job that must be accomplished and documented on a regular basis so that the server(s) can be restored in the event of failure.

This chapter will explore the reasons for regular backups and will explore several methodologies for backups. It will also give the student the opportunity to design an effective backup strategy for a given business scenario. Finally, it will examine the built-in backup utility for

NetWare 4.11 as an example of a backup system that a network administrator might use for backing up a NetWare 4.11 system. Since many classrooms do not have tape equipment available and since the SBACKUP utility itself is not commonly used, an actual backup will not be performed.

# Why Take the Time to Perform Backups?

There are really only two reasons for performing **backups**:

**Hardware and software failure**

**Human error**

With that said, it is apparent that neither of these reasons for backup can be successfully eliminated; therefore, regular backups must be performed so that a company can survive hardware and software failures and can recover from human error.

Regardless of the type of hardware utilized in a system, hardware can and does fail or malfunction. Hard drives fail; memory chips fail; other hardware components fail. Software, especially system software, is highly tested before it is released, but even well-tested software programs can have bugs that can adversely affect the data stored on a file server. Although systems may have other, more easily used, methods for data recovery, regular backups are the standard method of recovery from hardware and software failure.

Humans sometimes make mistakes. A user may inadvertently save a new file on top of an older, but still needed, file. A backup of the system gives the network administrator the ability to recover the user's previous file. A user may inadvertently erase a file, and this erasure may not be detected for some time. A consistent backup plan and methodology for archiving backup media can assist in restoring erased files.

Backups are commonly made to tape media although other media such as optical disks are gaining popularity.

# Common Backup Methodologies

The most common backup methodologies usually involve doing daily backups. They are:

**Full Backup:** This method involve making a full system backup of each server, including files, directories, and NDS, on a daily basis. The Archive flag for each file and directory backed up on a full backup is reset.

**Incremental Backup:** This method involve making a full system backup on the first day of the week and then making a backup daily of only those files, directories, and NDS items that have changed since the last backup, whether incremental or full. Each incremental and each full backup resets the Archive flags for the files backed up.

**Differential Backup:** This method involve making a full backup on the first day of the week and then backing up all the files, directories, and NDS items that have changed since that backup each day until the next full backup is made. This type of backup does not reset the Archive flag for any file. Only the full backup resets the Archive flag.

Regardless of the method chosen, the backup needs to be set so that it occurs automatically, in an unattended fashion. Historically, a backup that requires human intervention, either to set up the backup or to change tapes during the backup translates to a backup that does not get done on an on-going basis.

Ideally, as long as there is enough time available for a backup to be performed and for the backup to be verified during off-hours for the system, full backups should be performed on a daily basis, and tapes should be retained for a significant period of time. This method provides the best options for recovery should a given backup tape fail. Obviously, in the event of a failure, the latest backup tape would be the preferred restore medium, but if there is a problem with this medium, yesterday's full backup would be available. If there were a problem with yesterday's full backup tape, the previous day's full backup would be available, and so on.

Unfortunately, there may come a time for a business when it is no longer possible to complete a full backup on a daily basis. In this situation, a full backup must still be periodically created, perhaps during "down" hours over a weekend. Then, either incremental or differential backups can be performed during the week.

The trade-off between incremental and differential backups is that incremental backups require less time to create because they include only those files and directories that have changed since the previous day's full or incremental backup, while a differential requires a longer time to create each day. However, in the event of a failure, restoring a system with an incremental backup approach depends on restoring more tapes than the differential approach would require.

|  | Full Backup | Incremental Backup | Differential Backup |
|---|---|---|---|
| **Time to Back Up Daily** | Most | Least | Grows daily, medium |
| **Time to Restore** | Least | Most | Medium |
| **Archive Bit** | Reset | Reset | Not Reset |

**Figure 15-1.** Main characteristics of Full, Incremental, and Differential backups.

Figure 15-1 shows the various characteristics of the three main backup methodologies for an 8 a.m. to 5 p.m., five days per week business that makes its full backup tape on Friday.

Notice that the tradeoff essentially becomes time spent daily versus time and number of tapes that must be used to restore a system.

Now, consider a seven days per week/twenty-four hours per day operation. For a business of this sort, special considerations must be made. Perhaps the system must be made totally unavailable for a period until a full backup can be created on a less than daily basis. Another approach would be to have fault tolerant servers such that a given server is really two servers that are updated simultaneously. Then, on a periodic basis, the link between the servers could be severed with one server continuing to service the company's needs and the other server being backed up. In any event, regular backups must be made.

# The Backup Tape Archival Approach

Ideally, for a five days per week operation that can still make full backups, the following is a backup approach that will provide significant fault tolerance. It provides a large number of alternatives for restoration in the event that a given tape cannot be restored due to media malfunction or if something like a natural disaster destroys the servers and the computer room in which these servers are kept.

The process essentially requires 25 backup tapes to be used for daily backup, 5 tapes to be taken off-site for weekly backups in a secure, separate area, and 12 tapes per year that must be taken off-site and retained for a long period or perhaps forever, depending on the type of business the network is supporting.

There are 25 tapes utilized for backing up on a daily basis, perhaps numbered Daily W-D where W is the week number, 1-5, and D is the day number, 1-5. Tape Daily1-1 would be used for the backup on the first day of the first week, Daily 1-2 would be used for the backup of the second day of the first week, and so on.

Then, on a given day during each week, the daily tape would be exchanged with the previous weekly tape (from off-site), thus meaning that one tape per week is taken off-site for extra backup security.

At the end of a month's processing, perhaps the last day of the month or perhaps the day just before the month's accounting close, the daily tape is taken off-site for permanent retention, and a new tape is placed into the rotation.

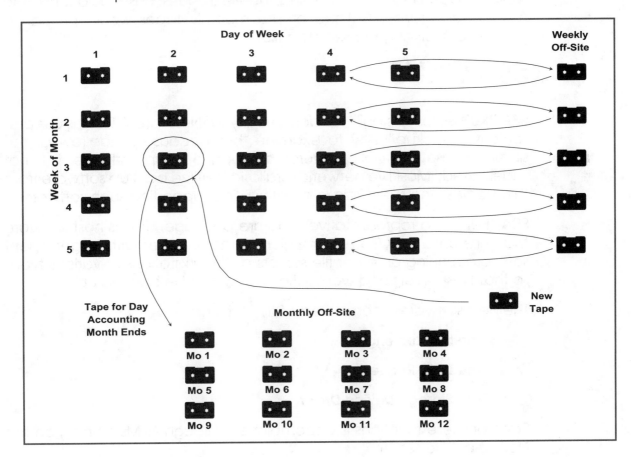

**Figure 15-2.** A comprehensive backup method.

Figure 15-2 depicts this tape backup method.

The advantage of the above approach is that it provides maximum fallback positions should a single backup tape fail or should the computer site be totally destroyed.

For example, let's say that the backup tape is taken off-site after the fourth day of the week and let's say that a disaster happened during the fourth day of the second week. This disaster occurs before the weekly backup tape was made. The network administrator would first attempt to restore from the backup tape labeled Daily 2-3. If there were some problem with this tape, the Daily 2-2 could be used. If there were some problem with this tape, the Daily 2-1 could be used, and so on. If a total disaster were to occur, the weekly tape from the fourth day of the previous week is kept off-site, and the network administrator would attempt to use it. If that weekly backup tape were bad, the previous week's backup tape could be used, and so on.

Also, let's say that a user uses a specific spreadsheet only once per year and at the end of the year, and let's say that he inadvertently erases the spreadsheet only a month into the new year. The daily and weekly backup tapes containing the file in questions would long ago have been erased, but the off-site monthly tapes would provide a vehicle for restoring the required file.

# SBACKUP

**SBACKUP** is Novell's built-in backup utility for NetWare 4.11. It is a representative backup utility to examine, but because it has few of the simple to use desirable features of good backup software, it is not widely used. Most live network installations utilize backup software from thirdparties who specialize in creating and supporting such software.

SBACKUP, as a representative software package, utilizes host software that runs on a host file server which communicates with target agent software running on other file servers and workstations of various types so that files servers and workstations alike can be backed up.

The Host software is composed of three parts:

> **The backup engine**
>
> **The Data Requester**
>
> **The Storage Device Driver.**

Each of these functions is accomplished through NLMs running on the NetWare 4 file server.

The Target Agent software takes the form of an NLM when running on a target file server or a TSR (Terminate and Stay Resident) program when running on a target workstation. The Target software for SBACKUP is available to back up other NetWare 3.1x and 4 servers and NDS, as well as DOS, Windows 95, OS/2, and Macintosh workstations.

SBACKUP is initiated from the NetWare 4 file server. The network administrator can then select the targets to be backed up. Once the backup has been accomplished, the tape must be recorded and taken off-site as needed.

# Practical Considerations for Backups and Restores

Backups must be made so that restores can be done when needed. The method of backup must fit the business hours of operation and the business needs. In general, performing full backups is the safest approach to take although the time available sometimes does not permit this approach. Regardless of the approach taken, though, several things can be done to ensure accuracy of the backup and availability of the backup media when it is needed.

## Backup Responsibility

One of the most important people in a business is the person who is responsible for performing and documenting the backup. This person does not necessarily need to be the network administrator, but the person must first and foremost be responsible and meticulous about detail. The backup should be set up by the network administrator such that it initiates automatically on a daily basis; therefore, the person who performs the backup should need only to ensure that the backups actually get made and document which tape contains which backup data. To determine whether or not the backup was successful, the daily backup person must be taught to examine the verification logs for error messages and to notify the network administrator if error messages do occur. Further, the backup person must meticulously document the tape library and must be responsible for seeing that those tapes that should be stored off-site actually do get taken off-site for storage.

## How to Determine Whether or Not a Backup Is Good

Every time a backup is made, a verify operation should be performed. This operation compares what is on the tape to what is actually still on the hard disk of the server. As accurate as most verification software is, it is possible that the verify program could malfunction and report that a tape is good when it is not.

The best way to help ensure that backup tapes are actually good is to perform a sample restore on a periodic basis, perhaps monthly, whereby a file in the middle of the tape is actually restored to the file server and examined for accuracy. This extra effort can prove invaluable should a backup tape actually be needed for restoration.

# What to Back Up

While it is desirable and easy to back up everything every day, it might be impossible to do given business hours of operation and other needs. It is sometimes, possible, though, to perform a full backup of those volumes of the server that are likely to change on a daily basis and avoid the possible downside of performing incremental backups by segregating programs and data on different volumes of the server. For example, the SYS: volume could be reserved for only NetWare system-specific programs and files. This volume could perhaps be fully backed up only once per week or even less often. Another volume could be reserved for just software programs that do not change frequently. This volume, too, could be fully backed up perhaps once per week or less often. Data, then, could be placed on other volumes, and could perhaps be fully backed up daily. This would be a nice compromise that would take maximum advantage of the time available for backup.

# Summary

System backups must be performed to ensure recovery in the event of hardware or software failure and to recover from human error. There are three common methodologies for backups: Full, Incremental, and Differential.

The full backup method requires that NDS and every file be backed up on each server daily. This method provide the most fall-back positions in the event of tape media failure, and it required the fewest tapes and therefore the least amount of time to recover from failure.

The incremental backup method requires that a full backup be performed on a set day of the week. Then, each day after that, only those files that have changed since the last full or incremental backup are backed up. This method requires the least amount of time daily to perform the backup, but it requires the most time to restore and provides little fall-back in the event of tape media failure.

The differential backup method also requires that a full backup be made on a set day of the week. Then, each day thereafter, the differential backup includes those files that have changed since the last full backup. The amount of time needed for daily backup grows daily until the next full backup tape is made, but the time to restore falls between the full and the incremental backup, and this method provides several fall-back tapes that can be used should there be a problem with the media on a given differential backup tape.

SBACKUP, as a representative of backup software, functions via host software that runs on the NetWare 4 server, which communicates with Target software that runs on other NetWare 4 servers and workstations.

# Questions

1. Explain the advantages and disadvantages of adopting the Full backup methodology.

2. Explain the advantages and disadvantages of adopting the Incremental backup methodology.

3. Explain the advantages and disadvantages of adopting the Differential backup methodology.

4. Explain the components of SBACKUP, specifically the host software and the Target Agent software.

5. Why should backups be performed?

6. Why should backups periodically be taken off-site?

# Projects

## Project 1 Objectives:

Design a backup strategy for each of the following business scenarios. Be sure to pay special attention to how your strategy performs in the following three situations:

1. The file server hard disk fails on the day before the next full backup is to be made, and a backup or backups must be restored.

2. A user erased a file almost a year ago, and she absolutely must have the file restored.

3. The computer room has been flooded, and limited operations must be set up off-site.

### Business Scenario 1:

The Jefferson Hospital District is supported by a NetWare 4 network that supports patient records and billing. The hospital is open 7 days per week, 24 hours per day, but patients normally do not check out between 12 midnight and 6 a.m., although some patients, mostly emergency cases, do check in.

## Business Scenario 2:

The Scamp Radio Company is a radio manufacturing company that runs two shifts, 7 a.m. to 3 p.m., and 3 p.m. to 11p.m. The business is a six days per week operation supported by a NetWare 4.11 network, and the system must be up during normal hours of operation. A full backup and verify takes 10 hours.

## Business Scenario 3:

Midway Community College retains all its student records and accounting functions on a NetWare 4.11 network. Business hours are normally 8:30 a.m. until 8 p.m. M-F, and 8:30 a.m. until 2:00 p.m. on Saturdays. A full backup and verification takes 12 hours.

# Project 2 Objectives:

Research and document at least three of the most popular backup software packages and devices. Prepare a written report and a short presentation to the class explaining your findings. Which of the three software and hardware solutions would you choose for each of the three business scenarios detailed above?

# 16
# Troubleshooting Methodology and Tidbits

## Objectives

After completing this chapter, the student will

1.  Be familiar with a solid troubleshooting model for analyzing and resolving many networking-related problems.

2.  Know about several sources available for troubleshooting information.

3.  Know when to use NetWare 4.11's volume repair utility, VREPAIR.

4.  Be familiar with several troubleshooting tips and techniques.

## Key Terms

Troubleshooting Model

NetWire

CompuServe

Novell Support Connection/NSEPro

VREPAIR

## Introduction

Running a network requires installing, configuring, and managing the network. These tasks are all proactive tasks that focus on performing a particular task correctly. Running a network also includes troubleshooting because neither the network hardware nor the people using the network or configuring portions of the network are perfect.

A full discussion of network troubleshooting is well beyond the scope of this textbook. In fact, the topic of network troubleshooting is itself at least an entire course. However, this textbook will discuss a solid outline for a troubleshooting model that will keep a network support specialist's troubleshooting activities focused and effective, regardless of the type of problem that is being solved. Additionally, two sources for supplemental information for use in troubleshooting are discussed. These are Novell's NetWire through CompuServe and the Internet and Novell Support Connection (formerly called NSEPro), Novell's Support Encyclopedia. Both are available by subscription. Finally, the textbook examines several Troubleshooting Tidbits, focusing on several common network problems and an approach for their solution. Example problems discussed address the following problem statements:

"The application I want to run won't run."

"I can't print."

"The SYS volume won't mount."

While these problems are in no way comprehensive with respect to the types of network problems a network support specialist can expect to encounter, they do provide a framework for explaining and applying the solid troubleshooting model presented earlier in the chapter.

# A Solid Troubleshooting Model

Troubleshooting is by the nature of the word a reaction to trouble. The word carries with it a sense of urgency to solve the reported problem so that normal work can continue. Synonyms for the word trouble include annoyance and adversity. Thus it is easy to understand why the word commonly implies a pressured situation, which can cause the network support specialist to react rather than act and therefore sometimes to forget to follow a solid **troubleshooting model** in solving the problem. Often, failure to follow a solid troubleshooting model can cause the troubleshooting process to be even more difficult and lengthy, usually leading to more pressure and more reactionary behavior, which is counterproductive in general. The purpose of this chapter is to fully explore a framework for logical, methodical troubleshooting which, when followed, helps ensure that a given problem can be resolved as efficiently as possible.

For many years, troubleshooting has been considered almost totally art. This is largely due to the reality that many of those using computers and the networks connecting them have little or no technical expertise and stand in awe of those who do. In fact, though, while troubleshooting does rely to some extent on the creative capabilities of the troubleshooter, successful troubleshooting relies mostly on following a logical troubleshooting model and applying the previous experience of the troubleshooter.

There are many renditions of the following troubleshooting model, but most are very similar, relying on logical problem analysis and methodical examination of possible problem solutions until the problem is solved. The troubleshooting model examined here includes the following steps:

1. Begin to document the problem from its onset.

2. Verify that the problem exists.

3. Gather information about the problem.

4. Formulate possible solutions and prioritize these possibilities.

5. Apply possible "quick fixes" one at a time.

6. Apply other possible solutions, in priority order and one at a time.

7. Resolve and document the problem.

# Begin to Document the Problem

From problem report to problem resolution, documentation of the problem and the steps used to resolve the problem must be done. Given that the troubleshooting activity is a pressured one, it would be easy to neglect documentation as an unnecessary activity that slows the troubleshooting process. In fact, though, creating troubleshooting documentation has several advantages.

1. Trouble call documentation helps ensure that the problem is clearly stated and the user is efficiently serviced. A possible trouble call report form is shown in Figure 16-1 at the end of this chapter.

2. It gives order to the troubleshooting process itself, reducing the possibility that the troubleshooter will go in circles, repeatedly trying out the same possible fix because he or she cannot remember whether or not the fix has been tried. As ridiculous as this seems, after several hours of trying to solve the same problem, repeating of steps can easily occur if complete documentation is not created throughout the troubleshooting process. Refer to Figure 16-2 at the end of the chapter for a possible troubleshooting form for the troubleshooter's use.

3. It gives a historical perspective on the particular station or user that might assist in problem resolution. Documentation of a problem and its solution gives the troubleshooter a knowledge base from which to draw for future problem resolution.

Many companies, especially the larger ones, utilize what is often called "Help Desk" software, which supports recording and following up on the trouble call and the knowledge base documentation. In any event, whether software is available or not, some procedures for problem documentation and problem resolution documentation must be developed and followed.

## Verify That the Problem Exists

Simply put, users sometimes overreact. Sometimes, there isn't really a problem, and sometimes the problem may be caused by the user himself. Before spending a great deal of time troubleshooting a problem it is a good idea to validate that there truly is a problem beyond user error. At this point, the troubleshooter's customer service skills are very important because he or she must work with the user to determine whether or not the problem is a system problem without insulting or offending the user.

The ideal method of determining whether or not the problem is caused by user error is for the troubleshooter to physically go to the user's station and watch as the user repeats the process he or she says is a problem. Unfortunately, physically witnessing the problem is often not practical, and the process must be handled by talking with the user over the phone or by using management software to take over the user's desktop. Regardless of the method used, the purpose of this step is to have the troubleshooter observe the user repeat whatever he or she was doing in an attempt to recreate the problem. The troubleshooter must be very clear in communicating with the user at this stage so that procedural errors can also be observed and pointed out.

If the reported problem is one that could be caused by equipment not being properly connected or turned on, it would be prudent to ask the user questions similar to the following, depending on the stated problem:

1. Is the network cable securely plugged into the network card in the workstation?

2. Is there anything crimping the network cable?

3. Is the power cord for the computer and/or printer plugged into the wall?

4. Is the printer turned on, and is the online button pressed?

Once the troubleshooter is convinced that there is a problem, then he or she is ready for the next phase.

# Gather Information About the Problem

Gathering information about the problem actually begins with the trouble call and proceeds through verification of the problem and throughout the entire troubleshooting event. Once the problem is verified as real, the troubleshooter begins to ask more detailed questions in an attempt to characterize the environment that existed when the problem occurred. Some of the questions that might be asked, depending on the type of problem being reported, are:

When did the user last do what is now causing trouble? If it the answer is never or several months ago, the problem must be handled differently than it would be if the answer were 30 minutes ago or yesterday. The latter indicates that something has recently been done to the system that possibly caused the problem. The former answer actually gives few clues.

What else was going on in the system while the user was trying to do the function that caused the trouble? Were any of these simultaneous functions new or recently new?

Who else was using the network when the problem occurred?

How heavily was the network used at the time the problem was reported? It may be that there really was no error, just slow response time because of heavy traffic.

What else can the user tell the troubleshooter? Often, the user has additional information that he must be coaxed to provide. For example, when a computer is beeping and/or keyboard keys create different characters from what they should produce, and when the troubleshooter has not been able to physical verify the problem, the troubleshooter may suspect that liquids have gotten into the keyboard. The user, though, may be unwilling to answer questions about spilling liquids because he is afraid of being blamed for causing the problem.

Once the troubleshooter thinks he or she understands the problem and the circumstances surrounding the problem, it is time to formulate possible solutions.

## Formulate and Prioritize Possible Solutions

Equipped with a good understanding of the problem and the circumstances surrounding it, the experienced troubleshooter can often pinpoint several possible educated guesses as to the cause of and the solution to the problem. The less experienced troubleshooter may want to consult other resources such as NetWire or Novell Support Connection, discussed later in the chapter, before formulating a list of possible problem causes and solutions. In either case, the purpose of this step is to determine possible solutions and to prioritize these possible solutions.

Prioritization of possible solutions is based on the length of time a possible solution would take to test and the probability that the possible solution will actually result in a solution. Generally, possible solutions that take small amounts of time are called "quick fixes" and are tested first. Possible solutions requiring a longer time to test are prioritized by the likelihood that a given change will result in resolution of the problem. Throughout this process, it is important to separate the possible solutions into the smallest testable change. Otherwise, changing two or more things simultaneously might mask the correct solution.

## Apply Possible "Quick Fixes"

"Quick fixes" are those changes that the troubleshooter reasonably thinks might fix the problem while also taking comparatively little time to check. When a solution is obtained in this manner, the troubleshooter is often considered to be an artist, a genius, or a brain. In reality, the troubleshooter is merely applying his or her experience to achieve a quick problem resolution. Even with "quick fixes," though, only one thing should be changed at a time (and put back in the original state if it did not result in problem resolution), and documentation must be maintained.

## Apply Other Possible Solutions

When "quick fixes" have been exhausted without problem resolution, each of the other possible solutions must be tested according to the likelihood that each will remedy the problem. Each possible fix must be tested one at a time, changing only one thing at a time, and putting the system back in its original state after trying each unsuccessful change. During this phase, it is very important to maintain detailed documentation in order to eliminate repetitive work. Further, even for the experienced troubleshooter, it may be necessary to access additional outside resources (such as NetWire and Novell Support Connection or contacts with other networking professionals) to obtain other ideas for problem resolution. Finally, when very complicated

NetWare problems arise, it may be necessary to contact Novell's consulting group for assistance.

## Resolve and Document the Problem

Once the troubleshooter believes that he or she has solved the original problem, it is imperative that the user reporting the problem be involved in evaluating the solutions. In general, troubleshooting for proper problem resolution is as much a social science as it is a computer science. The user reporting the problem must be convinced that the reported problem is gone and that other problems have not been introduced before the troubleshooter can say the problem is solved. Once the user is convinced that the problem is solved, it is a good idea to fully document the solution and to get the user to sign off on the problem resolution as shown in Figure 16-3 at the end of this chapter.

# Troubleshooting Resources

Depending on the type of problem, there are a variety of resource materials available to assist the troubleshooter in more efficient problem resolution. Several of the key resources for use in a NetWare 4.11 network will be discussed here. These are:

**Hardware and Software Documentation**

**NetWire on Novell's Internet Site**

**Novell Support Connection**

**Other Troubleshooting Resources**

## Hardware and Software Documentation

As simple as it seems, the documentation for the various hardware components and software components of a network can often be scattered and not readily available when problems occur. The prudent network manager will recognize that problems will occur and that it is imperative that the documentation be kept in a safe place. He or she will provide for a locked area to contain all hardware and software documentation. This area might perhaps be a bookcase in a locked room such as the file server room or a locking filing cabinet. The important thing is that all documentation, without fail, is placed in this area originally and is checked out and returned to this area when it is used. Many of the hardware and software manuals themselves have error or troubleshooting sections packed with troubleshooting tips and actual problem resolution steps. Referring to this documentation first can save a great deal of time in the troubleshooting process.

If documentation for a given hardware or software component is not available, the troubleshooter can often obtain information by contacting the manufacturer's Web site. A list of current Web sites is found in the appendix.

## NetWire on Novell's Internet Site

Novell's main Internet site can be contacted through www.novell.com. From this point, one can access a wealth of information including technical information documents and files containing patches and fixes. Originally, this information service was called NetWire and was available only through CompuServe Information Services through subscription. But, with the growing emphasis on the Internet, Novell has responded by providing most troubleshooting information on its Web site.

Since the Internet is very flexible, the information available through this means can change rapidly in response to customer need. At present, Novell's Web page provides technical information, product support information, file updates, an area regarding "What's New," Novell Program information, New User Information and Information about Sales and Marketing. Most sections have search capabilities that allow the user to perform keyword searches and filtering so that the most helpful information is displayed.

## Novell Support Connection

**Novell Support Connection**, Novell's Support Encyclopedia, is distributed monthly via a yearly subscription in the form of a CD-ROM. This CD-ROM provides a wealth of technical support information ranging from files with patches and fixes to technical information documents explaining particular problems to online copies of Novell's popular magazine, "AppNotes." Since Novell Support Connection is a monthly publication, it cannot contain the very latest information, but it does provide an extensive search engine for locating documents and files of interest for a particular topic. Each issue of "AppNotes" magazine is a wealth of detailed technical information about the latest software available from Novell. Currently, Novell Support Connection is available at a cost of $495 per year. A subscription to "AppNotes" is available for $99 per year. Of course, all prices are subject to change without notice.

## Other Troubleshooting Resources

In addition to the sources mentioned, the wise troubleshooter develops a human web of contacts with whom he or she shares technical issues and answers. This web can be developed as a normal course of business, and it can be accelerated by joining user groups, joining professional organizations, and taking Novell courses at local colleges and universities. In our technological world, the successful troubleshooter must keep strong contacts with other network professionals as well.

# Troubleshooting Scenarios

As explained earlier in the chapter, an extensive examination of network troubleshooting is beyond the scope of this textbook. This section will apply the troubleshooting model explained earlier and will outline a successful process for resolving the indicated problem. In some cases, additional outside utilities and tools will also be introduced as appropriate. By examining the problem solving techniques illustrated in these three scenarios, you will begin to develop your own troubleshooting skills.

## "The application I want to run won't run."

Sam Kinse calls in a trouble report that he cannot run the company's accounting package, specifically the Accounts Payable Vendor update program. The following is the problem verification and a list of questions, answers, and comments leading to an eventual solution:

### Problem Verification:

The troubleshooter calls Sam and asks him to go through logging into the network, calling up the accounting package, and attempting to access the desired program. He determines that Sam can access the accounting system and he can access the Account Payable vendor update program, but Sam cannot save any changes he attempts to make. He gets a message, "Access denied."

**Question for Sam:**

How long has the problem been occurring?

**Sam's Response:**

I don't know - I can't run the program today.

**Question for Sam:**

Have you ever been able to run this program?

### Sam's Response:

> I've never tried to run it, but I can run the rest of the Accounts Payable programs.

### Commentary:

If Sam has never been able to run the program, perhaps it wasn't set up for him to run. It might be a file system rights issue, but it is too early in the analysis to consider this the prime hypothesis. It is also important to verify that Sam is supposed to have the ability to run this program. Management may not want Sam to run this program. Before modifying the system so that he can run the program, appropriate management must be contacted to determine Sam's needs.

### Question for Sam:

> What other programs in the Accounts Payable portion of the accounting package can you run?

### Sam's Response:

> I'm able to run all the reports, but in actuality, I've never tried to run any of the update programs.

### Commentary:

After verifying that Sam is indeed supposed to be able to update vendors, the most plausible solution appears to be:

Checking to see that Sam has the appropriate file system rights to update the Accounts Payable Vendor file. This will likely require examination of the accounting system's documentation or checking out the file system rights for someone who is already able to run this program.

## Problem Resolution:

Sam had only the Read and File Scan file system rights to the directory containing the Vendor file. According to the Accounting system documentation, he also needed the Write, Create, Delete, and Modify rights. Once those rights were granted, Sam could run the program and signed the problem report showing that the problem had been resolved.

# "I can't print."

This problem is one of the most common and often one of the most complicated to resolve because of the many things that can cause a user not to be able to print. The following scenario gives one problem resolution sequence for a particular reason that a given user cannot print. Be aware that this problem resolution will certainly not resolve all printing problems. Also be aware that the user may actually have called in a problem that the network is down because he may equate his being able to print with the network's being "up."

## Problem Verification:

Katy Kirce calls to say that she cannot print her month-end reports. The troubleshooter in this case can physically go to Katy's desk to help her because her office is just down the hall. Therefore, many of the questions the troubleshooter would have asked Katy can be answered by observation and will be noted as such.

### Question for Katy:

> When could you last print? What printer do you use?

### Answer from Katy:

> I last printed just before leaving to go home last night. I haven't tried to print today until just now. I use this printer next to my desk.

### Question for Katy:

> Would you please show me the message you receive when you try to print?

### Answer from Katy:

> There wasn't an error message. My report just didn't print. I'll be happy, though, to show you how I run the report so that you can see for yourself. (She attempts to run the report again, and no message appears.)

### Observations and Commentary:

The printer is online and plugged into both power and to Katy's computer. The troubleshooter has Katy turn the printer on and off and reboot her computer just to make sure there isn't some simple problem, but these actions do not seem to fix the problem.

The troubleshooter develops the following educated guesses as to the cause of the problem, knowing that there is no error message:

1. Katy's printer might be redirected to another printer in the building.

2. There might be a problem with the queue/printer/print server hookup that Katy is using.

3. Maybe NPRINTER isn't loaded as a TSR on the computer that is attached to the printer Katy wants to use because the boot configuration files have been changed.

4. Maybe the print server isn't running.

All these hypotheses require that the troubleshooter verify the queue or printer to which Katy's print is directed. After examining her login scripts and her machine setup, the troubleshooter determines that Katy is redirected to a queue that is serviced by a printer down the hall because Katy had been working on another application earlier in the day. The troubleshooter and Katy find her output on that printer.

## "The SYS volume won't mount."

When bringing up a system or when troubleshooting why users can't log in, the troubleshooter determine that the SYS volume on a server won't mount either automatically as the server is brought up or when the troubleshooter issues the MOUNT SYS command at the console prompt on the server. Often when this happens, the system itself advises the operator to run **VREPAIR**, the volume repair utility. This utility is the first line of defense when a volume will not mount. Before running this utility, explained below, the troubleshooter should verify the circumstances surrounding why the volume will not mount. Was there a power failure? Do other volumes mount? Did the SYS volume run out of space because of a large print job, etc.? If the answers are "yes," then running VREPAIR can be a reasonable "quick fix." This option will be examined through the following Hands-On exercise.

# Hands-On with NetWare

To simulate the problem indicated, go to the console of the file server and do the following:

1. Dismount the SYS volume by entering:

   **DISMOUNT SYS**

2. Wait for the file server prompt to reappear.

3. Enter

   **LOAD C:\NWSERVER\VREPAIR**

4. Note that the VREPAIR NLM must be loaded from the C: drive directory because the SYS volume is dismounted. Fortunately, this utility was copied to the NWSERVER directory when the server was installed.

5. Select Set VREPAIR options and select Repair a Volume. A list of volumes to choose from will appear only if more than one volume is dismounted. In this case, you should not be asked to select a volume because SYS should be the only dismounted volume.

6. Change the current error settings so that the screen does not pause after each error and then choose the option to execute the repair. Wait for the utility to finish and then exit the utility.

7. Run VREPAIR one more time, and then mount the SYS volume.

The problem is usually resolved at this point, but care should be taken to make sure that the server is on a uninterruptible power source so that a power interruption will not cause the problem again and that there is plenty of free space on the SYS volume. When the SYS volume runs out of space, the various tables are corrupted so that the SYS volume cannot mount.

# Summary

Troubleshooting activities, while part art, must follow a solid troubleshooting model. This chapter examined the troubleshooting model that consists of the following steps:

Begin to document the problem

Verify that the problem exists

Gather information about the problem

Formulate possible solutions and prioritize these possibilities

Apply possible "quick fixes," one at a time

Apply other possible solutions one at a time

Resolve and document the problem

Special emphasis must be placed on documenting the problem both to eliminate redundant efforts troubleshooting a specific problem and to provide a historical reference for the future.

In addition to the troubleshooter's previous knowledge, several other resources for troubleshooting were examined. These include the hardware and software manuals that came with the system, the Web sites for the hardware and software for the system, NetWire through Novell's Web pages, Novell Support Connection, and the human network of other networking professionals. These resources are ready sources for additional information should the troubleshooter not be able to readily resolve the problem.

Finally, the chapter examined three troubleshooting scenarios as examples of troubleshooting techniques that led to problem resolution.

# Questions:

1. Why is documentation required before, during, and after the troubleshooting process?

2. What is a "quick fix"?

3. Why are the hardware and software manuals for the components of the system needed?

4. What types of information are available on Novell's Web page?

5. What is Novell Support Connection?

6. What is "AppNotes"?

7. What is VREPAIR and when is its use indicated? Where must VREPAIR be loaded from?

8. Do you think that troubleshooting is part art and part science? Why or why not? Where does the troubleshooter's experience enter in?

9. Why was it stated that troubleshooting is part social science? Give a troubleshooting scenario where social skills might be very important.

10. How do you verify that a problem is solved?

# Projects

## Objectives:

The purpose of these projects is to familiarize the student with various resources available for troubleshooting. Project I depends on making hardware and software manuals for the system available to the students for perusal. Project II requires the use of the Internet.

### Project I

Locate the hardware and software manuals for the classroom system. Examine each manual and summarize the types of troubleshooting information that is available.

## Project II

Access Novell's Web pages (www.novell.com) and do the following:

1.  Locate and document how to obtain the latest patches and fixes for NetWare 4.

2.  Locate and document information on Novell's Beta program.

3.  Locate and document information on the next version of NetWare.

| User Name/Extension: | Trouble Report Number: | Report Date: |
| | Person Taking Report: | Report Time: |
| Assigned to: | Date: | Time: |
| Problem resolution: | | Resolution Date: |
| | | Resolution Time: |
| User Signature indicating problem is resolved: | | |
| Problem Description: | | |
| When Was Problem First Noticed? | | |
| Other information about the problem: | | |
| User estimate of criticality of the problem | | |
| Intake person's estimate of criticality of the problem: | | |

**Figure 16-1.** Trouble Report form.

| User Name/Extension: | Trouble Report Number: | | Report Date: |
|---|---|---|---|
| | Person Taking Report: | | Report Time: |
| Assigned to: | Date: | | Time: |
| Questions Asked/Answers Given to Verify Problem Existence: | | | |
| | | | |
| | | | |
| | | | |
| Likelihood of Solution | Possible Solution | Results: | |
| | | | |
| | | | |
| | | | |
| | | | |

**Figure 16-2.** Troubleshooting Documentation form1.

| User Name/Extension:<br>Sam Kinse | Trouble Report Number:<br>A209<br>Person Taking Report:<br>JRB | Report Date:<br>10/26<br>Report Time:<br>9:30 am |
|---|---|---|
| Assigned to:<br>KRC | Date:<br>10/26 | Time:<br>10:00 am |
| Problem resolution: Gave Sam Write, Create, Erase, and Modify File System rights to the SYS:\ACCTG\AP\DATA directory on file server ACCT_MAIN | | Resolution Date:<br>10/26<br>Resolution Time:<br>11:30 am |
| User Signature indicating problem is resolved: Verbal approval by Phone, KRC | | |
| Problem Description: Cannot run the Vendor Update Program in the Accounting System | | |
| When Was Problem First Noticed? Today, but Sam hasn't ever run this program | | |
| Other information about the problem: Can run Accounts Payable reports | | |
| User estimate of criticality of the problem Moderate | | |
| Intake person's estimate of criticality of the problem: Moderate | | |

Figure 16-3. Sample troubleshooting documentation with user signoff.

# Appendix

## Where to Get Product Information and Technical Support

Usually, the best way of getting technical support or product information for a data communications or networking product is to access it through the Internet. Typically, a vendor will have a home page identified by www.vendorname.com. This home page usually will have links to various products and technical support for these products.

If you are unable to locate a given product's Web site, you might want to try using an Internet search engine. Through a search engine, you can search for information about a product by typing in key words. Two of the most popular search engines can be accessed through www.yahoo.com and www.lycos.com.

If you still need help, there are several technical support indices. These indices have search engines to locate technical support information via key words. Using these indices, you can obtain freeware and free technical support information not tied to a specific vendor.

Three of the current technical support indices may be accessed by:

CMPnet's Tech Helper at www.techweb.com/helper/

PC-Help Online at www.pchelponline.com/

Software.Net's Vendor Support Directory at www.software.net/directory.htm

# Vendor Listing

## Vendors of Communications-Related Hardware and Software

3Com Corp.

5400 Bayfront Plaza, Santa Clara, CA 95052

Telephone: 408-764-5000

Fax: 408-764-5001

Toll Free: 800-NET-3COM

E-mail: 3com@3mail.3com.com


Adaptec, Inc.

691 South Milpitas Blvd., Milpitas, CA 95035

Telephone: 408-945-8600

Fax: 408-262-2533

Toll Free: 800-655-3977


Alcatel Network Systems, Inc.

1225 North Alma Rd., Richardson, TX 75081

Telephone: 972-996-5000

Fax: 972-996-5409

Toll Free: 800-ALCATEL


Apple Computer, Inc.

1 Infinite Loop, Cupertino, CA 95014

Telephone: 408-996-1010

Fax: 408-974-5200

Cabletron Systems, Inc.

35 Industrial Way, PO Box 5005, Rochester, NH 03866

Telephone: 603-332-9400

Fax: 603-337-2211

E-mail: sales@ctron.com


Cheyenne Software, Inc.

3 Expressway Plaza, Roslyn Heights, NY 11577

Telephone: 516-465-4000

Fax: 516-484-3446

Toll Free: 800-CHEYINC


Cisco Systems, Inc.

170 West Tasman Dr., San Jose, CA 95134

Telephone: 408-526-4000

Fax: 408-526-4100


Compaq Computer Corp.

PO Box 69200, Houston, TX 77269

Telephone: 281-370-0670

Fax: 281-514-1740


Dell Computer Corp.

2214 West Braker Ln., Austin, TX 78758

Telephone: 512-338-4400

Fax: 512-728-3653

Toll Free: 800-289-3355

Digital Equipment Corporation

111 Powdermill Rd., Maynard, MA 01754

Telephone: 508-493-5111

Fax: 508-493-8780


Fujitsu Computer Products of America

2904 Orchard Pkwy., San Jose, CA 95134

Telephone: 408-432-6333

Fax: 408-894-1706

Toll Free: 800-626-4686

E-mail: info@fcpa.fujitsu.com


Hewlett-Packard Company

3000 Hanover St., Palo Alto, CA 94304

Telephone: 650-857-1501

Fax: 650-857-5518

Toll Free: 800-752-0900


Hitachi America, Ltd. / Computer Division

110 Summit Ave., Montvale, NJ 07645

Telephone: 201-573-0774

Toll Free: 800-225-1370


International Business Machines Corp.

New Orchard Rd., Armonk, NY 10504

Telephone: 914-499-1900

Fax: 914-499-6021

Intel Corp.

PO Box 58119, Santa Clara, CA 95051

Telephone: 408-765-8080

Fax: 408-765-1402

Iomega Corp.

1821 West Iomega Way, Roy, UT 84067

Telephone: 801-778-1000

Fax: 801-778-3450

Logitech Inc.

6505 Kaiser Dr., Fremont, CA 94555

Telephone: 510-795-8500

Fax: 510-792-8901

Toll Free: 800-231-7717

Lotus Development Corp.

55 Cambridge Pkwy., Cambridge, MA 02142

Telephone: 617-577-8500

Fax: 617-693-1197

MCI Communications Corp.

1801 Pennsylvania Ave. N.W., Washington, DC 20006

Telephone: 202-872-1600

Fax: 202-887-2023

Toll Free: 800-289-0073

Micron Electronics, Inc.

900 East Karcher Rd., Nampa, ID 83687

Telephone: 208-893-3434

Fax: 208-893-7395

Toll Free: 800-438-3343


Microsoft Corp.

One Microsoft Way, Redmond, WA 98052

Telephone: 425-882-8080

Fax: 425-936-7329


NEC America, Inc.

Corporate Center Dr., Suite 8, Melville, NY 11747

Telephone: 516-753-7000

Fax: 516-753-7041

Toll Free: 800-333-9549

E-mail: webmaster@nec.com


Netscape Communications Corp.

501 East Middlefield Rd., Mountain View, CA 94043

Telephone: 650-254-1900

Fax: 650-428-4091

E-mail: info@netscape.com


Network General Corp.

4200 Bohannon Dr., Menlo Park, CA 94025

Telephone: 650-473-2000

Fax: 650-327-2145

Toll Free: 800-SNIFFER

NORTEL Broadband Networks

5555 Windward Pkwy. East, Bldg. B, Alpharetta, GA 30201

Telephone: 770-661-4000

Fax: 770-661-4784


Novell , Inc.

122 East 1700 South

Provo, UT 84606

800-453-1267

www.novell.com


Oracle Corp.

500 Oracle Pkwy., Redwood Shores, CA 94065

Telephone: 650-506-7000

Fax: 650-506-7200

Toll Free: 800-345-DBMS


Packard Bell NEC, Inc.

1 Packard Bell Way, Sacramento, CA 95826

Telephone: 916-388-0101

Fax: 916-388-1109


Raytheon E-Systems / Richardson

1301 East Collins Blvd., PO Box 831359

Richardson, TX 75081

Telephone: 972-470-2000

Fax: 972-470-2466

Toll Free: 800-933-5359

Rockwell International Corp.

600 Anton Blvd., Suite 700, PO Box 5090

Costa Mesa, CA 92628

Telephone: 714-424-4546


Seagate Software, Inc. / Information Group

& Network Management Group

920 Disc Dr., Scotts Valley, CA 95066

Telephone: 408-439-2881

Fax: 408-342-4600


Storage Dimensions, Inc.

1656 McCarthy Blvd., Milpitas, CA 95035

Telephone: 408-954-0710

Fax: 408-944-1200


Sun Microsystems, Inc.

2550 Garcia Ave., Mountain View, CA 94043

Telephone: 650-960-1300

Fax: 650-969-9131


U.S. Robotice/3Com Corp. / Network Systems Division

1800 West Central Rd., Mount Prospect, IL 60056

Telephone: 847-797-6010

Toll Free: 800-USRCORP

Western Digital Corp.

8105 Irvine Center Dr., Irvine, CA 92718

Telephone: 714-932-5000

Fax: 714-932-6498

Toll Free: 800-832-4778


WorldCom, Inc.

515 East Amite St., Jackson, MS 39201

Telephone: 601-360-8600

Toll Free: 800-844-1009

E-mail: info@wcom.com


Xerox Corp.

PO Box 1600, Stamford, CT 06904

Telephone: 203-968-3000

Fax: 203-968-4566

Toll Free: 800-334-6200

# Glossary

**ASCII.** The acronym for American Standard Code for Information Interchange. This is a standard code for the transmission of data within the U.S. Standard ASCII is composed of 128 characters in a 7-bit format.

**Asynchronous.** A communication that places data in discrete blocks that are surrounded by framing bits. These bits show the beginning and end of a block of data. These framing bits are sometimes called start and stop bits.

**AUTOEXEC.BAT.** The batch file on a DOS workstation that is used to automatically run various programs when the DOS workstation is activated.

**AUTOEXEC.NCF.** The server file that functions similarly to the AUTOEXEC.BAT file when a file server is activated.

**Auto Load.** A printer that is designated as an auto load printer is physically attached to a file server running PSERVER and is automatically activated when PSERVER is run.

**Backup.** A copy of the files, directories, and NDS Directory structure of a network.

**Bandwidth.** The capacity of a media (often a cable) to carry data.

**Baseband.** A network cable that has only one channel for carrying data signals.

**Baud.** The rate of data transmission. Specifically, baud refers to state changes per second onto which data can be encoded.

**Bit.** An abbreviation for binary digit. A bit is the smallest unit of data for the computer.

**Bootable partition.** The partition of the hard drive that is designated for use in loading the computer's operating system into the computer when it is turned on.

**Boot Disk.** A disk used to load the computer's operating system into the computer when it is turned on.

**Bridge.** A device that divides a "too busy" LAN segment into two different collision domains.

**Broadband.** A network cable with several simultaneous channels of communication.

**Brouter.** Hybrid devices that incorporate bridge and router technology. Brouters make decisions on whether a data packet uses a protocol that is routable. Then they route those that can be routed and bridge the rest.

**Bulletin Board.** The electronic bulletin board system consists of a computer that is used to store, retrieve, and catalog messages sent in by the general public through their modems.

**Bus Topology.** A physical layout of a LAN where all nodes are connected to a single cable.

**Byte.** A combination of 8 bits.

**CAD.** Computer-aided design.

**CAPTURE.** A NetWare utility program used to redirect output from a printer port on the workstation to a network printer.

**CD-ROM.** A compact disk reader that is used to read digitally recorded compact disks.

**CD-ROM driver.** The software that controls the functioning of a CD-ROM reader.

**Cellular Radio.** A form of high-frequency radio transmission where the signals are relayed from antennas that are spaced in strategic locations throughout metropolitan areas.

**Channel Extender.** A device that links remote stations directly to a host system and operates at high speeds. It functions like a small front end processor to connect remote work stations and computers to a host. It can support auxiliary devices, including printers, disk drives, and microcomputers.

**Client 32.** Novell's latest 32-bit client communications software. Versions exist for DOS/Windows, Windows 95, and Windows NT.

**Client Computer.** The computer that functions as a workstation requesting information from one or more file servers.

**Cluster Controller.** A cluster controller is a device that supports several terminals and the functions required to manage those terminals.

**Coaxial Cable.** A cable consisting of a single metal wire surrounded by insulation which is itself surrounded by a braided or foil outer shield.

**CompuServe.** A public, subscription-only information service. NetWire has traditionally been housed on CompuServe.

**Concentrator.** An intelligent line-sharing device that allows multiple devices to share communication circuits.

**Common Name.** This is simply the name of the object without the names of any containers containing the object.

**Computer.** A electronic system that can store and process information under program control.

**CONSOLE.** The file server. Typically used to refer to the monitor and keyboard and console input and output devices.

**Container.** An NDS object that contains other objects.

**Container Login Script.** The login script associated with a container. This login script runs first for all users in a container.

**Control Code.** Special nonprinting codes that cause electronic equipment to perform specific actions.

**Country Object.** The object at the highest level in a Novell Directory Services Tree. This object represents a country and must be identified with a legal country code.

**CPU.** Central processing unit. The processor portion of the computer where the logic and control functions are performed.

**CSMA/CD.** Carrier Sense Multiple Access/Collision Detection. The method for media access for Ethernet networks. When a station wants to send data, it senses the line. If the line is open, it transmits. If a collision occurs, the stations waits a random amount of time and then reattempts transmission.

**CX.** Change context.

**Data communication.** The transmission and receipt of data.

**Device Driver.** A software program that enables a network operating system and/or the workstation operating system to work with devices such as network adapters, disk controllers, and other devices.

**Differential Backup.** A backup that backs up all files that have changed since the last full backup.

**Digital Line Expander.** A device that allows users to concentrate a larger number of voice and data channels into the bandwidth of a standard communication channel by using hardware and software techniques that make use of the entire bandwidth capability of a standard voice circuit.

**Directory Attributes.** Access rights attached to each directory.

**Directory Trustee Rights.** Trustee assignments made at a directory level.

**Disk Drivers.** The software that controls the functioning of the hard disk on a file server

**Distinguished Name.** The full name of an NDS object without regard for current context. The name begins with a period and contains the common name of the object and all containers back to the (ROOT) object, each name separated by a period.

**DOS.** Disk operating system. This term is usually a shortened notation for MS-DOS by Microsoft and PC-DOS by IBM.

**Drive Mapping.** An association of a virtual drive letter to a volume and directory location on a file server.

**Driver.** A memory resident program usually used to control a hardware device.

**Effective Rights.** The combination of directly assigned and inherited rights that determine what a user can do at a particular location in the file system or at a particular location in the NDS directory tree.

**Encryption.** The transformation of data from meaningful code into a meaningless stream of bits. To make this transformation, the data is sent through an encrypting algorithm with the result being the set of meaningless bits. To see the data in its original format, the scrambled data is sent back through the algorithm which in essence now works in "reverse," restoring the original message.

**Enterprise Network.** A network larger than a single file server type network that addresses the needs of a large business, often referred to as an enterprise.

**Feasibility Study.** The study performed in order to define the existing problem clearly and to determine whether a network is operationally feasible for the type of organization that it plans to serve.

**Fiber-Optic Cable.** A data transmitting cable that consists of plastic or glass fibers, surrounded by cladding. Data is transmitted over these fibers via light.

**File Attributes.** Access rights attached to each file.

**Full Backup.** A backup that backs up everything on a file server.

**File Server.** A computer running a network operating system that enables other computers to access its files.

**File Trustee Rights.** Trustee assignments assigned at the file level.

**Full Duplex.** In full duplex communication, data is transmitted and received over the same cable simultaneously.

**Gateway.** A device that acts as a translator between totally different systems.

**Group.** A collection of users.

**Group Rights.** Rights given to a collection of users via the group object.

**Half Duplex.** In half duplex communication, the terminal transmits and receives data over the same cable, but only one way at a time.

**Handshaking.** A set of commands recognized by the sending and receiving stations that control the flow of data transmission.

**Host.** In terminal/mainframe or terminal/minicomputer types of communication, a host is the mainframe computer or minicomputer. When the term host is used in a TCP/IP network, a host is any device, computer or otherwise, that has an IP address.

**Incremental Backup.** A backup that backs up only those files that have changed since the last full or incremental backup.

**Inherited Rights.** Rights inherited from a container or directory above.

**Inherited Rights Filter.** A filter attached to a directory or file that determines which rights can be inherited from above.

**Interface.** A communication channel that is used to connect a computer to an external device.

**Internetwork Packet Exchange (IPX).** One of the data transmission protocols used by NetWare.

**Interrupt.** An IBM PC or PC compatible central processing unit utilizes interrupt numbers for communication with the various devices attached to the PC. Only one device can utilize a given interrupt number, 0 to 15.

**Intruder Lockout.** A method for locking out a person who repetitively attempts to log in with a known user identification and an illegal password.

**IPX Internal Network Number.** The 8-digit hexadecimal number that uniquely identifies a file server.

**LAN.** Local area network. A network that typically encompasses a small geographical area. (This distinction is blurring as the quality and cost of worldwide communications improves.)

**LAN Drivers.** The software that controls the functioning of the network interface card.

**Leaf Object.** A object that represents an actual resource in a network. A leaf object can be contained in an Organization object or in an Organization Unit object. A leaf object cannot contain another object.

**Life Cycle.** The life cycle of a network is a representation of the phase through which a network proceeds before it becomes obsolete and ready for replacement.

**Line Monitor.** A device used to diagnose problems on a communication line or link. It attaches to a communication circuit, and a digital format of the data flowing through the circuit is displayed on a screen, printed to paper, or stored on an auxiliary device for further analysis.

**Line Splitter.** A device, similar to a port-sharing device, normally found at the remote end of a communication line, where the terminal or workstation is located while port-sharing devices are normally located at the host end of the communication line.

**Login Restrictions.** Restrictions covering such things as number of concurrent logins, account expiration date, and account disabled flag. Restrictions are stored per user in NDS.

**Login Script.** A login script contains commands that are executed when a user logs in. These commands set up the environment for the user usually through drive mappings and printer capture statements.

**Mainframe.** A computer that is the central computer systems that perform data processing functions for a business or industry.

**MAN.** A metropolitan area network is a network within a metropolitan area.

**Manual Load.** A printer that is designated as manual load must be activated by running NPRINTER.EXE if the printer is attached to a workstation or by running NPRINTER.NLM if the printer is attached to a remote file server.

**Memory Address.** Each network interface card usually uses at least some portion of the RAM memory of the PC itself for normal operation.

**Microcomputer.** A microcomputer is a general-purpose computer with a central processing unit. Microcomputers are computers like mainframes, but they are usually smaller and utilize a microprocessor for their central processing units.

**Microwave.** A line of sight communication that utilizes radio wave for communication between a sending and receiving station. Sending and receiving stations may either be physically on the earth or satellites orbiting the earth.

**Modem.** An electronic device that converts (modulates) digital data from a computer into analog signals that the phone equipment can understand. Additionally, the modem converts (demodulates) analog data into digital data.

**Multiplexer.** A device that supports the transmission of multiple signals over a single medium by replacing multiple low-speed transmission lines with a single high-speed transmission line or by combining several frequencies that do not overlap into one transmission.

**NDS. Novell Directory Services.** A tree-structured Directory of objects with properties that allows for a single log on to a Novell NetWare 4.11 system.

**NetAdmin.** The DOS-based text program that is used to administer NDS.

**NetWire.** Novell's support forum on CompuServe. Similar information is available on Novell's Internet Web site.

**NetWare.** A network operating system produced by Novell, Inc.

**NetWare Administrator. NW Admin.** The graphical version of a program that is used to administer the NDS tree.

**Network.** A data communications system connecting multiple devices such as computers, printers, etc.

**Network Address.** A hexadecimal number used to identify a network cabling system.

**Network Address Restrictions.** These restrictions control which stations can be used by a given user to log in.

**NIC.** The network interface card. A circuit board that is installed in the file servers and the workstations that make up the network. It allows the hardware in the network to send and receive data over the transmission media connecting workstations and servers.

**Network Management.** A plan to prevent network problems where possible and to prepare for network problems that will most likely occur. The plan must address monitoring and controlling hard disk space, monitoring network workload and performance, maintaining user login information and workstation information, monitoring and resetting network devices, performing regular maintenance on software and data files stored in the servers, and making regular backups of data and programs stored in the servers.

**Network Modeling.** The process of simulating a network prior to creating it to determine its expected operating parameters such as response time.

**Network Operating System.** A network operating system is the grouping of software programs that are used to control a file server and a client computer and the communications between them.

**Network Security.** Network security maintains control over the data stored and transmitted by the network with the major goals of preventing computer crime and data loss.

**Novell.** A company based in Provo, Utah, that produces the NetWare network operating system.

**Novell Support Connection/NSEPro.** Novell's subscription support CD-ROM service.

**NPRINTER.** The program that allows other workstations to print to a workstation's printer or to a printer attached to a file server not running PSERVER. NPRINTER.EXE runs on a workstation with a remote printer attached, and NPRINTER.NLM runs on a file server with a remote printer attached.

**Object.** An item in the NDS tree such as a container or a leaf object like a user.

**Object Rights.** Trustee rights assigned to an NDS object.

**Optical Fiber.** Optical fiber consists of thin glass fibers that can carry information at frequencies in the visible light spectrum.

**Organization Object.** The Organization object falls under the Country object and above the Organizational Unit object in a Novell Directory Services tree. An Organization object can contain leaf objects and Organizational Unit objects and aliases to these objects. It cannot contain another Organization object.

**Organizational Unit Object.** An Organizational Unit Object must be contained in either an Organization object or another Organizational Unit object. It can also contain leaf objects.

**OSI Model.** A 7 layer networking communications model created by the International Standards Organization with the purpose of making communication between heterogeneous devices easier.

**Packet.** A discrete unit of data bits transmitted over a network.

**Parallel Port.** A port, normally located on the back or a computer or a Centronics interface on a printer or other device, that transmits parallel communication. Using parallel communication, 8 bits of data are transmitted simultaneously.

**Password.** A secret word used to authenticate a user.

**Password Restrictions.** These restrictions cover password requirements and what a user can and cannot do with his or her own password.

**PBX.** A private telephone branch exchange (PBX), normally leased or owned by a company, to connect telephones, terminals and computers within the company.

**PCONSOLE.** A NetWare utility program used to configure and operate print servers. Its name stands for Print Server Console.

**PDN.** A network using packet-switching techniques for communication. Packet switching is a store-and-forward data transmission technique in which messages are split into small segments called packets.

**Port Address.** The memory address in the local PCs utilized for communication with the central processing unit.

**Printer.** The NDS object representing the printer itself. It is connected to a print server and to one or more print queues.

**Print Queues.** Definitions of the order and location in which a file is to be printed on the network.

**Print Server.** A computer program, PSERVER.NLM, that periodically checks the print queues to service completed print jobs by sending them to the appropriate printer.

**Profile Login Script.** The login script associated with a profile object. This object is normally associated with various users to form a group login script.

**Property.** A characteristic of an object in NDS.

**Property Rights.** Trustee rights assigned to one or more properties of an NDS object.

**Protocol.** A set of rules to be followed for two electronic devices to communicate.

**Protocol Converter.** A device that connects electronic devices with differing protocols so they can communicate with each other.

**PSERVER.** The print server program.

**Public network.** Public networks have standard interfaces that allow almost any type of computer or terminal to connect to other computers or terminals.

**RAM.** Random access memory.

**Relative Distinguished Name.** The partial NDS name of an object relative to current context.

**Remote Printing.** Printing to a printer that is not attached to the file server running PSERVER.NLM.

**Response Time.** The time that expires between sending an inquiry from a workstation or terminal and receiving the response back at the workstation.

**Ring Topology.** A network configuration that connects all nodes into a logical ring-like structure.

**ROM.** Read-only memory.

**Router.** A device, working at the network layer of the OSI model, that determines the most efficient data path between two networks.

**RS-232 Interface.** A serial communications standard commonly used for modem and other serial communication.

**Satellite.** A device which orbits the earth and is used to relay microwave transmission.

**SBACKUP.** Novell's backup utility.

**Search Drive.** A network drive mapping that functions similar to a directory listed in a path statement on a DOS workstation.

**Security Equal To.** A user may be made security equal to another uses. This means that the user has the security assigned to the other use as well as the security assigned to the user himself.

**Selected Property Rights.** Rights assigned to specific properties of an NDS object rather than to all properties of the object.

**Serial Port.** A port, normally located on the back or a computer that transmits serial communication. Using serial communication, 1 bit of data is transmitted at a time.

**Server Computer.** The computer that functions as the file server for a network.

**Single Login.** Single login allows a user to have access to resources throughout an enterprise network through NDS.

**SNA.** IBM's proprietary Systems Network Architecture.

**Software.** Programs used to control the functioning of a computer or other device.

**Star Topology.** A network configuration where each node is connected by a single cable link to a central location, called a hub.

**STARTUP.NCF.** The server boot file that functions similarly to the CONFIG.SYS file on a DOS workstation when a server is activated. The STARTUP.NCF file must, at minimum, contain the drivers for the hard drive(s) in the file server.

**Synchronous.** A method of communication using a time interval and a limited number of control characters to distinguish between transmitted blocks of data.

**TCP/IP.** A set of networking standards that grew from the Department of Defense initiatives in the early 1970s to interconnect systems made by different vendors. TCP/IP is now the underlying communications protocol for the Internet.

**Telecommuting.** The process of working from home via use of a telecommunications connection to an employer's computer systems.

**Terminal.** A term usually used to describe an electronic input station with no processing power that provides input to a central computer. The word terminal has become recently become more generic, often referring to input stations such as PCs that do have processing power.

**The Internet.** The worldwide network interconnecting computer systems and devices such that global communication can occur. The underlying protocol for the Internet is TCP/IP.

**Token.** The data packet used to carry information on LANs using the ring topology.

**Topology.** The manner in which nodes are connected on a LAN.

**Transmission Medium.** The physical means for communication between a sender and a receiver.

**Troubleshooting Model.** An organized methodology for troubleshooting a problem.

**Trustee.** A user or group that is given rights to the file system or to NDS.

**Trustee Rights.** Rights given to users or groups to access file system directories or NDS on the file servers.

**Twisted Pair.** Wire encased in plastic covering and twisted together to minimize interference and crosstalk. The cables are twisted in pairs because the electrical effect of one current is canceled by the electrical effect of the other, thereby reducing the amount of interference that the signal is subjected to. The signals from one pair of cables are prevented from interfering with the signals of another pair, a type of interference that is sometimes called crosstalk.

**Uninterruptible Power Supply.** A device that keeps computers running after a power failure, providing power from batteries for a short period of time.

**User Login Script.** Login script information specific to a user's requirements.

**Value.** A value is the current meaning of a property of an NDS object.

**Video Conferencing.** Conferencing that occurs through simultaneous, realtime video and audio transmission between two physically separate locations.

**Virus.** A computer virus is an executable computer program that propagates itself, using other programs as carriers, and sometimes modifies itself during or after replication. It is intended to perform some unwanted function on the computer system attached to the network.

**VREPAIR.** Novell's utility for repairing a volume that is structurally corrupt.

**Volume.** The highest level of the directory structure on a Novell file server. This level is often considered equivalent to a drive letter on a local computer.

**Wide Area Network.** A network that encompasses a large geographical area.

**Workstation.** A computer attached to a network.

**X.25.** A communication protocol used on public data networks.

# Index